Ernest Jones, Chartism, and the Romance of Politics 1819–69

Ernest Jones, Chartism, and the Romance of Politics 1819–1869

MILES TAYLOR

OXFORD
UNIVERSITY PRESS

OXFORD
UNIVERSITY PRESS

Great Clarendon Street, Oxford OX2 6DP

Oxford University Press is a department of the University of Oxford.
It furthers the University's objective of excellence in research, scholarship,
and education by publishing worldwide in

Oxford New York

Auckland Bangkok Buenos Aires Cape Town Chennai
Dar es Salaam Delhi Hong Kong Istanbul Karachi Kolkata
Kuala Lumpur Madrid Melbourne Mexico City Mumbai Nairobi
São Paulo Shanghai Taipei Tokyo Toronto

Oxford is a registered trade mark of Oxford University Press
in the UK and in certain other countries

Published in the United States
by Oxford University Press Inc., New York

British Library Cataloguing in Publication Data
Data available

Library of Congress Cataloging in Publication Data
Data applied for

ISBN 0-19-820729-8

1 3 5 7 9 10 8 6 4 2

Typeset by Regent Typesetting, London
Printed in Great Britain
on acid-free paper by
Biddles Ltd,
Guildford and King's Lynn

Preface

In 1848 two different forces met and converged across much of the globe. One was literary romanticism enjoying its final swan-song, the other was the fledgling first steps of democratic protest. Leading the various movements which made up the 'springtime of the peoples' were neither hardy artisans nor hardened ideologues, but poets, dramatists, and racy journalists. Alphonse Lamartine in Paris, Massimo D'Azeglio in Rome, Lajos Kossuth in Budapest, William Smith O'Brien in Dublin, Ferdinand Freiligrath in Cologne, and Henry Parkes in Sydney are just a few examples of the men of revolution whose contributions to poetry and prose were as substantial, if not as enduring, as their impact on politics. The new style of leadership which these men brought to the barricades—part-demagogue, part-chivalrous hero—was to alarm and inspire politicians for the next three decades. In their own different ways, Benjamin Disraeli and William Gladstone in England, Giuseppe Garibaldi in Italy, Horace Greeley in America, Charles Stewart Parnell in Ireland, and Ferdinand Lassalle in Germany all learned lessons about mass politics from the example of 1848. And whilst popular political protest may have disappeared from view after 1848 until the 1860s when white adult male urban democracy was extended across much of Europe, America, and parts of the British empire, the idea of the people came alive in the media of the period. The 1850s and 1860s were the heyday of the serialized sensation novel, pioneered by Charles Dickens and Wilkie Collins, the speaking tours of evangelical preachers such as Charles Spurgeon, and the melodrama and theatrical spectacle of new dramatists such as Dion Boucicault. All were outgrowths of romanticism and all signalled the arrival of demos in fact and fiction. Yet the interrelationship between the style and content of late romanticism and the emergence of mass politics at mid-century has seldom been studied in depth. This is partly because literary scholars and historians tend not to talk to one another, or when they do their own disciplinary patois preclude useful dialogue. But it is mainly because assumptions about class and ideology still dominate our understanding of 1848 and after. The voice of one noisy newspaper columnist in 1848—Karl Marx—has tended to drown out the cacophony of verse and oratory produced by political romanticism. The following study attempts to redress the balance and show how the tone of mass politics in the later 1860s was influenced by the tragicomic men of 1848.

Ernest Jones was England's outstanding contribution to the gallery of nineteenth-century romantic populists. As is generally well known, he was a lawyer who rose to prominence in the Chartist movement in 1848, kept the remnants of working-class protest alive during the 1850s, and reappeared in the parliamentary reform campaigns at the time of the second reform bill in 1866–7. Unlike most of his fellow political poets and dramatists on the Continent, Jones has not been the subject of a full modern biography and his considerable literary output has never been given its due. He has gone down in history as the principal English ally of Marx and Friedrich Engels, yet this friendship tends to distort his real significance. Jones wrote hundreds of poems, several dramas and full-length serial novels, as well as editing or contributing to a dozen or so newspapers. He was a man of letters as much as a man of the people, steeped in German, French, and English romanticism, the London stage, and classical history. He not only wrote poems, but also read them aloud to appreciative mass audiences, and wrote about the function of literature in the modern age as well. Jones perceived himself to be a democratic writer. Accordingly, any account of his politics must start and end with a proper appreciation of how democracy and literature functioned together in the mid-Victorian age. To make sense of Ernest Jones in this way is also to look again at the character of mid-Victorian popular politics. For Jones's suffusion in late romanticism was not a hindrance, as some of his biographers have suggested, but rather the perfect preparation for a political career in mid-Victorian Britain. As scholars have begun to recognize more and more, the arts of democratic oratory were often indistinguishable from the conventions of the stage, the bar, and the pulpit. In his time Jones played all these parts, and the story of his life is thus also a small chapter in the history of the coming of the golden age of mass politics.

Jones's life is like a jigsaw puzzle for which there is more than one solution. Many people have helped me find the pieces, although I remain wholly responsible for the final assembly. Michelle Hawley and Elaine Hadley first tempted me to take on Ernest Jones, and a seminar paper to their romanticism workshop on a wild moonlit evening in Chicago gave me a perfect start in more ways than one. Owen Ashton, Clyde Binfield, Clare Brant, Sally Ledger, and Michael Thompson kindly invited me to their seminars and colloquia as my work progressed and helped keep the momentum going. Jones's papers and writings are now fairly far-flung, and I have taken advantage of friendships near and distant in order to accumulate material. David Armitage in New York, Fabrice Bensimon in Paris, Colleen Forrest in Texas, Austin Gee in Munich, Anne Le More in Berlin, John Morrow in Edinburgh, Michihiro Okamoto and Hideo Koga in Japan, Frank Trentmann at Harvard, and Chris Waters in Williamstown have all helped track down or eliminate elusive sources. Nearer to home I would like to thank the following for information, suggestions, and leads: Malcolm Chase, Ian Haywood, John Hargreaves, Nicholas Hope, Stephen Roberts, Mike Sonenscher, Ted Royle, and Roy Vickers. I would particularly like to single out Owen Ashton at Staffordshire University's Centre for the Study of Chartism for his unremitting supply of Jones references and for his hospitality on my visits to Stoke. Without Owen's enthusiasm Chartist studies in this country would not be what they are, and my own knowledge of mid-Victorian popular politics and literature considerably less than it is. Similarly I could not have undertaken this work without the helpful advice of two of the most eminent historians of Chartism: John Saville and Dorothy Thompson. Dorothy in particular has been a generous and spontaneous source of much material and many suggestions, and although the end result may be unexpected my gratitude to her is no less profound. Special thanks too to Esther Rowlands, who over tea and cake in New York City helped me make sense of Jones's complicated personal life. Thanks also to Ian Patterson for showing me his Ernest Jones jug. Andrea Cross was my guide to the topography of downtown Manchester and the Pennine uplands and deserves special praise. A whole host of librarians have eased my passage through Jones's scattered papers, and it is a pleasure to acknowledge their contribution: in particular that of Judith Baldry and Paula Moorhouse at Manchester Central Library, but also Thomas Bardelle of the Lower Saxony State Archives, Frank Baudach at the Eutiner Landesbibliothek, Lady de Bellaigue at the Royal Archives in Windsor, Barbara Clark of Cumbria Record Office, Bernard Crystal at Columbia University Library, New York, Frau Dr Rheinhart in the State Archive in Lüneburg, Ralph

Thompson of the Discovery Museum in Newcastle, and Lesley Whitelaw at the Middle Temple Library in London.

For permission to cite materials I wish to acknowledge the following: Yale University Library; the Rare Book and Manuscript Library of Columbia University, New York; Manchester Archives and Local Studies, Manchester Central Library; Margaret McFarlane of the Northern Circuit; Chetham's Library, Manchester; London Metropolitan Archives; the National Library of Wales; the International Institute of Social History, Amsterdam; the Bishopsgate Library at the Bishopsgate Institute; the British Library; and the University of Hull Brynmor Jones Library. Citations from the Middle Temple records are made by kind permission of the Masters of the Bench of the Honourable Society of the Middle Temple.

For permission to reproduce portraits and illustrations I would like to thank the following: Manchester Archives and Local Studies, Manchester Central Library (Plates 1, 8–10); Dover Museum (Plate 2); the Syndics of Cambridge University Library (Plate 3); the British Library (Plates 4–6); and the Bishopsgate Library at the Bishopsgate Institute (Plate 7).

Several friends have been kind enough to read parts of this book in draft: David Craig, Michelle Hawley, and Stephen Roberts, and two—Rohan McWilliam and Peter Mandler—have been resilient enough to read it all. To each of them I am indebted, as I am to my two editors: the outgoing Tony Morris for his friendship and loyalty over many years, and the incoming Ruth Parr for her patience over many months. Finally, I am as ever grateful to my own family—Ann, Helena, Patrick, and Sarah—for their companionship. They are usually my toughest critics, but also, I suspect, my warmest fans.

M. T.

Contents

List of Plates

Abbreviations

BGI	Jones papers, Bishopsgate Institute, London
BJH	Jones papers, Brynmor Jones Library, University of Hull
BL	British Library, London
CL	Jones papers, Chetham's Library, Manchester
CN	*Cabinet Newspaper*
COSL	Co-operative Society Library
EJD	Jones diaries, 1839–47
EJLD	Jones legal diaries, 1860–6
HG	*Halifax Guardian*
IISH	Jones papers, International Institute of Social History, Amsterdam
MCL	Manchester Central Library
ME	*Manchester Examiner and Times*
MECW	Karl Marx and Friedrich Engels, *Collected Works* 48 vols. (London: Lawrence and Wishart, 1975–2001)
MG	*Manchester Guardian*
NP	*Notes to the People*
NS	*Northern Star*
PP	*People's Paper*
PRO	Public Record Office, London
SC	Jones papers, Seligman Collection, Columbia University Library, New York
Yale	Yale University Library

Introduction

I

ON A STORMY Saturday afternoon at the end of January 1869 thousands of mourners and spectators thronged the rain-swept streets of central Manchester to watch the slow passage of the funeral cortège of Ernest Jones, the last of the Chartist leaders. By all accounts it was one of the largest public gatherings of its kind that the northern English city had seen for many years. There was genuine emotion and shock displayed that day. Jones had died suddenly from pneumonia four days earlier, the day after his fiftieth birthday. He had been on the verge of his greatest achievement—selection as a Liberal candidate for the next parliamentary election. To add further pathos, Jones seems to have had an uncanny premonition of his early death. His parting words at what proved his last public meeting were reported as, 'he desired soon to get into the House of Commons . . . he could not afford to wait very long. What little work he had in him must be taken out speedily, or it would soon be lost altogether.' Alongside the grief there was political spectacle too. The northern department of the Reform League had taken over the organization of the funeral, attempting to make the occasion a show of respectable working and middle-class liberalism. The mutes who led the procession were veterans of the Peterloo massacre of 1819, the coffin-bearers were old Chartists from the heady days of 1848, and the pall-bearers included the city's Liberal MPs and the executive members of the Reform League in Lancashire. In the sixty or so carriages which followed the coffin were the rest of the city's elite—councillors, police chiefs, doctors, clergy, and even the Conservative Mayor.[1] The great and good of Manchester—the citadel of Victorian liberalism—seemed to be burying one of their own.

[1] *ME* (1 Feb. 1869), 3. On the Reform League's attempt to orchestrate the funeral, see: A. D. Taylor, 'Commemoration, Memorialisation and Political Memory in Post-Chartist Radicalism: The 1885 Halifax Chartist Reunion in Context', in Owen Ashton *et al.* (eds.), *The Chartist Legacy* (Woodbridge: Merlin Press, 1999), 267; Paul Pickering, *Chartism and the Chartists in Manchester and Salford* (London: Macmillan, 1995), 173–4. For Jones's last speech: *ME* (27 Jan. 1869), 5.

But not all went to plan. The departure of the cortège from Jones's house in Higher Broughton was delayed because of the sheer number of people who wanted to view the corpse before the lid of his coffin was nailed down, and by the time the principal mourners got underway the waiting crowd was already a mile in length. As if in homage, the procession meandered along a route dotted with memories and reminders of the dead man's dramatic life, a life which had little in common with the sanitized liberalism that the Reform League were keen to convey on that midwinter day. Down the Bury New Road filed the crowds, past the Manchester Assizes, where Jones had defended scores of the city's labouring poor, and then into Victoria Street, so named in 1837, four years before Jones was presented to the young queen. They crossed the top of Deansgate, home to Heywood's, for over twenty years the publishers of some of Jones's romantic poetry, 'penny dreadful' novels, and political pamphlets, and then turned into Market Street, traversing Cross Street, from where Jones had run his busy legal practice since settling in the city in 1860. Through the dense and narrow city centre flowed the mourners, past the People's Institute, where Jones had given his first Chartist speech in the city in 1847, where he had presided over the 'Labour Parliament' in 1854, and where he had survived an assassination attempt the same year, past the Mosley Arms hotel in which he was arrested on a charge of sedition in 1848 at the height of the Chartist agitation, before turning into Piccadilly and onto the London Road, where the numbers swelled again as working-class men and women joined from nearby Ancoats and New Cross, neighbourhoods which had turned out in force to support Jones's election campaign of the previous year. Finally, the procession reached the gates of Ardwick cemetery, half-a-mile away from the Hyde Road railway bridge, where a policeman had been killed by escaping Fenian prisoners whom Jones went on to defend in a famous showtrial in 1867. By now the gloom was gathering, there had been no letup in the rain, and only the city worthies were allowed into the chapel for the short service led by the Unitarian minister, the Revd Saul Steinthal. But the crowds stayed on and were allowed to fill up the graveyard, waiting for the burial.

Those inside the chapel heard an excerpt read from the 39th Psalm: 'Lord, make me know mine end, and the measure of my days', in which David thanks God for giving him a voice: 'I was dumb, I opened not my mouth; because thou didst *it*.' There was a reading from St Paul's epistle to the Corinthians on the resurrection: 'Death is swallowed up in victory.' Then the coffin was taken outside once more. Edmond Beales, the President of the Reform League, paid tribute to Jones. 'In him', Beales told the crowd, 'you had combined the erudition of the scholar, the genius of the poet, the fervid eloquence of the orator, and the courageous soul and fervent spirit of the undaunted patriot whom no persecution could frighten from the advocacy of his principles, whilst no temptation or threatened loss of fortune could tempt him to betray them.' The burial ensued, and at the final sprinkling of the earth on the descended coffin 'many of the mourners there were unable to restrain their feelings'. One of them felt moved to verse:

> For you, he gave up place and pelf;
> For you renounced the claims of self;
> And nobly closed the course he ran,—
> Pleading for universal man.[2]

A few weeks later Saul Steinthal and another local vicar, John Hopps, gave funeral orations on Jones at a packed meeting of over 1,000 people in Stalybridge. Hopps praised Jones as a 'high priest' who had 'never swerved from the cause he so religiously adopted', whose 'solemn earnestness and burning fervour' were 'heaped upon . . . the altar of the people's freedom'.[3] Two years later, its costs supported by public subscription, a tombstone was erected over Jones's grave, memorializing the dead 'patriot and poet' who had 'freely toiled and suffered on behalf of the wronged and oppressed', and setting in stone his own words for the sake of posterity: 'Democracy is but Christianity applied to the politics of our worldly life.'[4]

By mid-Victorian standards, the death and funeral of Ernest Jones was an extraordinarily melodramatic affair.[5] On the eve of the

[2] William Stokes, *Lines on the death of Mr Ernest Jones* [n.d.].
[3] *Ashton Reporter* (20 Feb. 1869), 4.
[4] 'Record of Tombstones in Ardwick Cemetery', Manchester Archives and Local Studies, MCL, M74/5/35/1; *ME* (10 Apr. 1874), 4; William Lewis, *The Ardwick Cemetery from 1836 to 1906* (Manchester: William Harris, 1906). The phrase is taken from Jones's *Democracy Vindicated: A Lecture Delivered to the Edinburgh Working Men's Institute on the 4th January 1867* (Edinburgh: Andrew Elliot, 1867), 23.
[5] For the decline in extravagant public funerals after mid-century, see: Pat Jalland, *Death in the Victorian Family* (Oxford: Oxford University Press, 1996), ch. 9; cf. John Wolffe, *Great Deaths: Grieving, Religion and Nationhood in Victorian and Edwardian Britain* (Oxford: Oxford University Press, 2000), ch. 6.

opening of the new parliamentary session at Westminster, the Reform League had done its best to make political capital out of the occasion. But the elements, the crowds, and the preacher had all conspired to turn Jones's last journey into something altogether more spiritual, in which the talk was of sacrifice and life after death. What was celebrated on that rainy day in 1869 and for a long time afterwards was not Jones's contribution to the Liberal political cause or even to Chartism, but rather the parable of his life and death as a poet and as a patriotic martyr. In the months and years that followed his death, like the man at his graveside, Jones's friends and followers would burst into poetry at the mention of his name, reciting his verse, or their own attempts at emulation. Published soon after his death, a 'Sonnet suggested by the death of Mr. Ernest Jones' ran thus:

> How futile are Man's purposes! In vain
> He struggles onward, and with patient soul
> Strains to the landmark of some distant goal,
> In steadfastness of mind, and heart, and brain
> That know no daunting: for one darling Hope—
> Whate'er it be—Ambition, Riches, Fame—
> That aery phantom of a lofty name—
> He all things dares, defies.[6]

And in the popular obituaries, memoirs, and biographies of Jones that poured from the press over the next thirty years, the picture was painted over and again of a man of privilege who had renounced his prospects and devoted himself to the working classes and suffered and died as a result. Writing in the *Illustrated London News*, a journalist who had known Jones as a young man lamented that 'he sacrificed himself and his social position for the sake of convictions, for which he suffered long and has died early'.[7] Many thought that there was something saintly about his life. Recording his memories for one of Jones's biographers, an old friend from the 1850s, William Mitchell, suggested that Jones was quite unlike other public men: 'for whom public esteem sunk to zero when seen in private. For they had ceased to pose and became their real selves.' Jones was different, Mitchell explained:

---

[6] *Freelance* (30 Jan. 1869), 36.
[7] *Illustrated London News* (6 Feb. 1869), 143. The author was probably Charles Mackay.

But with Ernest Jones it was not so, he was the same all through, in private life the same unselfish patriot as in public, the same gallant gentleman where he was not known as where he was well known. Frank, cheery, bright and transparent alike in word, act and thought, and ever charitable in his judgment of others. And yet he was misunderstood and maligned; so universally was he defamed he might in his late time have used words to represent his own case which he puts into the mouth of one of his ideal heroes—'Mine has been a talked of name, Slandered till slander's grown to fame.'[8]

Political allies offered similar recollections. Robert Applegarth, the trade unionist, remembered how Jones had 'refused affluence and high social position, though placed within his reach, in exchange for political freedom and penury; with what sublime indifference he suffered two years, not only imprisonment, but of deliberately planned torture; and how he finally died in harness, advocating the cause of the people.' Others recalled the 'chivalry' with which Jones suffered his humiliation.[9] The memory of W. E. Adams, the radical journalist, was even more poignant. He recalled seeing Jones in 1857: 'the pinched face and the threadbare garments told of trial and suffering. A shabby coat buttoned close up round the throat seemed to conceal the poverty to which a too faithful adherence to a lost cause had reduced him.'[10] Others spelled out the tragedy of his final days. In a biography of Jones rushed into print in 1869 by Farrah's, the London publisher, Mansfield Marston noted, '[l]ike the hero of his own great poem, 'The Painter of Florence', he died just as he was about to pluck the fruits of his former labours', or as Louis Blanc put it even more dramatically, at his last public meeting Jones 'avait entendu la voix de l'invisible et austère messager qui l'appelait'.[11] Jones's erstwhile Chartist colleague George Jacob Holyoake later added pathos to this by remembering Jones's own premonition of his mortality. Holyoake recalled how just months before his death Jones

[8] William Mitchell to A. B. Wakefield, 3 Jan. 1891, Wakefield corresp., MCL. The final line is taken from Jones's own Percy Vere (pseud.), *My Life* (London: T. C. Newby, 1846).

[9] Robert Applegarth, 'People I have Known' *Newcastle Weekly Chronicle* (18 Apr. 1896), 5; *Lloyds Weekly London Newspaper* (7 Feb. 1869), 6; G. J. Harney, 'The Late Ernest Jones', *Social Economist* (1 July 1869), 1–2; John Page Hopps, 'Ernest Jones: A Retrospect', *University Magazine*, NS 3 (Mar. 1879), 357–62.

[10] W. E. Adams, *Memoirs of a Social Atom*, 2 vols. (London: Hutchinson & Co., 1903), i. 230.

[11] [M. Marston], *Life and Labours of Ernest Jones, Esq., Poet, Politician and Patriot* (London: F. Farrah, 1869), 4; Louis Blanc, *Dix ans de l'histoire d'Angleterre* (Paris: Calmann Lévy, 1880), 38.

had spoken to him on 'his favourite theme', which was 'the manner in which an actor on the stage of the world should quit it'.[12]

Jones was thus remembered and revered by his contemporaries not as a politician, but as a popular icon. He became immortalized not for what he did, but for the tragic manner of his death and the moral tale that was his life. Long after he passed away, Jones aroused emotional and poetic sentiments in some of the most staid Victorian labour leaders. He became a cult figure around whom a mini-industry of jugs, almanac covers, and cheap engravings grew up, and about whom many legends and rumours began to circulate. In death Jones won a following of devoted admirers that had often eluded him in life, and like a sect they stood guard over his reputation. An instance of this came in January 1879, when an anniversary dinner was held in the Manchester Junior Reform Club, presided over by Dr Richard Pankhurst, husband and father of the famous suffragettes. There were several political speeches that evening, but most of the time between endless maudlin toasts was taken up with readings of Jones's poetry and singing of his songs. The centrepiece of the occasion was the viewing of Jones's manuscripts, amongst which '[t]he most precious relics' were the leaves cut out of a prayer book on which he wrote several poems whilst imprisoned in 1849. 'The history of these poems is quite romantic,' stated the account of the dinner: '[w]hen the author was denied the use of pens, ink, and paper, he improvised a pen out of a crow-quill he picked up in the courtyard of his prison, and used as ink, blood drawn from his wrist.'[13] For the next twenty years these manuscripts or relics were passed on to a succession of Jones's friends in the hope that someone would prepare an edition of his poems. Like more modern icons in film and popular music, Jones did wonders for his posthumous status by dying relatively young and whilst in the public eye, by leaving behind a body of unknown work, and, above all, by living a life which seems to have been scripted for the stage.

---

[12] G. J. Holyoake, *Sixty Years of an Agitator's Life*, 2 vols. (London: T. F. Unwin, 1892), ii. 559.

[13] James Mosley (ed.), *In Memoriam: Ernest Jones* (Manchester: Co-operative Printing Society, 1879), 5.

2

The manner of Ernest Jones's death and the ways in which he was memorialized tell us a great deal about his life, and for that reason it is appropriate to begin a biography of Jones with the final instalment. At first sight, it may be difficult for a modern reader to understand the adulation that surrounded Jones. It has been said that high failure is better than low success, and of few men would this be truer than Jones. Judged by the usual political criteria he was a conspicuous under-achiever. Jones left behind him no political ideology, no legislative achievement, and no grateful constituents to remind us of his contribution to the Victorian era. He joined the Chartist movement in 1846 at the nadir of its fortunes, and became its de facto leader in the aftermath of 1848, its greatest failure. Unlike John Wilkes in 1762 or Feargus O'Connor in 1843, there was no symbolic victory over the government at his trial in 1848, and unlike Henry Hunt in 1820 or Richard Oastler in 1840, there was no opportunity to turn his two-year imprisonment into an instant propaganda success by carrying on his campaign from his cell. Whereas other Chartist editors—Thomas Cooper, William James Linton, and G. W. M. Reynolds all spring to mind—were able to translate notoriety as political agitators into commercial success as poets, artists, or newspaper proprietors, Jones did not. In conditions of mid-Victorian boom for the middlebrow novel, lowlife yellow paperback, and daily broadsheet, Jones was a business disaster, to the extent that he was declared insolvent more than once, and was forced to rely on the support of the Royal Literary Fund and the generosity of leading literati to help him through his poorer times. Towards the end of his life he built up a successful practice as a barrister, but nothing to rival better-known advocates such as W. P. Roberts or J. A. Roebuck, both of whom in their day earned the sobriquet of 'people's lawyer'. By even the flexible standards of radical hagiography Jones was several leaves short of a laurel. His only real victory of note came in a much-publicized libel action against G. W. M. Reynolds in 1859, in which Jones upheld his reputation against Reynolds's mischievous charge that he was not all that he claimed or seemed.

Yet that sole success—a vindication of his character—after years of adversity suggests two reasons why the life of Ernest Jones possesses significance beyond the merely biographical. First, Jones belonged to the last generation of what has been called the tradition of 'gentlemanly radicalism' in Hanoverian and Victorian Britain.[14] Britain was the first industrial nation, the home of the world's first urban proletariat, yet until the advent of the Labour party in 1900 working-class movements tended to be led by the rural gentry. From the time of John Wilkes and Horne Tooke in the reign of George III, Sir Francis Burdett and Henry Hunt in the Regency years, through to Sir Wilfrid Lawson, Sir Charles Dilke, and Henry Hyndman at the close of the century, there were always men of wealth and education who chose to turn their talents and resources to plebeian politics. In an age when the language of working-class protest remained anti-industrial, constitutionalist, and seldom inflected by modern notions of class, the gentlemanly status of these men gave their politics a credibility that other radical leaders lacked.[15] Their independent wealth usually managed to deflect prying questions about their motives, their privileged upbringing lent their political rhetoric a learned air, and their non-industrial backgrounds gave them a neutral viewpoint from which to observe the social tensions of the towns. At the same time, the whiff of suspicion and scandal was never very far away from men who so deliberately flaunted caste and convention. As Wilkes found out, a man could be acclaimed as a patriot one day, and denounced as a scoundrel the next. The French revolution, mediated through the lurid prose of Edmund Burke, Thomas Carlyle, and Charles Dickens, raised the spectre of the rural gentleman as at best an insouciant dandy, and at worst a scheming demagogue or religious zealot, manipulating the mob.[16] By the

[14] John Belchem and James Epstein, 'The Nineteenth-Century Gentleman Leader Revisited', *Social History*, 22 (1997), 174–93; Patrick Joyce, *Democratic Subjects: The Self and the Social in Nineteenth-Century England* (Cambridge: Cambridge University Press, 1994), 214–17; Eugenio F. Biagini, *Liberty, Retrenchment and Reform: Popular Liberalism in the Age of Gladstone, 1860–1880* (Cambridge: Cambridge University Press, 1992), ch. 7; Rohan McWilliam, *Popular Politics in Nineteenth Century England* (London: Routledge, 1998), 66.

[15] Of course not all scholars would subscribe to this characterization of working-class protest. For some key works which do, see: Craig Calhoun, *A Question of Class Struggle: Social Foundations of Popular Radicalism During the Industrial Revolution* (Oxford: Blackwell, 1982); Gareth Stedman Jones, 'Rethinking Chartism', in *Languages of Class: Studies in English Working-Class History, 1832–1982* (Cambridge: Cambridge University Press, 1983), 90–178; David Cannadine, *Class in Britain* (London: Yale University Press, 1998), ch. 3.

[16] For Burke's demonology, see J. G. A. Pocock, 'The Political Economy of Burke's Analysis of the French Revolution', in *Virtue, Commerce and History: Essays on Political Thought and History, Chiefly in the Eighteenth Century* (Cambridge: Cambridge University Press, 1985), 193–212. For Burke's lament at the end of

time of the mid-Victorian years pleading political virtue and dis-interestedness was simply not enough. In an age preoccupied with evangelical respectability and commercial probity, gentleman radicals had to prove their social and financial morality as well. The ethos of the gentleman had become overlain with expectations about masculinity, asceticism, and—the word is unavoidable—earnest-ness.[17] Jones's life, or more accurately, the careful ways in which he refined and defended a particular version of his life, offers a case-study of the increasingly contested role of gentlemanly radicalism in the nineteenth century.

Secondly, Jones's passage into memory as a 'poet and patriot' offers confirmation of the persistence of romanticism in the *mentalité* of mid-nineteenth-century popular politics. In literary analysis the 1840s and 1850s are conventionally described as 'post-romantic' or 'Victorian', insofar as poetry and prose fiction moved away from the idealism and naturalism of the era of the Lake poets and Byron and Shelley, and became preoccupied instead with religious doubt, material change, and artistic introspection.[18] But although polite literary culture may have become recognizably 'Victorian', popular poetry, drama, and prose did not. Gothic melodrama, cheap romances of domestic life, and epic historical verse flourished in the early Victorian age. Penny-dreadful publications such as those of John Cleave and Reynolds rivalled improving, utilitarian serials such

chivalry: Tim Fulford, *Romanticism and Masculinity: Gender, Politics and Poetics in the Writings of Burke, Coleridge, Cobbett, Wordsworth, De Quincey and Hazlitt* (London: Macmillan, 1999), ch. 1. On Carlyle's denigration of the Jacobins as fanatics see: John D. Rosenberg, *Carlyle and the Burden of History* (Oxford: Clarendon Press, 1985), 64–5, 103–4. For Dickens: Ian McCalman, 'Controlling the Riots: Dickens, Barnaby Rudge and Romantic Revolution', *History*, 84 (1999), 458–76.

[17] Stefan Collini, 'The Idea of Character: Private Habits and Public Virtues', in *Public Moralists: Political Thought and Intellectual Life in Britain, 1850–1920* (Oxford: Clarendon Press, 1991), 91–118; Herbert Sussman, *Victorian Masculinities: Manhood and Masculine Poetics in Early Victorian Literature and Art* (Cambridge: Cambridge University Press, 1995); James Eli Adams, *Dandies and Desert Saints: Styles of Victorian Masculinity* (London: Cornell University Press, 1995); Mark Girouard, *The Return to Camelot: Chivalry and the English Gentleman* (London: Yale University Press, 1981), esp. chs. 6, 9.

[18] Isobel Armstrong, *Victorian Poetry: Poetry, Poetics and Politics* (London: Routledge, 1993); Donald Thomas, *The Post Romantics* (London: Routledge, 1990); Patrick Brantlinger, *The Spirit of Reform: British Literature and Politics, 1832–1867* (Cambridge, Mass.: Harvard University Press, 1977); Catherine Gallagher, *The Industrial Reformation of English Fiction: Social Discourse and Narrative Form, 1832–1867* (London: University of Chicago Press, 1985).

as the *Penny Magazine*, as the onset of urban industrialism was perceived by the media through a haze of escapist storytelling and excursions into imaginative lyric. 'Olden time' history set in the Elizabethan and Jacobean eras—exemplified in the fiction of authors such as Harrison Ainsworth—vied with the cult of medieval chivalry in the competition for readers of the nation's history.[19] The persistence of romanticism was not, however, simply a descent into sensationalism or costume drama. The Lake poets, and later on Byron and Shelley, supplied mid-Victorian radical poetics with a pastoral vision which has been expertly documented in recent work.[20] And in Shelley's celebration of the poet as the 'legislator of the world', the romantics bequeathed to Victorian culture the persona of the artist as prophet and seer, a role that set a challenge to writers and poets such as Thomas Carlyle, J. S. Mill, and Alfred Tennyson.[21] It is the claim of this study that the meaning and context of Ernest Jones's career as the last Chartist leader cannot be understood properly without registering this long reach of the age of romanticism.

---

[19] On melodrama: G. Kitson Clark, 'The Romantic Element, 1830–50', in J. H. Plumb (ed.), *Studies in Social History: A Tribute to G. M. Trevelyan* (London: Longmans, 1955), 229, 234; Louis James, *Fiction for the Working Man, 1830–1850: A Study of Literature Produced for the Working Class in Early Victorian Urban England* (London: Oxford University Press, 1963); Martha Vicinus, *The Industrial Muse: A Study of Nineteenth-Century British Working Class Literature* (London: Croom Helm, 1974); Rohan McWilliam, 'Melodrama and the Historians', *Radical History Review*, 78 (2000), 57–84. On the press: Patricia Anderson, *The Printed Image and the Transformation of Popular Culture, 1790–1860* (Oxford: Clarendon Press, 1991). On medievalism and the 'olden time' in popular history: Girouard, *Return to Camelot*; Peter Mandler, ' "In the Olden Time": Romantic History and English National Identity, 1820–50', in Lawrence Brockliss and David Eastwood (eds.), *A Union of Multiple Identities: The British Isles* (Manchester: Manchester University Press, 1997), 78–92; Rosemary Mitchell, *Picturing the Past: English History in Text and Image, 1830–1870* (Oxford: Clarendon Press, 2000).
[20] Anne Janowitz, *Lyric and Labour in the Romantic Tradition* (Cambridge: Cambridge University Press, 1998).
[21] Carl Woodring, *Politics in English Romantic Poetry* (Cambridge, Mass.: Harvard University Press, 1970), chs. 5–6; David Duff, *Romance and Revolution: Shelley and the Politics of a Genre* (Cambridge: Cambridge University Press, 1994); Joseph Bristow, 'Reforming Victorian Poetry: Poetics After 1832', in Bristow (ed.), *The Cambridge Companion to Victorian Poetry* (Cambridge: Cambridge University Press, 2000), 1–24.

3

Ernest Jones has long evaded a full biography. Twelve authors—ten men and two women—have begun biographies, written short sketches, or edited parts of Jones's work, but only one, George Howell in 1898, completed a full biography. Despite being commissioned by the Ernest Jones Memorial Committee to write the work, Howell was unable to find a publisher, although his manuscript was serialized in the *Newcastle Weekly Chronicle* in 1898. Over 130 years after his death Jones continues to defy attempts on his life. He remains an unconquered peak of popular radicalism, and amongst his personal papers is a telling trail of letters from one defeated, exhausted, or frustrated would-be biographer to the next young challenger. It is worth tracing the fortunes of Jones's previous biographers, if only to point out the pitfalls which have lain along their path, and which this biography has tried to avoid. For what emerges from a survey of the various efforts to subject Jones to biography is how the distance of time since his death in 1869 has served to obscure the romanticism which enveloped his life.

Within weeks of his burial attempts were made to commemorate Jones's literary accomplishments. Soon after his death a Memorial Fund Committee was established, mainly to provide for his widow and children and for a memorial, but also for a life and edition of his prose and verse works.[22] Some of Jones's manuscripts, including his unpublished poetry, his prison poems, and his diary from the 1840s, were entrusted to two members of this committee, James Crossley and Eli Sowerbutts, his literary executors, but nothing came of this enterprise, although selections of Jones's verse did eventually appear in A. H. Miles's *Poets of the Century* in 1892.[23] Instead, in the decades after his death a series of short, potted sketches of Jones's life appeared, but all of them drew heavily and uncritically on Jones's

[22] 'Ernest Jones Memorial Fund', Resolutions, (1869–70), George Howell papers, BGI. The Memorial Fund did organize some lectures, for example: F. R. Lees, *In Memoriam: An Oration on the Death of Ernest Jones, The People's Friend* (Leeds: J. W. Petty, 1874).

[23] Miles included eight poems by Jones: A. H. Miles (ed.), *The Poets and the Poetry of the Century: Frederick Tennyson to Arthur Hugh Clough* 10 vols. (London: Hutchinson & Co., 1892), iv. 547–62; A. H. Miles to George Howell, 21 Mar. 1892, Howell papers, BGI. In 1897 Thomas Costley claimed Jones as a great Salford poet, and regretted that there was no local monument to him: *Lancashire Poets, and Other Literary Sketches (In a Series of Lectures)* (Manchester: Abel Heywood & Sons, 1897), 72–5.

own reminiscences.[24] It was not until the late 1880s that a serious attempt was made to produce a scholarly biography, based on hitherto unused sources. And by then the trail had begun to go rather cold. Jones's eldest son, Ernest, stirred the Halifax free-thought lecturer A. B. Wakefield into action, and in January 1891 the Memorial Committee was resuscitated at a meeting in Halifax, with Jones's second son, Edmond Stanley Jones, being appointed secretary.[25] The Committee suggested that George Jacob Holyoake, Gerald Massey, or George Julian Harney be invited to write the biography. Further meetings at Manchester and Birmingham were held later in the year. Wakefield also gave lectures in support of the project, and his own short life of Jones was published.[26] The following year various enquiries were made by the Committee as to the whereabouts of Jones's writings, and this move turned up copies of his *Notes to the People* of 1851–2 and his *Evenings with the People* of 1856.[27] Finally, in May 1892 an agreement was reached between the Memorial Committee and the publishers T. Fisher Unwin for two works. There would be a biography and an edition of Jones's writings and speeches. Initially, the volume containing the literary works was to be edited by W. E. A. Axon, the Manchester antiquarian, with the biography to be written by Henry Dunckley, the former editor of the *Manchester Examiner and Times*.[28] But by April 1892 George Howell had been entrusted with the task instead, for a fee of £250.[29]

In some ways, Howell was a natural choice as a biographer. He had known Jones during the Reform League campaigns of the mid-

[24] Marston, *Life and Labours of Ernest Jones*; J. M. Davidson, *Weekly Dispatch* (26 Jan. 1890), 2; Frederick Leary, *The Life of Ernest Jones* (London: Democrat Publishing, 1887); D. P. Davies, *A Short Account of the Life and Labours of Ernest Jones. To Which is Appended Several of his Poems* (Liverpool: Journal of Commerce Printing Works, 1897).

[25] Ernest Beaufort Jones to Wakefield, 7 Oct. 1886, Wakefield corresp., MCL; *Halifax Courier* (24 Jan. 1891), 3.

[26] A. B. Wakefield, *Ernest Jones: The People's Friend* (Halifax: privately published, 1891); id., 'Ernest Jones as Reformer and Poet', lecture at Ancoats, Manchester (31 Jan. 1892), Howell papers, BGI; id., 'The Poetry of Ernest Jones: Notes for Address at Manchester Literary Club' [1891], Wakefield correspondence, MCL.

[27] Thomas Garbutt to Edmond Jones, 19 May 1892, IISH.

[28] 'Ernest Jones Memorial Committee' (fliers 1891–2), Jones MSS, Nuffield College, Oxford, Spec. Coll. CD37; 'Memorandum of an Agreement between T. Fisher Unwin and E. R. Stanley Jones' (16 May 1892), Howell papers, BGI.

[29] Howell to A. B. Wakefield, 17 April 1892, Wakefield correspondence, MCL; F. M. Leventhal, *Respectable Radical: George Howell and Working Class Politics* (Cambridge, Mass.: Harvard University Press, 1971), 212.

1860s, he had already written several histories of the labour movement in Britain, and he had a reputation for honest efficiency. But in
other respects, Howell was a strange choice. He had little affinity
with the working-class milieu of Jones's adopted home of industrial
Manchester and the West Riding of Yorkshire, his political career
had been devoted to reclaiming the respectable face of working-class
politics from the demagoguery of the men of 1848, of whom Jones
was a prominent example, and above all, Howell was a self-educated
Methodist, unsympathetic to the early Victorian preoccupation with
Byronic romanticism. Howell could be relied on to deliver homage to
a radical politician, but not to produce an appreciation of a lost
literary talent and seer, which is what men like Wakefield really
desired. Nonetheless the manuscripts which had been lovingly
sheltered by Sowerbutts and Wakefield now duly passed, via the
Manchester Library, to Howell, and further enquiries yielded other
lost gems from the Jones backlist.[30] However, all did not go well. By
January 1893 Howell was complaining that he was being delayed by
the reluctance of the committee to finance his researches; two
years later he protested at having no support whatsoever from the
committee. When he finally downed tools on completion in 1896, he
denounced the 'scandalous treatment' of the committee, who had
not only proved mean, but had held on to manuscript materials.[31]
Howell turned to old friends at the *Newcastle Weekly Chronicle*, a
paper well known for its interest in the heroes of mid-Victorian
radicalism, and the life of Jones joined a queue awaiting publication,
behind the serialized biographies of Jessie White Mario and Charles
Gavan Duffy.[32] There was some substance to Howell's animus. The
uncooperative committee had also so mismanaged Jones's widow's
fund that it had to be relaunched in 1903.[33] And the surviving Jones

[30] Howell to A. B. Wakefield, 21 Apr., 24 Apr. 1892, Wakefield corresp., MCL;
Charles Goss to C. W. Sutton, 31 July 1911, 2 Aug. 1911, IISH. For loans of or information as to the whereabouts of materials relating to Jones's life, see: F. Boorman to
Howell, 29 May 1892. Ernest Jones jr. to Howell, 30 May 1892, 2 June 1892,
A. B. Wakefield to Howell, 11 Feb. 1895. Ernest Jones jr. told Howell that he had in
his possession two large boxes, with 'thousands' of letters, but for one reason or
another Howell did not consult them. These were the family papers eventually
purchased by Edward Seligman for the library at Columbia University, New York.
[31] Howell to A. B. Wakefield, 28 Jan. 1893, 14 Feb. 1895, 28 May 1896, Wakefield
corresp., MCL; Howell, 'Ernest Jones, The Chartist: Poet and Orator, Patriot and
Politician', *Newcastle Weekly Chronicle* (1 Jan. 1898), 9.
[32] Joseph Cowen to Howell, 10 Feb. 1892, George Howell papers, BGI.
[33] 'A Fund for the Assistance of the Widow of the Late Ernest Jones' (1903), BGI;
L. Atherley Jones to Anon., 22 Apr. 1899, IISH.

family were of not much use either. Despite, or perhaps because of, being a prominent Liberal MP and aspiring author, Jones's youngest son, Llewellyn Atherley-Jones, offered little assistance to the Committee or to Howell. Instead, Atherley-Jones preferred to remember his father as a proto-Gladstonian liberal, a caricature which eventually found its way into his own autobiography published in 1925.[34] Howell was left with access to two of Jones's diaries and to his published poetry, and he diligently put together all the reviews of Jones's published work. But family memorabilia and correspondence did not come Howell's way, with the result that his resources were rather limited, and he padded out over a third of the book with a narrative history of reform politics in the first half of the nineteenth century. By the time it appeared Howell's biography was several years overdue, but in reality it was twenty years too late. Howell hoped that his biography would 'keep green the memory of a man whose talents and energy, sacrifices and sufferings, entitle him to be ranked among the heroes of freedom'. It did not. In 1908 *Reynolds's Newspaper* could refer to Jones as a 'forgotten hero'.[35] By then his grave in Ardwick cemetery had fallen into disuse. A few years later the suffragette campaign and the reappearance of political prisoners in Britain did rekindle a little interest in Jones. In 1913 the Manchester and Salford Trades Council repaired and rededicated the memorial, where it remained undisturbed until the whole cemetery was bulldozed to make way for a recreation ground in the late 1950s.[36]

So by the turn of the century Jones had largely disappeared from the pantheon, respectable or otherwise, of radical liberalism. To an early twentieth-century Labour party leadership keen to emphasize its authentic working-class origins, a silver-tongued gentlemanly radical was of limited political use and Jones, along with Feargus O'Connor, became nudged out in favour of Fabian gradualists such

---

[34] L. Atherley-Jones, *Looking Back: Reminiscences of a Political Career* (London: H. F. & G. Witherby, 1925), 1–9. Atherley-Jones was the author of the pseudonymous *The Fall of Lord Paddocksha* (London: William Heinemann, 1901) by Lionel Langton, the plot of which—a gentleman seducing a servant girl—bore an uncanny resemblance to his own father's *The Lass and the Lady* of 1853 (see below, Ch. 5). On Atherley-Jones's version of his father's life, see A. D. Taylor, 'Commemoration, Memorialisation and Political Memory', 268.

[35] Howell, 'Ernest Jones', *Newcastle Weekly Chronicle* (1 Jan. 1898), 9; *Reynolds's Newspaper* (2 Feb. 1908), 2.

[36] *Manchester Courier*, (1 Sept. 1913), 3; TUC *46th Annual Report* (Manchester: Trades Union Congress, 1913), 46–7.

as Francis Place and William Lovett. Only the Social Democratic Federation, with H. M. Hyndman at its head—perhaps the last example of the patrician strain in working-class radicalism—found in Jones a stick with which to beat moderates in the labour movement.[37] The half-century since his death had not been kind to Jones's memory. On the centenary of his birth Jones was remembered mainly by the socialist left: by J. B. Glasier in the *Labour Leader*, Ben Turner in the *Yorkshire Factory Times*, and Charles Glyde in the *Vanguard*.[38] The first wave of scholarly histories of Chartism published either side of the First Word War did begin to remedy this neglect, painting a picture of Jones as an outsider, a cosmopolitan socialist, his views the outcome of his German background and his contact with Marx and Engels.[39] In part, this reflected nostalgia both in Europe and America for an international socialist movement which was torn asunder in 1914. Some of these historians, particularly those with access to Manchester, used new evidence about Jones. None of them, with the exception of Dolléans, seem to have consulted Howell's biography. They did, however, generate new interest in Jones, leading to the researches of Ella Twynham in the 1920s. Twynham twisted more aid out of Jones's sons than Howell had managed, but her manuscript biography of Jones never saw light of day, although it did provide some of the basis for G. D. H. Cole's account of Jones in his *Chartist Portraits* (1941).[40] By the time of the Second World War the memory of Ernest Jones had become so

[37] *Justice* (26 July 1884), 5; *Social Democrat*, 2 (May 1898), 131–3; Henry Mayers Hyndman, *The Record of an Adventurous Life* (London: Macmillan & Co., 1911), 12.

[38] *Labour Leader* (23 Jan. 1919), 6–8; *Yorkshire Factory Times* (23 Jan. 1919), 3; C. A. Glyde, 'The Centenary of Ernest Jones', *Bradford Socialist Vanguard* (Feb. 1919), 3; (Mar. 1919), 2; (May 1919), 2–3.

[39] Édouard Dolléans, *Le Chartisme, 1830–48*, 2 vols., (Paris: H. Floury, 1912–13), ii. 338; P. W. Slosson, *The Decline of the Chartist Movement* (New York: Columbia University Press, 1916), 196; Julius West, *A History of the Chartist Movement* (London: Constable, 1920), 231–2; Mark Hovell, *The Chartist Movement* (Manchester: Manchester University Press, 1918), 280–1; M. Beer, *A History of British Socialism*, 2 vols. (London: G. Bell & Sons, 1920), ii. 159; Theodore Rothstein, *From Chartism to Labourism: Historical Sketches of the English Working Class Movement*, 2nd edn. (London: Lawrence & Wishart, 1983), passim; F. E. Gillespie, *Labor and Politics in England, 1850–1867* (Durham, NC: Duke University Press, 1927), 73.

[40] Ella Twynham, 'The Life of Ernest Jones', unpublished typescript, Cole collection, Nuffield College, Oxford; G. D. H. Cole, *Chartist Portraits* (London: Macmillan & Co., 1941), ch. 12; Ernest Jones jr. to Twynham, 8 Feb. 1923, Jones MSS, Nuffield College, Oxford.

insignificant that a chain of Jewish jewellers based in the north of England could rename their stores 'Ernest Jones and Co.' on the grounds that it sounded like a neutral and authentically English appellation.

The last major attempt on Jones's life came shortly after the Second World War as Marxist historians began to loosen the grip that Fabian and radical-liberal historiography had held over British working-class history since the death of Victoria. Dorothy Thompson (née Towers) began Ph.D work on a biography of Jones and became the first scholar to make extensive use of the Jones family papers.[41] John Saville put together an edition of Jones's principal political writings, including excerpts from his speeches, political pamphlets, and extracts from the newspapers he edited, and prefaced the volume with the most reliable account of Jones's life yet to appear.[42] In addition to picking up the by now familiar paper-trail of Manchester memorabilia and ephemera, both Thompson and Saville made use of the hitherto unpublished correspondence between Jones and the exiled Marx and Engels. Some of this material was beginning to become available in the East German edition of Marx and Engels's collected works, but the good contacts of the Communist Party Historians' Group were also able to obtain as yet unseen letters direct from the archives in Moscow. Neither Saville nor Thompson was particularly interested in Jones's literary aspirations. This was a surprising blind-spot, given how at the same time Edward Thompson, another member of the Communist Party's Historians' Group, was re-evaluating William Morris, and another member, Francis Klingender, was exploring the relationship between romantic expression and the industrial revolution.[43] Nonetheless, between them, Saville and Thompson contributed a great deal to putting Jones in a new perspective. Saville saw Jones, influenced by Marx and Engels, as the intellectual cornerstone of a new Chartist ideology, which embraced socialism and republicanism after the defeat of 1848, whilst Dorothy Thompson found via Jones's

[41] Some of her findings on Jones appeared in: Dorothy Towers, 'The Chartist Poets', *Our Time*, 7 (Apr. 1948), 168–9; Dorothy and Edward Thompson, 'Halifax as a Chartist centre' (unpublished typescript, n.d., *c.*1955), Calderdale District Archives, Halifax; Dorothy Thompson, 'Letters from Ernest Jones to Karl Marx, 1865–1868', *Bulletin of the Society for the Study of Labour History*, 4 (1962), 11–23.

[42] John Saville, *Ernest Jones, Chartist* (London: Lawrence & Wishart, 1952).

[43] E. P. Thompson, *William Morris: Romantic to Revolutionary* (London: Lawrence & Wishart, 1955); Francis D. Klingender, *Art and the Industrial Revolution* (London: Lawrence & Wishart, 1947).

activities in the West Riding evidence of the communal working-class culture which sustained the movement for so long. As Chartist studies entered its golden years in the 1960s and 1970s, Jones, shorn of all romantic ideological baggage, had been successfully accommodated within the new Marxist social history of the period. But still he awaited a full biography.

Why has Jones proved so insurmountable? The problem is not lack of interest, although as the above potted survey makes clear, Jones has been subject to a series of appropriations by radical and Marxist historians and this has rather distorted his significance, exaggerating his political contribution at the expense of his literary reputation. Nor is there want of material. Jones kept virtually everything—family letters, business papers, manuscript copies of all his poems, reviews of his work, diaries, legal notebooks, sketchbooks, and calling cards.[44] Piecing together evidence from his diaries in the 1840s, the newspapers he edited and largely wrote during the 1850s, and his legal notebooks in the 1860s, as well as using information from other sources, it is possible to establish what Jones was doing or where he was on virtually every day of his adult life, from the moment he and his family returned to England from Holstein in 1838 though to his death in Manchester over thirty years later. Yet there is little that has been published in the last hundred years that adds materially to our knowledge of his life. We know now more about his relationship with the town of Halifax,[45] his friendship with Marx and Engels,[46] his attempts to seek the patronage of the mid-Victorian literary establishment,[47] and his involvement in Manchester politics at the time of the second reform act.[48] However,

[44] For a fuller account of the principal locations of Jones's manuscripts, see my entry on Jones in Neville Kirk and David Howell (eds.), *Dictionary of Labour Biography*, vol. 11 (forthcoming, 2003); cf. Hideo Koga, 'Some Notes on Evaluations and Materials of Ernest Jones: Chartist', *Journal of the Faculty of Liberal Arts (Yamaguchi University)*, 23 (1989), 13–25.

[45] Dorothy and Edward Thompson, 'Halifax as a Chartist Centre'; Kate Tiller, 'Late Chartism: Halifax, 1847–58', in James Epstein and Dorothy Thompson (eds.), *The Chartist Experience: Studies in Working-Class Radicalism and Culture, 1830–60* (London: Macmillan, 1982), 311–44.

[46] Saville, *Ernest Jones*, app. 1; Thompson, 'Letters from Ernest Jones to Karl Marx'.

[47] Thomas W. Porter, 'Ernest Jones and the Royal Literary Fund', *Labour History Review*, 57 (1992), 84–94.

[48] A. D. Taylor, 'Ernest Jones: His Later Career and the Structure of Manchester Politics, 1861–9', MA thesis, Birmingham University (1984); id., ' "The Best Way to Get what He Wanted": Ernest Jones and the Boundaries of Liberalism in the Manchester Election of 1868', *Parliamentary History*, 16 (1997), 185–204.

apart from the correspondence with Marx and Engels and the revelations about Jones's appeal to the Royal Literary Fund, there is nothing in general here that could not be gleaned from a perusal of Howell's biography. By contrast, far greater advances have been made in recent years in our appreciation of Jones's poetry and novels, and the biography that follows is considerably indebted to the insights and ideas of this body of work.[49] But even here there is little in terms of source material that was not already known. The bulk of Jones's published poems have long been available in modern editions.[50] Recent Jones scholarship has thus deepened our knowledge of certain moments of his life, and begun to restore his literary accomplishments to somewhere near their proper place. But for all his renowned transparency, the actual events of Jones's life remain curiously opaque. For the real problem in writing the life of Jones is that Jones got there first. On more than one occasion, whilst he was still alive, Jones told versions of his life-story—versions which quickly became standard, and which over time have been accepted unquestioningly by most historians.

4

The most famous rendition of Jones's life-story came in 1868, in a pamphlet entitled *Ernest Jones: Who is he? What has he done?* This penny pamphlet, published by Abel Heywood on behalf of the Reform League, was brought out to aid Jones during his 1868 election campaign in Manchester. Thirty thousand copies were printed, and although it was published anonymously, it seems certain that it was put together at Jones's own dictation by James Crossley, one of his allies from the Manchester Manhood Suffrage League.[51] It was thus very much a work of autobiography, although a selective one at

---

[49] Ulrike Schwab, *The Poetry of the Chartist Movement: A Literary and Historical Study* (Dordrecht: Kluwer Academic, 1993); Anne Janowitz, *Lyric and Labour*; Ian Haywood, *The Literature of Struggle: An Anthology of Chartist Fiction* (Aldershot: Scolar Press, 1995), 16–17, 20–1, 142–56, 195–202; id. (ed.), Ernest Jones, *Woman's Wrongs* (Aldershot: Ashgate, 2001).

[50] Y. Kovalev, *An Anthology of Chartist Literature* (London: Central Books, 1956); P. Scheckner, *An Anthology of Chartist Poetry: Poetry of the British Working Class, 1830s–1850s* (London: Associated Universities Presses, 1989).

[51] The copy in MCL has the following pencilled note on the title-page: 'This was written at the dictation and proofs corrected by Ernest Jones himself.' *Ernest Jones. Who is he? What has he Done?* (Manchester: The Reform League, 1868); cf. the entry on Jones in *Men of the Time*, 7th edn. (London: Routledge, 1868), 454–5.

that. The version of events which Jones retold in the 1868 pamphlet went as follows.

The first part of the pamphlet was devoted to establishing Jones's impeccable pedigree, rooting it in Britain's feudal past, but also in the nation's royal and heroic present. Born in Berlin in 1819, Jones came from a privileged background. His father's family were of Welsh origin, but had been settled in England for 500 years. Jones's father was a wounded war-hero, a veteran of the Peninsular campaign and of Waterloo, and with the peace after 1815 had become equerry to the Duke of Cumberland, the 'uncle to our Queen'. Jones senior had married the daughter of a large landowner from Kent, and after Ernest's birth he had retired to an estate in Holstein in northern Germany. The pamphlet then turned to the naturalistic idyll that was Ernest Jones's childhood. An only child, Jones 'passed his boyhood' in this 'lonely and purely agricultural region . . . the solitude and romantic scenery, no doubt, tending to develope [*sic*] the germs of that poetic spirit which has since borne fruit in his mature years'. His literary ability already evident in the poetry he had published as a 10-year-old, Jones was also a precocious friend of the people, running away in 1830, apparently to join the Poles in their revolt. But the free spirit was also a hard-working young man, and in his later teens, so the pamphlet went on, he attended the exclusive St Michael's College in Lüneburg, normally a school reserved for the German nobility; but its doors were opened to Jones after a 'letter patent' had been granted by the King of Hanover. There Jones excelled, giving an early indication of his oratorical skills by making a farewell address in German to 'a great concourse of the surrounding nobility and gentry'. So good was the speech that the college had it published, and the certificate he gained on leaving the college was one of the highest ever given. In 1838 the family returned to England, and now the pamphlet set to work on describing how Jones moved effortlessly into the aristocratic and court circles of metropolitan London. He 'was now launched into the vortex of fashionable life'. He was presented to the Queen, 'and was, for some years, a regular visitor at court'. He married the daughter of a Cumbrian landowning family—but 'neither this alliance with an old Conservative family, nor the blandishments of society, appear to have weaned him from his love of liberty and his devotion to literature'. Jones's first novel was published, to widespread acclaim in the reviews, and he was called to the bar.

And then, the pamphlet explained, all changed. 'In 1845, although with the most promising professional prospects, he abandoned the active pursuit of the latter and the allurements of the fashionable life, to devote himself to the interests of the working classes.' Jones joined Feargus O'Connor at the *Northern Star*, and for the next twenty years 'passed from town to town throughout Great Britain, teaching political and economical truths . . . probably attending more meetings and delivering more lectures . . . than any man now living'. But such was his morality that he never accepted payment for labour. Indeed, the pamphlet asserted, he used his own wealth to support the righteous: 'all the income he derived from his labours as a literary man, unconnected with politics, and from private business, over and above what was needed for a household conducted with the most rigid economy, he spent on the popular cause.' The account then turned to what proved the centrepiece of this version of Jones's life: his arrest, trial, and imprisonment in 1848. Alarmed by his oratory the Whig government had him arrested and 'left nothing undone to secure a conviction'. A long, detailed account of the harshness of his two-year imprisonment was then given. Kept in solitary confinement for most of the time, denied pen, ink, and paper, as well as visits from his family, Jones could only keep his dignity by refusing to pick oakum. For this infringement he was put on a bread-and-water diet, denied his Bible, and placed in a cell recently occupied by a victim of the cholera: 'the Whig oligarchy finding they could not break his spirit were resolved on his destruction.' By the second year of his imprisonment Jones was 'so broken in health, that he could no longer stand upright'. He was taken to the prison hospital, 'and then told that if he would petition for his release and promise to abjure politics for the future' his sentence would be ended immediately. This Jones refused to do, but according to the pamphlet this was a mere preliminary to his ultimate act of defiance. As final proof of his courage when denied pen, ink, and paper, 'he wrote some of the finest poems in the English language' on the fly-leaves of his prayer book, by using a quill fashioned from a rook's feather, an ink bottle made from soap, and blood drawn from his own veins.

Eventually released from prison, the account continued, Jones persisted in his newspaper and lecturing work, despite a wealthy uncle, 'whose heir at law' he was, threatening to cut off his inheritance unless he dropped his political views. His uncle died soon after and left his entire fortune to a stranger, but only in 1859, when he sued G. W. M. Reynolds for libel, did Jones reveal the full extent of this self-sacrifice, and received widespread public sympathy as a result. Forced to return to the bar, he built up a successful practice which climaxed in his defence of the Fenians in 1867, for which he received the praise of the judge. But still Jones did not allow professional success 'to lure him from the people's cause'. He returned to public lecturing at the time of the American Civil War and the Schleswig-Holstein crisis, and since the mid-1860s had been working for the Reform League. Jones, the pamphlet concluded, assuring its readers, was neither a penniless adventurer nor a political dandy.

He is not a rich man, it is true, but he has voluntarily resigned a large fortune that he might serve the people—he has sacrificed more in his profession than would have placed him among the wealthy in the land . . . but even thus he is not poor: he is in the enjoyment of a large practice in a lucrative and honourable profession, and heir, by settlement, to some land in Cumberland, and some thousands of pounds of funded property.

The pamphlet of 1868 was not the only occasion on which Jones told his patriotic tale. Indeed, the telling of the story can be seen as integral to his whole political career. When Jones first joined the Chartist movement, he used elements of the same tale, in verse form, in order to introduce himself to the working-class cause. In January 1846 he gave to the *Northern Star*, the principal Chartist newspaper, his poem *My Life*, signed pseudonymously by Percy Vere. The first few verses of the poem described an idealistic aristocratic youth breaking with custom and convention, refusing the comforts and rewards of a privileged lifestyle in order to devote himself to humanity, in spite of all the obloquy it would bring. Freed from prison in 1850, Jones sought to re-establish himself amongst the Chartist leadership and did so by emphasizing his social descent. In a 'Letter to the Aristocracy', he told the readers of his *Notes to the People* that 'I moved among your order once—but I have left it now, and I have grown vulgar—shockingly vulgar—plebeian, down-right plebeian—and I glory in it'. A year later he described to the same readers how, unlike other Chartist leaders like George Julian Harney, who had risen from the ranks of poverty to 'broadcloth, ease and literary competence', he, by contrast, 'has blighted the happiness of his home, and the prospects of his life . . . has steeped himself in poverty to the lips . . . thrown from all the world offers of prosperity, to embrace all it offers of adversity—for what? not even for the hope of gain—but for the sake of truth'.[52] In 1852 Jones resorted to legal action to clear his name after a financial dispute with other Chartists over the running of the *People's Paper*, and in 1859 he defended himself from Reynolds's charge of financial misdemeanours by accusing him of libel. In both cases Jones's defence was based on the revelation of his misfortunes and suffering.[53] It is also apparent that Jones regaled his working-class followers with stories of his privileged youth. One of them later recalled being enraptured late at night by the 'proper account of his origin' given by Jones, and noting how much had changed for Jones since his early days: 'Kissing the Queen's hand had not had that influence over Mr Jones it had over some Radical politicians that I have known in my time.'[54]

Sacrifice was thus the central motif of Jones's version of his life. His well-heeled parentage and marriage, his familiarity with the court of Queen Victoria, his literary vocation and promising legal career were all things he had forsaken on behalf of the cause of the people. As a result he had been persecuted by the government, almost died in prison, been ostracized by his wealthy relations, and lost his fortune, inheritance, and health. But he had kept his name and reputation—his victory over Reynolds in the libel case of 1859 was a key landmark in the story—because he had stuck to his principles in the face of all attempts to buy his silence. His political views might be faulted and the ardour with which he advocated his cause might be considered too extreme, but no one could doubt his consistency, or the nobility of his character and honesty of his motives. Such was the portrait offered by Jones in 1868, completing the sketches and studies that he had dashed off earlier in his career. It was a self-portrait that few questioned at the time, and few have questioned it since. Jones told the tale of his virtuous fall from aristocratic grace so often and so well that everyone believed it. Soon after meeting him Feargus O'Connor declared that Jones was 'the young sprig of aristocracy promoted to the rank of democracy'. Writing the first history of the Chartist movement, Robert Gammage, who was acutely perceptive about Jones in many other respects, assumed he

[52] *NP* (5 July 1851), 184–6; (25 Apr. 1852), 1015.
[53] See below, Ch. 5.
[54] Benjamin Wilson, 'Reminiscences of Ernest Jones, Chartist, Poet, and Orator', *Halifax Courier* (31 Jan. 1891), 7.

was an aristocrat.[55] Over time, the story of his fall became conventional wisdom too. 'Who suffered for the working man?' cried out a voice in the crowd at a Manchester election rally in 1868, 'Ernest Jones', came the chorus; 'Who suffered for his country?' 'Ernest Jones.'[56] The essential ingredients of the tale he told in 1868 were repeated verbatim in all the obituaries that appeared in 1869, and in most of the ensuing short biographies and sketches down to Howell's work in the 1890s, even by contemporary radicals who knew Jones very well, and who had not always been well disposed to him.

However, Jones's tale of his own life was just that: a tale. As the following biography reveals, in all the important details—his family background, his education, his literary and legal prospects, his finances, his imprisonment, his conduct during the Fenian trial—Jones's account of his life was either wrong, or at best concealed people and events which did not fit his chosen narrative of a patriotic martyr. But that does not make Jones's self-invention less interesting. On the contrary: establishing why he chose to present himself to his fellow politicians and to his working-class followers in this melodramatic way, and moreover why they all, colleagues and supporters alike, accepted his story to the letter, can tell us a great deal about the influence of romanticism on mid-Victorian popular politics. What follows, then, is a life of Ernest Jones, and in that sense it aspires to be a conventional biography, working through the obvious chronology of his life from birth to death. Using the voluminous materials that Jones accumulated during his lifetime, and the other standard tools of biographical research, the book aims to reconstitute from the available evidence the most plausible account of Jones's activities, speeches, and writings. It serves as a corrective to the wilder things that Jones chose to tell about his life, and to some of the even wilder things that he suppressed. Readers with an interest in Chartism and radical liberalism, the events of 1848, the influence of European republican and socialist exiles, the campaign for parliamentary reform in the mid-1860s, and the Irish question will find these issues dealt with as prominently as would be expected in a study of Jones. I hope also that readers with an interest in mid-Victorian literature, especially poetry, will find the discussion of

---

[55] O'Connor, quoted in Robert Gammage, *History of the Chartist Movement, 1837–1854* (London, 1855), 282.
[56] *MG* (21 Aug. 1868), 3.

Jones's engagement with romanticism illuminating. But the book is also an unconventional biography. It is an account of how Jones invented and retold his own life-story for political and literary effect, and in so doing achieved his only real success. My overriding concern is to show how Jones created the persona of 'poet, politician and patriot', and why that character—that version of Ernest Jones—proved so charismatic and potent to a mid-Victorian audience, to the extent that when he was finally laid to rest on a wet January afternoon in Manchester Jones had acquired the following of a cult-leader and the esteem normally reserved for a saint.

A German Childhood

ERNEST JONES was born on 25 January 1819 in the Vonschen Palace in Berlin. Heavily pregnant with 'dumpy', Charlotte, the baby's mother, had arrived in the snowy Prussian capital a few weeks earlier, and Captain Charles Jones hurried from his duties in the royal household at Neu Strelitz in Mecklenberg to join her in time for the birth. Several days later the baby was christened in a ceremony at the English ambassador's house on the Unter den Linden. Lord Charles Murray, the son of the Duke of Atholl, stood as godfather, and the newborn child was given two names. One was Charles, after his father, and this became the name always used by his own family. The other was Ernest, after the royal prince whom Charles Jones had served as a cavalry officer during the Napoleonic wars, and latterly as aide-de-camp: Ernst Augustus, the Duke of Cumberland, the fifth son of George III.[1] Ernest Jones thus entered the world in a foreign court in a faraway land, but in another sense he had landed in England in 1819, or at any rate in Percy Bysshe Shelley's version of it, 'England in 1819', for the lives of Jones's parents and the circumstances surrounding his own birth were immediately bound up with the Hanoverian regime satirized so savagely by Shelley: 'Princes, the dregs of their dull race, who flow | Through public scorn,—mud from a muddy spring.'[2] It was as part of the royal entourage that Jones's parents came to Berlin in the first place, and it was the messy nature of Charles Jones's retirement from the Duke of Cumberland's service in 1821 which was to prevent the family from returning to England as Charles Jones had wished. Instead, they were exiled in Holstein for the first nineteen years of Ernest Jones's life. In later life

---

[1] Charlotte Jones to Charles Jones, 25 Oct. 1818, Charles Jones to Charlotte Jones, 16 Dec. 1818, SC; Births and Christenings, BGI.

[2] P. B. Shelley, 'England in 1819', in *Complete Poetical Works*, ed. Thomas Hutchinson (London: Oxford University Press, 1960), 574–5; James K. Chandler, *England in 1819: The Politics of Literary Culture and the Case of Romantic Historicism* (London: University of Chicago Press, 1998).

Ernest Jones would evoke his German childhood as an idyllic prelude of innocence and nature. Looked at in more detail, and from his parents' perspective, however, an altogether more sinister tale unfolds.

I

Charles Jones, Ernest's father, was a colourful character of whom, were the records not so obscure, an intriguing and interesting life-story might be written. He was born some time in the mid-1770s in Sudbury in Suffolk,[3] and was married for the first time to a 'Miss Braybrooke', the granddaughter of Henry Sleech, a Fellow of Eton and related, by marriage, to Richard Neville, Lord Braybrooke (1750–1825), making Ernest Jones an unlikely and certainly unknowing distant relative of William Gladstone.[4] His first wife seems to have died young, for in August 1807 Charles Jones began his career in the army, buying a commission in the 15th King's Hussars, the regiment commanded by the Duke of Cumberland. Jones was promoted to lieutenant the following spring, and became a captain in October 1813.[5] With the 15th Hussars Charles Jones saw active service in the Peninsular campaign, most notably at Sahagun in 1809 where his regiment fought alongside that of Sir John Moore, although Ernest Jones's later claim that his father was at Moore's side when he fell was a little embroidered, for so too were many hundred other officers. Captain Jones himself received a severe

---

[3] According to notes Ernest Jones made in 1847, his paternal grandfather owned two houses in Sudbury whilst his great uncle William owned Wood Hall, also in Sudbury. William Jones, who died aged 65 in 1835, was an alderman of the town: Ernest Jones, 'Diary, 1839–47', MCL; Walter Copinger, *Manors of Suffolk: Notes on Their History, and Devolution, with Some Illustrations of the Old Manor Houses*, 7 vols. (London: T. F. Unwin, 1905–11), i. 234–5; *Bury and Norwich Post* (8 Apr. 1835), 2.

[4] Catherine Glynne, Gladstone's wife, was a second cousin of 'Miss Braybrooke's' father, Thomas Dampire, the Bishop of Rochester (1748–1812). 'Miss Braybrooke' was almost certainly a Miss Dampire, but writing in 1847 Ernest Jones may have been more familiar with the Braybrooke name, the 2nd Earl having become famous for his edition of the diary of Samuel Pepys: 'Diary, 1839–47', MCL; 'Notes on the History of the Neville, Aldworth, Howard, Audley, Calandrini and other Associated Families from the 15th century', (c.1811, comp. 2nd Lord Braybooke), Braybrooke papers, Essex Record Office, D/Dby F60, 'Printed Pedigree of the Aldworth Neville Family from the 16th century' (1833), ibid., F38 ; Thomas Harwood, *Alumni Etonenses; or, a Catalogue of the Provosts and Fellows of Eton* (Birmingham: T. Pearson, 1797), 96.

[5] Commander-in-Chief's Memoranda, 27 Aug. 1807, 10 Mar. 1808, PRO, WO 31/235,/248; *Army List* (1808–18); H. C. Wylly, *The Fifteenth (The King's) Hussars, 1759–1913* (London: Caxton Publishing Co., 1914), 423.

facial injury at Sahagun.[6] In addition to his cavalry duties, Charles Jones was entrusted with keeping the regimental diary for the whole period of his service between 1807 and 1815, thereby bringing him into fairly close contact with the Duke of Cumberland, the commander of the regiment. These diaries were no more than the usual diurnal records of movements, manoeuvres, stores, and supplies, but when Jones left active service he took the diaries with him, becoming in effect the custodian of the regiment's war archive, called upon throughout the 1820s by former fellow officers and on occasion the War Office to verify the events of the previous decade. The diaries languished in the Jones family home, finding their way into the young Ernest's nursery, where the 4-year old filled up the excess pages with watercolours and a cursive alphabet.[7] Back in 1814 Charles Jones went on to half-pay and returned to England, only to be called up the following year as part of the renewed campaign against the resurgent Napoleon. At Waterloo he was temporarily upgraded to a brigade major in the combined 5th cavalry regiment, and was part of the force that moved eastwards into the German states after the battle to extinguish the final embers of French influence. He emerged from the campaign with a Waterloo Medal, gainfully earned, and also, not so gainfully won, the misleading title of 'Major' which he proved reluctant to give up.[8]

At the peace Charles Jones returned to England, but instead of retiring from service, as did many thousands of officers, he accepted the invitation to join the Duke of Cumberland's household as aide-de-camp, or 'secretary', as the Duke himself referred to his position. Some of his duties seem to have been an extension of wartime service, mainly confined to military matters—supervising the disbanding of the regiment and executing the Duke's orders with regard to disciplinary offences committed by other officers.[9] But Captain

---

[6] *Ernest Jones. Who is he? What has he Done?* (Manchester: The Reform League, 1868), 3; Major Lord Carnock (ed.), *Cavalry in the Corunna Campaign (As Told in the Diary of the Adjutant of the 15th Hussars)* (London: Society for Army Historical Research, 1936).

[7] Carnock (ed.), *Cavalry in the Corunna Campaign*. The sixteen volumes of regimental diaries are now held in the Discovery Museum, Newcastle. Ernest Jones's juvenile contributions are in the volume for 1813–14. For War Office queries, see: Charles Jones to R. Browne, 27 Feb. 1823, SC.

[8] Wylly, *Fifteenth Hussars*, 423; Charles Dalton, *The Waterloo Roll Call* 2nd edn. (London: Arms and Armour Press, 1971), 24.

[9] 'Regimental Diary (15th Hussars)', 1815, Discovery Museum, Newcastle; Duke of Cumberland to the Adjutant-General of the Forces, 12 Apr. 1817, MCL.

Jones was quickly drawn into the political intrigue surrounding the Duke, occasioned above all by Cumberland's decision in 1815 to marry a divorcee, Frederica Sophia-Charlotte, Princess of Solms, the sister-in-law of Frederick-William III of Prussia. Until the accession of his elder brother George, the Prince of Wales, in 1820 and the ensuing controversy over his attempt to divorce his estranged wife, Queen Caroline, it is fair to say that the Duke of Cumberland was the least popular of the royal princes, all of whom were looked upon with a mixture of incredulity and apprehension, especially since, in the absence of any other legitimate heir, they were all potential future kings. But Ernst Augustus had none of the redeeming features of his brothers. He was no sailor, nor did he patronize the arts. He was vehemently anti-Catholic, and had the means to enforce his views, with the patronage of several parliamentary boroughs at his disposal and the allegiance of many peers in the House of Lords. And as an unmarried prince in the eye of a public becoming well used to titillation and outrage at royal expense in the wake of the Mrs Clarke affair of 1809, scandal inevitably attached to his name—although as scandals go, the so-called Sellis affair of 1810 was quite spectacular.[10] At the end of May 1810 the Duke was found in his apartments in St James dangerously wounded from a sword-attack, and the body of his valet, Sellis, was found, his throat cut, in another part of the palace. It was quickly concluded that Sellis, jealous of another valet, bore a grudge against the Duke, had attacked him, and then taken his own life. But the rumour-mill suggested otherwise, and radical journalists put it about that the Duke had murdered Sellis, possibly after he was discovered *in flagrante* with Sellis's wife, or possibly because Sellis was threatening him with blackmail. In 1813 one such journalist—Henry White, editor of the *Independent Whig*—was prosecuted for libel, and a jury headed by the radical tailor, Francis Place, found him guilty. But the dust on the case never really settled. As late as 1840 pamphlets were still circulating, pinning the guilt for Sellis's murder and other assorted black deeds on the Duke.[11]

[10] The definitive biography remains: G. M. Willis, *Ernest Augustus: Duke of Cumberland and King of Hanover* (London: Arthur Barker, 1954).

[11] On the Sellis affair, see: A. Aspinall (ed.), *The Correspondence of George, Prince of Wales, 1770–1812*, 8 vols. (London: Cassell, 1963–71); vii. 5–8; Willis, *Ernest Augustus*, ch. 8. For later attempts to stoke up charges against the Duke, see: T. Norton, *The Duke of Cumberland, and a Word, By the Way, of Cant and Slander* (London: C. G. Cabban, 1832); [Anon.], *Secret Life and Extraordinary Amours of Ernest, King of Hanover* (London: J. Thompson, 1840). For royal scandals in the

In 1815, however, when Charles Jones joined the Duke's house-hold, flitting between residences at Kew, Worthing, and St James, there was a new twist to Ernst Augustus's damaged public reputa-tion. Against the wishes of his mother, the Duke married the divorced Princess Frederica in May, and a long stand-off ensued between Ernst Augustus and the rest of the court, with his mother refusing to see him if accompanied by his new wife. Captain Jones acted as a rather hapless intermediary, carrying letters between the Duke and his mother, letters which both sides refused to open.[12] The marriage also provoked further public furore over the Duke, when a large addition to the Civil List was proposed for the upkeep of his expanded household in England and now in Mecklenberg too.[13] Although only a bit-player in this royal soap-opera, Charles Jones clearly found it inspiring, for in 1816 he began to employ the blank pages of the regimental diary for the draft of a story set at court and involving a plot centred on the royal succession.[14]

In 1817 Charles Jones found something else to occupy his leisure hours: the affections of Charlotte Annesley, whom he met when the Duke of Cumberland was visiting his younger brother, Augustus Frederick, the Duke of Sussex. Charlotte Annesley was the only daughter of Alexander Annesley, a wealthy lawyer who lived at Hyde Hall in Hertfordshire, and who on his death in 1813 was said to be worth £50,000, with properties in London and Brighton and extensive farmland in Kent.[15] By 1817 Charlotte was a relatively old spinster, having been born in 1779, and the wife of one of her three brothers, Hutton, was expressing her concern that she should make

Regency years, see: Peter Spence, *The Birth of Romantic Radicalism: War, Popular Politics and English Radical Reformism, 1800–15* (Aldershot: Scolar Press, 1996), ch. 6; Philip Harling, 'The Duke of York Affair (1809) and the Complexities of War-time Patriotism', *Historical Journal*, 39 (1996), 963–84.

[12]   Charles Jones to Herbert Taylor, 25 Dec. 1815, 26 Dec. 1815, Royal Archives, Windsor, RA 47,557, 47,559. For Queen Charlotte's disapproval: *The Taylor Papers, Being a Record of Certain Reminiscences, Letters and Journals in the Life of Lieut.-Gen. Sir Herbert Taylor, etc.*, arranged by Ernest Taylor (London: Longmans, Green & Co., 1913), 167–9.

[13]   Willis, *Ernest Augustus*, ch. 8. George Cruikshank captured the controversy in a scurrilous print, complete with Sellis clutching a blood-spattered razor: 'A Financial Survey of Cumberland or the Beggar's Petition' (1 Aug. 1815), repr. in G. S. Layard, *Suppressed Plates, Wood Engravings, Etc, Together with Other Curiosities Germane Thereto* (London: A. & C. Black, 1907), 60–8.

[14]   'Regimental Diary (15th Hussars)' (1813–14), Discovery Museum, Newcastle.

[15]   Ernest Jones, 'Diary, 1839–47', MCL; *Gentleman's Magazine*, 84 (Jan. 1814), 94–5.

a good marriage soon.[16] Charlotte was part of the Duke of Sussex's household, based mainly at Tunbridge Wells and St James, and she and Charles Jones met on different occasions throughout 1817 whenever the itineraries of the two brothers coincided.[17] In November of that year the tragic death in childbirth of Princess Charlotte, the Prince of Wales's daughter (and bearer of the dynasty's hopes for an heir), afforded Charles and Charlotte an unexpected opportunity to spend more time together. Charles Jones arranged for Charlotte to move into apartments in Bury Street in St James, and they both joined the fashionable court set of the neighbourhood, including the salon of Lady Catherine Stepney, the novelist. In February 1818 they were married at St George's in Hanover Square, with the Duke of Cumberland giving away the bride. By June Charles and Charlotte were informing family friends of her pregnancy and her hopes for a period of domestic stability.[18] However, the interweaving of the Jones household with the affairs of the royal households of the princes continued unabated. The Duke of Cumberland only extended his stay in London long enough to be present at the double royal wedding in July of the Dukes of Clarence and Kent—a significant occasion, for it considerably improved the prospects of a new generation of heirs to the throne (Princess Victoria was born to the Duchess of Kent the following year). In the middle of July the Duke of Cumberland's party packed up and left for Spa, from where they made a quick visit to Berlin in October to celebrate the Crown Prince of Prussia's birthday, before moving on to Neu Streilitz, the Duchess's home, and finally returning, the day after Christmas, to Berlin. The court life of London became transposed to Berlin, and Charlotte and Charles Jones befriended, among others, the family of Louis Ferdinand Radziwill, nephew of Frederick the Great. The Duke and the now pregnant Duchess remained in Berlin throughout 1819, their son George being born in

---

[16]   Giovanna H. Annesley to Charlotte Annesley, 24 Dec. 1816, SC.
[17]   The following letters give a flavour of the developing relationship: Charles Jones to Charlotte Annesley, 15 Feb. 1817, BJH; Charles Jones to Charlotte Annesley, 15 Oct. 1817, Charlotte Annesley to Charles Jones, 5 Nov. 1817, Charles Jones to Charlotte Annesley, 24 Dec. 1817, SC.
[18]   Charles Jones to Charlotte Annesley, 27 Jan. 1818, SC; *St James Chronicle*, (5 Feb. 1818), 1; J. H. Annesley to Charles Jones, 11 June 1818, SC. On Princess Charlotte's death and funeral, which Charles Jones attended, see: Stephen Behrendt, *Royal Mourning and Regency Culture: Elegies and Memorials of Princess Charlotte* (London: Macmillan, 1997).

May—news of the baby's arrival delivered to the Duke by his faithful attendant, Charles Jones.[19]

So, amidst an intense cycle of royal nuptials, mourning, and births, Ernest Jones slipped into the world, his parents squeezing in time to begin their own family whilst their princely paymasters were frantically trying to secure the Hanoverian lineage. And although it took two more sons of George III, and an act of parliament in 1830, to deny the Duke of Cumberland the imperial crown of Britain and Ireland—under Salic law he did become King of Hanover in 1837—the seeds were literally sown in 1818 and 1819 for the perpetuation of the British monarchy. No wonder that in later life Ernest Jones could convince himself and others that his own destiny was tied up with the fortunes of nations and dynasties. However, in complete contrast to the House of Hanover, the affairs of the Jones household went from bad to worse in the decade after Ernest's birth. Ill-health, debt, blackmail, and a disputed inheritance combined to render Charles Jones and his family involuntary exiles in northern Germany.

Charles Jones left the service of the Duke of Cumberland in 1821. Poor health was given as the reason, with the court's doctors advising him to seek rest and recuperation in the German spa-towns for wounds incurred during his military campaigns. For the next three years, together with Charlotte and the infant Ernest, Charles Jones passed from 'one bath to another' without much improvement in his condition. In September 1821 he was advised to seek southern sun in Lisbon, and although he attempted to make the passage from Hamburg to Toulon in the pursuit of Mediterranean climes, he got no further than the German port, where he collapsed and was forced to remain, adopting the Hanseatic town as his home from home.[20] Charles Jones's ill-health proved expensive, with hotel bills quickly eating into his income. He remained on half-pay, having rejoined the list in 1817, but at the end of 1821 the Duke of Cumberland stopped his salary as aide-de-camp. Captain Jones protested that were he able to serve the Duke he would, and was thus entitled to continue drawing his salary. But it was also clear that ill-health was not the only reason for his service being terminated. Writing in 1827, Charles Jones told of his resentment at not being released after his marriage

---

[19] For the royal itinerary, see: *St James Chronicle* (18 July 1818), 4; (27 Oct. 1818), 2; (7 Jan. 1819), 3. On the royal birth: Willis, *Ernest Augustus*, 163; Charles Jones to the Duke of Cumberland, 27 May 1837, SC.

[20] Charles Jones to Charles Greenwood, 10 Sept. 1821, Charles Jones to J. R. Birnie, 12 July 1822, Charles Jones to Col. Palmer, 30 Mar. 1823, SC.

and of the deterioration of his relationship with the Duke in the two years after the royal household's return to Berlin.[21]

The captain's financial woes in Germany were compounded by troubles he had left behind him in England. Before his marriage, it transpired, he had moved into a lodging house of ill-repute run by a Miss de Grays and her mother. Once married to Charlotte, mother and daughter began to pursue Charles Jones, claiming that he was the father of Miss de Grays's two children. Jones denied the claims, but to avoid scandal settled the sum of £39 per annum on Miss de Grays. But the blackmail did not go away. By 1821 'the worthless strumpet' was at his heels again, via a London lawyer. Jones proposed a final settlement, taking away the annuity but giving over a 'cottage' he owned in Brompton for the perpetual use of Miss de Grays and her mother.[22] This allayed the demands of Miss de Grays, but robbed Charles Jones of an English nest-egg. Whether Charles Jones sacrificed a lucrative property in the suburbs of west London out of paternal guilt, or merely to avoid tainting his and the Duke of Cumberland's name with scandal, is impossible to determine at such a distance of time. Suffice to say that after the Jones family's return to England in 1838, Charles Jones did resume contact with a long-lost daughter, Fanny, sending her an explanatory poem which began: 'My father he went to a far distant land | And left me as 'twere wide at sea | Unknowing I pressed his hand | For then I was in infancy.'[23]

In a further twist to the Jones family fortunes in the 1820s, Charlotte, Captain Jones's wife, turned out not to be such a rich heiress after all. At the end of 1821 Charles Jones began to complain of how Charlotte's eldest brother, acting as executor to the Annesley estate, had swindled his sister out of her share of their father's legacy.[24] The affair hung over the Jones family for another twenty-five years. Only in the mid-1840s, on Charlotte's death, would Ernest Jones properly investigate the conveyance of the Annesley

[21] Wylly, *Fifteenth Hussars*, 423; 'Charles Jones' Memoir' (Sept. 1827), repr. in Aspinall (ed.), *Correspondence of George Prince of Wales*, vii. 373–8; Charles Jones to Charles Greenwood, 2 Jan. 1823, SC.

[22] Charles Jones to Col. Palmer, 30 Mar. 1823, Charles Jones to Herbert Taylor, 26 July 1823, Charles Jones to Charles Greenwood, 8 Aug. 1824, SC.

[23] Charles Jones to Fanny, 26 Dec. 1839, BJH. Ernest Jones later penned a poem entitled, 'To my Sister', describing a reunion after many years apart: *NP* (15 Nov. 1851), 572.

[24] Charles Jones to Charles Greenwood, 16 Dec. 1821, SC.

estate, and to his horror, find the charge of fraudulence to be base-less. But the scheming of wicked uncle Hutton became an item of hand-me-down rancour in the Jones household, one of those grudges that inscribes itself over time into family history. On several occasions Charles Jones attempted a rapprochement with Hutton, inviting him to Germany in 1821 and in 1825 seeking him out as temporary cover against his English creditors.[25] But, along with the Duke of Cumberland and Miss de Grays, Hutton Annesley became, in Charles Jones's eyes, part of the world's conspiracy against him.

In this way, Ernest Jones grew up in northern Germany largely against his father's wishes. By 1824 Charles Jones had given up hope of returning to England, no longer because he was unfit to travel, but because of the queue of creditors who would await him on his arrival. In the autumn of 1824 the nomadic Jones bathers finally settled in Reinbek, on the outskirts of Hamburg, in a modest farm-house which was to become their home for the next fourteen years. Charles Jones continued to protest his case over his stopped salary, but to no avail, and the family was forced to practice the strictest frugality, with only the captain's half-pay on which to survive. Payments fell behind on the family piano.[26] In September 1827 matters came to a head, and Charles Jones, embittered and worn out by the Duke of Cumberland's 'black ingratitude',[27] produced his last trump card. It was his account of the infamous Sellis affair, as told to him by the only surviving witness: the Duke himself.

'Compelled by some irresistable [sic] power which seems to call me from the grave (to which I feel I am fast approaching) to set down ere I depart & bring to light a crime which has laid buried in dark mystery for nearly 18 years'—so began Charles Jones's memoir of the confession that he alleged the Duke of Cumberland had made to him during Christmas 1815.[28] Troubled by his mother's opposition to his marriage, according to Charles Jones, the Duke unburdened himself to his aide-de-camp, revealing that he was forced 'to destroy [Sellis] in self-defence' as 'the villain threatened to propagate a report & I had no alternative'. The Duke swore Captain Jones to secrecy,

[25] Charles Jones to Hutton Annesley, 12 July 1822, Charles Jones to Mr. Myers, 1 Feb. 1825, Charles Jones to Charles Greenwood, 21 Jan. 1826, SC.

[26] Charles Jones to Charles Greenwood, 30 Nov. 1824, Charles Jones to George Wilkinson, 14 Mar. 1825, SC.

[27] Charles Jones to Charles Greenwood, 21 June 1827, SC.

[28] 'Charles Jones' Memoir', in Aspinall (ed.), *Correspondence of George, Prince of Wales*, vii. 373–8.

and he duly held his tongue, but thereafter saw the Duke in a very different light. 'From this time I became gloomy, lost all spirit and energy', Charles Jones recollected, and vowed to leave the Duke's service at the earliest opportunity, which he thought had arrived with his own marriage in 1818. Jones's memoir, like so many of the complaints and accounts he scribbled during the unhappy 1820s, did not see the light of day. Captain Jones intended that his executors should make it public in the event of his death, but he recovered his health in 1827 and lived for another sixteen years. The memoir was locked away, only to be dusted down and passed on months before the final dramatic demise of Charles Jones in 1843. Blackmailed he may have been, blackmailer he was not.

Having cleared the Duke's confession off his chest in 1827, Charles Jones seems to have given up his campaign to be reinstated to his salary. Cut off from the court, estranged from family, with no immediate prospect of returning to England, the Jones household was marooned on its little farm-holding in Holstein. Charlotte and Charles, ageing parents in straitened circumstances, devoted all their attention to their precocious son Ernest, or Carl as he was known— a 'beautiful' boy, although 'a pickell [sic] and a sprite'.[29] All the dashed ambitions of the father—literary dabbling, a gentry lifestyle, public acclaim—became reinvested in the son.

2

If the public life of Ernest Jones is best understood as a series of invented personae, in which the events of his own life were recast as the romantic history of a man of the people, his own childhood stands as an early case-study of that process. The autobiography that Jones dictated in 1868 told of a lonely but privileged upbringing on his father's estate. Inspired by the 'solitude and romantic scenery', the young Ernest had his first poetry published when he was only 10, and the same year ran away to join the Poles in their revolt against Russia. His grooming as a Byronic gentleman, so the 1868 version of his life went, was completed by his attendance at a royal finishing-school in Hanover—St Michael's College in Lüneburg—where, although a foreigner, he distinguished himself in oratory and left with the highest academic honours.[30] At one level this was a heavily

[29]   Charles Jones to Hutton Annesley, 12 Feb. 1822, SC.
[30]   Ernest Jones, Who is he?, 3.

doctored account of his early life. The glimpses that the evidence yields of Jones's infant years—the forced frugality, the recycling of his father's journals for drawing-paper, the family moving to a farm-house, the disputed piano—all suggest an environment of genteel poverty rather than sedate retirement. And, as will become clear, Jones's recollection of his precocious literary talent and his schooling obscured as much as it revealed. But what cannot be disputed is the fact that the young Ernest Jones grew up in an environment in which he was afforded the materials for viewing the world in a highly romanticized way. Even if the events of his own childhood and adolescence did not conform to a standard *Bildungsroman*, by the time he left Germany in 1838 he was equipped with the literary means required to transform the mundane into art.

Ernest Jones's schooling began and remained at home for many years. Not until he entered college in 1836 did he leave the family farmhouse. Until then he was taught by his parents and, in later years, by two house-tutors. Neither Captain Jones nor Charlotte spoke particularly good German, so Ernest seems to have received a steady diet of classics, French (Voltaire, Racine), and English literature (Scott and Shakespeare in particular).[31] The family took in the English-language press available in Reinbek: notably, from 1828 onwards, the *Hamburg Reporter* and its literary supplement, the *Gleaner*, which reproduced periodical literature from the reviews in Britain and North America. Both parents liked to try out their own poetry, and they certainly encouraged the muse in their son, as the tale of Ernest's first literary outing attests.

In April 1830 the Hamburg publishing house of Nestler advertised a forthcoming collection of poems, *Infantine Effusions*. The book was the work of Ernest Charles Jones, a youth 'under ten years of age', and was 'considered so extraordinary' that his friends had been induced to publish it.[32] The book contained a dozen poems. Not all were original. One was a translation from Monsieur de [*sic*][33] Voltaire's *Henriade*; another an extract from Rodolski. There were acknowledged imitations of Shakespeare ('Rodriguo' and 'Lines on

---

[31] Acquaintance with Shakespeare and Voltaire is evident in Jones's *Infantine Effusions* (Hamburg: F. H. Nestler, 1830), and with Scott in his unpublished 'Alboin of Lombardy' (see below). Charlotte Jones mentions the family's familiarity with Racine in a letter to Charles of 4 Dec. 1836, SC.

[32] *Hamburg Reporter* (27 Apr. 1830), 4.

[33] Charles Jones had a habit of adding 'de' to names, in order to denote status. For example, in Berlin Charlotte Jones was known as Madame de Jones, née d'Annesley.

England') and an unacknowledged pastiche of Scott ('The Minstrel'). But there were several poems which bore the hallmarks of a child prodigy. These were verses with authentic-sounding date-stamps: 'Lines written 23rd July 1828', 'Lines Written when Eight Years of Age', and 'Pyrenean Adventure'—apparently 'written on reading an extract from a novel' in 1829. And there were verses which treated of legitimate subjects in the young Ernest Jones's life: 'Lines on the Land of my Birth' (about Prussia) and 'Lines Written on the Death of my Godfather, the Late Lord Charles Murray' (who had died in the Greek War of Independence). The range of vocabulary, together with the confident syntax and metre, suggested a raw talent, well worth the puffing-up given by the publisher. To take the earliest verse, 'Lines Written when Eight Years of Age', for example:

> In a valley rural-place,
> I this day, did guide my pace,
> Where the river purls along
> Rolling with a current strong.
> Flowers, wav'd by a zephyr's breath—
> Its borders were bestudded with;
> Mountains—at some distance were—
> With mist-crown'd tops which kiss'd th'air;
> Majestic frowning on their brow—
> Ancient Elms—and Beeches grow.

In the same year the infant Jones produced another effusion. Charles Jones submitted a story by Ernest, entitled 'The Invalid's Pipe', to a miscellany published in London devoted to stories for children (though not necessarily by children). The story duly appeared—described as 'the genuine production of the son of a British officer, only nine years of age'—and so 'C.E.J.' appeared in print alongside other budding English talents including Geraldine Jewsbury and the not quite so juvenile Howitts and the Strickland sisters.[34] The 'Invalid's Pipe' told the tale of a wounded old Hussar, and in prose, as in poetry, the style suggested a maturity beyond the author's years.[35] On closer inspection, however, it is doubtful

[34] C. E. J., 'The Invalid's Pipe' in *Ackermann's Juvenile Forget-me-not* (London: R. Ackermann, 1830), 189–92.

[35] The story begins: 'It was not far from the Castle of Fürstenstein, near the spot where the gallant Blucher, with the brave army of Silesia won such glory, that the Baron of Fürstenstein met a maimed soldier, who was endeavouring to reach Berlin to claim his pension, and whose age denoted that his wounds had long been his honourable though painful companions.'

whether this tale or the poems were, as Nestler, the Hamburg publisher, claimed, 'precisely as they came from the pen of the child, without any correction whatever'.[36] Charles Jones went to great lengths to ensure that the poems saw the light of day, badgering both the publisher and the *Hamburg Reporter* on several occasions, and his role may have gone beyond that of a zealous parent promoting his child's talent.[37] Another piece of Ernest Jones juvenilia survives from the same period, and in terms of basic grammatical ability, let alone literary merit, it does not bear comparison with *Infantine Effusions* or 'The Invalid's Pipe'. In December 1833 Jones drafted a long dramatic verse entitled 'Alboin of Lombardy'.[38] It is not clear what stimulated this idea—possibly a French version of Bandello's classic tale of love and death in feudal Verona. But what is revealing is the laboured and predictable poetic manner in which Jones, now almost 15, composed his tragedy. For example, the poem begins:

> Three flowers bloom so fresh and fair,
> Beneath the tall oaks favouring share
> And many a blossom buddeth there,
> That decks the earth and scents the air.

> They bloom upon the mountain high,
> Or open in the lowly glade.
> And many a tempest sweeping by,
> Left them blooming fresh and fair
> As first the Summer saw them there

The inconsistent stanzas, the rather desperate choice of rhyming couplet, and the excessive piling-up of naturalistic imagery suggest an amateurish adolescent and certainly not one who had won his literary spurs several years earlier. 'Alboin of Lombardy' needed a correcting pen, retaining the content but paring down the flowery vocabulary and tightening the rhythm. Either Jones had regressed as a poet since the publication of *Infantine Effusions*, or, more plausibly, his father and mother had altered and improved their son's poetry on the first occasion, but not on the second. One further clue adds weight to this explanation. *Infantine Effusions* contains a poem entitled 'Pyrenean Adventure', not dissimilar to one which Charles

---

[36] *Infantine Effusions*, p. i.
[37] Charles Jones to Eduard von Hopstrauss, 15 Apr. 1830, BGI.
[38] 'Alboin of Lombardy' [1833], Ernest Jones Manuscript Poems, MCL, Ms. F821.89.J5/20.

Jones himself doodled twenty years previously, as the 15th Hussars made the long trip home from the Peninsular campaign.[39]

If *Infantine Effusions* was not really the stunning literary debut that Jones would later claim it to be, it is nonetheless a significant reminder of the care and determination that Charles and Charlotte Jones took in nurturing and honing their son's talent. But they could only take his studies so far. Consequently, in his adolescent years they turned to private tutors to continue and expand his education. The first such man was Friedrich Binge, a graduate in theology from Kiel, who was tutor to Jones until 1834, when he left to become pastor at the Lutheran church on the island of Sylt in Schleswig, and later at Kellinghusen in Holstein. The second tutor was Johann Schwarke, another theology graduate, this time from Halle, who tutored Jones during 1834–5, and later went on to become pastor for many years at the Lutheran church in Malente in Holstein, where he also stood as deputy for the Landtag in 1848.[40]

Binge and Schwarke rounded out Jones's education, improving his command of the German language and expanding his curriculum in line with Charles Jones's hope that he would eventually go on to university. The two theologians may also have introduced Jones to German patriotic poetry, and they almost certainly gave him a deeper acquaintance with the teachings of the Lutheran church, the effects of which would later be seen in the evangelical tone of much of Jones's Chartist poetry and speeches. Both men hailed from Holstein, and would eventually return to serve as pastors there. In the nineteenth century Holstein was a seedbed for nationalism, but of a conservative kind, invoking the traditions and spirit of the *Volk*, rather than the democratic aspirations of the people.[41] Throughout the nineteenth century Holstein was hemmed in on all sides by stronger neighbours: Napoleonic France, royal Hanover, imperial Prussia, and covetous Denmark. Eventually in the 1860s the

---

[39] 'Regimental Diary (Fifteenth Hussars)', 1809, Discovery Museum, Newcastle.

[40] For Binge, see: Rudolf Möller, 'Die Pastoren der evangelisch-lutherischen Kirchen gemeinde Keitum (Sylt) und ihre Familien', *Zeitschrift für Niederdeutsche Familienkunde*, 4 (1991), 397. For Schwarke: Eduard Alberti, *Lexikon der Schleswig-Holstein-Lauernbugischen und Eutinischen Schriftseller von 1829 bis Mitte 1866*, 2 vols. (Kiel: Akademische Buchhandlung, 1867), ii. 381; Walter Körber, *Kirchen in Vicelins Land: Eine Eutinische Kirchenkunde* (Eutin: Struve's Verlag, 1977), 291.

[41] On this distinction, see: F. M. Barnard, *Self-Direction and Political Legitimacy: Rousseau and Herder* (Oxford: Clarendon Press, 1988); F. C. Beiser, *Enlightenment, Revolution and Romanticism: The Genesis of Modern European Thought* (Cambridge, Mass.: Harvard University Press, 1992).

Holstein question became a major diplomatic problem, and one on which Ernest Jones claimed he had extensive knowledge. In the 1830s, however, Holstein was just one of several German duchies and kingdoms straining at the leash of the Prussian-controlled German Bund, and in these circumstances patriot poets such as Arndt and von Stolberg enjoyed renewed popularity.[42] By the time he settled in England Ernest Jones was familiar with the work of these poets, and began to publish translations of them, and it seems more than likely that Binge and Schwarke had supplied the original introductions.

As recent theology graduates, destined for clerical careers, Jones's two tutors also played an important part in his religious education. Charles and Charlotte Jones do not seem to have been particularly devout Anglicans, even when they returned to London in 1838. In Reinbek they themselves attended the local Lutheran church, and taking on Lutherans as tutors to their son would have been a natural step. But, having studied in the 1820s at Halle University, the great centre of the revival of a radical Lutheranism, Schwarke in particular was no ordinary pastor. Halle imparted grounding in an anti-rationalist, living theology, in which the heart was deemed as important a part of faith as the head, and the impetus was towards creating an active church rather than a receptacle of dry doctrine. Such German theology had quite an impact on the Tractarian movement back in Britain, and as later chapters demonstrate it found its way into Jones's cosmology too.[43] Schwarke tutored Jones for a whole year, and then prepared him for entry into St Michael's College, to which Charles Jones applied for his son's admission at the end of 1835.

---

[42] William Carr, *Schleswig-Holstein, 1815–48: A Study in National Conflict* (Manchester: Manchester University Press, 1963). For the anti-French tone of the German patriot poets, see: Geoffroy Remi, 'Le Liberté allemande selon Ernst Moritz Arndt: poete politique allemand en dix-neuvième siecle', in Roger Sauter (ed.), *Visages de Liberté: recherches lexicales et litteraires* (St Étienne: Université Jean Monnet, 1992), 119–44; Bruno Lieser, ' "Les Françaises font magnifique besogne": Les idées politiques de Fr. L. Stolberg (1750–1819) jusqu'à la Revolution Française' in H. Kreuzer *et al.* (eds.), *Von Rubens zum Dekonstruktivisimus: Sprach-, Literatur-, und Kunstwissenschaftische Beiträge: Festschrift für Wolfgang Drost* (Heidelberg: C. Winter, 1993), 61–84.

[43] Nicholas Hope, *German and Scandinavian Protestantism, 1700–1918* (Oxford: Clarendon Press, 1995), 448–9.

3

In the spring of 1836 Ernest Jones finally left home to study for two years at St Michael's College in the garrison town and provincial capital of Lüneburg, some 25 miles away from Reinbek. Although only a carriage-ride southwards beyond the River Elbe, the college in Lüneberg was in many ways a whole world away. Jones had never been parted from his parents before. The tale of running away to join the Polish rebels in 1830 is almost certainly apocryphal.[44] And rather than a natural step in the education of a young gentleman, Jones's college years were a brutal introduction to the outside world—a harsh break from the cosseted childhood and adolescence he had enjoyed amidst the farmyard animals of Holstein. St Michael's College, or the Ritter-Akademie as it was also known, was one of the last of the aristocratic finishing schools which dated back to the sixteenth century. By the 1830s most had become cadet schools or ordinary *Gymnasien*, but the college in Lüneburg retained the trappings of an elite institution. A special royal patent from the King of Hanover was required to allow Jones, a foreigner, to enter, and Captain Jones was accordingly charged higher fees. The principal was a military man: one Colonel Knesebeck. The number of academicians was limited to twelve, and they endured a rigorous syllabus. Lessons were held on six days of the week, beginning at seven in the morning and frequently going on until five in the afternoon. The curriculum covered the usual mixture of humanities and sciences, but the essentials required of men of good breeding were provided as well: riding, landscape painting, and dancing.[45] Cooped up in such a masculine and martial environment, the young men inevitably played out barbaric rituals of inclusion and exclusion. In short, Jones, foreign and delicate, was badly bullied.

It is not difficult to work out why Captain Jones sent his son to such a college. He not only intended Ernest to complete his studies, he also hoped to restore to him some of the trappings of nobility that a childhood of cottage-economy on the north German plain had

[44] It is not mentioned at all in any of the copious family correspondence of the 1830s, whereas the minor illnesses of the young Carl are carefully documented.

[45] Charles Jones to Colonel von Knesebeck, 21 Dec. 1835, St Michaelis, Lüneburg, Rep. Aa 29, nr. 29, Stadtarchiv, Lüneburg; Charles Jones to the Directors of the Cloister of St Michaels, Lüneburg, 4 Jan. 1836, ibid., nr. 13; Col. Knesebeck to Charles Jones, 6 Feb. 1836, SC; 'Stundenplan' (1836), SC; Charlotte Jones to Ernest Jones, 15 June 1837, BJH.

taken away. Where better to seek the stamp of status than in royal Hanover, among the scions of the German aristocracy, in an ancient military town. In 1841 Ernest Jones described the town and the college in terms which suggest that his father had achieved his aim. He recalled Lüneburg as a 'city of an olden age'—'the oldest seat in the house of Guelph'—bedecked with Gothic turrets and church spires: a town which furnished some of the 'bravest battalions' in the fight against Napoleon. As to the college, Ernest Jones described it thus:

[i]ts students are . . . almost all sons of noble houses of the country; the glories of romantic eld still cling around their ancient dwelling place, replete with memorials of former days, and as they wander down the arched aisles and see the arms and effigies of their ancestors, through generations, gathered around them, we may understand the pride and love with which they look on those monastic walls[46]

But Jones's grooming as a gentleman was evidently a painful one, and much more traumatic than this rose-coloured account written several years later suggests. He entered the college in 1836 somewhat below the standard of the other pupils. His first report at the end of the Easter term spoke of elementary problems in his command of the German language, and in his understanding of the sciences. And the college described his intelligence as 'emotional' rather than 'philosophical', his behaviour towards his fellow academicians as 'soft and yielding'.[47] This was probably a coded way of saying that Jones was being mistreated, but it was not until he returned home for the summer vacation with a badly swollen face, bloodshot eyes, and covered in bruises that the full extent of the bullying became known to his parents. The college attributed the injuries to a combination of Jones's clownish behaviour, the 'chummy treatment' of his fellow scholars, and his unusually sensitive skin. Disconcertingly, they also advised Captain Jones that toughening of the body and physical fatigue were 'highly desirable'.[48] For his part, Ernest Jones confessed to having been beaten on a daily basis for three months. His father

[46] 'King Ernest's Arrival', *Morning Post* (30 Apr. 1841), 6. On the awkward mix of traditional monarchy and urban modernity in nineteenth-century Hanover, see: Michael John, 'National and Regional Identities and the Dilemmas of Reform in Britain's Other Province', in Lawrence Brockliss and David Eastwood (eds.), *A Union of Multiple Identities: The British Isles* (Manchester: Manchester University Press, 1997), 179–82; Adolf M. Birke, *England and Hanover* (Munich: K. G. Saur, 1986).

[47] Professor A. Herrmann to Charles Jones, 2 July 1836, SC.

[48] Professor A. Herrmann to Charles Jones, 31 July 1836, SC.

called in physicians who confirmed the extent of the injuries and condemned the 'immoral and murderous behaviour' of the other pupils.
Within days Charles Jones was accusing the Ritter-Akademie of a
cover-up, and threatened to withdraw his son. But he was appeased
by a visit to Reinbek from one of the college masters, Professor
Hermann, and at the beginning of Michaelmas term Ernest Jones
resumed his studies.[49] The bullying ceased, and the college report of
December 1836 noted that he was now in the highest grade.[50]

His nightmarish first term behind him, Jones remained at the
Ritter-Akademie until the end of the Lent term of 1838. In the new
year of 1837 Charles Jones did think of sending him to Oxford,
but decided against it on the grounds that he was too young, and,
presumably, would be too far away should any further ill-treatment
befall him.[51] By the time Jones left Lüneburg he had become part of
the drinking and dancing camaraderie of the college, proved himself
a classicist and a poet, but had not excelled in any other way.[52] There
is no record of him leaving the college, as he later claimed, with the
'highest honours', although he did depart with fees in arrears, as
Captain Jones was routinely reminded on his return to England.[53]

The young Ernest Jones also left Lüneburg as a royalist, or at any
rate, as a sworn supporter of the man who was crowned King of
Hanover in 1837, and whose processional route passed through the
college town. Ironically, Ernst Augustus, the same royal prince who
had been the bane of the Jones's household in the 1820s, now
became the young Ernest's model of patriot kingship. This is a
significant point. One fiction that Ernest Jones upheld above all
others throughout his later life was that he entered politics in 1846
with his creed very much a tabula rasa. Until his late twenties, he
always insisted, he was all insouciance and ignorance, with only the
abortive childhood mission to save the Poles as evidence of his democratic credentials. However, in 1841 Jones contributed to the

[49] 'Report' [on Ernest Jones' state of health], 2 Aug. 1836, SC; Charles Jones to
Professor A. Herrmann, 24 July 1836, St Michaelis, Lüneburg, Stadtarchiv, Lüneburg
Rep. Aa 29, nr. 30; Charles Jones to Professor A. Herrmann, 7 Aug. 1836, SC; Charles
Jones to Col. Knesebeck, 22 Aug. 1836, SC; Professor A. Herrmann to Charles Jones,
4 Sept. 1836, SC.
[50] Professor A. Herrmann to Charles Jones, 23 Dec. 1836, SC.
[51] Charles Jones to Prince Radziwill, 21 Feb. 1837, SC.
[52] Charles Jones to Prince Radziwill, 21 Feb. 1837; Eduard von Bülow to Ernest
Jones, 6 May 1838, SC.
[53] College Secretary to Charles Jones, 2 Apr. 1841, St. Michaelis Lüneburg, Stadt
Archiv, Lüneburg, Rep. Aa 29, nr. 34.

Morning Post a trilogy of articles about 'King Ernest's Accession' four years earlier, based on his own eyewitness testimony.[54] On becoming King of Hanover in 1837, Ernst Augustus immediately suspended the constitution which his younger brother, the Duke of Cambridge, had granted as viceroy in 1833. This outraged liberals and radicals across Europe, including some MPs in England who tried to have Ernst Augustus removed completely from the line of succession.[55] But Ernest Jones leaped to his defence. He described how Hanover was in a state of great discontent in 1837, the new constitution having brought onto the stage a fickle public, the spirit of anarchy and cabal, and abuse of power. A resident monarch with a firm hand was needed, and for that reason Ernst Augustus, according to Jones, was right to annul the constitution. And the manner in which he did it carried great conviction. He appeared 'unattended' in Hanover in front of the haranguing and 'infuriated populace', he demanded of the liberal professors of Göttingen an oath of loyalty, shaming those who refused, and thus mollifying the German student, a type 'ever prone to disturbance, though a noble and enlightened character'. He went out of his way to mingle with the people, and so the once 'turbulent' subjects of Hanover rediscovered their ancient feelings of reverence for a resident monarch. Ernst Augustus was undoubtedly severe—according to Jones, he abhorred umbrellas as degenerate[56]—but there was none of the 'cold and informal parade' of other Continental monarchs. He encouraged the *volkish* customs of his people, for example, happily presiding over the Schützenfest archery competition. More practically, he restored the more monarchical constitution of 1819, a move which made sense given that Hanover, ringed by expansionist powers, was no longer protected by the United Kingdom.

The Ritter-Akademie in royal Hanover thus concluded Ernest Jones's German education in more ways than one. It is hard not to read into the above account of Ernst Augustus's accession the rebarbative and illiberal *Weltanschauung* of the boorish officer-class alongside whom Jones had attended the college. But the influences on Jones's adolescent years were more diverse than this, and his

---

[54] The series, by 'Karl', comprised three articles: 'King Ernest's Accession', *Morning Post* (10 Apr. 1841), 'King Ernest's Arrival' (30 Apr. 1841), and 'King Ernest in his Dominion' (7 May 1841).   [55] Willis, *Ernest Augustus*, chs. 18–19.

[56] The umbrella was a common metaphor for sham liberalism, associated especially with King Leopold of Belgium and Louis Philippe of France, both of whom were often depicted with brollies. It would later be used against Jones. See below, Chs. 4, 7.

eulogy to Ernst Augustus can be read in a number of ways. Jones's evocation of a Hanoverian *Volk*, devoted to their traditions and contented in their Gothic, gabled towns, suggests that he subscribed to a romanticized 'German' view of patriotism as rooted in the land and in the past, rather than believed in its 'French' versions: that is, a set of liberal and hence possibly partisan constitutional forms.[57] More complex still is Ernest Jones's relationship to his father's former master. To declare his support for an absolutist constitution passed in the year of his birth and reinstated in the year of his majority by the man his father considered the author of all his own family's misfortune, suggests breathtaking innocence or lack of tact on Ernest Jones's part, or a more complex psychology of almost Oedipal proportions on which it is wiser not to speculate. All that can be said with certainty is that the larger-than-life presence of the Duke of Cumberland, now the King of Hanover, preoccupied Ernest Jones as a young man much as it had tormented his father as a new parent. As far as Jones had any political views on his return to England in 1838 they were focused around the idea of a patriot king, sweeping away faction and earning the love of his people. Above all, Jones's colourful recollections of his adopted homeland reveal the influence of his two doting parents, isolated in foreign parts, suffocating their only child with historical tales and romantic verse, mixed up with family stories of chivalrous soldiers and cheating relatives. By the age of 18 even Jones's mother was conceding that her son was 'too highly wrought', and warned him 'that by revelling in a fairy & unreal creation of too romantic feelings you may become . . . too visionary for the world of common place reality in which in this present age we live'.[58] Although some mothers may have expressed themselves more eloquently, few can have known their sons quite so well.

---

[57] Further evidence of Jones's support for the idea of the 'patriot king' is provided in the extraordinarily long poem on the French Revolution which he wrote as a schoolboy. It is undated, but judging from the handwriting and spelling mistakes, it must be from sometime between 1835 and 1838. The poem located the roots of upheaval in King Louis XVI's soldiers' experience of republicanism whilst serving overseas in America. After describing the rivers of blood that accompanied the Jacobin seizure of power, the regicide, and the seizure of church property, the poem concluded by heaping praise on the counter-revolutionary rising of the King's youngest brother, the Comte d'Artois (later Charles X), and regretting that the Duke of Brunswick had been unable to aid Artois and defeat the republic at the Battle of Valmy: Ernest Jones, Manuscript Poems, MCL, Ms. F821.89 J5/66.

[58] Charlotte Jones to Ernest Jones, 31 May 1837, BJH.

2
Karl, or Literary Life in London, 1839–1845

IN THE SUMMER of 1838 the Jones family—Charles, Charlotte and the 19-year old Carl (i.e. Ernest)—sailed back to London. Their return was closely connected to the fact that Ernest was soon to come of age, and required completion of his studies in England. Three years later Charles Jones proudly told the Crown Prince of Hanover that his son had by then 'left the German and English universities' and entered the Middle Temple.[1] Jones minor certainly entered the Middle Temple—in March 1841 under the direction of the ageing Lord Wynford, an ultra-Tory chum of the Duke of Cumberland from the days of the reform bill[2]—and dutifully dined and drank his way to the bar, but he never passed through the portals of any university, English or German, ancient or modern. Nor did he launch 'into the vortex of fashionable life' and become a 'regular' at the court of the Queen Victoria, as he claimed in 1868.[3] True, Jones was presented to the youthful Queen at a levée in May 1841, and that same year married into a landowning family—the Atherleys of Cumberland. But thereafter he spiralled downwards as his life became beset with literary failure, personal tragedy, financial ruin, and religious crisis. In later versions of his life-story Jones was in denial about these formative years. He highlighted his aristocratic and royal connections, and boasted of his literary fame. In so doing he was able to emphasize the complete break signalled by his becoming a Chartist in 1846. He was a social renegade, a cultural apostate—in O'Connor's words, 'a young sprig of the aristocracy'. Throughout the 1850s and 1860s Jones was able to validate his 'conversion' to Chartism by drawing this stark contrast between the

---

[1] Charles Jones to the Crown Prince of Hanover, 21 July 1841, SC.
[2] Charles Jones to Lord Wynford [n.d., c.1841], SC.
[3] *Ernest Jones. Who is he? What has he done?* (Manchester: The Reform League, 1868), 4.

opulent world he had renounced and the humble cause he took up.
Inevitably, the real story was somewhat more complex. Jones's move
to Chartism was indeed a conversion, but as this chapter describes,
one of an altogether religious kind.

I

More is known about the early adulthood of Ernest Jones than any
other period of his life, for from the summer of 1839 until the spring
of 1847 he kept a diary. All of Jones's biographers from George
Howell onwards have known of this diary and some have made use
of it, although with varying effect.[4] For the most part the diary has
been used in a realist mode, that is, as a record of what Jones did
before he became a Chartist and during the first year of his Chartist
activities. Even in this mode, the diary has been used sparingly, and
no attempt has been made to re-create the social world in which
Jones moved, of which the diary gives ample evidence. Stranger still,
no questions have ever been asked about why Jones kept a diary at all
and why he stopped, what use he made of it, and what the text of a
diary can tell us about the self-identity of a young man in the early
1840s. Diaries are not simply transparent records through which a
life can be viewed unproblematically. People keep and people kept
diaries for different reasons. Most are simply appointment books,
their entries made long before the day itself, some are records of
travels or residence away from home, or records of interesting phases
in a person's life, sometimes compiled days or weeks after the events
have transpired, and often written in the knowledge that others—
family, friends, or even a public readership—will find them of
interest. Others are journals or notebooks, which might comprise
anything from random jottings to full-blown accounts of mental and
bodily health, from idle thoughts and sketches to longer drafts of
prose and verse. Others still are forms of Protestant confessional in
which the diarist renders a daily account of deeds done, good and evil
thoughts, and protestations of right faith and future conduct.[5]

---

[4] EJD, MCL. The most extensive analysis is that of Stan Broadbridge who edited
the extracts published by the Historians' Group of the Communist Party of Great
Britain in its *Our History* series: 'Diary of Ernest Jones, 1839–47', *Our History*, 21
(1961). Unfortunately, Broadbridge's meticulous work has been completely neglected
by modern scholars.

[5] Arthur Ponsonby, *English Diaries: A Review of English Diaries from the 16th to
the 20th Centuries with an Introduction on Diary Writing* (London: Methuen & Co.,

Moreover, people usually keep diaries at particular periods of their lives. Marathon diarists such as Gladstone or Farington are the exception. Most early Victorian diarists of whom there is record tended be young men and women in their early twenties, who used the diary as a form of self-knowledge, offering more room for introspection than private correspondence, and more opportunity for authenticity than commercial writing.[6] Such diaries might take the form of a manual of correct etiquette, or a record of self-enlightenment through reading and study, or a repository of inner thoughts. Whatever the form, the fashion for diaries amongst young people in the early Victorian years was above all dictated by the desire to describe in detail a journey of discovery. Diaries were the means of fashioning their own self, their own identity, whether that was measured by a standard set by Debrett, *Émile*, or God.

Jones was not the first in his family to keep a diary. His father, as we have seen, had been charged with keeping the regimental diary of the Duke of Cumberland's Hussars during the Peninsular and Waterloo campaigns. In 1837 Charlotte, Ernest Jones's mother, began a diary, although after four pages of entries it became a draft of a play.[7] Jones's own diaries, spanning nearly eight years, are a mixture of notebook-type journals, engagement calendars, and introspective meanderings. Dinner-guest lists nestle side by side with rough versions of poems and plots, details of social calls and church attendance sit with florid descriptions of the weather and long, Keatsian-style walks across west London, holiday itineraries with dramatic descriptions of his emotional state. Jones wrote predominantly in English, but sometimes in German, and on one or two occasions lapsed into Greek. The diaries commenced with a note of an unsuccessful visit (the first of many) to a publisher in July 1839 and closed with an entry on Jones's first visit to Halifax in May 1847. They are a remarkably full record of the young Ernest's inward and outer life in his pre-Chartist days, written with the expectation that someone, someday would read them. In March 1844, in a fit of pique, Jones refused to record where he had been that day, so 'that

1923); Robert A. Fothergill, *Private Chronicles: A Study of English Diaries* (Oxford: Oxford University Press, 1974).

  [6] Kathryn Carter, 'The Cultural Work of Diaries in Mid-Century Victorian Britain', *Victorian Review*, 23 (1997), 251–67; Rebecca A. Steinitz, 'Shared Secrets and Torn Pages: Diaries and Journals in Nineteenth-Century British Society and Literature', DPhil. thesis, University of California, Berkeley (1997).

  [7] Charlotte Jones, 'Journal' (1837), SC.

prying eyes when they look over these Pages shall not have the gratification of satisfying their propensity for mental larceny by reading them'.[8] Mental larceny or not, the diaries are a crucial source in the evolution of Jones into a Chartist.

On their return to England the Jones family settled in west London—in Bedford Place in Kensington. In 1839 Charles Jones lobbied hard for reinstatement to the army's retired list on full pay, regretting his 'fatal resolution' of 1821 to go onto half-pay.[9] With preferment probably in mind, he also renewed old social acquaintances from Regency days: military families such as the Dundases, the Gillies, the Manners, and the Betts. Ernest himself spent much of 1839 and early 1840 writing and rewriting his 'Valdine', later to become *The Wood Spirit*. He records reading Shelley, and Southey's 'Madoc', taking long walks, especially in Kensington Gardens, which, whatever the season, proved evocative. After walking there for over three hours on the first Saturday in August, he enthused: 'Splendidly splendid day of Splendour. There is an air. There is a sky. There is a gentle breeze. There are perfumes.' By October the Gardens were 'Delightful, beautiful and melancholy. The beauty of the Gardens is inexpressible. I looked on the old Palace, and the sunset that built a Palace of gold and crimson over it in Heaven.'[10] There were other distractions too. No doubt at his parents' prompting Ernest was introduced to a series of eligible young women, although he proved adept enough at spying them out for himself, recording on one occasion that he '[l]ooked for almost 3 hours through the telescope at Miss Bush who was sitting in her Garden'.[11] Beyond sharing pews in church and promenades in the park it was all innocent enough. But the heady mix of nature and women moved the young Jones to verse of a fairly predictable kind. There was sweet sorrow on parting:

> Weep, Agatha!—Those tears like dew from heaven
> Fall on my parched and burning heart—

---

[8] Diary entry, 14 Mar. 1844. One later reader did find them 'mental larceny'. Preparing Howell's biography for serialization in the *Newcastle Weekly Chronicle* in 1898, W. E. Adams commented that he 'was considerably surprised that so able a pen-man should not have left a livelier account': Adams to Howell, 3 Feb. 1898, Howell papers, BGI.

[9] Charles Jones to Sir Edward Hermans, 7 Nov. 1839, SC.

[10] EJD, 3 Aug., 13 Aug., 16 Aug., 27 Aug., 13 Oct. 1839.

[11] Ibid., 7 July 1839.

> Weep on! Weep on!—For in those tears is given
> A hope—a solace—tho' we part![12]

And women and summer days:

> Lady sat in the garden of flowers
> And happy the fate she knew
> Had nought but hope to mark the hours
> And joy to guide them through[13]

And parting from women on summer days:

> The time of love and sweets and flowers.
> When song is soft in honied bowers . . .
> . . . And many a link, that may not part
> 'Fore pleasure's thrill or sorrow's smart
> Is bound for ever 'round the heart
> By nature's kindly ministry.[14]

By the close of 1839 Jones had completed 'Valdine' but had been unable to persuade any publisher to take it, unless it was at the author's expense. Help was at hand, however, for the following year the young Ernest made what proved the best literary contact of his life. During the spring of 1840 Lady Catherine Stepney, an ageing 'silver fork' novelist, moved to the centre of the Jones' family's social calendar. Lady Stepney, née Pollok, was the widow of Sir Thomas Stepney (who died in 1825), a former groom to the Duke of York who was known to Charles Jones from his days at court in the years immediately after Waterloo. By 1840 Lady Stepney was enjoying what proved to be the final bloom of a glittering literary career. Three society novels, loosely set in the 1800s—*The New Road to Ruin* (1833), *The Heir Presumptive* (1835), and *The Courtier's Daughter* (1838)—had already been published to popular acclaim, and in 1841 *The Three Peers*, set in the 1720s, appeared.[15] Her home in Henrietta Street, off Cavendish Square, became a fashionable rendezvous for the London literary set. By the late summer of 1840 Jones was visiting her salon on a daily basis, in November he was given a pre-publication copy of her *Three Peers*, and she herself spent Christmas Day 1840 with the Jones family. Lady Stepney opened a

---

[12] 'To Agatha', MCL, Ms f 821.89.J5/31.
[13] 'Lady sat', MCL, Ms f 821.89.J5/58.
[14] Lines Written in the Countess of M . . .'s Album', MCL, Ms. f821.89.J5/31.
[15] Alison Adburgham, *Silver Fork Society: Fashionable Life and Literature from 1814 to 1840* (London: Constable, 1983), 102.

door for Jones on the London literary scene, and it is hard to imagine his work every seeing the light of day without her aid. She introduced Jones directly to Bulwer-Lytton, who proved a lifelong ally, probably gave him introductions to the *Court Journal*—the first magazine to take his poetry—and put him in touch with T. and W. Boone, the publishers of his first novel, *The Wood Spirit*.[16] Over time the Stepney salon yielded Jones other significant friendships too: with the Strickland sisters, the Wordsworths' daughter Jemima Quillinan, and a host of theatrical names, of which more shortly. Reading between the lines of a poem he dedicated to her, Jones's debt to his new patron was not difficult to discern:

> Calling high visions from the depth of years
> A fair magician waves the mighty wand,
> Till in her mirrors magic space appears,
> How bright the beings that dwell in fancy's land.[17]

The immediate fruit of Lady Stepney's magic came in the form of a book deal with Boone, the New Bond Street publisher. In July 1840 his firm undertook to bring out *The Wood Spirit*, although they recommended delaying publication until 'next season when that class of persons with whom you have influence are returning to town'.[18] Jones's romance was eventually published anonymously in two volumes in the spring of 1841. Set on the bleak coastland of Jutland, *The Wood Spirit* is a rambling epic, telling the story of Altren, a warring knight who returns from fighting under the flag of Conradin of Hofstaufen against the French in the Apennines, to reclaim his castle on the northern edge of Europe. On his return he faces two foes. One is the sea, which, having already inundated the coastal lands and surrounding hamlets of Jutland, threatens to do so again. The other enemy is Lyndarn, the abbot in charge of the local monastery of St Emmeran. Lyndarn has taken control of Altren's domain in his absence, taxed the local peasants to the hilt, and become involved in war and subterfuge with Altren's neighbouring lords. Inspired by the memory of his ancestor, Rolf 'the Wave

---

[16] Jones met Bulwer-Lytton at Lady Stepney's in May 1840: EJD, 24 May 1840. Lady Stepney certainly interceded with the *Court Journal* on Jones's behalf in 1844, so may have done so earlier too: Ella Twynham, 'The Life of Ernest Jones' (unpublished typescript, *c*.1930), 9–10. It is likely Lady Stepney is among the 'friends' referred to in the letter of Boone's to Jones of 29 July.

[17] 'Acrostic to Lady Stepney', MCL, Ms. f 821.89.J/27.

[18] T. and W. Boone to Jones, 29 July 1840, SC.

Tamer', Altren sets out to curb the power of the sea, and with the peasants' aid builds a granite wall as a sea-defence. He is also befriended by Valdine, a celestial sprite who appears one evening as he muses over Rolf's cenotaph in a nearby wood. But Altren is less successful in the battle against his worldly enemy, Lyndarn. The abbot, aided by the spirit of the sea—the Sea-King—and by rival warlords, defeats Altren. However, in allying with pagan warriors Lyndarn has betrayed his Christian faith, and his destiny is sealed. Altren, with the help of Valdine and assorted peasants and Christian nobles, eventually triumphs over the greedy abbot. *The Wood Spirit* is quite a convoluted story. A Swedish sub-plot, with a second hero named Karl Folkungar, works its way into the narrative at the end of the first volume, only to disappear from view thereafter, and Lyndarn is reworked into a tragic misunderstood hero by the end of the tale. But the work did unveil settings (days of medieval chivalry) and themes (the power of nature, the importance of Christian faith) which were to recur in Jones's poetry and prose for the next decade, including his Chartist oeuvre.

Critics liked what they read. Most reviewers located the romance within a bardic tradition, likening it to the Ossianic tales of the eighteenth century or even the Scaldic martial verse of ninth-century Iceland. The *Morning Post* was nearer the mark when it described the work as 'essentially German',[19] for the most obvious source for *The Wood Spirit* was Friedrich de la Motte-Fouqué's fairy tale *Undine* (1811), in which a water-sprite marries a human being. Jones would have been familiar with this popular German story, set as an opera by E. T. A. Hoffmann in 1813, but he would also have known of Fouqué's reputation amongst German nationalist poets. Fouqué had lectured on literature at Halle university, where Johann Schwarke had studied immediately before joining the Jones household as tutor to the young Ernest.[20]

Further evidence of the immersion of the young Jones in German patriotic poetry is provided by his own first published poetry, which

[19] *Morning Post* (7 May 1841), 5; cf. *Morning Herald* (10 July 1841), 6; *The Argus* (16 May 1841), 312; *Naval and Military Gazette* (22 May 1841), 327.

[20] On Fouqué's *Undine*, see: Gisela Dischner, 'Friedrich de La Motte-Fouqué: *Undine* (1811)', in P. M. Lützeler (ed.), *Romane und Erzählungen der Deutschen Romantik: Neue Interpretationen* (Stuttgart: Philipp Reclam, 1981). And on English enthusiasm for Fouqué's tales of medieval chivalry: Mark Girouard, *The Return to Camelot: Chivalry and the English Gentleman* (London: Yale University Press, 1981), 107–8.

began to appear in the *Court Journal* in the autumn of 1840. Between September 1840 and July 1842 this magazine carried thirteen of Jones's own poems, and another eleven translations by him of the verse of an assortment of Holstein and Swabian nationalist poets, such as Arndt, Rückert, von Stolberg, and Ühland, as well as Schiller.[21] In January 1843 the *Court Journal* also published the prose tale, 'Confessions of a King', which was to prove a hardy perennial in the Jones repertoire. All of these poems—Jones's own verse and the translations—are shot through with sublime, elemental imagery. Nature, be it mountains, forests, the sun and moon, or the night-skies above, is invested with a protean and tempestuous power, as in Arndt's 'Stars' or Rückert's 'The Two and the Third', but this power, or spirit, is restrained by the captive state of the people, who for too long have been in thrall to monarchs (Ühland's 'Minstrel's Curse'), or to 'reason' ('The Two and the Third'). The heroes of these poems are the young nobles, such as Stolberg's 'German Boy', or the travelling minstrels (Ühland) or the shepherd boy (Ühland), who, because they are closer to nature, whether nature be defined as youth, song, or pastoral abundance, are more likely to heed the call of the spirit. In the German patriotic poets' version the call of the spirit was equated with military valour. Stolberg's 'German Boy' promises: 'I'd die, O father, proud as thou, | The death for Fatherland.' Uhland's 'mountain shepherd boy' declares that he will: 'descend and join the file, | And swing my sword and sing the while.' Jones aped these themes in his own poetic contributions to the *Court Journal* in three main ways. First, in poems such as 'To Her' and 'Lines on Adelaide Kemble' he equated nature with true feeling. In 'To Her' it is, not surprisingly, love—'Love so deep that it must be | An agony or ecstasy'—which is elemental: 'flame as wild | As comet sent | Athwart a burning firmament, | Yet lasting as a sun.' In 'Lines on Adelaide Kemble' the naturalistic element was provided by song. He praised the singer for her music, 'the heav'n of sound':

> It calls the spirits of the heart
> From slumbers long and deep,

[21] For Arndt and von Stolberg, see above, Ch. 1, n. 42. For Rückert, see: Jürgen Erdmann (ed.), *Friedrich Rückert, 1788–1866: Dichter und Gelehrter* (Coburg: Landesbibliothek, 1988). For Ühland, see: Victor G. Doerksen, *Ludwig Ühland and the Critics* (Columbia, SC: Camden House, 1994), ch. 2.

> Till it makes tyrants start
> To find that he can weep

Secondly, Jones copied the German polarity between nature and the spiritual world on the one side, and the austerity of the man-made world on the other. In the 'Geister-Ahnung' (Ghost-idea) Jones described how a 'fairy strain' and a moonbeam flooded a 'ruined mansion hall'. In the 'Glocken-ruf' (Bell cry) he showed how the peal of a bell could summon thousands to God, whereas a priest could not: 'Zum Herze spricht das Herz allein' ('The heart speaks to the heart alone'). Finally, Jones warmed to the chivalric settings of the German school. Nowhere was this better exemplified than in his 'Confessions of a King' which ran over several issues of the *Court Journal* in January and February 1843, and which combined the mystic timelessness of *The Wood Spirit* with the enthusiasm for nature of his verse of 1840–2. In its depiction of a tragic historical figure overtaken by fate it also gestured towards Bulwer-Lytton's *Rienzi*.[22] The 'Confessions', later republished in the Chartist *Labourer*, told the story, apparently found hidden within the pages of a bible, of the King of Aldi, originally a son of the soil— 'surrounded by sea, moor, heath, and forest'—who as a young man was befriended by a Pilgrim. The Pilgrim recognized genius in the youth, but saw too its shadow, in the form of ambition. No surprise then that years later the youth, now a man, usurped a kingdom by turning a virtuous prince's subjects against their natural ruler, only to find himself defeated by his own conspiring father-in-law. The moral of the tale was clear. Nature had bestowed talent on the youth, but he had lacked higher guidance: 'man cannot stand', warned the narrator, 'without the aid of God'. The King of Aldi had all the higher qualities except religion, and so although he had risen to power through his own strengths, he was then left at the mercy of fate: 'I had, as yet, apparently created my past; my future existence was to be the creature of events', so the king reflected.

With these works Jones was introduced to the reading public—or at any rate, the readers of the *Court Journal*, a sort of *Tatler* of its day. Of course it was not Jones who made his literary debut, but 'Karl, author of *The Wood Spirit*'. After signing his first contribution, 'The Dying Girl', with the initials 'E.C.J', Jones adopted 'Karl'

---

[22] For which see E. A. C. Christensen, *Edward Bulwer Lytton: the Fiction of New Regions* (Athens, Ga: University of Georgia Press, 1976), 124, 127–8.

as his nom de plume thereafter. By re-Germanizing the Anglicized name by which he was known in his family, Jones gave emphasis to his Continental literary credentials at a time when Thomas Carlyle, amongst many, in print and on the podium, were giving wider publicity to the work of Goethe, Schiller, and others.[23] In 1842 Jones attempted to enhance his cosmopolitan reputation further by establishing (as he informed Lord Aberdeen, a would-be patron), along with 'several other literary characters' a weekly newspaper—the *Foreign Post and Political Review*—which would treat foreign events alongside domestic news.[24] But Jones's German pretensions were more than simply a commercial ploy. The poetic idiom with which he was most familiar was actually German patriotic verse, and although he sometimes seems to have been better at hamming rather than emulating his literary heroes, slipping into romantic nature-worship came easily. Above all, Jones adopted the German romantic persona of the lyricist as the authentic observer of the human experience. Already at this early stage his vision of the poet as a bard or minstrel, awakening the virtue of the people, was evident. Poetry, he declared in a review of Maria Abdy's work in 1842, should guide feelings in the right way.[25]

In 1840, around the same time that he became acquainted with Lady Stepney and embarked on a fledgling literary career as 'Karl', Jones also met Jane Atherley, whom he married the following summer. Jane, a few months older than the young Jones, played an important part in the construction of Carl's or 'Karl's' literary identity, for she gave him (and the Jones family more generally) an English pedigree that was hitherto lacking. In the manner of these things, their romance was a rapid affair. Within weeks of their meeting love-letters were going back and forth, his sealed with a stag's head, hers singing the praises of his story 'The Invalid's Pipe' (published ten years previously). By early April he had exchanged his miniature portrait for her ring and lock of hair, and the two families were in regular contact.[26] Jane Atherley was quite a catch for Jones, for although her family were untitled they had a more stable landed

[23] Rosemary Ashton, *The German Idea: Four English Writers and the Reception of German Thought, 1800–60* (Cambridge: Cambridge University Press, 1980), ch. 2.

[24] It would be an 'essentially conservative' paper, Jones promised Aberdeen: Jones to Aberdeen, 14 Mar. 1842, BL, Aberdeen papers, Add. Ms., 43, 239, fos. 85–6.

[25] *Metropolitan Magazine*, 35 (Oct. 1842), 41–4.

[26] Ernest Jones to Jane Atherley Jones [1840], CL, MUN. A.0.10/2; EJD, 6 Apr. 1840.

lineage than the Joneses and had better connections in the political world than those afforded by the military veterans on whom Charles Jones tended to rely. Jane Atherley was the daughter of Edmond Gibson (who, in addition to his own, assumed his mother's name Atherley on her death in 1817) and Jane, née Stanley, the younger sister of Edward Stanley, MP for West Cumberland between 1832 and 1852. Edmond Gibson Atherley came from a line of Cumbrian attorneys and magistrates, owned land at Barfield near Whitehaven, and had a busy practice in Grays Inn in the twenty years or so after the peace of 1815. He edited a common law digest and had written his own guide to the law of marriage.[27] Gibson Atherley was a rentier and not a working landowner. In 1826 he supported freer admission of foreign corn, denying that it would harm English landowners, but he remained an obdurate opponent of the Tories' currency measures, claiming that his own estate and those of his 'Family connexions' had been ruined by Peel's premature return to cash payments in 1819.[28] Jane Stanley, his wife, was some eighteen years younger, Jane Atherley was their only child, and mother and daughter were particularly close, as the extensive correspondence between them attests.

Throughout 1840 Ernest and Jane seem to have enjoyed a leisurely courtship, taking tea and walks, dining, partying, and going to the theatre at the Haymarket and at Covent Garden. Then in the early summer of 1841 the pace quickened. The two were presented by the Duke of Beaufort to the Queen at a levée on 12 May,[29] and within a fortnight were scouring central London for a new home. Jane was expecting their first child, duly born at the end of December (Ernest Beaufort Annesley Jones). The pregnancy possibly alarmed Jones. Shortly before the levée he left town for several days on his own, taking the steamer down to Woolwich and then walking from village to village through Kentish London. On his return wedding preparations were under way, and the two were married, Jane now three months pregnant, in the middle of June at St George's in Hanover Square. As Jane's aunt tartly observed, it was not a union

[27] *Notes & Queries* (8 Jan. 1898), 31; C. Roy Hudleston, 'Millom Families', *Transactions of the Cumberland & Westmoreland Antiquary Society*, 93 (1993), 94–5; E. G. Atherley, *Practical Treatise on the Law of Marriage* (London: W. C. Clarke & Sons, 1813); id. (ed.), *Sheppard's Common Assurances*, 8th edn. (London: Samuel Brooke, 1826).

[28] E. G. Atherley, *Letter to the Earl of Liverpool . . . on Objections to the Admission of Foreign Corn* (London: Ridgway & Sons, 1826), 23; id. to Robert Peel, 17 Apr. 1848, BL Add Ms 40,600, fos. 138–9.

[29] *Court Journal* (15 May 1841), 1200.

'clad in roses', and thereafter Jones's relations with Jane's father seem to have soured.[30] But to all the world it appeared to be a 'dashing' (Jones's own description) society wedding, attended by the Stanleys and others.[31] The newlyweds spent a fortnight in Richmond, settled into their new home in Upper Montagu Street, where they remained for the next two years, and in September took a tour through France, staying in Paris before returning via Rouen and Le Havre. One observer was particularly enthusiastic about the young Ernest's good fortune. Charles Jones proudly informed the Crown Prince of Hanover that through his marriage his son had now become connected with 'many of the most noble families of England & Scotland'. In later years the legend grew that the Atherleys were in fact descended from the Plantagenet kings.[32]

It was at the time of his marriage that, through Lady Stepney, Jones was introduced to the world of the London stage.[33] The Jones family were fairly regular theatregoers in 1840 and 1841, but after the birth of his first child, with Jane nursing the baby away from home, Jones became particularly keen, attending nearly fifty performances of comedies, farces, dramas, and a few tragedies in just over five years. His first contact came in December 1841 and was with Charles Matthews, the manager of the Covent Garden theatre and the husband of the famous tragic actress Madame Vestris. Jones was introduced to Matthews at Lady Stepney's, and from him Jones got to know the leading London dramatic writers and performers of the early 1840s—Dion Boucicault, Charles Kean, Charles Kemble, William Macready, and William Oxberry, all of whom his diary records meeting during 1842. He also befriended Henry Vandenhoff, brother of George Vandenhoff, a young actor in Matthews's company, who later found fame as an expert on elocution, and who may have influenced Jones's interest in oratory.[34] Initially Jones

---

[30] Mary Gibson to Jane Atherley, 8 June 1841, SC; diary entry, 17 May 1842.

[31] EJD, 15 June 1841; *Court Gazette* (12 June 1841), 388; *Court Journal* (19 June 1841), 1303.

[32] Charles Jones to the Crown Prince of Hanover, 21 July 1841, SC; *PP* (14 Jan. 1854), 4.

[33] Virtually all of Jones's biographers have overlooked his connections with the theatre, leading one recent scholar to assert that Jones experimented with all genres of literature, *except* the theatre: Hugues Journés, *Une littérature revolutionnaire en Grande-Bretagne: la poesie chartiste* (Paris: Publisud, 1991), 119.

[34] EJD, 29 Dec. 1842. The relationship with Vandenhoff is suggestive. In contrast to some of the stilted and declamatory traditions of delivery associated with Kean and Macready, Vandenhoff championed a performative manner of speech-making,

hoped to get Matthews interested in an operatic version of *The Wood Spirit* which he had prepared. He also sent Madame Vestris one of his songs—'Clouds'—which had been set to music the previous autumn by Michael James Balfe, of 'Come into the garden, Maud' fame. Matthews undertook to stage the opera, but unfortunately his theatre failed before it could be performed. But Jones did not give up. By the summer of 1842 he was frequently to be found backstage at Covent Garden or the Lyceum watching rehearsals or first nights. The Shakespearean actor-manager Charles Kean, in particular, became a close friend, judging from the number of meetings that Jones's diary records between the two of them, either at the Haymarket or at each other's respective homes.[35] Jones was also witness to the burgeoning reputation of the young Irish dramatist Dion Boucicault, at that stage veering between pastiches of Restoration comedy and adaptations of French historical drama.[36] Jones was spurred into writing his own dramas. Between the close of 1841, when he completed 'The Folkungar', and February 1844, when he concluded 'The Libertin', he dashed off eight plays. Unfortunately none of these have survived, as they were all turned down by the various London theatres, with one exception. 'St John's Eve' was accepted by the Lyceum in February 1844, but, as with Matthews's staging of *The Wood Spirit*, the theatre company failed before it could be performed. Jones did publish a dramatic poem of the same name in *The Labourer* in 1847, and assuming it is substantially the same work, its Gothic and melodramatic themes (which are discussed in the following chapter) might be taken as indicative of the content of his dramas as a whole. The titles of the other plays he

arguing that 'a nervous and elegant style of Elocution, are as essential, almost, as force of argument and grace of language'. He argued that gesture was essential, and recommended that orators should take advice from fencing masters. Vandenhoff also warned (prophetically in the case of Jones) that '[h]e who would touch the heart, "and wield the fierce democracie" ' must be able to quell tumult as well as rouse it: George Vandenhoff, *The Art of Elocution; from the Simple Articulation of the Essential Sounds of Language, up to the Highest Tone of Expression in Speech, Attainable by the Human Voice* (London: Wiley & Putnam, 1846), 12–13, 208–10; cf. id., *Dramatic Reminiscences; or Actors and Actresses in England and America* (London: T. W. Cooper, 1860), 14–15.

[35] For the background on this phase of Kean's career, see: M. Glen Wilson, 'Charles Kean at the Haymarket, 1839–50', *Theatre Journal*, 31 (1979), 329–42; Richard W. Schoch, *Shakespeare's Victorian Stage: Performing History in the Theatre of Charles Kean* (Cambridge: Cambridge University Press, 1998), 3, 24–6.

[36] Richard Fawkes, *Dion Boucicault: A Biography* (London: Quartet Books, 1979), ch. 3.

wrote—'Lavagna', 'Love and the Monkey', 'The Gray Man', 'King Death', and 'The Fairy of Montberceau'—are not especially suggestive, although the latter sounds like a variation on the themes of *The Wood Spirit*. However, one letter of rejection has survived and it provides a further clue. Written to Jones by Thomas Serle, the manager of the Drury Lane company, it explained that had the theatre been a 'melodramatic company', 'St John's Eve' would have had a chance, but 'with us it would only be a tragedy at second-hand with the best actors left out'.[37] In the growing breach between the professional theatre of comedy and tragedy and the more demotic world of the melodrama, it appears that Jones's work was already tending in the direction of the popular.

Shortly after meeting Jane Atherley and Lady Stepney, Jones noted in his diary that he had begun work on a piece entitled 'The man in search of himself'.[38] Like so many of Jones's efforts it never saw the light of day, although unlike most of his other unpublished 'literary effusions' he did not see fit to file it away and keep it. Perhaps he had no need. By 1842 the young Ernest had, to some extent, found himself, or at least created a self with which he was comfortable. He was an up-and-coming author—of poetry and prose, shot through with fashionable German angst. In April 1842 he was elected a Fellow of the Society of Arts.[39] He had a developing sideline in drama, although his efforts in this direction seem to have been rejected as effortlessly as they were written. He was cramming his way, in all senses of the word, to the bar. And he was a society name: he habituated the salons of west London, he had been presented to the Queen, and he had married into the Stanley family—granted, they were the Stanleys of Cumberland and not of Alderley—but, as so often in Jones's life, if you did not look too closely the general effect was really quite impressive. Into this contrived world, towards the end of 1842, real tragedy began to intrude.

2

George Howell, the last of Jones's Victorian biographers, was the first to reveal the extent of his financial misfortunes in the mid-1840s. In chapter entitled 'The Kearsney Estate—Financial

[37] T. J. Serle to Jones, 28 Jan. 1843, BL Add Ms 52,477, fos. 260–1.
[38] EJD, 23 May 1840.
[39] Ibid., 11 Apr. 1842; *Transactions of the Society . . . for the Encouragement of Arts, Manufactures and Commerce*, 54 (1841–2), p. xxi.

Disaster', Howell described how in September 1844 the 25-year-old Jones invested £57,000 in a house and 1,100-acre estate in Kent. Within months, according to Howell, Jones was forced to sell this property at a reduced price of £16,000, and he was subsequently pitched into insolvency proceedings, from which he only emerged, a discharged bankrupt, in March 1846, shortly before he joined the Chartist movement. As John Saville has since observed, had anyone known of Jones's insolvency at the time of his falling in with the Chartists, or indeed during his skirmishes in and out of the libel courts during the 1850s, then his opponents would have had a field day, for no democrat liked a bankrupt on the make, particularly during the later 1840s when political and commercial boomers and busters often went hand-in-hand. But contemporaries did not know of Jones's financial troubles and his reputation for honesty and transparency remained intact. And there his biographers have closed their inquiries on the Kearsney estate, concluding that Jones's finances were 'involved in obscurity', that his investment may possibly have been connected with an attempt to enter Parliament, but had no bearing on his becoming a Chartist in 1846.[40] His family papers tell a rather different story. The picture that emerges is of the Kearsney Abbey speculation being the last fatal twist in a series of tragedies which beset the Jones family in the 1840s.

Despite appearances, the Jones family income was in a precarious state in the early 1840s. Charles Jones had never been returned to the full-pay retirement list, and by 1842 his position seemed parlous. In September he pleaded with both the Crown Prince of Hanover and his father, the King, to grant him some 'pecuniary succour', but to no avail.[41] Two months later he drew up a series of instructions relating to his finances which his wife was to implement in the event of his death.[42] This memorandum revealed that Charles Jones would be effectively leaving Charlotte and Ernest without any income, for although enjoying a military commission, Captain Jones was without a full pension. He did, however, have some life assurance.

---

[40] George Howell, 'Ernest Jones, The Chartist: Poet and Orator, Patriot and Politician', *Newcastle Weekly Chronicle* (12 Feb. 1898), 7; John Saville, *Ernest Jones. Chartist* (London: Lawrence & Wishart, 1952), 16.

[41] Charles Jones to the Crown Prince of Hanover, Charles Jones to King Ernst, 23 Sept. 1842, Niedersachsen Hauptstaatsarchiv, Hanover, Dep. 103, nr. 39/45, Dep 103 II, nr. 2/36.

[42] 'Private memorandum for the attention of my wife' (2 July 1841, revised 9 Nov. 1842), BJH.

Charles Jones blamed his misfortunes on his former master, the King of Hanover—referred to in the memorandum as 'that villain' to whom all the Captain's 'loss of rank & property may be justly attributed'. The Captain closed his instructions by suggesting that his wife might now finally publish his 'memoir' of the King's murder of his manservant Seliss in 1810. Notwithstanding the fact that time and time again the Duke had seen off his accusers in the libel courts, Captain Jones, it seemed, knew something else: 'I have done great wrong to society', he told his wife in the memorandum, 'in screening him from the penalty of the law & the due execrations of mankind which would have long ago rolled him into the abyss of infamy, had I have published half what I know.' However, the Captain's secrets were never revealed. He overdosed on laudanum at the beginning of September.[43] And then five months later in February 1843, on the eve of returning to Hanover to visit the King, he was killed while cleaning out his pistols. It was not thought to be a suicide, reported *The Times*,[44] but given the circumstances, the possibility that Charles Jones, embittered by wrongful treatment at the hands of the King of Hanover and contemplating financial ruin, had taken his own life cannot be ruled out.

The family were devastated by Charles Jones's death, and even more so when it became evident that the Britannia Life Insurance Company was not going to pay out. Ernest Jones, accompanied by Thomas Wakley, the Middlesex coroner, and Colonel Gillies, a family friend, made frantic visits to the offices of the Britannia and to the magistrate, but were unsuccessful in reversing the company's decision.[45] There was also a question-mark over the will—John Hutton Annesley, Charlotte's brother, refusing to act as executor.[46] Within weeks the remaining Joneses had given up the Bedford Place parental home, rented out 33 Upper Montagu Street, and all— Ernest, Jane, baby, and Charlotte—moved into a house in Sussex Gardens. Charlotte lobbied the Horse Guards, calling in person and

---

[43] EJD, 7 Sept. 1842.

[44] *The Times* (17 Feb. 1843), 6. Laudanum (opium) overdoses and shooting were reasonably common forms of suicide in Victorian times, and as a wounded veteran Charles Jones had easy access to both means. *Felo de se* suicide verdicts invariably led to life assurance companies not paying out: Olive Anderson, *Suicide in Victorian and Edwardian Britain* (Oxford: Clarendon Press, 1987), 221, 364–70; Victor Bailey, *'This Rash Act': Suicide Across the Life Cycle in the Victorian City* (Stanford, Calif.: Stanford University Press, 1998), 62, 141.

[45] EJD, 25 Feb., 2 Mar. 1843.

[46] Hutton Annesley to Jones, 3 Mar. 1843, SC.

writing to Lord Anglesey and the Duke of Somerset. She also contacted the King of Hanover, from whom it was hoped an appointment might be found for Ernest. Jones himself badgered the Duke of Beaufort.[47] And when the King of Hanover visited London during the summer, Jones called on him on ten separate occasions in the space of two months. What took place during those visits we shall never know, but it is not too far-fetched to suggest that Jones went with blackmail in mind. He had access to his father's personal papers after his death and may have felt that natural justice entitled him to some recompense. None was forthcoming.

His father's death also seems to have had a deep impact on Jones personally. Overnight he became the head of the household, with all the patriarchal and financial responsibilities that entailed. Within a week or so of his father's death he was hauling a drunken servant off to the police,[48] and his days became filled up with business appointments of one sort or another. Most significantly of all, writing ground to a halt. Between laying down his pen on 'St John's Eve' at the beginning of 1843 and taking it up again just over two years later, Jones produced very little—he churned out another drama, 'The Libertin', in the late summer of 1843, and had two poems published in the *Morning Post* around the turn of the year.[49] He began to take his vocation more seriously, making sure that he kept the requisite number of dinners at the Middle Temple, where he was eventually called to the bar in April 1844. Gradually, his life as a social butterfly began to wind down, and by 1844 most of his spare time was spent in the company of three close friends: Archer Gurney, a writer and poet whom he befriended at the bar in 1842, Michael Conan, an Irish barrister, and Joseph Cholmondeley, the family's doctor, who lived a few streets away near Regent's Park.[50] Gurney in particular, as will become clear, played an important part in Jones's unfolding personal crisis.

In the short term Jones's main concern was money. His father had left him nothing except a few unpaid bills, and although a careful

[47] EJD, 7 Mar., 23 May 1843; J. G. Atherley to Jane Atherley Jones, 4 Apr. 1843, SC; Duke of Beaufort to Jones, 12 Mar. 1843, BJH.

[48] EJD, 26 Feb. 1843.

[49] 'To Chateaubriand' and 'New Year's Eve', *Morning Post* (13 Dec. 1843), 5; (1 Jan. 1844), 5; diary entry, 27 Aug. 1843.

[50] Michael Conan, the eldest son of a Dublin merchant and a graduate of Trinity College, Dublin, was a Middle Temple barrister and a literary dabbler. His translation of epigrams of the Latin poet Martial appeared in *Bentley's Miscellany*, 11 (May 1842), 537. For Gurney, see below.

financial settlement was granted to Jane Atherley, Ernest's wife, upon their marriage, it provided income but no capital except in the event of their deaths.[51] Here lay some of the background to Jones's seemingly rash purchase of Kearsney Abbey. The estate was intended to provide an income. For Kearsney Abbey was not a real abbey, but a mansion which began construction in 1812, built in the 'monastic' style by John Minet Fector (1754–1821), the son of an Anglo-Dutch merchant of Huguenot descent. In 1814 Fector had entertained the King of Prussia there. 'Its romantic scenery', boasted a local guide, 'engages the attention of every passing stranger', but apparently not that of its owner, John Minet Fector the younger, who, having sold off his father's business to the National and Provincial Bank in 1833, set about divesting himself of his father's folly as well.[52] The estate was huge, embracing not only the house, but landscaped pleasure-gardens, two large farms, four smaller farms, eight cottages, several houses, corn mills, and one or two individual plots of land. All the adjoined property was occupied, bringing a sizeable annual rent.[53] Jones had no intention of living on the estate. Like his father-in-law and countless other Victorian gentlemen, he would become a rentier.

Jones first came across the Kearsney estate in the summer of 1844, although he may also have got to hear of it during a long autumn holiday spent at the Kent seaside the previous year. The family spent all of June 1844 on holiday in Dover. They saw much of their friends the Manners, and it is likely that Captain Manners told Jones of the impending sale of Kearsney. Towards the end of the month Jones was shown the house and surrounding lands by Martin, the vendor's agent. He also met with Coleman, the occupier of the principal farm on the estate. Jones visited the estate six times, mostly on his own, and then the whole family returned to London. Back in London Jones immediately set about raising money for his venture, visiting Coutts the bankers and a Mr Campbell, one of a series of bill-brokers in whom Jones entrusted his hopes over the ensuing months. He obtained a copy of a valuation of the estate with a view to estimating the rental value of the farms and other properties. Fector's agent's

[51] W. Hammond to Charles Nuttall, 10 Mar. 1869, BJH.

[52] William Batcheller, *The New Dover Guide* (London: Simpkin & Marshall, 1845), 170; William Minet, *Some Account of the Family of Minet* (London: Spottiswoode & Co., 1892), 150; Douglas Welby, *Reflections of River: The Kentish Village* (Dover: Crabwell, 1977), 22–3.

[53] There is a complete guide in the 1854 sale particulars: East Kent Archives Centre, Dover, EK/U844/E37.

valuation came to around £55,000 for the whole estate, which, given that Fector senior was reckoned to have spent £72,000 on the house and gardens alone, represented something of a bargain. Mansell, Jones's own agent, largely agreed with the valuation, suggesting to Jones that the 'Abbey'—the main house—might be a summer residence with potential for shooting, and that Coleman, the principal tenant, might be persuaded to rent or even buy some of the smaller farms, including Whitfield farm, whose tenant had allowed it to become very dilapidated. All told, Mansell's estimate was that a rental income of around £1,500 per annum might be secured from the estate, two-thirds of which might be derived from the farms and other business concerns.[54] By September Jones had concluded that it was a worthwhile investment, and anticipating the date set for the sale by auction of the estate by a month or so, he made Fector junior an offer of £57,000. The offer was accepted and a contract duly changed hands on 27 September.[55] The following month Jones set about maximizing the potential return on his forthcoming purchase. A notice to quit was served on the tenant of the unproductive Whitfield farm, and in November the Gothic heap that was Kearsney Abbey, along with its grounds, was offered for sale for £16,000 to a Captain Stevenson. This amounted to a £2,000 profit, as Fector's valuation had originally been that it was worth £14,000.[56] Thus, by the beginning of November Jones was on the verge of completing a nifty piece of business. At a knockdown price he was about to become a substantial landowner in Kent, and he was making a handsome return on his investment almost immediately. At the same time Jones was toying with the idea of standing for Parliament.[57] The only problem was that he had to raise the capital to complete his side of the contract. And he had to raise it as soon as possible.

The London money market in the mid-1840s was not unlike the West End stage. It flattered and encouraged those on the rise, and was merciless and cruel to those whose reputations took a dive. Jones spent most of November 1844 dashing hither and thither across

[54] Valuation of Kearsney estate [n.d.], SC; *Dover Chronicle* (5 Oct. 1844), 2; Charles Bischoff to Jones, 10 Dec. 1844, SC.

[55] *Dover Chronicle* (7 Sept. 1844), 1; (5 Oct. 1844), 2; EJD, 27 Sept. 1844.

[56] EJD, 2 Oct. 1844, 8 Nov. 1844; William Cross to Jones, 8 Oct. 1844, BJH.

[57] At the beginning of November he was sounded out about a vacancy at Andover, where it was rumoured Lord William Paget was about to resign. Nothing came of this: Diary entry 4 Nov. 1844; *Hampshire Chronicle* (14 Sept. 1844), 1.

London in a brougham carriage, borrowed from a friend and driven by Charles, his manservant, seemingly at all hours of the day and evening, chasing down possible bills and loans, meeting his agent, and trying to keep Fector's agents at bay. By the new year it was clear that Jones was not going to be able to raise sufficient finance on the London bills market, and he turned his attention to securing a mortgage. The Gray's Inn firm of Wilton and Blackman were consulted with this end in view, but they began to worry about the validity of some of the titles to the estate. By now Fector's solicitors were running out of patience, and on 27 January politely enquired of Wilton and Blackman as to Jones's private resources. Within days Coleman, Jones's main prospective tenant, informed Martin, Fector's agent, that the purchase appeared to be off. Jones's creditors in London got wind of this and called in their bills.[58] The house of cards was collapsing. By the middle of February the family's Sussex Gardens home was possessed by auctioneers. Jones was 'hiding from his creditors' and had taken to only going out with a stick and a dagger. The family escaped to a small cottage at the lower end of Hampstead Heath, taking only their 'clothing and a few pct. books and boxes'. Other china, glass, and books had all been claimed. 'My position', declared Jones in his diary, 'is critical in the extreme.'[59]

Critical, but actually nowhere near as bad as Howell and other biographers have made out. Jones did not buy for £57,000 and sell for £16,000, which even in the annals of mid-Victorian business failure would have been unusually careless. He had simply signed a contract on a large estate which he then could not complete. His eyes were bigger than his bank-balance. Kearsney Abbey was never actually his to sell or to let. The contract incomplete, Fector withdrew, and the estate went back on the market in May 1845. With the exception of the house and the principal farms, all the lots were auctioned off.[60] As for Jones, he sought 'protection' under the Insolvency Act of 1842. As he explained to the readers of *Notes to*

[58] Wilton and Blackman to Jones, 21 Jan. 1845, 27 Jan. 1845, Charles Bailey to Jones, 14 Feb. 1845, SC.

[59] EJD, 25 Feb. 1844.

[60] *Dover Telegraph* (8 Mar. 1845), 8; (31 May 1845), 8. Ironically, part of the estate was bought (and sold two years later) by a consortium which included Jones's namesake, Lord Ernst Augustus Bruce, the Vice-Chamberlain to the Queen (and later the 3rd Marquess of Ailesbury): Indenture (16 Mar. 1847), Laurie Mss, East Kent Archives Centre, Dover, EK/U491/T38.

the People several years later, he was left owing around £3,000 (his Chartist opponents claimed £9,000) to assorted bill-brokers.[61] But the whole episode, following on from his father's death, had clearly proved traumatic for the family above and beyond the dire financial straits into which they were plunged. Charlotte, Jones's mother, had fallen seriously ill two months before Jones made the offer for Kearsney, with what seems to have been some kind of brain tumour. She died at the end of August 1845. Moreover, Jones became a father for a second time in September 1844 (of Edmond Stanley Radziwill Jones).[62] The gulf between the status of an independent gentleman that he desired and the desperate dependency in which he lived could never have been greater.

Jones responded to this impasse in his life—the first of many—in several ways. First, perhaps flushed with the acumen that his new status as a barrister gave him, he decided to pursue his mother's brother, John Hutton Annesley, for what he believed to be a fraudulent conveyance of his maternal grandfather's estate. Charlotte's father had died a wealthy man in 1813, his estates worth at least £50,000, but his will had been executed by Hutton Annesley. Jones came to suspect, possibly from papers left by his own father, that his mother had been defrauded of an inheritance of the livings of some dozen farms in Kent, and residential property in Lincoln and in Brighton. The issue turned on whether Charlotte, as a co-beneficiary with her two brothers—Hutton and Robert—had signed the conveyances involved in the selling on of various parts of the estate. Jones contacted his other uncle, Robert Annesley, and had some of his suspicions confirmed. In June Jones spent a few days going over the former Annesley farms in the Gillingham area of Kent with his lawyer, Fesenmeyer, making enquiries about the details and circumstances of their sale. As a result of this visit and the discussion with Robert Annesley, Fesenmeyer drew up a schedule of the various properties and the way in which they were conveyanced. In only two cases did it seem that Charlotte had not signed the conveyance, and as another lawyer, Capron, from whom Jones sought advice in July, pointed out, since the original sales had all taken place nearly thirty years ago fraud would be difficult to prove—it would depend on the purchaser knowingly participating in the fraud as well as the

---

[61] *London Gazette* (12 Feb. 1846), 353; (5 Mar. 1846), 670–1; *NP* (14 Feb. 1852), 817–18; cf. *NS* (31 Jan. 1852), 1.
[62] EJD, 16 July 1844.

vendor.[63] However, both Fesenmeyer and Edmond Atherley, Jones's father-in-law, seemed to have convinced Jones that there was still a moral case for Hutton to answer, and at the end of 1845 he went down to Hampshire to visit his uncle and demand out-of-court retribution. The two men met, Jones was rebuffed, and he returned to London threatening legal action.[64] Nothing ever came of this, but the seed of another sub-plot within the Jones life-story had been sown. Jones never forgave Hutton, and in future years he would return to the dramatic claim that he had been denied his inheritance by a wicked uncle who, disliking his nephew's politics, had left his fortune to his gardener.[65] This was complete nonsense. When he died in 1858 Hutton Annesley's estate was valued at only £1,000, and the principal beneficiary was not his gardener but his wife.[66]

Following the trials and tribulations of the previous two years, Jones's second strategy was to seek gainful employment. He wrote to Lord Ashley. Feelers were put out to the Anti-Corn Law League, and to their figureheads, John Bright, Richard Cobden, and Charles Pelham Villiers, proposing the start-up of a new newspaper. In July Jones applied to become Auditor of the Essex District, and in September 1845 finally found a job as secretary with the Leek and Mansfield Railway Company, charged with seeing their bill through Parliament.[67] Parliamentary draughtsmanship at 4 guineas a week was not the berth to which the young Ernest had aspired on the family's return to England seven years previously. Not that it lasted very long. The company was launched with a prospective capital of £600,000 for the purpose of forming a junction between the North Wales and Lincolnshire railways, thereby allowing passengers to be 'wafted from Holyhead to Boston and back again in 16 hours'. However, it foundered, and to this day the traveller from the Wash to Wales must change at Crewe. By January 1846 Jones was paying off the remaining bills of the company.[68] But it did not really matter, for Jones had rediscovered the muse. His third and final way of

[63] Robert Annesley to Ernest Jones, 10 Apr. 1845, Robert Annesley to Charlotte Jones, 19 Apr. 1845; 'Memorandum on conference with Robert Annesley' (8 May 1845), SC.
[64] EG Atherley to Jones [n.d.], BJH; FW Fesenmeyer to Jones, 27 Aug. 1845, SC; EJD, 13 Dec. 1845; Jones to Hutton Annesley, 14 Dec. 1845 [copy], SC.
[65] Ernest Jones. Who is he?, 10.
[66] Calendar of Grants of Probate (27 Sept. 1858).
[67] EJD, 5 June, 10 June, 14 June, 27 July 1845.
[68] Railway Times (20 Sept. 1845), 1600; (4 Oct. 1845), 1774; EJD, 15 Jan. 1846.

coping with his personal and financial traumas was to pick up his pen again. At the end of February, 1845 he noted in his diary that he had '[r]ecommenced writing'. And he now had plenty of material: royal blackguards, wicked scheming uncles, wronged fathers, defrauded mothers, landed families ruined by the ravages of commerce, and righteous sons bent on revenge—Jones did not have to look far for a plot. But there was another, new dimension to Jones's writing when he resumed his literary vocation in 1845: religion.

3

Outwardly, Ernest Jones in his mid-twenties was a fairly observant Anglican. Although he had clearly imbibed something from Binge and Schwarke, the two Lutheran pastors charged with his adolescent education, there was nothing in his behaviour in the first half of the 1840s to suggest that he was anything other than a normal church-goer of the early Victorian period. True, some of his poetry in the *Court Journal* sounded somewhat deistic, but a poet should be allowed due licence. The Jones family attended church most Sundays, usually at St John's, Kensington, occasionally further afield, for example, St Barnabas' in Finsbury. Sometimes Jones fasted for Lent, but equally he often worked at his desk on a Sunday. He steered clear of Roman Catholicism, on one occasion, for example, accompanying his friend Conan to the 'French chapel' at Regent's Park but making a point of not going in.[69] After the death of his father Jones continued to attend services regularly, but there was now a marked shift to low church venues and preachers. On Good Friday 1844 he went to the service led by Baptist Noel at Well Walk chapel. Noel was on his way out of the Anglican church, becoming a Baptist in 1848 in reaction to the Gorham controversy of that year. He had been an interventionist church voice in the condition of England politics of the 1840s, writing a tract opposing the corn laws in 1841, and in 1846 advising young men to help alleviate poverty in London and the surrounding agricultural districts by becoming city missionaries.[70] Jones also took an interest in the Presbyterian

[69] EJD, 10 Dec. 1843.
[70] Baptist Noel, 'On the Means of Acquiring Influence', in Henry Raikes *et al.*, *The Claims of Missions upon the Young of England: Eleven Lectures by Clergymen of the Church of England* (London: John F. Shaw, 1846), 125–42. K. R. M. Short, 'Baptist Wriothesley Noel: Anglican, Evangelical, Baptist', *Baptist Quarterly*, 20 (1963), 51–61; D. W. Bebbington, 'The Life of Baptist Noel: Its Setting and Significance', ibid., 24 (1972), 389–41; Donald M. Lewis, *Lighten their Darkness: The Evangelical*

ministry. A month or so before his conversion to Chartism in 1846, Jones recorded attending the 'Scottish kirk' and found Peter Lorimer's sermon to be 'the most magnificent piece of oratory I ever heard', while of his fellow Presbyterian preacher, McClymont, Jones wrote, '[o]f course I cannot agree with all their tenets, although I admire their fervour, argumentative power and eloquence'.[71] Lorimer was a founding figure in the English Presbyterian church, taking up a Chair in Hebrew and Biblical Criticism at the English Presbyterian College in Leicester Square. He had a particular expertise on the pre-Reformation English church, translating a German biography of Wycliffe towards the end of his life.[72] Although Jane and Ernest's church of choice remained the new, small wooden hut that was the temporary Anglican chapel in Rosslyn Hill,[73] the effect of this exposure to the anti-clerical and social-reforming low churchmanship of Noel and Lorimer was to be revealed in Jones's conversion to Chartism, as the next chapter makes clear.

Further evidence of Jones's religious preoccupations at the time of his family tragedy in the mid-1840s comes from the most vital friendship of his early adulthood—that with Archer Gurney. Gurney (1820–87) was born in Tregorny in Cornwall, the son of an official in charge of the royal tin-mines. Like Jones, Gurney had lived on the Continent—in Vienna—and was enamoured of German authors. In 1836 he translated Schiller's *Turandot* into English, and six years later did the same with Goethe's *Faust*. The two men met in June 1842, soon after Gurney had entered the Middle Temple. They quickly became inseparable. Gurney's father also died in 1843. Gurney would frequently stay over for the night in Upper Montagu Street, and he and Jones would read aloud their works to one another. Gurney later dedicated poems to the Jones family, and became godfather to Jones's third child, born in January 1847 (Llewellyn Archer Atherley Jones), and attended the christening of

Missions to Working-Class London, 1828–60 (London: Greenwood Press, 1986), ch. 3; In 1854 Jones's *People's Paper* featured a portrait and appreciative article on Baptist Noel: *PP* (27 May 1854), 2.

[71] EJD, 19 Apr. 1846.

[72] G. V. Lechler, *John Wycliffe and his English Precursors*, trans. Peter Lorimer (London: C. K. Paul, 1878); W. B. Shaw, 'A Biography from the Fasti of our Church', *Journal of the Presbyterian Historical Society of England*, 1 (1917), 135–6; ibid. 3 (1924), 193–4; George G. Cameron, *The Scots Kirk in London* (Oxford: Becket Publications, 1979), 112–13.

[73] For which see: F. M. L. Thompson, *Hampstead: Building a Borough, 1650–1964* (London: Routledge & Kegan Paul, 1974), 382.

his fourth child in 1851 (Walter Charles Augustus Jones, whose third name was also that of Gurney's younger brother). Their career paths were later to diverge. Gurney became a curate in Exeter and then Soho in London, and later chaplain to the Court Chapel in Paris. But in the mid-1840s they shared an interest in poetry and drama. Like Jones, Gurney was an aspirant writer. A play of his, 'Alboin', 'a drama of the Spanish school' set in fourteenth-century Sweden, was performed in Edinburgh in 1846, and a collection of his poems appeared in 1850.[74] And it was Gurney who first introduced Jones to political agitation. At the end of 1845 he began to deliver pro-corn law lectures in Devon and Cornwall, and in January 1846 he and Jones attended protectionist and Anti-Corn Law League meetings together. Perhaps most significantly, Jones in turn appears to have been a sounding-board for Gurney as he gravitated towards becoming a cleric, a move completed with his ordination in 1849. The summer they met Jones recorded in his diary that the two of them 'sat here disputing about religion for 5 hours'.[75]

What they were disputing Jones unfortunately does not say, but something of its substance might be reconstructed from Gurney's contribution to the *Theologian* in 1845. Gurney published an article there which was prompted by the work of the evangelical poet Robert Montgomery, whose *Ideal of the English Church*, published the same year, had called for 'evangelic churchmanship in the Church of England' and 'an embodied church as well as an abstract creed'. Gurney argued that the Reformation had been fatal for Episcopal and Apostolic government in the church, especially in Germany, where 'ecclesiastical insubordination' had now become fearfully prevalent. By contrast, in England and in Ireland, and particularly within the Presbyterian church in Scotland, the 'purer Ideal of the Reformation'—that is, 'Catholic discipline and individual faith'—had been preserved. Now, in modern times, the 'Ideal of the Reformation' faced its greatest challenge. It had 'to bring the influences of her system to bear upon the poor of our manufacturing and mining districts, and upon the citizen, or middle classes in all districts of our country'. Writers and clerics had a responsibility in this respect. The middle classes were:

[74] Gurney to Thomas Serle, 23 Oct. 1842, BL, Add. Ms. 52, 478, fo. 251. There is a copy of 'Alboin' in the Lord Chamberlain's plays: BL, Add. Ms. 42, 994, fos. 208–51.

[75] EJD, 10 Aug. 1842.

already greatly influenced by the literature which she [the church] has evolved; the manners and customs she has developed: not so the majority of the laboring [sic] classes. These require to have the Gospel preached to them in its pure integrity, and a heavy debt is incurred if we strive not by every means in our power to draw them within the visible fold of Christ.[76]

Paternalistic leadership was required as well. In 1846 Gurney penned a historical dramatic poem in honour of Charles I, prefacing the work with the hope that it might awaken 'the friends of the Church and State, and the protectors of the Rights of Labor'.[77] There is no record of Jones's own immediate response to Gurney's published views in 1845, but as the next chapter describes, the two men went on disputing through 1846 and 1847, their earnest discussions reaching a very public climax in the spring of 1847, when they appeared together on a Chartist platform to debate the social and political questions of the day. By then Gurney had renounced German romanticism and had turned to embrace the more quietist religious poetry of Robert Montgomery. Jones, by contrast, was finding in German, as well as French and Russian, romanticism and in Chartism itself a vehicle for poetry as a means of political engagement. Both men were responding in different ways to what appeared to them to be a vacuum at the heart of English society.

In the shorter term, Jones's lyrical imagination returned to him fairly easily during 1845. After walking on the heath in mid-March he entered his thoughts in his diary: 'a beautiful and exquisite walk ... Moon and starlight in the avenue and grove of firs on the Upper Heath at its Eastern verge. Beautiful. The striking of the distant church clocks of London are faint on the ear like a head under pillows.'[78] And he resumed his varied output, producing in March 1845 a series of poems in German for the *Deutsche Londoner Zeitung*, a translation of Thomas Babington Macaulay's poem, 'The War of the League', as well as a letter, entitled 'Wealth and Debt', sent to *The Times*.[79] These aside, Jones devoted himself on recommencing writing in the spring of 1845 to three longer pieces of

---

[76] [Archer Gurney], 'The Ideal of the Reformation', *Theologian*, 2, (1845), 418–19; cf. Robert Montgomery, *The Ideal of the English Church: A Sketch* (London: Smith, Elder and Co., 1845), 16, 42. In the 1830s and 1840s Montgomery's reputation and sales ranked him alongside Byron, his mentor.

[77] Gurney, *King Charles I: A Dramatic Poem in Five Acts* (London: William Pickering, 1846), p. xv.   [78] EJD, 12 Mar. 1845.

[79] The three poems were: 'Der Deutsche Sprachschatz', 'Politisches', and 'Licht und Spracht': *Deutsche Londoner Zeitung* (25 Apr. 1845), 16.

dramatic verse: 'Corayda' not to see publication until 1860; 'Lord Lindsay', eventually published in the *Labourer* towards the end of 1847 and by MacGowan in 1848 (and republished as *The Battle Day* in 1855); and *My Life* (or *Percy Vere*, as it became known), which was brought out later that year by T. C. Newby of Mortimer Street. 'Corayda' and 'Lord Lindsay' were two long epic poems—verse versions of the themes Jones had explored in 'Confessions of a King'. 'Corayda', set in 'the glorious, gallant days | Of hero feats and poet lays', told the tale of a poor youth called up to fight, who became part of the King's retinue and fell in love with Amorine, a maid of the royal line. Implicated in a conspiracy to assassinate the King, Corayda is sentenced to death, only to be reprieved at the last minute when Sir Guivro, a rival to the King, is revealed as the chief wrong-doer. Corayda is freed but banished, and returns to his valley, a 'wanderer' in exile. Earning his spurs in peace and war, Corayda eventually comes back to the court to find the monarch facing the mob:

> Then rose the mass, then led the few,
> But why nor led, nor leader knew;
> They chose a cause, they seized a name,
> No matter which, 'turns all the same.

Although the masses razed the city to the ground, 'with none to guide' they yielded to the unscrupulous Sir Guivro. Enter Corayda to rescue the King and help him to escape. Sir Guivro laid siege to the palace, but God was not on his side, and Corayda triumphs, becoming king and marrying the royal maid. Similarly, 'Lord Lindsay' saw Jones on familiar ground. To a mid-1840s readership the name Lindsay might have conjured up the history of the feuding Scottish family of the Elizabethan age. But with its north German setting and chivalric characters, Jones was back in feudal times once more. The heroic Lindsay seemed to have everything—an ancient name, a beautiful young bride, and military valour. But he was 'spirit-cold', and Jones's conclusion was predictable. Leaders without faith were doomed to fail. And so on the day of battle:

> Delay and doubt did more that hour,
> Than bayonet-charge and carnage shower

And Lindsay dies on the battlefield:

> So high a heart—so sad a fate!
> Wanting but faith to have been great.

'Corayda' and 'Lord Lindsay' were examples of Jones doing what he did best by the mid-1840s—mystical tales of chivalry in far-off places. They were admittedly derivative. Reviewers in 1848 likened 'Lord Lindsay' to Walter Scott's *Lay of the Last Minstrel* (1805).[80] Moreover, Alfred Tennyson, who Jones recorded reading in June 1845, and Bulwer-Lytton too, had the market cornered as far as the early Victorian cult of chivalry was concerned.[81] But Jones was at least consistent, depicting characters who, lacking religious faith, were destined to fall victims to the vagaries of fate. However, in *My Life*, his third major verse drama of 1845, Jones attempted for the first time a dramatic monologue, a story of love and revenge in high places, but one narrated not by the poet, 'Karl', but instead by an actual character in the story. By making the supposed author of the poem—'Percy Vere' or 'Perseverando'—a part of the plot, Jones created a device whereby his protagonist both expressed feeling and recounted events, achieving a greater degree of authenticity than were he simply the poet, an outside observer.[82] Again, Tennyson may have been the inspiration, both literally—his 'Lady Clara Vere de Vere' had appeared in his *Poems* three years previously—but also in prompting Jones to experiment with the dramatic monologue, for *My Life* bears some similarity to Tennyson's 'Locksley Hall', also included in the 1842 collection.

Jones's poem was prefaced with an introduction in which 'Percy Vere' introduced himself to his readers, describing how 'My Life has been a wild, strange life, | Now lulled in love—now wrapped in strife'. The introduction makes it clear that *My Life* is a cautionary tale, written for the enlightenment of the unprincipled aristocracy. The narrator-cum-protagonist describes how he has seen many of his ilk give up patriotism for party, and turn away from the multitude, a

---

[80] *Wakefield Journal*, (18 Feb. 1848), 6; *Naval and Military Gazette* (11 Mar. 1848), 167.

[81] Girouard, *Return to Camelot*, ch. 12; Stephanie Barczewski, *Myth and National Identity in Nineteenth-Century Britain: The Legends of King Arthur and Robin Hood* (Oxford: Oxford University Press, 2000), ch. 2.

[82] On the dramatic monologue, see: Robert Langbaum, *The Poetry of Experience* (London: Chatto & Windus, 1957); Dorothy Mermin, *The Audience in the Poem: Five Victorian Poets* (New Brunswick, NJ: Rutgers University Press, 1983); Ralph W. Rader, 'Notes on Some Structural Varieties and Variations in Dramatic "I" Poems and their Theoretical Implications', *Victorian Poetry*, 22 (1984), 103–20; Herbert F. Tucker, jr., 'From Monomania to Monologue: "St. Simeon Stylites" and the Rise of the Victorian Dramatic Monologue', ibid., 121–37; Cornelia D. J. Pearsall, 'The Dramatic Monologue', in Joseph Bristow (ed.), *The Cambridge Companion to Victorian Poetry* (Cambridge: Cambridge University Press, 2000), 67–88.

multitude who, despite their rude turbulence, love them best. He describes how he has seen men settle down to a life of unfulfilling wealth—'[d]eath's images before the grave'—only to long to live again and to break with custom. Percy Vere offers his story not out of egotism, but because he is 'now an altered man, | Not haught of heart as I began':

> And in my time from low to high
> I've seen so many do as I,
> Methought it might a warning be,
> And that save you which ruined me.

In renouncing social convention, Percy Vere suggests that he has become a kind of everyman, who can speak of all manner of strife: from 'scenes of courtly state' to 'huts and factories—camps and mines'. But his heterodoxy in the name of humanity has also led him to disregard the niceties of lyrical form:

> I've half unlearned the Poet's art,
> And only kept the Poet's heart

The introduction of *My Life* is then followed by the story of Percy Vere. He is the son of a peer, his father having an income of £6,000 a year, but the son refuses to follow in the family way. As a boy he 'recked more of deeds than of descent' and read heroic tales of 'bold patriots', of which his father was dismissive, advising him to '[l]eave Roman thoughts to dusty shelves'. So Percy Vere remains fettered to his aristocratic lifestyle, meeting rich pale girls—'toys of glass for baby kings'—and looks on as a terrible family tragedy unfolds. Percy Vere's parents are Lord and Lady Caerleon, but theirs is a loveless marriage, Lady Caerleon only having consented to wed in order to gain a title. Percy Vere has an elder brother, Philippe de Vere. Into their lives one day comes Clare, a country orphan, who had initially been sent 'To Hell's great masterpiece—the town', but now entered the Caerleon household as a servant, where her spirits improve rapidly, with lustre in her eye and melody in her voice. Lady Caerleon mistakes this blooming for the effects of social refinement, and Philippe falls in love with her. But Clare has fallen for Warven, a pale student in the family's employ as secretary. Lady Caerleon and Philippe, united in their jealousy, conspire to oust Warven, and he is forced to leave their service. Warven removed, Philippe seizes upon Clare, kisses her, and takes her silence as an assent to marriage. Warven reappears and a fight ensues, Philippe's behaviour brings disrepute on the family, and the father is forced to flee to foreign climes.

It is not an entirely successful poem. Percy Vere himself starts out as a protagonist and tragic hero of the piece, only to become no more than the narrator by the time of main tale. The plot rather fizzles out in the frantic final scenes, and the concluding twists and turns seem rather tame and cursory when compared with the opening build-up. But what Jones was doing with 'Percy Vere' was akin to other exponents of the dramatic monologue, such as Tennyson and Browning. He was conveying the action and drama of a novel through verse, and he was attempting to make his poem a commentary on social issues, albeit in rather a hackneyed manner. After all, dramatizing the lives of decadent aristos was hardly an innovative art-form by the 1840s. Most important of all, however, was that with 'Percy Vere' Jones unleashed the persona who was to dominate so much of his poetry and prose during his first years as a Chartist: the fallen peer, the knowing and humane aristocrat. It was this verse-drama, now revealingly retitled *My Life, or Our Social State*, that Jones was to present as his introduction to the Chartists six months later. And in that sense, the ambivalence over 'Percy Vere's' identity and role within the plot of the poem—was he part of the tragic saga of the Caerleons, or merely its chronicler—served Jones's purpose well. *My Life* was a disguise, hinting at the real world of the author, but distancing him from it as well. It was a balancing act that Jones was to play for much of his public life. In an age so conscious of class, status, and pedigree, Jones, aka Percy Vere, would keep everyone guessing.

4

Shorn of much, though perhaps not all, of the mystery which came in time to shroud his early adulthood, Jones's position on the eve of his 'conversion' to Chartism begins to make more sense. Professionally and privately he had been moving in a decidedly downward direction since his father's death at the beginning of 1843. He had failed to build on the early literary success of *The Wood Spirit* and the contributions to the *Court Journal*, his dramas were unable to secure a home amidst the fickle and competitive new world of the deregulated London stage after 1843, and his sporadic attempts at journalism and reviews came to nothing. By the beginning of 1846 Jones was in need of a new audience, a new market for his wares. Furthermore, his family fortunes were at an all-time low, as he joined the long list of business failures in the trough years of the mid-1840s and also became caught up in an inheritance dispute of Dickensian proportions. To cap it all, his mother died in the late summer of 1845, and judging from the long, reflective entry Jones made in his diary, this was a great impasse in his life.[83] By 1845 he was thus also in the midst of a personal crisis, and as with many Victorian men, it seems to have taken a spiritual form, hence the switch to low church attendance and the intense debates and discussions with Gurney, the outcome of which—a determination to become a kind of social missionary—became clearer during 1846 and 1847. To some extent Jones's private emotions and public mishaps were writ large in his verse and prose—the heady idealism of his early patriotic poetry, the tragic chivalry of his dramatic verse, and the more complex family drama that is 'Percy Vere'. At the same time, his literary output, whilst clearly fashioned towards whatever market or genre he thought most appropriate, does show a consistent theme: the need for poetry to address natural feeling and humanity in the face of the repressive realities of the modern world. On becoming a Chartist poet these themes were to flourish and develop.

There remain one or two pieces of the jigsaw to put into place. By the close of 1845 Jones was meeting regularly with his friend Michael Conan at the Irish Society's rooms off Piccadilly, and references to the *Nation*—the newspaper of the Young Ireland movement which sought repeal of the Union—began to appear in his diary.[84] It is tempting to read this as a piece of the puzzle that points to Jones's growing democratic nationalism, and some have erroneously recalled Jones appearing in the *Nation* before his debut in the *Northern Star*.[85] Jones's Irish politics were rather more moderate. During 1844 he had taken an interest in the trial of Daniel O'Connell in the House of Lords, and had even met up with John Martin, John Mitchel's great ally in 1848. Jones met Martin at the dinner table of Dr Costello, who was the manager of Wyke House, the hospital in Hanwell where the dying Charlotte Jones was being looked after. But this was before Martin had split from O'Connell.

[83] EJD, 30 Aug. 1845.
[84] Ibid., 25 Nov., 10 Dec. 1845.
[85] Charles Gavan Duffy, *Young Ireland*, 2 vols., (Dublin: M. H. Gill & Son, 1887), ii. 161 n. The first reference to Jones in the *Nation* did not come until 1848, when the paper published an excerpt from 'Lord Lindsay': *Nation* (19 Feb. 1848), 122.

As for the Irish Society—or the Irish Society of London for Promoting the Education of the Irish People Through the Medium of their Own Language—this was not so much a hotbed of nationalism as a vehicle for evangelical missionaries such as Baptist Noel.[86]

It was not Ireland but Archer Gurney who finally flushed Jones out into the public political sphere. Returning from addressing protectionist meetings in Devon at the close of 1845, Gurney took Jones along to a public debate in Willis's Rooms between himself and George Thompson, the anti-corn law lecturer.[87] It was Jones's first ever political meeting—he made a short speech—and he clearly enjoyed the experience. For the greater part of the next quarter of a century addressing political meetings came to be what he did best.

[86] It might be suggested that O'Connell's self-styling as a Gaelic chieftain appealed to Jones's sense of patriot kingship, but there is no evidence to support this. EJD, 5 Feb. 1844, 10 Aug.1845. There is also no evidence to suggest that Jones did more than read in the Irish Society's rooms, which were in an arcade off Piccadilly. On the Irish Society, see: H. J. M. Mason, *History of the Origins of the Irish Society Established for Promoting the Education of the Native Irish Through the Medium of their Own Language* (Dublin: Goodwin & Sons, 1844).
[87] EJD, 21 Jan. 1846; *Globe* (22 Jan. 1846), 3.

3
The Poet as Patriot, 1846–1848

IN JANUARY 1846 Jones began the move which led him from the fringes of the London literary scene and the bar to centre-stage in the Chartist movement. He did not so much cross the Rubicon as wander over the road. The offices of the *Northern Star* lay round the corner from Jones's old theatrical haunts in the Haymarket, while the headquarters of the Chartist Co-operative Land Society (later the Chartist Land Company) were only a few streets away from the Middle Temple, where he had taken to dining at the end of the day's work in the City. Years later, during his libel action against G. W. M. Reynolds, Jones explained his 'conversion' to Chartism in the following manner: '[i]n the winter of 1845, having accidentally seen a copy of the *Northern Star*, and finding the political principles advocated harmonised with my own, I sought the executive and joined the Chartist movement.'[1] However, his actual motives at the time seem to have been somewhat less lofty. Jones's diary entries for late January make it clear that he had not given up hope of employment with the Anti-Corn Law League, and as late as May he was still doing the rounds of various theatres in the hope of finding someone to stage his dramas.[2] Putting out feelers to the Chartists was almost certainly part of an attempt to get work and find an audience, rather than a democratic leap from the closet. On 28 January, clutching a sheaf of poetry, Jones spent a busy day meeting up with Christopher Shackleton, who ran the Chartist Hall in Holborn, and with Thomas MacGowan, who published the *Northern Star*. In turn they seem to have put him onto Thomas Wheeler, the London correspondent of the paper, and Philip McGrath, one of Feargus O'Connor's staunchest Irish allies in the Chartist Land Society. These hardy

[1] CN (16 July 1859), 2.
[2] EJD, 28 Jan. 1846, 4 May 1846, 5 May 1846.

stalwarts of Chartist agitation must have been mystified by the well-heeled young man in their midst. For Jones introduced himself not with a speech, nor with a declaration of his political principles, nor even with a routine denunciation of Britain's ruling elite. Instead he gave to the *Northern Star* a copy of *My Life*, the long dramatic monologue which Newby had published the previous year. Curiously enough it worked. Four months later on 5 May, in a letter to the *Northern Star*, Jones formally offered himself as a candidate for the next Chartist Convention, 'thus giving one more example', he declared, 'to those classes, with whom early associations have connected me, of how unworthy one of their own order thinks them of the privileges they enjoy, and of the powers they arrogate'. The paper reacted to this letter with caution, advising 'those who may be disposed to appoint Mr Jones their representative to fully satisfy themselves as to the "orthodoxy" of his principles'. But about *My Life*, extracts of which the paper included in the same issue, the *Northern Star*'s editors entertained no such reservations. The poem was 'glorious proof of the progress of democratic principles, that in spite of force and fraud, political and social persecution, such men as Mr Jones are avowing themselves as converts to Chartism'.[3] Clearly, Jones's poem reached parts that conventional forms of address could not. Indeed, as this chapter explains, it is difficult to understand Jones's almost instant success within the Chartist movement without a proper appreciation of his poetry. Not only did he from the very beginning present his Chartist credentials in the form of a lyrical vitae, but his poetry also proved the making of his reputation. His *Chartist Poems*, published in October 1846, went through five editions by the end of the year, and also sold many thousands more in a penny edition, entitled *Chartist Songs and Fugitive Pieces*. With some credibility Jones could boast by October that he was 'pouring the tide of my songs over England, forming the tone of the mighty mind of the people'.[4] Moreover, during 1846–7, alongside political lectures he gave lectures on poets and on poetry, and in the pages of the *Labourer* in 1847–8, which he co-edited with Feargus O'Connor, he not only published more poems but also wrote a great deal on poetic form. What was it about Jones's poetry that catapulted him from relative obscurity into the Chartist leadership?

---

[3] *NS* (9 May 1846), 3.   [4] EJD, 8 Oct. 1846.

I

One simple answer is that by 1846 Feargus O'Connor, the beleaguered leader of the Chartist movement, needed a new ally, and preferably one with poetic abilities. Jones was not the first poet in the Chartist ranks. The movement already boasted many poets—George Binns, Edward Mead, Thomas Cooper, Allen Davenport, and Ebenezer Jones amongst the most prolific—and during the 1840s the columns of the *Northern Star*, under the discerning eye of William Hill, and those of other Chartist newspapers became filled with the verse of a largely autodidact generation of artisan-poets, some of whom might have been better advised to take up a pike rather than a pen.[5] Even the Chartist leaders—Harney and O'Connor, for example—turned their talents to poetry, to ominous critical silence in the case of the latter. To some extent Chartist poetry was a continuation of the kind of agitational verse of the 1830s, for example, that of Ebenezer Elliott, the Sheffield 'Corn-Law Rhymer'. In other respects Chartist poetry blurred the distinction between oral and print expression, for many of the poems were songs or hymns, intended to be sung outdoors at Chartist meetings.[6] But above all, Chartist poetry of the 1840s represented a popular appropriation of romanticism, and specifically of the work of Byron and Shelley. Cheap editions of Byron's verse appeared regularly from 1837 onwards, a cottage industry led by William Milner, a Halifax printer and bookseller, who also helped to distribute the *Northern Star*. The leading Chartist and Owenite newspapers and periodicals devoted a great deal of attention to both men's works and to their lives. Some of Byron's 'tales'—for example, *Mazeppa* and *The Reformed Transformed*—were turned into penny novels, and poems such as *Don*

    [5] Y. Kovalev (ed.), *An Anthology of Chartist Literature* (London: Central Books, 1956); id., 'The Literature of Chartism', *Victorian Studies*, 2 (1958), 117–38; Brian Maidment (ed.), *The Poorhouse Fugitives: Self-Taught Poets and Poetry in Victorian Britain* (Manchester: Carcanet, 1987); Peter Scheckner, *An Anthology of Chartist Poetry: Poetry of the British Working Class, 1830s–1850s* (London: Associated Universities Presses, 1989); Ulrike Schwab, *The Poetry of the Chartist Movement: A Literary and Historical Study* (Dordrecht: Kluwer Academic, 1993); Hugues Journès, *Une littérature revolutionaire en Grande-Bretagne: la poesie chartiste* (Paris: Publisud, 1991); Stephen Roberts, *Radical Politicians and Poets in Early Victorian England: The Voices of Six Chartist Leaders* (Lampeter: Edward Mellen, 1993).
    [6] Roy Palmer, *The Sound of History: Songs and Social Comment* (Oxford: Oxford University Press, 1988), 14, 262–4; Timothy Randall, 'Chartist Poetry and Song', in Owen Ashton *et al.* (eds.), *The Chartist Legacy* (Woodbridge: Merlin Press, 1999), 171–95.

Juan, Childe Harold, and *The Prisoner of Chillon* were regularly reprinted. Where Byron was admired by the Chartists mostly on the grounds of literary merit and sometimes for his extravagant praise of liberty, Shelley was seen as a 'poet of the people'. His 'Mask of Anarchy', 'Queen Mab', and, above all his 'Men of England' became inspired rallying-calls for Chartists at different stages of the movement between 1839 and the later 1850s.[7] A generation after their deaths, Shelley and Byron still had a radical political message for the living. Byron, his sexual libertinism carefully airbrushed out by his publisher, John Murray, was seen as a champion of liberty prepared to die for the cause, whilst Shelley's attacks on priestcraft and monarchy, as well as his millennial tone, guaranteed him notoriety as a critic of 'old corruption'. But there was more to the popular legacy of romanticism than this. As Anne Janowitz has shown in her important study, romanticism supplied some of the stock ingredients of Chartist forms of address, especially in the latter half of the 1840s.[8] The romantic celebration of nature and of rural England fed into the Chartists' back-to-the-land, 'people's farm' rhetoric of the Land Company years.

Of all the Chartist poets who did most to popularize Byron and Shelley, and who also imitated much of their style, the most prominent was Thomas Cooper, the undisputed 'poet laureate' of Chartism. Cooper had been imprisoned for two years in 1843, and whilst incarcerated he composed an epic poem—*The Purgatory of Suicides*—which envisaged the social utopia that awaited the prisoner on release and the working class on emancipation from

---

[7] Bouthaina Shaaban, 'Shelley in the Chartist Press', *Keats–Shelley Memorial Bulletin*, 34 (1983), 41–60; id., 'The Romantics and the Chartist Press', *Keats–Shelley Journal*, 38 (1989), 25–46; id., 'Shelley and the Chartists', in Betty T. Bennett and Stuart Curran (eds.), *Shelley: Poet and Legislator of the World* (Baltimore, Maryland: John Hopkins University Press, 1996), 114–25; Ronald Tetreault, 'Shelley Among the Chartists', *English Studies in Canada*, 26 (1990), 279–95; Paul Thomas Murphy, *Towards a Working Class Canon: Literary Criticism in British Working Class Periodicals, 1816–1858* (Columbus, Ohio: Ohio State University Press, 1994), 139–42; Keith Walker, *Byron's Readers: A Study of Attitudes Towards Byron* (Salzburg: University of Salzburg, 1979), 101–3; Andrew Elbentein, *Byron and the Victorians* (Cambridge: Cambridge University Press, 1995), 85–7. For William Milner, see: D. Bridge, 'William Milner: Printer and Bookseller', *Transactions of the Halifax Antiquarian Society*, (1969), 75–83.

[8] Anne Janowitz, *Lyric and Labour in the Romantic Tradition* (Cambridge: Cambridge University Press, 1998), chs. 5–6. See also her earlier 'Class and Literature: The Case of Romantic Chartism', in W. C. Dimock and M. T. Gilmore (eds.), *Rethinking Class: Literary Studies and Social Formations* (New York: Columbia University Press, 1994), 239–66.

their slavery. The poem made quite an impact, partly because of the dramatic circumstances in which it was written. Denied writing materials, Cooper claimed he had composed each stanza orally and then committed it to memory. But the poem also had substantial literary merit. It was replete with classical imagery, deployed a Spenserian and Miltonic style, and attempted to challenge the 'liberal detachment' of contemporary mainstream poets.[9] On his release Cooper found himself lauded by not only the Chartist faithful, but by some of the literary reviews as well, as an authentic working-man's poet. He was befriended by popular writers such as W. J. Fox and William Howitt, praised by Carlyle, Disraeli, and Wordsworth, and eventually in the 1850s found a job at Somerset House through the influence of Charles Kingsley. Moreover, when Cooper returned to the Chartist leadership in 1846 he did so as a critic of Feargus O'Connor, whom he had once eulogised as the 'lion of freedom'. Cooper was particularly critical of O'Connor's alleged mismanagement of the monies invested in the Chartist Land Society. In 1846 Cooper joined the London-based People's Charter Union, in which Chartists rubbed shoulders with more moderate radicals in opposition to O'Connor's militancy.[10] In May of that year Chartists gathered in a soirée to celebrate the anniversary of Cooper's release from prison, and although O'Connor attended the meeting and denied friction between the two men, it was clear that there was not room for two monster reputations in one movement. The appearance of Ernest Jones in the new year of 1846, clutching *My Life* and a handful of favourable reviews of his work, could not have been more timely as far as O'Connor was concerned. Here was another poet, with a growing literary reputation, ready to oust Cooper.[11] It was no coincidence that the same issue of the *Northern Star* which reported Cooper's soirée in early May introduced Jones to the Chartists.

Jones's ascent thus mirrored Cooper's demise. In May Jones was adopted as Chartist delegate for Limehouse in east London, in the same month he joined George Julian Harney in the executive of the

[9] Janowitz, *Lyric and Labour*, 166–72; Philip Collins, *Thomas Cooper the Chartist: Byron and 'The Poets of the Poor'* (Nottingham: University of Nottingham, 1969); Stephen Roberts, 'Thomas Cooper: A Victorian Working-Class Writer', *Our History*, 16 (1990), 12–26.

[10] Roberts, 'The Later Radical Career of Thomas Cooper, c. 1845–55', *Transactions of the Leicestershire Archaeological and Historical Society*, 64 (1990), 62–72.

[11] *NS* (9 May 1846), 6; Janowitz, *Lyric and Labour*, 172.

Polish Committee (or the Democratic Committee for the Regeneration of Poland as it was officially known), and through the same conduit, the Fraternal Democrats. In the following year he would meet Karl Marx while speaking on the same platform at a Polish meeting.[12] But it was on O'Connor's less internationalist wing of the Chartist movement that Jones was to make his most decisive impact in the summer of 1846, when he attended the Chartist conference at Leeds. On the first Sunday in August, high up on the Pennines astride the Yorkshire and Lancashire border in the natural amphitheatre that is Blackstone Edge, Jones made his first outdoor speech—'his maiden speech to his new allies'. Later that day he spoke at the Chartist Hall in Manchester. The following day the Chartists convened at Leeds, and here Jones moved for the expulsion of Thomas Cooper following the latter's demand for O'Connor to explain the whereabouts of Land Society monies.[13] Cooper was hounded out, and like a daring young warrior proving his worth to his chief, Jones was duly rewarded. A fortnight later he led the triumphal procession which opened O'Connorville, the Chartist estate in Hertfordshire, at the end of September he became secretary to the Land Society, and by the end of the year he had been put in charge of the second leader column and the correspondence of the *Northern Star*.[14] At last Jones had found a purpose and an audience. Entering Nottingham a few days after Cooper's expulsion, he told Jane that he had found 'all the walls placarded with bills, in which the name of Ernest Jones figured in letters one foot long'.[15] His journey and his diary were nearing completion. As he recorded in October:

Wonderful! Vicissitudes of life—rebuffs and disappointments countless in literature—dry toil of business— . . . legal and social struggles,—dreadful domestic catastrophes,—poverty—domestic bickerings—almost destitution—hunger—labour of mind and body—have left me, through the wonderful providence of God, as enthusiastic of mind—as ardent of temper—as fresh of heart—and as strong of frame, as ever! Thank God! I am

[12] *NS* (4 Dec. 1847), 1; John Saville, *Ernest Jones: Chartist* (London: Lawrence & Wishart, 1952), 27.

[13] *NS* (8 Aug. 1846), 8; *Leeds Times* (8 Aug. 1846), 8; Roberts, 'Later Radical Career of Thomas Cooper', 65; Janowitz, *Lyric and Labour*, 177–8.

[14] *NS* (22 Aug. 1846), 8. In 1847 Jones worked for the Chartist Land Bank as well, and earned a salary of £2 per week as a lecturer for the Land Society: Alice Mary Hadfield, *The Chartist Land Company* (Newton Abbot: David & Charles, 1970), 25, 33, 36; Thomas Frost, *Forty Years Recollections: Literary and Political* (London: Sampson Low, 1880), 183.

[15] Jones to Jane Atherley Jones, 7 Aug. 1846, SC.

prepared to rush, fresh and strong, into the strife or struggle of a nation, to ride the torrent, or guide the rills if God permits[16]

In the space of a few months Jones had replaced Cooper as the noble patriot, and the persona of the fallen peer had displaced the artisan poet. As John Arnott, of the Fraternal Democrats, eulogized Jones in October:

> Estranged Aristocrat! What leave the favoured few,
> Regardless of fortune and prospects in view,
> Noble democrat to join the Chartist band,
> Eschewed, despised, and scouted through the land[17]

2

Jones's impact as a Chartist poet was more than simply fortuitous, however. By all accounts there was also something captivating about his poetry, and it is worth devoting some more detailed attention to the forty or so poems that made up the cycle which appeared in the *Northern Star* and the *Labourer* between the early summer of 1846 and the new year of 1848, a dozen of which were reproduced in *Chartist Poems*. Jones's reputation—admittedly limited—amongst literary scholars has usually rested on the claim that he was a class poet, or at least a poet in the romantic tradition who inflected his poems with a greater degree of social realism than most of his contemporaries. Jones, it is claimed, took radical poetry down an industrial road, in which the site of struggle became the factory and not the land, and the agent of change became the collective working class and not the lyrical observer. Jones, in other words, proletarianized the pastoral.[18] Such an interpretation of his poetry fits with the prevailing theme of Jones's biographers—that he converted to Chartism, and had the more polished edges of his world-view roughened up by his exposure to the working class and by his meeting with Karl Marx and Friedrich Engels in 1847. There has been

---

[16] EJD, 8 Oct. 1846.
[17] John Arnott, 'An Acrostic, to Ernest Jones, barrister-at-law', NS, (17 Oct. 1846), 3.
[18] Kovalev, 'The Literature of Chartism', 133–5; H. Roßler and I. Watson, 'In defence of Ernest Jones', *Gulliver: Deutsch–Englische Jahrbücher*, 12 (1982), 134–9; Stephan Lieske, 'Ernest Jones' Contribution to the Development of Working-class Poetry', *Zeitschrift für Anglistik und Amerikanistik*, 35 (1987), 118–27; cf. Janowitz, *Lyric and Labour*, 179–85; Michael Sanders, 'Poetic Agency: Metonymy and Metaphor in Chartist Poetry, 1838–52', *Victorian Poetry*, 39 (2001), 111–35.

some disagreement about precisely when his verse and prose began to register this turn to class. Some commentators attribute it to *Chartist Poems*, others to the *Labourer*, whilst others still to the poetry he produced in prison. But there is little scholarly doubt over Jones's eventual emergence as a democratic or even socialist poet.

For a class poet Jones wrote surprisingly few poems about the industrial working class. In fact, he wrote only one: 'The Factory Town', published in the first volume of the *Labourer* in January 1847. It is a poem which, given its subject, has not surprisingly received an inordinate amount of scholarly attention. However, it is a poem which is about something other than class. 'The Factory Town' presents a vision of modern industry as a fiery hell, in which men, women, and children are slaves to the spinning wheel—'the modern rack'—suffocated and parched in the dungeon that is the factory system. Jones spares no detail in describing the sadistic treatment of form and flesh. The heat and noise of the factory are a subversion of nature:

> . . . though 'twas night of summer
> With a scent of new mown hay
> From where the moon, the fairies' mummer,
> On distant fields enchanted lay!
>
> On the lealands slept the cattle,
> Slumber through the forest ran,
> While, in Mammon's mighty battle
> Man was immolating man!

More than that, the factory town was a rejection of God's design— 'red Mammon's hand was robbing | God's thought-treasure' from the minds of the workers. The factory was a false deity—the 'fierce steam-horses, England's mighty *Juggernaut*!' Those who might have resisted Mammon—the priest and the nobility—capitulated to its temptations:

> While the priest, from drowsy riot,
> Staggered past his church unknown,
> Where his God in the great quiet,
> Preached the livelong night alone!
>
> Still the bloated trader passes,
> Lord of loom and lord of mill;
> On his pathway rush the masses,
> Crushed beneath his stubborn will.

And in silent protest, the darkened skies and the tempestuous elements seemed to confirm God's displeasure at the mutation of nature brought about by the factory:

> Over all the solemn heaven
> Arches, like a God's reproof
> At the offerings man has driven
> To Hell's altars, loom and woof!

> And the winds with anthems ringing,
> Cleaving clouds, and splitting seas,
> Seem unto the People singing:
> 'Break your chains as we do these!'

In place of the inferno of the factory, the poem envisaged a pastoral idyll:

> . . . many a happy village
> Shall be smiling o'er the plain,
> Amid the corn-field's pleasant tillage,
> And the orchard's rich domain!

Two themes stand out in Jones's 'Factory Town', and both have been unduly neglected in the rush to claim the poem as a celebration of the rights of the urban proletariat. First and foremost, the poem continues and extends the religious motif in Jones's verse which, as we have seen in previous chapters, arose out of his schooling in Germany, his acquaintance with the patriot poets of Holstein, his exposure to low church preaching in London, and from his friendship with Archer Gurney. Secondly, Jones's vision of modern industry, as far as he had a coherent view of it, was derived not from an understanding of the class struggles of the 1830s and 1840s, nor even from a radical agrarian tradition embodied in the idea of the people's farm. Rather, his depiction of class relations in the hungry 'forties rested on a quaint but idealized view of the collapse of the medieval social order, whereby the labouring poor had been deserted by the nobility and the church. 'The Factory Town' is thus one example of how Jones's poetry in 1846 and 1847 was interwoven with a primitive Christian theology, and an 'olden time' sense of history. There are many other examples. Some of the best are contained in *Chartist Poems* itself.

Chartist Poems opens with 'The Better Hope', a poem which, like a calling-card, introduced the character that Jones was to make his own—a man of privilege devoting himself to the people. Like *My Life* and *Lord Lindsay*, 'The Better Hope' describes 'a child of the hard-hearted world . . . with a rich old name' who leaves the cold solemnity of his home to embrace the 'broad, laughing world'. His father's house, though rural and grand, was unnatural:

> My father's hall was a dark old spot,
> With a dark old wood around,
> And large quiet streams—like watery dreams,
> On the verge of a haunted ground.
>
> And the dwellers were filled in that solemn place,
> With the trance of a sullen pride:
> For the scutcheoned grace—of a titled race,
> Is the armour the heart to hide.

But going forth past 'hamlet and town', the son finds 'the gloom of what should have been bright'—'the noonday was darker than the night'. The factory has appeared:

> For a giant had arisen all grisly and grim,
> With his huge limbs, loud, clattering and vast,
> And he breathed his steam breath—through long channels of death,
> Till the soul itself died on the breath.

Rather than turn away, however, this latter-day saint straps on his 'armour to face the rough world'. Jones may have been having fun in 'The Better Hope', perhaps mocking the pastoral as much as subverting it. There are shades of St George and the dragon, and Jack and the Beanstalk here, as well as Jones's usual Sadean goriness: 'Like a wine press for mammon to form a gold-draught, | It [the wheel] squeezed their best blood through its fangs.' It is not difficult to imagine how audiences might have warmed to these melodramatic images. But his underlying theme is that God made nature a bounteous world, and between them the old and the new rich have undermined man's inheritance. The contrast between a workers' world shrouded in darkness, in which the withered and pale bodies (of women and children in particular) are devoured by work, or the soulless and haughty world of the nobility in which all feeling has been lost, and the natural world of light, warmth, humanity, and sturdy workers (now mainly men) and paternal nobles, is a feature of virtually all of the poems in *Chartist Poems*, for example, 'Our Summons':

> Up! Ye labourers in the vineyard!
> We call you to your toil!
> For the sun shines in the furrows,
> And the seed is in the soil.

Or in 'Our Destiny', where the labourer is urged to 'unclasp God's book of nature', and reveal how 'God has poured around us his paradise of light!' It is true that Jones's vision is a pastoral utopia, nowhere better described than in the poem 'O'Connorville', but what is being idealized is the reuniting of a people with God through the reappropriation of the land. 'The Coming Day' and 'Onward and Upward', the two poems with which Jones concludes the collection, sees this restoration of the natural order as the people's true aspiration. In 'The Coming Day' it is prophesied that the sun would one day rise on a world where 'man shall cease for aye to bend unto each sceptered clod', and in which a 'household God' would dwell 'in every home and heart, | Not sought alone in piles of stone—encaged by monkish art'. Similarly, in 'Onward and Upward' Jones forecast the freeing of the 'spirit' '[f]rom priestcraft—to nature and God'. And in perhaps the most powerful imagery of the whole collection, in 'Blackstone Edge', Jones recalls the great gathering of crowds on that Sunday in mid-August as a rediscovery of humanity—of the senses—and of God:

> Then every eye grew keen and bright,
> And every pulse was dancing light,
> For every heart had felt the might
> Of truth, presaging victory.
>
> And up to Heaven the descant ran,
> With no cold roof betwixt God and man,
> To dash back from its frowning span,
> A church prayer's listless mockery.

In 'O'Connorville', the longest poem in the collection, the labourer's passage from the crowded town to the Chartist estate—the 'promised land'—is described as a journey out of the unlit, unnatural world of church, nobility, and the towns:

> There towers the church, with finely tapering spire,
> Type of the lessening of pure desire;
> Thus dies the flame, the glory thus departs,
> On marble cradled, but not nursed in hearts!

> There looms the massy mansion of the great,
> That steals from gladness what it gives to state . . .

> There distant towns uplift their clouded sin,
> As though to hide from heaven the hell within . . .

and into '[n]ature's rich blazonry of green and gold', where the
elements and manmade world are in harmony: 'O'er scenes the Lord
of thunder bade be still; | Nor looms the palace-pinnacle and dome, |
As though man felt in nature not at home.'[19]

In *Chartist Poems* the pastoral theme is thus more about man's
relationship with God than the struggle between the classes in the
modern world, and in that sense Jones's early Chartist poetry shows
considerable continuity with the prose and verse of his pre-Chartist
years. The absence of a true religious faith that Jones and Gurney had
decried in the material world, Jones was now rediscovering in the
redemptive English labourer. This theme was not only central to his
Chartist Poems, it also lay at the heart of his oratory during 1846 and
1847. From the moment when Jones appeared on Blackstone Edge
on a summer Sunday—a 'holy day', as he reminded the 25,000-
strong gathering—to his final outdoor appearance before his arrest
on Whit Sunday in 1848 in Bishop Bonner's Fields, Jones's platform
speaking was shot through with the imagery and potency of an evangelical preacher. The egalitarian Christianity and evangelical style of
much Chartist oratory has been noticed by historians of the movement.[20] But they have invariably focused on men of the cloth, like
J. R. Stephens or Arthur O'Neill, who became embroiled in
Chartism, rather than looking at those ostensibly secular Chartist
leaders who aped evangelical style and sentiment. Jones was one of
these.

Contemporaries singled out the power of Jones's oratory, its effect
all the more pronounced as he was a small man and, especially in his
twenties, of delicate build. His appearance was also striking. In
later years his hair thinned considerably, his clothes became more
dishevelled, and he took to wearing first, a monocle, and then a pair
of ordinary glasses. At the outset of his Chartist years, however, he

---

[19] Cf. 'Song for May', *Labourer* (May, 1847), 193–5.
[20] Eileen Yeo, 'Christianity and Class Struggle in Chartism, 1838–42', *Past &
Present*, 91 (1981), 109–39; Eileen Groth Lyon, *Politicians in the Pulpit: Christian
Radicalism in Britain from the Fall of the Bastille to the Disintegration of Chartism*
(Aldershot: Ashgate, 1999); Owen Ashton, 'Orators and Oratory in the Chartist
Movement, 1840–48', in Ashton *et al.* (eds.), *Chartist Legacy*, 48–77.

had a shock of red hair and went to great lengths to maintain a gentlemanly appearance, giving his wife Jane precise details about which items in his elegant wardrobe she was to send to him whilst on his speaking tours. He also had the oratorical style, not so much of an agitator as of an actor or preacher. Benjamin Wilson, himself a former Methodist preacher, recalled that he 'had a powerful voice with a musical ring, and was a perfect master of elocution'. J. B. Leno compared him to other popular preachers, such as Henry Vincent and George Dawson.[21] This evangelical effect was heightened by the timing and venue of his speeches. Jones often spoke on a Sunday morning or afternoon, or a day in the religious calendar, and sometimes shared his pitch with itinerant religious preachers, competing with them for the attention of the passing weekend crowds. There was also a theatrical element to Jones's speeches, especially in the way he often began a speech by introducing himself as a fallen peer. For example, at his first ever public speech, at Limehouse at the end of May 1846, he wondered out loud: 'Perhaps it was a novelty to have a connection of the aristocracy with them, but he did not see why, because his forefathers held Conservative opinions, he was not to hold and believe sincerely democratic opinions.' His prologue, or signature-tune over, Jones would then settle into his main theme. Usually, it was not long before the state church became the target of his criticism. Again, his first speech at Limehouse in May 1846 was typical:

Let them save the millions of fellow-beings—keep men from the factory women from the looms and perish ten times two million sterling from the revenue. Let the deficiency be made up by less expensive, less salaried and fewer offices of state, fewer palaces of royalty, and smaller stables for the royal horses . . . [Where was] the sympathy enshrined in a bench of bishops who, to the God of Peace proffered thanksgiving for terrible slaughter, but could not offer a petition to parliament for their poor and starving countrymen? From the bishops, who rolled in luxury, while their brethren in Christ were perishing from want? While the churches separated the poor from the rich and smiled on the great man's half-empty pew, while the pauper stood shivering on the stones.[22]

[21] Benjamin Wilson, *Struggles of an old Chartist* (1887), repr. in David Vincent (ed.), *Testaments of Radicalism: Memoirs of Working Class Politicians, 1790–1885* (London: Europa Publications, 1977), 205; J. B. Leno, *The Aftermath* (London: Reeves & Turner, 1892), 79; Jones to Jane, 12 July 1847, SC.
[22] *NS* (30 May 1846), 6.

Several aspects of this excerpt stand out: the simple dichotomies of the attack on 'old Corruption', a form of delivery which recalls the rhyming couplets of Jones's poems. Or the way in which melodramatic caricatures—starving paupers and bloated bishops—stand in as class descriptions. But above all it was Jones's attack on a church which had lost its sense of mission which became his abiding theme in so many of his speeches. On Blackstone Edge he:

congratulated the meeting on the imposing array of numbers in which they had mustered, they had chosen a holy day, and they could not have signalised it by a more holy deed—for they were assembled in defence of right, justice, and liberty, and well would it be, if bishops and pastors were to be found preaching on the hill top in honour of the God of peace, instead of expounding dogmas of the God of war, in stately churches to listless hearers in well-cushioned pews.[23]

In contrast to the corrupt modern church Jones sang the praises of simple Christian faith. Jones's mission, he told a Tower Hamlets meeting in October 1847, was 'to reunite those whom God united, and man has parted', for Christianity was the 'foundation of democratic institutions'.[24] The modern world was repugnant to the laws of God, he told an audience in Brighton, in a speech that he described in his diary as the best he ever made. The voice of the people was the voice of God and so it would eventually be heard.[25] Such religiosity could lead to some rather idiosyncratic views. Take, for example, Jones's view of the Irish famine. The terrible hunger in Ireland, Jones told a meeting at St Pancras in London in October 1846, had been permitted by God to remind men of their evil, and to impel them to act. At another meeting, in February 1847, Jones suggested that God's design lay behind the famine and it was intended to be the agent of revolutionary change.[26]

A similar continuity in Jones's world-view before and after his first contact with Chartism is evident in his preoccupation with the medieval past. In *Chartist Poems*, for example, there were striking examples of the same Gothic setting that Jones had chosen for *The Wood Spirit* and 'Lord Lindsay'. Take 'The Two Races' for example.

[23] NS (9 May 1846), 1.
[24] NS (4 Nov. 1847), 8.
[25] NS (23 Jan. 1847), 3; EJD, 14 Jan. 1847. A local paper had a different view, reporting that 'a slender intelligent-looking young man . . . failed by the utmost efforts of oratory, which sometimes took the highest flights into the regions of hyperbole, to stir the meeting into any very warm enthusiasm': Brighton Herald (16 Jan. 1847), 3.   [26] NS (27 Feb. 1847), 7.

This poem is an appeal to the 'old race', that is, the 'gentlemen of England', 'peers of Plantagenet', 'conquerors of the Gaul', and 'sons of Saxon chivalry'. Jones turns to them as the 'champions of old liberty', as the men:

> Who bearded York and Lancaster,
> And John on Runnymede;
> Who tamed the tyrant's tyranny,
> And soothed the people's need.
>
> Who welcomed honest poverty
> To shelter and to feast,—
> And broke on his own infamy
> The crozier of the Priest.

Now they are needed to 'punish purse-proud guilt', as the:

> Lords of Trade are stirring
> With their treasures far and nigh;
> They are trampling on the lowly,
> They are spurning at the high.

In other words, a 'new race' has arisen: the aristocracy of artificial wealth and fashion. This race is immoral ('lurers of the village-maid') and effete ('a worn-out generation | In body and mind. | They've buried all their manhood | In silk, and plume, and gem'). Jones made similar appeals to old England in other pieces in *Chartist Poems* and elsewhere. In 'Labour's History' he told of how God had given the land to his children, but had seen it taken away by the three out-laws—the king, the priest, and the soldier, who in turn had handed it over to the 'gold-king'. In 'Our Rally' and in three poems originally printed in the *Northern Star* but not included in the subsequent collection or elsewhere—'A Chartist March', 'Britannia', and 'Patriot's Test'—he summoned the 'freemen' and 'yeomen' who won at Marston Moor, Trafalgar, and Waterloo to rise again against the 'miserable knaves | Who sink in silken revelries what starving labour craves'.[27]

Jones's poems thus presented a somewhat particular version of the class struggle, in which the onset of modern industry—'the lords of the loom'—was only the latest stage in a series of usurpations of the natural order which had been going on for many centuries and in

---

[27] 'A Chartist March', NS (13 June 1846), 3; cf. 'Britannia', NS (18 July 1846), 3; 'The Patriot's Test', NS (19 Jan. 1848), 3.

which the church, the monarchy, and the 'lords of corn' had played their part. In the first two volumes of the *Labourer*, published in 1847, Jones began to root this theme in a firmer historical narrative. The *Labourer*, co-edited and largely co-written by O'Connor and Jones, began to appear on the newspaper stalls in the new year of 1847, some three months after *Chartist Poems*. The magazine featured another fifteen of Jones's poems—notably 'The Factory Day' and 'The Age of Peace'—as well as republications of 'Onward and Upward' and 'Lord Lindsay'. The *Labourer* also introduced the Chartist readership to Jones's prose for the first time—novellas, serials, advice manuals, reviews, and histories—on the grounds, as the editors informed their readers in the opening number, that as 'we are convinced that all which elevates the feelings or heightens the aspirations, can but strengthen the political power of a people, we have placed poetry and romance side by side with politics and history'.[28] As far as Jones's contributions were concerned it would be more accurate to say that the magazine conflated romance and history, rather than ran them in parallel. For example, in a pair of articles entitled 'The insurrection of the working classes' and 'The progress and prospects of society', Jones located the story of 'how the people lost their lands and liberty' back in the early middle ages, when the church and the nobility expropriated common land. In these accounts the 'rise of democracy' was located in the fourteenth century. Jones singled out the *Jacqueries* and the revolts of Picardy in France, or the peasant revolt against the nobility led by Rienzi in Rome, or the rise of the Juts and other Danish and Swedish peasants. The 'constitutional' state, 'under which we now live', was simply the enactment in law of the monopolistic form of land-ownership which had arisen across Europe in the medieval epoch.[29]

As with Jones's anticlericalism, there was considerable overlap between the medieval tone and setting of his poems and the content of his speeches during 1846 and 1847. Much of his venom during

---

[28] 'Preface', *Labourer* (Dec. 1847), p. i. Unfortunately none of the articles in the *Labourer* are attributed, although Thomas Frost later claimed that Jones 'furnished most of the contents—politics, history, fiction, and poetry': Frost, *Forty Years Recollections*, 185. Since Jones himself later republished many of his contributions to the *Labourer* in his newspaper ventures of the 1850s, we can be reasonably certain of his authorship. O'Connor's main contribution to the *Labourer* seems to have been the long series of articles on husbandry and smallholdings, several of which reappeared in his *National Instructor* (1850–1).

[29] 'The Insurrection of the Working Classes' ran from Jan. to Dec. 1847; 'Progress and Prospects of Society', *Labourer* (Feb. 1847), 70–3.

1847 was reserved for the Poor Law, which he saw as a means of denying God's natural bounty to the rural working man. A fairly typical attack came in a speech at the 'Crown and Anchor' in London in June 1847, when he accused the peer, the soldier, the sporting hunter, the parson, the landlord, the Queen, and the manufacturer of enjoying a 'rich law' at the expense of the poor. Whereas, 'God has written the proper Poor Law on the broadland he has given us. Its statutes are inscribed on many millions of acres of rich corn and pasture, that say to the hungry: come and be fed! to the naked, come and be clothed.'[30] Jones's aspiration was to turn back from the modernity of the factory system and embrace the small-producer idyll of past centuries. The same nostalgia can be seen in his support for nationalism on the Continent. His was not a nationalism of a modern republican or socialist variety, but support for peoples such as the Poles or the Italians, whom he believed were throwing off the modern yoke of despotism and rediscovering their former liberties. At a meeting of the Fraternal Democrats in October 1847, Jones thus heaped praise on Pope Pius IX:

why has Italy fallen! She once was free, when the first peasants founded their agrarian republic on the banks of the Tiber. But the Caesars defaced her— building the palaces of kings, which are gravestones of liberty. Then, when these sank before the northern swords of more potent tyrants, forth from their ruins crept priest-craft like a bloated spider, spreading its slimy web around the growth of ages and hiding the light of truth, not under a bushel, but under a mitre. (Immense applause). Is there a change? Is the veil broken? Does the light flash through? There is a man named Pius. Why do we honor him? Because he is more of the Roman than the priest, more of the Italian than the Roman, more of the man than the Italian.[31]

In other words, Jones did not require immersion in the ideas of Marx and Engels to arrive at a cyclical view of history. His version of the class struggle was located in the same distant epochs as his earlier dramatic verse and tales, as was his understanding of how monarchy and priest-craft had given way to the nobility who in turn yielded to the greedy millocracy: 'The grub, royalty, was transformed into the feudal oligarch; then the middle class spun its cotton web around the torpid noble; and now the people are breaking their flimsy chains, and from the perishing frames of decaying systems, bright-winged Liberty shall soar above the garden of its own creation.'[32]

[30] NS (12 June 1847), 1.   [31] NS (16 Oct. 1847), 1.
[32] NS (5 Feb 1848), 8.

In a similar vein, Jones chose medieval settings for virtually all of the stories he wrote for the *Labourer* in 1847 and 1848. For example, 'Confessions of a King' (originally composed by Jones in 1843) was set in fourteenth-century Italy. 'St John's Eve' (which appeared in the third volume of the *Labourer* in 1848, and was most probably a reworking of his drama of the same name written in 1843) involved former serfs. Even 'The Romance of a People', though set in Poland in 1831 and often claimed as an example of Jones's commitment to Continental nationalism, actually had a medieval theme.[33] It took as its hero and heroine Wladimir, the leader of a peasant army, and Zalesha, the daughter of a serf. And closer to home Jones penned tales of families forced from the land into the factory ('An English Life'), Irish peasants taking on the merchant and the military ('The meal-mongers; or, food riots in Ireland' and 'The Murdered Trooper'), and a motley crew of brigands, bandits, and pirates ('The Price of Blood' and 'Pirates' Prize').[34] These were entertainments. They were high on melodramatic convention and fairy tale. The principal characters in 'St John's Eve', for example, were Rupert, an old widower, and his beautiful daughter Gemma. Gemma is in love with Rudolf, a huntsman, but Rupert wants something better for his daughter. A stranger appears offering to kill Rupert, to which Gemma agrees, only for a phantom to appear just as the dastardly deed is to be done on St John's Eve. Rudolf gets the blame and is accused of sorcery, Gemma is whisked away to marriage by a knight, but one year later, in the graveyard of a Catholic cathedral, she dies.

Jones's combination of history and romance seems far removed from a vision of class struggle. True, he did choose some industrial settings for his stories, but these were outnumbered by his preference for the Gothic and the rural. Insofar as a political message was being carried by Jones's fiction, it was not a particularly radical or subversive one. In no way was Jones evoking an urban proletariat ready to seize power, or even a communitarian utopia based on an equal

---

[33] 'Confessions of a King' ran from Feb. 1847 until Mar. 1848; 'St John's Eve' from May to Nov. 1848; and 'The Romance of a People' from Jan. to Dec. 1847. For a reading of 'The Romance of a People' as a parable of Continental nationalism, see: Ian Haywood, *The Literature of Struggle: An Anthology of Chartist Fiction* (Aldershot: Scolar Press, 1995), 16–17.

[34] 'An English Life', *Labourer* (June 1847), 277–80; 'The Meal Mongers', ibid. (Apr. 1848), 186–97; 'The Price of Blood', ibid. (Sept. 1847), 129–41; 'The Pirates' Prize: A Tale of the South', ibid. (Mar.–Apr. 1847), 143–9, 168–80.

division of the land. If these histories had a 'people' as their subject, then the people were simple peasant folk, their lives bedevilled by rapacious soldiers, predatory nobles, and hypocritical and libidinous clergy. Primitive rebels perhaps, but nothing more. It was Wagner rather than Marx, Cobbett and not O'Connor. To interpret Jones's literary contribution to Chartism as proto-socialism rather misses the point. What he envisaged in his prose, as in his verse and oratory, was a noble but simple peasantry who without proper leadership were fated to suffer. They needed a modern Rienzi, and there were no prizes for guessing who that might be.

3

Jones's early Chartist poetry and oratory were thus distinctive for their evangelical tenor and Gothic, melodramatic sense of history, rather than their appeal to class solidarity. At the same time Jones did see himself as a 'democratic' poet, articulating the sufferings of the poor. Alongside his considerable output of poems in 1846–8 Jones also wrote about the proper function of the poet in the modern age. Whilst grander and more commercially successful poets such as Browning, Clough, and Tennyson were becoming increasingly reluctant to express themselves on the great political and social issues of the day, Jones rehabilitated the idea of the poet as the conscience of the people. Not for him Clough's poet distracted by the 'vain titillation of a moment's praise', or Browning's 'Patriot' who 'leaped at the sun' and ended up on the scaffold, stoned by the populace, or Tennyson's poet who faces 'irreverent doom'.[35] In going down this road, Jones was to break finally from his friend Archer Gurney, who looked instead to religious poetry for social salvation, and who eventually heeded the call of the Church of England, becoming ordained in 1849.

[35] Clough, 'Look You, My Simple Friend' (1849, sometimes known as 'The Poet'), in F. L. Mulhauser (ed.), *The Poems of Arthur Hugh Clough* (Oxford: Clarendon Press, 1974), 25–6; Browning, 'The Patriot: An Old Story' (probably written in 1849), in John Pettigrew and T. J. Collins (eds.), *Robert Browning: The Poems*, 2 vols. (London: Yale University Press, 1981), i. 611–12; Tennyson, 'To ——, After Reading a Life and Letters' (1849, written about either Byron or Keats), in Christopher Ricks (ed.), *The Poems of Tennyson*, 3 vols. (Harlow: Longman, 1969), ii. 297–8. On the rise and fall of the engaged poet, see Joseph Bristow, 'Reforming Victorian Poetry: Poetics after 1832', in Bristow (ed.), *The Cambridge Companion to Victorian Poetry* (Cambridge: Cambridge University Press, 2000), 1–24; Isobel Armstrong, *Victorian Poetry: Poetry, Poetics and Politics* (London: Routledge, 1993), ch. 7.

Jones's most extensive writing on poetic form came in a series of reviews published in the *Labourer* during 1847 and the beginning of 1848. In his first major literary survey Jones noted that a 'democratic tendency' had begun to pervade English literature, commencing with Byron and Shelley, and now to be found in Elizabeth Barrett Browning, Tennyson, and even Bulwer-Lytton. Jones singled out for praise Barrett Browning's 'Lady Geraldine' and her 'Flight of the Duchess of May', as well as Tennnyson's 'Lady Vere de Vere'. At the same time he lamented the simplistic and unrealistic treatment of ordinary people which often lay at the heart of such works. In this respect he focused on Ebenezer Jones, another Chartist poet, whom he accused of degenerating 'into unintelligible obscurity . . . fond of transposing words, neglectful of the harmonies of rhythm, and partial to placing his heroes and heroines in the most preposterous and extraordinary situations'. Here, Jones's determination to eliminate yet another Chartist poet pretender—and especially one who shared his most prized asset, his name—is barely disguised. But he had a wider point, which was that the ornate vocabulary of poetry needed to avoid a 'forced simplicity' when dealing with ordinary people as its subjects, otherwise it became simply 'irresistibly comic'. 'It is necessary', declared Jones, warming to his manifesto, 'that democratic poets should in their pages, *elevate* and not endanger the dignity of the democratic character'. And he recommended that English writers take a leaf out of foreign literature, whose writers were 'tuned to the popular key', to the extent that an author's works would 'descend to future times' because they were a 'faithful exponent of their own'.[36] In order to nudge English authors in the right direction Jones then commenced a series of articles on 'National Literature'. He began with Poland, reviewing Count Krasinski's *Infernal Comedy*, which he singled out as an example of how democratic dramatic verse should *not* be written. Krasinski, whom Jones had met shortly before Charles Jones's death, produced characters which were too brutal and one-dimensional, and, Jones noted: 'the author has made his democratic hero inaccessible to all feelings of humanity; a cold, mighty intellect, removed from human sympathy; whereas the strength, the promise and pride of modern democracy is the triumph of the *humane*.'[37] German literature, and

[36] 'Literary Review: Ebenezer Jones', *Labourer* (Nov. 1847), 235–40.
[37] 'National Literature: Poland', ibid. (Jan. 1848), 212–13; diary entry, 25 Jan. 1843.

in particular Schiller's *Robbers*, was for Jones a much better model to follow. Although the morality of Schiller's tale of a son of the aristocracy falling on hard times and taking up with a gang of thieves was often misunderstood, Jones thought that the central message of the book came when the hero, realizing that so much of his life remained incomplete, refuses to commit suicide and face the retribution of God. Here, suggested Jones, Schiller had proved himself to be: 'a noble advocate of religion, for he makes his hero, through the effort of *worldly reasoning* alone, come to the same conclusions (though with different feelings), as the religious man—proving that *faith* is founded on the *real*, as well as the *ideal*'.[38]

As well as singling out foreign dramatic poetry for praise, Jones also found much that was exemplary in the lives of foreign poets. He admired Pushkin, who, 'disgusted with the venality and despotism disgracing every branch of the public service . . . dedicated his leisure to the muse', facing censorship and exile as a result of his outspoken views, eventually achieving a martyr's death.[39] In a similar fashion Jones had high praise for Mirabeau, the French revolutionary orator. Tyrannized by his father, ostracized and unloved by the rest of his family, his wealth taken from him, he devoted himself as tribune to the people's cause. As Jones explained:

He was an orator because he had suffered—because he had failed—because, at the age when the heart expands and seeks sympathy and intercourse with others, he had been repulsed, mocked, humiliated, despised, defamed, hunted, plundered, outlawed, exiled, imprisoned, condemned—because, like the people of 1789, of whom he was the type and symbol, he had been held in minority and tutelage long beyond the age of manhood—because paternity had been as cruel to him as royal fatherhood had been to the people.[40]

In one of his last contributions to the *Labourer* Jones developed this idea of the democratic poet as a suffering patriot in a fictional form. In a short story entitled 'Pride and Prejudice', Jones told the story of Carl Wonrad (Schiller's hero in *The Robbers* had been Carl Moor).[41] Wonrad is of a privileged background and through his

[38] 'National Literature: Germany', ibid. (Nov. 1848) 227.
[39] 'National Literature: Russia', ibid. (Mar. 1848), 130–5.
[40] 'Mirabeau', ibid. (Oct. 1848), 153. It is perhaps not too mischievous to note that here Jones anticipates the Freudian interpretation of kingship put forward by his most famous namesake: Ernest Jones (1879–1958).
[41] 'Pride and Prejudice; or the Martyr of Society', ibid. (May 1848), 228.

father's influence gains high office, one of the duties of which is to detect sinecurism and corruption. Finding the public accounts to be falsified he seeks their reform, only to find that the nefarious powers that be blame *him* for all wrongdoing. Dismissed from office and shunned by colleagues and peers alike, he turns to 'the tribes of the earth' and devotes himself to democracy. Alarmed by his new political views and new allies, his father disinherits Wonrad, and his detractors accuse him of being a needy gentleman, 'troubling the waters of society, that he might fish a treasure from their current'. Such accusations enrage Wonrad, for all the world seems to have forgotten that 'democracy had caused the loss of his property and position'.

For Jones, then, the role of the poet and of 'poesy', as he liked to call it, was clear. Poets should be less preoccupied with form and elegance, and instead, heeding the spirit of the age, they should direct their poetry towards democratic subjects and the positive nature of humanity. Hence the heroes of Jones's pre-Chartist dramatic monologues, such as 'Lord Lindsay' or *My Life*, with their 'feeling' and imaginative natures which were at odds with the heartless and emotionally inert world of the nobility, could reappear without any incongruity in his Chartist poetry. Their democratic credentials lay not in their political agenda or their social class, but in their ability to feel and express their humanity. They might not be understood: their motives might be impugned by both the well-to-do and the down-at-heel; but the important thing was that they be true to their faith and convictions.

Just as Jones was recommending the secular heroism of French and German romanticism, his friend Archer Gurney was denigrating it at every turn. Writing in the *English Review* in 1848, Gurney complained that in Germany writers such as Immanuel Kant and poets such as Ühland, Rückert, and Schiller (all among Jones's heroes) had given silent assent to a dangerous form of liberalism, which denied the importance of spiritual life. Only in England, with the exception of Byron and Shelley, had literature upheld Christianity, and Gurney cited Coleridge, Southey, and Wordsworth as examples of this. Gurney set out his own position on the proper place of poetry in a long introduction which he wrote in 1847 to a selection of the works of Robert Montgomery.[42] Gurney lamented the fact that whilst in the

---

[42] [Gurney], 'The German Mind', *English Review*, 10 (1848), 374–5, 377–8, 380–1; Gurney, 'Introductory essay', in *Religion and Poetry: Being Selections*

material world there was more attention than ever being devoted to the collection of positive facts, in the spiritual world any attempt to assert positive truths was seen as too philosophical. For this reason Gurney welcomed Montgomery's poetry, for he saw it as based on an unashamed patriotism in which England was seen as the champion of God's truth and the guardian of the rights of humanity. Such poetry was required to see off any Romanist tendencies, as in Montgomery's best-known poem 'Luther', but Gurney also noted that Montgomery was alive to the 'possibility of social anarchy which may blast over our Institutions in Church and State, and eventually destroy the nation's Christianity'. This social anarchy Gurney named as Chartism, and quite clearly he saw religious poetry as one of its best antidotes.[43] As well as a religiously minded literature, Gurney wanted an active ministry. Too often, he complained, the 'voices of the people' were not heard in the Church of England, hence the rival attractions of Roman Catholicism. What was required was a church which might produce 'the spiritual and intellectual exertion requisite for catholic communion'.[44]

Since Jones and Gurney remained in close contact throughout 1847 it is fairly certain that their very different views on the function of poetry in the modern age were the outcome of some heated discussions. Whereas Gurney thought that the poet should, in a passive fashion, assert positive spiritual truths—the ideal—Jones believed that the task of the poet was to find faith in humanity—the real—and to do so by revealing the sufferings of the people. A poem by each of the two men neatly captures the gulf that now separated them. In Jones's 'The Poet's Mission'—a poem reworked for a Chartist audience from an earlier one entitled 'To Byron'—the calling of the poet as patriot is clear:

> Who is it in love's servitude,
> Devotes his generous life,

Spiritual and Moral, From the Poetical Works of the Reverend Robert Montgomery, etc (London: privately printed, 1847), 9–10, 28–9, 52–3, 67–8.

[43] Gurney's argument bears some resemblance to the Tractarian view, developed in Keble and Newman's work above all, that poetry was a 'divine medicine' which might relieve the affective and imaginative side of the mind responsible for stress: G. B. Tennyson, *Victorian Devotional Poetry: The Tractarian Mode* (Cambridge, Mass.: Harvard University Press, 1981), 26–8, 34, 50, 58–9.

[44] [Gurney], 'Review of J. H. Newman's *Loss and Gain*', *English Review*, 10 (1848), 75.

> And measures by his heart's own good
> A world with evil rife?
>
> The Bard—who walks earth's lonely length
> Till all his gifts are given;
> Makes others strong with his own strength,
> And then fleets back to Heaven.[45]

By way of contrast, in his 'An Angry Hour' Gurney was to propose a far less heroic course:

> Friend, have you rattled your thunder?
> Believe, you're not the last man nor first,
> To groan out wrath raving, and wonder;
> Pray groan, lest the safety-valve burst!
>
> Doubtless the age has its weakness:
> Yet, friend! our life's claims are not few:
> Just stand in the circle, with meekness,
> And you shall find something to do.[46]

Jones also distanced himself from his friend's Toryism, using the pages of the *Labourer* to damn with faint praise Gurney's historical drama *King Charles I.*[47] He called it a work of 'genius and prejudice', and 'magnificent as a poem' but a failure as a political essay, for Gurney had mistaken the 'spirit of the age' if he thought common sense would revert to the 'standard of medieval chivalry'. And in what was perhaps the most remarkable episode of their whole friendship, Jones lured Gurney into two public debates on the merits of the Charter in February and April 1847.[48] On the first occasion Gurney offered to debate with Jones, as well as O'Connor. But Jones refused, arguing that 'since you belong to my own order of society and profession' it would be better if a working man spoke instead, 'thus proving to your order and profession, that the working men of England are able to defend the cause of justice without *Heraldry* or *Blackstone*'. Thomas Clark duly deputed in the first debate, but on the second occasion Jones took up the challenge. The debate was

---

[45] 'The Poet's Mission', *NS* (17 Oct. 1846), 3. In fact the original version was an ode to a patriot king ('A monarch greater than a throne') entitled 'To Louis Philippe'. It was then reworked to become 'To Lord Byron' before reappearing as 'The Poet's Mission': Ernest Jones Manuscript Poems, MCL, MS. f 281.89 J5/30.

[46] 'An Angry Hour', in Archer Gurney, *Poems* (London: Longman, Green, Longman & Roberts, 1860), 300–1.

[47] *Labourer* (Feb. 1847), 94–6.

[48] *NS* (6 Feb. 1847), 1; (20 Feb. 1847), 6; (17 Apr. 1847), 6.

advertised as 'an important discussion between Archer Gurney and Ernest Jones, esquires, barristers at law'. Jones spoke second, pouring scorn on Gurney's attack on socialism, and his defence of the mixed constitution, the inequality of the laws of nature, and the freedom of the press. The theatricality of this debate in the South London Chartist Hall in Blackfriars Road might have been lost on the audience, for no mention was made of the fact that the two men were close friends. But for Jones the occasion was more than just another Chartist lecture. It was a means of affirming his new vocation to his closest friend, and a very public way of denouncing the society and profession that he had renounced and that Gurney represented. By such devices Jones was able to make his identity as a Chartist more authentic, bridge the gulf between his own status and that of his followers, and head off questions about his motives in joining the movement. By the autumn of 1847 Jones's Chartist credentials had become watertight. With no intended irony, he introduced a Chartist meeting in Tower Hamlets, east London, thus:

When I look at this meeting, and the individual by whom it is presided over, I feel proud, as a democrat, to take part in its proceedings. I see a numerous assemblage of men convened here, not for a selfish purpose, not to further their own end and aims, but to render help to men of other lands, strangers by clime, country, language and tradition. And whom have we in the chair? Not an aristocrat, not a man of wealth. Yes! An aristocrat, for he belongs to the noble order of the working men! Yes, a man of wealth, for he earns what little he possesses. Time was, when such a meeting would not have been held, had not a lord, baronet, or sire been in the chair. Times are changed. We prefer the man with coronet inside of his head, instead of outside . . . We have learned to speak for ourselves. We no longer go cringing to a pursled peer, or pursue proud commoner, saying: 'God gave us a tongue, but we don't know how to use it' . . . Let the pensioner represent the plunder he has gorged, the soldier the blood he has shed, the lawyer the fees he has pocketed; but the hardy hand and the hearty shout shall represent the working man; he shall speak for himself, and thank God! he need not be ashamed of his identity.[49]

This was typical Ernest Jones: stagy alliterative rhetoric as though he was penning rhyming couplets, biblical allusion (he had used the same passage from the 39th Psalm in his debate with Gurney), and an inversion of the meaning of aristocracy to imply nobility of feeling and not social status. Above all, Jones was playing guessing-games with his audience about his own identity, just as the fictive characters

[49] NS (16 Oct. 1847), 1.

of Percy Vere and Carl Wonrad had done with his readers. For how did the assembled working men of London's East End know that Jones was not a typical lawyer pocketing fees, or a 'pursled peer'? Judging from the enthusiastic response he received from audiences up and down the country during his first year on the Chartist executive, Jones had learned to play his part as the outcast aristocrat with great conviction.

4

Jones's reputation as the Chartist poet laureate was secure by the new year of 1847, and during the rest of that year he completed his own metamorphosis from literary man about London into a Byronic man of the people. The honing of his credentials as a Chartist leader took a little longer. In the elections for the Chartist executive held in March 1847 Jones only received nominations from four places: Liverpool, Halifax, Bermondsey, and Camberwell. In terms of popularity he trailed in fifth place, some way behind O'Connor, McGrath, Thomas Clark, and Thomas Wheeler.[50] However, three things happened in the ensuing year to confirm Jones's emergence as one of the key Chartist leaders: the election campaign he fought in Halifax in the summer of 1847; the legal services he rendered through the pages of the *Northern Star* throughout the year; and finally his frequent appearances on the Chartist platform during the momentous months of February through to June 1848.

Jones had first come to know Halifax, the small mill-town nestling in the Calderdale valley on the Yorkshire side of the south Pennines, in the summer of 1846. A Halifax man, Benjamin Rushton, had chaired Jones's memorable debut up on Blackstone Edge, and the following day at the Leeds convention Jones had been urged by Halifax delegates to stand for election in the town.[51] At the beginning of May 1847 Jones renewed his acquaintance with the town, speaking to an 'immense meeting' and getting a 'tremendous reception' in

---

[50] *NS* (27 Mar. 1847), 1.

[51] *NS* (8 Aug. 1846), 4; for the background, see: G. R. Dalby, 'The Chartist Movement in Halifax and District', *Transactions of the Halifax Antiquarian Society*, (1956), 94–111; Dorothy and Edward Thompson, 'Halifax as a Chartist centre' (unpublished typescript), 54–65; Kate Tiller, 'Late Chartism: Halifax, 1847–58', in James Epstein and Dorothy Thompson (eds.), *The Chartist Experience: Studies in Working-Class Radicalism and Culture, 1830–1860* (London: Macmillan, 1982), 311–25.

the evening, then spending the following day there in the misty drizzle before moving on to Dewsbury and Bradford.[52] Towards the end of June he returned to announce his intention to contest the constituency at the forthcoming election. This may have been good news for Jones who, having found his public calling, put down his private journal and made no more entries. It was undoubtedly good news for the Chartists of Halifax. But these were not welcome tidings for Jane, Jones's wife. She objected vehemently, fearing that there would now be no change in the 'mode of living' to which Jones had subjected his family.[53]

In contesting Halifax, Jones joined forces with Edward Miall, the proprietor of the *Nonconformist* newspaper, and one of the leading critics of the Whig government's proposals to bring in a system of national education, thus threatening to override voluntary and non-Anglican educational provision. In Halifax, Miall and Jones took on the Whig candidate, Sir Charles Wood, and although neither Miall nor Jones were successful, the liberal unity which had prevailed in the town since 1832 was shattered, the Tory candidate was elected alongside Wood, and the government of Lord John Russell was given a bloody nose. To some extent the alliance of Miall and Jones was purely tactical. Although Miall came out in support of the Charter, and the local Whiggish newspaper labelled him a Chartist in 'politics and religion', there was little if any contact between the two men. Miall's *Nonconformist* did not carry any of Jones's election addresses or speeches. The joint election ticket was very much the work of the Methodist shopkeepers who turned their backs on the local Whig-liberal elite.[54] Jones's anticlericalism was not, however, simply a badge of convenience. The bulk of his election address, issued on 21 June, a month or so ahead of polling and long before there was any talk of a pact with Miall, was forthright enough in its criticism of the state church. In addition to the Charter, Jones called

[52] EJD, 7 May, 9 May 1847.

[53] Jones to Jane, 30 June 1847, SC. In fact Jane did join her husband in Halifax a few days later. It proved to be the first of only two public appearances she ever made with Ernest Jones (the other occasion was at a soirée organized by the Fraternal Democrats in July 1850, to celebrate Jones's release from prison). See below, Ch. 4.

[54] 27% of Methodist voters 'plumped' (that, is gave both their votes) to Jones and Miall: J. A. Jowitt, 'A Crossroads in Halifax Politics: The Election of 1847', *Transactions of the Halifax Antiquarian Society* (1973–4), 19–36; John A. Hargreaves, 'Methodism and Politics in Halifax, 1832–48', *Northern History*, 35 (1999), 139–60; id., *Halifax* (Edinburgh: Edinburgh University Press, 1999), 104–5; Wilson, *Struggles of an Old Chartist*, 204–5; HG (17 July 1847), 4.

for the separation of church and state, the restoration of church property to the poor, and for the clergy to be supported by their own followers.[55] Those who had heard his virulent attacks on the Church of England throughout the previous year would have recognized the consistency of his views. If anyone was making a convenient marriage in Halifax in 1847 it was Miall the Chartist, and not Jones the scourge of the Anglican establishment.

Jones also put his legal acumen to good use in the *Northern Star*. The correspondence columns of the paper had always been more than just a platform for the venting of political views. News of the movement's activities, calls for funds, searches for missing persons, and criticisms of the paper itself found their way into the letters column, as did requests for legal advice. Until February 1847 such legal matters were passed onto W. P. Roberts, the Manchester-based solicitor, but in the middle of that month the legal department of the *Northern Star* became properly established with the division of the correspondence column into 'miscellaneous', handled by Harney, and 'legal', dealt with by Jones.[56] Within a couple of months Jones was besieged with letters—some forty per week by the spring of 1847—together with accompanying legal documents. The English may not have been the most revolutionary working class in Europe, but they were certainly its most litigious. Their concerns were mainly over property rather than employment law. Enquiries concerning paternity disputes, inheritance, small debts, tenancy agreements, and the sale of goods flooded in, presenting Jones with two immediate problems: postage and imposture. By April Jones was insisting that postal costs must be paid by the correspondent, especially if they required a private answer to their query. By May he was refusing all requests for personal interviews.[57] Jones also found himself having to discriminate between bona-fide Chartist requests for legal aid, and those coming from men of property. Soon after he commenced his pro bono service he admonished one correspondent, 'KOL', thus: 'Your transaction is a swindle. We are here to assist men in the recovery of their rights and not to aid them in the commission of

---

[55] *NS* (3 July 1847), 1.

[56] *NS* (21 Nov. 1846), 5; (13 Feb. 1847), 5; Stephen Roberts, 'Who Wrote to the *Northern Star*?', in Owen Ashton *et al.* (eds.), *The Duty of Discontent: Essays For Dorothy Thompson* (London: Mansell, 1995), 55–70; For Roberts's legal services to the Chartists, see: Raymond Challinor, *A Radical Lawyer in Victorian England: W. P. Roberts and the Struggle for Workers' Rights* (London: I. B. Tauris, 1990), ch. 11.

[57] *NS* (3 Apr. 1847), 5; (10 Apr. 1847), 5; (15 May 1847), 5.

wrong. As you have not called yourself a Chartist we hope and believe you are not one.'[58]

But of course, as Jones himself knew only too well, it was easy for the well-to-do to pass themselves off as Chartists. By June he was fed up with requests for gratuitous legal advice from men 'whose very letters prove them to be men of property', so he instituted a sliding scale of fees from 5s. up to half a sovereign, according to length of case and ability to pay, for rich men seeking private advice.[59] But still the letters kept coming in, and they mounted up during his absence from the *Star* office at the time of the Halifax election. At the beginning of August Jones declared that 'the number of communications exceeds the possibility of reply', and henceforth until further notice he would only answer privately letters accompanied by a fee of 5s., and publicly in the paper only those from correspondents evidently unable to pay.[60] Eventually this new policy began to have some effect. By the turn of the year the number of enquiries receiving replies had dwindled to a handful each week, though whether this was a fall in demand or supply is not clear.

In resorting to charging fees for 'private work' Jones was undoubtedly trying to ease his way out of the tangled web his generosity had woven. Until the new year of 1848 he continued to give pro bono advice, and although his tone was always peremptory and sometimes officious, he seems to have gone to some lengths to keep up with statute law, and two cases in particular suggest that he did pursue a series of cases with due care. In September 1847 he appeared before Lincolnshire magistrates, representing the family of a man killed by a policeman during an election riot at Sleaford.[61] And in the following month Jones's diligence towards his Chartist clients landed him in hot water. He took up a case of one John Broadbent, who claimed that a property near Glossop rightly belonged to him although it was currently occupied by someone else. Jones contacted

---

[58] *NS* (20 Feb. 1847), 5.

[59] *NS* (12 June 1847), 5.

[60] *NS* (7 Aug. 1847), 4. Returning to Halifax in late August Jones arranged for a 'professional friend' (probably Roberts) to take over his business: *NS* (28 Aug. 1847), 4.

[61] *NS* (4 Sept. 1847), 3; *Lincoln Mercury* (20 Aug. 1847), 3. Jones seems to have based an episode in his story 'The London Doorstep' on this incident: *Labourer* (May 1848), 228–32. For a later defence of his role in the Sleaford election case, see *PP* (20 Jan. 1855), 4. Jones's familiarity with contemporary statute law is provided in his series 'The Poor Man's Legal Manual', which ran in the *Labourer* from July 1847 until April 1848.

a Manchester solicitor called Halsall, checking information about the dispute, only to find that Halsall went off and checked up on Jones and duly reported him to the Middle Temple for offering his services in the *Star* 'without intervention of attorney or solicitor'. The Masters of the Bench at the Middle Temple took the matter very seriously and summoned Jones to appear before them. Jones also took the matter seriously. He threatened Halsall with a libel action and invited him to appear with him at a public meeting to hear his charges. He also defended his policy, confirming that he had given direct legal advice to poor men, 'finding that they were the victims of knavish legal practitioners', and had only introduced the fee system to check the volume of correspondence and to cover 'the great expense in postage, searches for wills, documents in the various courts, cab-hire, etc'. Throughout the first half of 1848 he refused to appear before the Masters of the Bench, and it was not until November 1850 that the case was finally heard. Jones was severely censured for 'irregular and unprofessional' conduct, but no further action was taken.[62] He was lucky to escape being struck off the Law List. The intervening years of his imprisonment were probably the mitigating factor. But as usual, out of real adversity Jones created a new dramatic twist, claiming days after the Kennington Common meeting of 10 April that the Bench of the Middle Temple had called him to account for his extreme political views.[63]

By the New Year of 1848 Jones had become one of the hardest-working members of the Chartist executive, dividing his time between dispensing legal advice, working for the Land Company as a paid lecturer, writing for the *Northern Star* and the *Labourer*, and serving as the unofficial representative of the working people of Halifax. His political and poetic identity complete, the *Northern Star*, after much delay, finally presented an engraved portrait of Jones gratis with its New Year edition. The picture, by Thomas Martin, depicted Jones the man of letters, standing next to a writing table, back to a window, through which can be seen trees framed against the sky.[64] At the end of February Jones was entrusted with a

---

[62] Minutes of Parliament, Middle Temple (1847–55), 14 Jan. 1848, pp. 37–8; 28 Jan. 1848, pp. 42–5; 27 Nov. 1850, p. 127; Middle Temple Library, London, MT.1/MPA/14; Jones to Halsall, 22 Jan. 1848, Jones to D.W. Eldred, 23 Feb. 1848, SC.

[63] *The Times* (14 Apr. 1848), 6.

[64] *NS* (1 Jan. 1848). For other similar portraits by Martin of Chartists and radicals, see: Stephen Roberts and Dorothy Thompson, *Images of Chartism* (Woodbridge: Merlin Press, 1998).

mission to Paris, where along with Harney and McGrath of the Chartist executive, and three German members of the Fraternal Democrats (Bruno Bauer, Josef Moll, and Karl Schapper), he presented an address of support to the new Republican government.[65] And at the beginning of April, when the Chartist National Convention convened in the wake of the revival of the parliamentary reform movement in Britain, Jones was returned as delegate for Halifax. Amidst so much toil something had to give. O'Connor expressed his disapproval of the way in which the domestic department of the *Northern Star* was being managed,[66] and persuaded Jones to relinquish it and devote himself to the Convention. This he did, playing a key role in the planning of the mass demonstration on Kennington Common on 10 April 1848. But what really secured his reputation as the most notorious of the Chartist leaders was his role during the weeks that followed.

The events leading up to the Kennington Common meeting in April have been described many times, and from most angles. Jones was there on that famous day, sitting alongside O'Connor and Harney, other leading members of the Land Company (McGrath, Wheeler, and Christopher Doyle), and members of the press in the second of the three cabs that accompanied the huge petition. The convoy proceeded slowly along the southern bank of the Thames, all routes over the river blocked by an assorted mix of Chelsea pensioners, special constables, and armed mounted police, forcing them eventually to turn back to the Common.[67] Individuals seldom alter the course of tumultuous events such as the Kennington Common meeting, but in a curious way Jones did make a difference, although perhaps not as he intended. More than any other Chartist leader in the spring of 1848, Jones expressed 'physical-force' Chartism. Whereas O'Connor was particularly careful in the

[65] *NS* (18 March 1848), 5; *Le National* (7 Mar. 1848), 4; *La Réforme* (10 Mar. 1848), 4.

[66] O'Connor to Harney, 4 Jan. 1848, repr. in F. G. and R. M. Black (eds.), *The Harney Papers* (Assen: Van Gorcum, 1969), 61–2.

[67] David Large, 'London in the Year of Revolution', in J. Stevenson (ed.), *London in the Age of Reform* (Oxford: Blackwell, 1977), 177–211; John Saville, *1848: The British State and the Chartist Movement* (Cambridge: Cambridge University Press, 1987), 102–20; David Goodway, *London Chartism, 1838–48* (Cambridge: Cambridge University Press, 1982), 129–42; Henry Weisser, *April 10: Challenge and Response in England in 1848* (London: University Press of America, 1983), esp. ch. 3; Stanley Palmer, *Police and Protest in England and Ireland, 1780–1850* (Cambridge: Cambridge University Press, 1988), 484–90.

days leading up to the Kennington Common meeting to couch Chartist claims in peaceful and constitutional language, likening the petitioners to the reformers of 1831 and declaring his affinity with the moderate, organic Whiggism of Edmund Burke and Charles James Fox, Jones was defiantly militant. Possibly inspired by the role of the National Guard in Paris in February, Jones called for the rank and file of the army to join up with the Chartists. He advocated simultaneous mass petitioning of the Queen, bypassing Parliament, and invited 200,000 people to accompany the petition on 10 April. At the Chartist convention in the days before the Monday demonstration he urged the delegates to support meetings all over the country, argued that they should adopt the tricolour as their flag, and, warming to his theme, also suggested they attempt to put up a green flag of liberty in Downing Street to show sympathy for their Irish brethren.[68] Flags, soldiers, mobs, and monarchs: there was something rather quaint about Jones's sense of strategy in the run-up to 10 April, as though the chivalric heroes from the pages of 'Lord Lindsay' or 'Corayda' were coming to life. But of course inciting the military and encouraging conspiracy were serious treasonable offences, and it was no wonder that from this moment on Jones began to be singled out as worthy of police surveillance.

If Jones was a physical-force Chartist by day in the week leading up to 10 April, by night he was a resident of Bayswater, sitting around the dinner table with his wife, three small boys, and his great friend Archer Gurney. On 9 April the two men quarrelled about the day ahead, and so alarmed was Gurney at the scale of the planned procession that he went directly from Jones to the Home Office, and intimated to George Grey that the Chartist leaders were frightened and that they would be prepared to settle for a demonstration on the Common, without the planned crossing of the river into Westminster. Seldom can the avoidance of revolution have pivoted on a tiff between two overwrought young men. In fact the authorities had determined to hold back the procession anyway, but Grey drew comfort from Gurney's advice.[69] For his part Jones pressed on regardless of Gurney's concerns. He returned to the National Convention on 14 April and called for simultaneous meetings to be

---

[68] *NS* (11 Mar. 1848), 1; (8 Apr. 1848), 8; *The Times* (7 Apr. 1848), 5; (8 Apr. 1848), 7.

[69] George Grey to Lord John Russell, 9 Apr. 1848, repr. in Spencer Walpole, *The Life of Lord John Russell*, 2 vols. (London: Longmans, Green & Co., 1889), ii. 69.

held across the country on Good Friday. According to the Chartist journalist Thomas Frost, it was at this point that Jones took strategic command of the Chartist organization, decreeing that associations up and down the land be divided into wards, and thence into classes of ten men each, in order to facilitate rapid mobilization. To spur on the movement Jones planned to travel northwards to Scotland. Promising Jane that 'we will be so happy and domestic when I return', he left London a week later.[70]

Jones spent a week in Scotland, addressing Chartist supporters in Dundee, Edinburgh, and Greenock. He compared the Chartists to the Covenanters, and urged the men of Scotland to prepare to demonstrate and petition in unison with the English movement. At the end of April Jones returned to London, and inverted the message, encouraging the movement in London not to lag behind the efforts of their northern counterparts. He also rounded on the moderate parliamentary reformers, led by the veteran Joseph Hume, who were calling for a 'Little Charter' of household suffrage, triennial parliaments, and the ballot. Jones accused Hume, and other MPs such as John Bright and Richard Cobden, of being in the pay of the government.[71] Having given up his post at the *Northern Star*, Jones himself was in need of being in someone's pay. Thomas MacGowan, the publisher of the *Northern Star*, had lent him some money but now wanted it back, and his other creditors from the insolvency settlement of 1845 were hot on his heels. In the middle of May he wrote to O'Connor's friend, the stockbroker Thomas Allsop, appealing for financial assistance which the latter duly gave. Jones assured Allsop that his mother-in-law, Mrs Atherley, was worth £5,000 and he would thus one day be able to honour the debt. 'Chartism', explained Jones, 'has left me without a friend' and debtors' prison beckoned within days unless he found the money.[72]

Prison did indeed beckon for Jones a few weeks later. In London, the meeting on Kennington Common was by no means the end of Chartist activity. Throughout May each weekend saw Chartist demonstrations, as plans were made to match the April mass turnout with similar marches over the Whitsuntide weekend at the beginning

---

[70] Frost, *Forty Years' Recollections*, ch. 9; Ernest Jones to Jane, 16 Apr. 1848, SC.

[71] *NS* (29 Apr. 1848), 6; (20 May 1848), 7; (27 May 1848), 8.

[72] Jones to Allsop, 12 May, 18 May 1848, Yale. Ironically, Jones was offered the editorship of the *North British Express*, based in Newcastle, but the letter does not seem to have reached him in time: John Grant to Jones, 24 May 1848, SC.

of June. By now the first of the state trials under new emergency legislation (the Crown and Government Security Act) had begun, the first defendant being John Mitchel, one of the leaders of the 'young Ireland' agitation for repeal of the Union. This trial took place in Dublin, but news of the sentence (fourteen years transportation) passed on Mitchel travelled fast, and by the end of May the cause of Ireland had become an integral part of the cause of the English Charter. On 29 May, 80,000 people marched from Stepney Green through the City of London to Trafalgar Square and heard calls for the release of Mitchel. Six days later, on Whit Sunday, simultaneous meetings were held at Paddington, addressed by Peter McDouall, and on Bishop Bonner's Fields, addressed by Jones. Around 300,000 Chartists milled around the east London park, amidst the holiday crowds. At the edge of the park in the church of St James the Less, 'K' division of the Metropolitan Police waited, hidden from sight, but with a clear view of the meeting.[73]

Jones arrived at Bishop Bonner's Fields at around 5.00 p.m., and began to speak once Alexander Sharp had finished addressing the crowd. What he had to say was not especially novel. He stressed the importance of the Chartists being well organized and peaceable, remaining in their wards and classes should the authorities move against them, but urging them to demonstrate simultaneously in order to create national unanimity—there must be no 'partial outbreaks', he warned. Jones denounced his detractors, repeating the charge that Cobden was in the pay of the governing classes, and denying newspaper reports that he (Jones) had been a Tory ten years previously. As proof he declared that he had fought on several occasions for the principles he now upheld, revealing that 'I bear one of the bayonet wounds of the King of Hanover's soldiers about my person'. Jones's address was fairly brief. He was due on the mail-train to Manchester, but he finished with a flurry, calling for the flying of the green flag over Downing Street, and for Lord John Russell and not John Mitchel to be transported to Australia. At 6.30 p.m. Jones and Sharp left, and the meeting began to break up. As the crowds drifted away, some youths spotted the policemen secreted in the church, began throwing stones at them, and a full-scale brawl quickly developed. Church windows were shattered and mounted

[73] The account that follows is based on: *The Times* (5 June 1848), 8; *NS* (10 June 1848), 6; 'Indictment of Ernest Jones', PRO, TS/11/376; Correspondence relating to Bishop Bonner's Fields (June 1848), PRO, HO 45/2410, Pt. 1, fos. 590–650.

police reinforcements were called in. There were several injuries, and in the days that followed the local courts filled up with the apprehended rioters. Some local residents complained that the police had been drinking in the church throughout the afternoon and had themselves precipitated the violence, but most of the householders living along the edge of the Fields denounced the Chartists and provided the magistrates with telling evidence against Jones and Sharp.

Evidence of what? For of course the two Chartist speakers had actually left the park well before the rioting began. Moreover, Jones had said virtually nothing that day that he had not previously propounded in the meetings of the Chartist convention. However, for once someone was listening to his every word. James White, a shorthand writer and itinerant supplier of copy for some of the London dailies, was in attendance as a police spy and recorded Jones's speech verbatim. The authorities had their man, now they needed the body.

4

The Poet as Martyr, 1848–1850

AS HIS REPUTATION grew during 1847 and 1848 Jones began to attract the interest of the satirical magazines. *The Man in the Moon* was first off the mark towards the end of 1847, running an article on the 'poet-teacher of the people', a clever skit on the author of a so-called work entitled 'Voices from the Crowd', and featuring an in-depth review of one poem in particular: 'Starve us all; or the Queen's good example', the close resemblance of which to Jones's own 'Royal Bounty: a legend of Windsor' was fairly obvious. In Jones's poem, published in the first volume of the *Labourer* earlier in 1847, the Royal Family gave leftover meat from their plates to their dogs, and the breadcrumbs from their table to the poor. *The Man in the Moon*'s version, by contrast, has Prince Albert popping out to the baker's for a 'stale three-farthing penny roll' for the royal progeny. The magazine sarcastically heaped praise on the poet's achievement, singling out the '*felicitas curiosa* of the metaphors' and the 'very abstraction of entity' of the allusions. Not to be outdone, *Punch* followed up several months later, just after the Bishop Bonner's Fields meeting, following which Jones was arrested, reprinting another poem from the 'Voices from the Crowd' collection entitled 'Wait a little longer'. With its refrain, 'There's a Special now coming, boys, a Special now coming; | Let's knock the hat extremely flat', it was probably a pastiche of Jones's own 'Song of the gaggers' which had just appeared in the *Labourer*, as well as a teasing reminder of how the Chartist speakers on that Whit Sunday afternoon had left before the police appeared.[1] To this sending-up of Jones's poetry

---

[1] 'The Poet-Teacher of the People', *Man in the Moon*, 2 (1847); 'The Clerkenwell Poets', *Punch* (10 June 1848), 246. Jones himself wrote a poem entitled 'The Song of the Specials' which remained unpublished (Ernest Jones Manuscript Poems, MCL: Ms f821.89 J5/7). *Punch* may have known of this poem, or, equally plausibly, Jones may have penned his own version in response to *Punch*'s pastiche.

the magazines added their own amusing caricature of Jones the politician. Jones fits the profile of *Punch*'s 'model agitator' published in February 1848: 'born with the bump of Notoriety . . . [h]e heads all the rows', a rebel from his family who goes to the bar, before finding his true vocation as 'a hearty hater of every Government'; the 'only thing he flatters is the mob': 'He excites the people to arm themselves for the worst; but begs they will use no weapons. His talk is incendiary, his advice nothing but gunpowder, and yet he hopes no explosion will take place. His is an Arsenal wishing to pass for a Chapel or a Baby-linen warehouse.' And of course, *Punch* went on, the 'model agitator' liked to go out in style: 'A Monster Meeting is his great joy, to be damped, only, by the rain or the police. He glories in a prosecution . . . He asks for it: shrieks out to the Government— "Why don't you prosecute me?" . . . The favour is at length granted. He is thrown into prison, and grows fat upon it; for from that moment he is a martyr, and paid as one accordingly.'

Bored with lampooning O'Connor the carpetbagger and Reynolds the gullible Francophile, and overtaken by their rivals in racist mimicry of William Cuffay, the black Chartist, *Punch* now had a new burlesque: Ernest Jones, the melodramatic Chartist. As he lay in his cell in Newgate, awaiting trial at the end of June, *Punch* offered a composite caricature of Jones and Peter McDouall, the militant Lancashire Chartist. 'A great demonstration' depicted McDouall as a kid-gloved dandy threatening a magistrate with his rolled-up umbrella and denouncing the judge, in the words Jones had uttered at Bishop Bonner's Fields, as 'a myrmidon of the brutal Whigs', before promising to advise his comrades to go home to their tea.[2] The following month *Bentley's Miscellany* added to the fun with a mock autobiography of a convicted Chartist, entitled 'How I became a Chartist'. Purportedly the account of a barrister, who out of boredom had become a regular theatregoer before beginning to attend Chartist meetings, it was clearly modelled on Jones. The

---

[2] 'The Great Demonstration', *Punch* (24 June 1848), 261; 'The Model Agitator', ibid. (18 Mar. 1848), 130. 'Mymirdon' was the term used by Richard Cobden in the House of Commons to describe the deluded followers of O'Connor: *Hansard*, 3rd ser., 98 (23 May 1848), 1311. Richard Altick has identified Charles Cochrane, organizer of the Trafalgar Square demonstration at the beginning of March, as *Punch*'s 'model agitator', but Cochrane was, unlike Jones, neither a barrister nor, as the illegitimate son of a lieutenant-colonel, a rebel from his family: Richard D. Altick, *Punch: The Lively Youth of a British Institution, 1841–51* (Columbus, Ohio: Ohio State University Press, 1997), 294.

autobiographer explained that he was drawn to Chartism, or 'any other *ism*' which promised excitement, the prospect of a new career, and the opportunity for exhibitionism. Above all, Chartism was a 'rendezvous' for the bored and 'used-up' of the world, where indolent young men could 'play over again their respective parts in the most imposing *incognito*—where they can meet with the homage and respect in the unknown which is denied to them amongst the known quarters of their existence'.[3]

Jones's popular verse and his theatrical manner on the platform were of course easy and obvious targets for the satirical weeklies, staffed as they were by world-weary West End critics, bent on stopping the creeping influence of the French drama, and no strangers to writing comic doggerel themselves.[4] Some of them probably knew Jones personally, but there was more than *Schadenfreude* to their wit. The caricature of Jones which emerged in the London satirical press during 1848 was also an indication of the very self-conscious way in which Jones chose and played the roles of mob-orator and political martyr during the course of 1848. After all, this was a man who modelled himself on Mirabeau and Pushkin, who had written a poetic tragedy on the 'French Revolution', and who had sat backstage at Covent Garden and the Haymarket whilst Kean and Macready honed their reputations as tragedians. For Jones, politics was high drama, and in sending him up the satirists were confirming his mastering of the art. Yet the satirists were also contesting the legitimacy of Jones's attempt to articulate his politics through theatrical and poetic forms of address. Down to the summer of 1848 Jones had succeeded in passing himself off as the fallen peer, teasing his audiences with allusions and hints concerning his real identity, but also largely satisfying doubts about his sincerity and consistency. After his arrest in June 1848, Jones's political persona was no longer put to the test in front of Chartist crowds, or even erstwhile literary colleagues, but in the theatre of the courtroom. This

---

³ [James Ward], 'How I became a Chartist', *Bentley's Miscellany*, 24 (July 1848), 101–6. For the increasingly hostile caricature of Chartism in 1848, see: Stephen Roberts and Dorothy Thompson, *Images of Chartism* (Woodbridge: Merlin Press, 1998), 5; Celina Fox, *Graphic Journalism in England During the 1830s and 1840s* (London: Garland, 1988), 258–9. On *Punch*'s burlesque of Chartism, see Altick, *Punch*, 294–302.

⁴ On *Punch*'s xenophobia over the state of the English drama, see: Janice Nadelhaft, 'Punch and the Syncretics: An Early Victorian Prologue to the Aesthetic Movement', *Studies in English Literature*, 15 (1975), 627–40; Altick, *Punch*, 728.

chapter chronicles Jones's attempts to play the part of orator and martyr with conviction during the remainder of 1848 and over the next two years. The story begins on the stage of the courtroom with Jones's trial for sedition in the early summer of 1848, before transferring behind the scenes to the prison cell where he served out his imprisonment. Finally, the chapter considers the carefully orchestrated release of Jones from prison in 1850.

I

Jones was arrested in Manchester three days after the Bishop Bonner's Fields meeting. A warrant for his arrest was telegraphed from London and he was picked up in the middle of his breakfast in the Mosley Arms hotel, having spoken at the City Music Hall the previous evening. He was taken back by train to London and charged with sedition at Bow Street Police Court. He accepted the charge, complimented the government informant on his correct copy, but denied that he had uttered anything untoward. Bail was set at £1,000—much higher than it had been for Alexander Sharp, Joseph Williams, and John Fussell, the three other Chartists arrested in London at the same time—and Jones languished in Newgate for over three weeks before the required sureties were found. O'Connor appeared at Bow Street almost immediately, where he was amusingly mistaken for a volunteer special constable, but his offer of bail was rejected as he was a Member of Parliament.[5] Back in Halifax, where Jones had been due to speak on the day he was arrested, protest meetings were held, and from Newgate he awaited trial with his usual air of defiance, as though this fate was the inevitable climax to his political career. Jones declared in the *Northern Star* that he would not conceal his feelings or true beliefs in the court. He explained, 'I never joined the movement without foreseeing the consequences, and I am not the man to shrink from the result'. He expected nothing other than calumny—in the letter he alluded to the indelicate criticism which had been made of his marital life; and rough justice— he explained that all the newspaper coverage of his purported comments at Bishop Bonner's Fields had prejudged the whole trial. Above all, Jones expected to be treated in court like a martyr: 'If, therefore, I am convicted, I shall go to my prison with a proud heart,

[5] *HG* (10 June 1848), 7; (17 June 1848), 3; (1 July 1848), 2.

and with the belief that I shall not be there long, for it will not be long before we have the Charter—at least if there are MEN in England. If otherwise, I may as well be in their gaols as not, for all England is but a prison for the people.'⁶

Jones's brave talk was not wholly misplaced. Since the 1790s English radicals had more often than not successfully taken on the Crown in state trials involving charges of sedition and treason, cleverly turning statute on its head by appealing to the authority of the common law, or by disputing the Crown's insistence on proving the intentions of protestors, or by simply stoking up unwanted debate by publishing court proceedings verbatim. When the language of the law proved so open to contest and public debate juries proved reluctant to convict. As recently as 1843 O'Connor had been acquitted on charges similar to those on which Jones now stood accused.⁷ By the summer of 1848, however, things stood rather differently. In the first place, although Jones was not accused of felony treason, a new class of crime which had been put on the statute book by the Whigs in April specifically to deal with Irish and English protestors, the sedition he did stand accused of was defined in unusually broad terms by the Crown, making conviction almost impossible to avoid. Secondly, the prosecution went out of its way to single out Jones's gentlemanly status as a contributory factor in his guilt. The Crown refused to treat Jones as a patriot appealing to the common-law right of resistance, or even, for that matter, as a poet. Instead, Jones was identified as a renegade barrister—a man of education and social position who had taken advantage of his status to mislead the London crowds and incite them to riot.

Jones's trial on 10 July in the Central Criminal Court came midway through the summer and early autumn of state trials. By the time

---

⁶ NS (1 July 1848), 1. For reactions in Halifax to his arrest, see Benjamin Wilson, *The Struggles of an Old Chartist* [1887], repr. in David Vincent (ed.), *Testaments of Radicalism: Memoirs of Working Class Politicians, 1790–1885* (London: Europa Publications, 1977), 199.

⁷ John Barrell, *Imagining the King's Death: Figurative Treason, Fantasies of Regicide, 1793–96* (Oxford: Oxford University Press, 2000); James Epstein, ' "Our Real Constitution": Trial Defence and Radical Memory in the Age of Revolution', in James Vernon (ed.), *Rereading the Constitution* (Cambridge: Cambridge University Press, 1996), 22–51. O'Connor's triumphant edition of his own trial proceedings was published in 1843: *The Trial of Feargus O'Connor, esq. . . . and fifty-eight others, at Lancaster, on a Charge of Sedition, Conspiracy, Tumult and Riot* [1843] (2nd edn., New York, A. M. Kelley, 1970). On Chartist trials in general, see: Jacqueline Fellaigue Ariouat, 'Rethinking Partisanship in the Conduct of the Chartist Trials, 1839–48', *Albion*, 29 (1998), 596–621.

he went into the dock most of the English Chartists arrested in the wake of the London disturbances during May had been tried and convicted (but not sentenced), although the bulk of the cases involving the young Irelanders had yet to take place. Two months after the Kennington Common meeting of 10 April public anxiety was again at fever-pitch as rumours circulated of mobs armed with pikes ready to spring Jones and his fellow prisoners from Newgate.[8] The determination of the Crown to secure conviction at all cost had already become paramount. The trial of John Fussell at the beginning of July had set the tone. In Fussell's trial Sir John Jervis, the attorney-general, had insisted that sedition meant not only the precise language used, but also the circumstances of the meeting at which the words were uttered and the subsequent consequences of the speech.[9] These were markedly different criteria from previous prosecutions for sedition, when the Crown had concentrated on determining the intentions of the speakers and the precise wording of their utterances. Now the burden of proof lay in determining the unforeseeable effects of such speeches. Jones, the consummate showman, found that the reactions of his audience had become part of the evidence used against him.

Opening the case for the Crown, Jervis, also a Middle Templar, confessed that he was embarrassed to state that Jones was a barrister, a member of his own profession. As a barrister, Jervis argued, Jones should have known better. He should have been aware of the fairness of English law, and of the fallacy of the doctrines he promulgated. The only merit in seeing Jones in the dock, explained Jervis, was that it served to refute the charge that there was one law for the rich and another for the poor. Jervis stated that the charge of riot was not being pressed against Jones, for he had left the meeting before the trouble began, but there still could be no mistaking the meaning of his language, referring as it did to an organized uprising in the provinces, his desire to see the green flag flying over Downing Street, and to see Lord John Russell transported to Australia.[10] It was left to

[8] David Goodway, *London Chartism, 1838–1848* (Cambridge: Cambridge University Press, 1982), 90.

[9] John E. P. Wallis (ed.), *Reports of State Trials . . . 1842 to 1848*, NS (1894), vol. 7, cols. 728, 760, 762–3, 770, 773; Jervis had helped draw up the Felony Treason Act: D. Freestone and J. C. Richardson, 'Sir John Jervis and his Acts', *Criminal Law Review* (1980), 5–16. For the significance of Fussell's trial, see: John Saville, *1848: The British State and the Chartist Movement* (Cambridge: Cambridge University Press, 1987), 179–84.

[10] *State Trials*, vii, cols. 785–6, 791–2, 796, 799.

Jones's defence counsel, Sergeant Wilkins, not only to deny the charges of sedition, but also to right the record as far as Jones's profession was concerned. Jones was, Wilkins pointed out, 'a young man entering on life with literary attainments, and with a liberal education . . . He is a member of the Bar, it is true, and if he had the most aspiring ambition that profession holds out to him the brightest prospects'. And, Wilkins stressed, it had been Jones's conscience alone that compelled him to speak out on behalf of the 'unprotected, wronged and injured', and his poetic naivety which had led him to utter loose phrases—'vapour'—such as his reference to Russell.[11] Neither judge nor jury were impressed with Wilkins's defence. In his summing-up Thomas Wilde drew the jury's attention back to Jones's colourful rhetoric. Wilde pointed out that the assembly of 3,000 people in east London on that fateful Whit Sunday was not illegal in itself, but being addressed by speakers inciting and encouraging unlawful organizations made it so. Equally there were things said by Jones which in other circumstances might have been uttered with impunity, but on this occasion were inflammatory. Wilde was especially critical of Jones's desire to bring 'the rich man's nose to the grindstone', and took time in his summation to point out to the jury that the rich kept the poor in employment by consuming their manufactures, and that industry and hard work created its own reward. It was mischievous, the judge argued, of Jones to suggest to the working men of the metropolis that it was otherwise. Duly directed, the same jury that had convicted Fussell took only thirteen minutes to find Jones guilty.[12]

Before being sentenced Jones was allowed the customary last word, and he used it to take issue with the two main arguments that had been used in his prosecution. He denied that his language had been inciteful or seditious, or amounted to an attack on the shop-keeping or jury classes, claiming that the judge had relied on incorrect reports of one speech. '[A] just estimation of the man', Jones pointed out, 'cannot be formed by that one speech alone, but must be formed by the whole tenor of that man's life.' The personal history of the speaker and not the disposition of the crowd, Jones remonstrated, were the real circumstances by which the speech should be judged. Jones also emphasized that his credentials were not those of an ordinary lawyer. Turning the attorney-general's

[11] *State Trials*, vii, cols. 802–3, 804–5, 806.
[12] Ibid., cols. 807–17.

charge back at him, Jones declared that he was ashamed of the legal profession if it was the case that a man 'never feels charity except when he is paid for it'. For his part Jones defended his actions thus: 'I was more entitled to speak . . . for this very reason—that I could speak more dispassionately, that I could speak more calmly, that I was not likely to be excited into the vortex of passion and likely to lead people astray in speaking from excited feelings, which might be induced from suffering felt by myself.'[13] But Wilde was unmoved. He objected to Jones's attempt to use the dock as a platform for a lecture—a 'harangue'—on the law of property, and refused to join in with speculations as to Jones's past conduct. In passing sentence Wilde returned to Jones's inflammatory speech which he stated, contrary to Jones's protestations, did not contain anything to indicate that 'the person who delivered it was influenced by right feelings and right objects'. And so, concluded Wilde:

What I have to look at is this—what was the speech there delivered . . . what was its tendency to public mischief delivered by a person perfectly competent from education and from natural powers to express his meaning fully, to guard it when it required guarding, to leave it at large where it was not his object to guard it? Taking you therefore to be a person possessed of those powers, addressing a promiscuous meeting, and using the language you did use . . . I am bound to act upon that.

Accordingly Wilde sentenced Jones to two years imprisonment and to be bound over to keep the peace for a further two years on his release.[14] So sentenced, Jones was led away, this time not to Newgate but across London beyond Parliament to Tothill Fields Prison, one of the toughest of the 'new model prisons' that had sprung up in the capital in the previous twenty years.

Jones's trial amounted to much more than a demonstration of his guilt. It had also been an inquest into the romantic political identity which he had constructed since joining the Chartist movement in 1846. At his trial—both through his counsel Wilkins and in his own pre-sentence speech—Jones had attempted to defend his actions as those of the humane and disinterested observer, motivated by feeling and compassion but not vanity or mischief. Had the judge

---

[13] *State Trials*, vii, cols. 823–9. For Jones's pre-sentence speech: NS (22 July 1848), 8. The whole proceedings were later issued as a pamphlet by MacGowan: *The Queen against Ernest Jones: Trial of Ernest Charles Jones for Sedition and Unlawful Assembly at the Central Criminal Court before Wilde (C.J.), July 10, 1848* (London: Thomas MacGowan, 1848).   [14] *State Trials*, vii, col. 830.

understood Jones's own life-story, or at least the version he had told and embellished before his Chartist following, then the sincerity of his actions would not have been called into question. But the Crown saw only a young, well-heeled firebrand with a dangerously republican countenance—'a barrister whose business was not over-whelming . . . with red whiskers and red hair', as a young Walter Bagehot described Jones earlier in the year. Instead of a well-meaning young poet whose powerful and violent imagery belied his patrician political views, the Crown saw a manipulative demagogue who should have been more circumspect. 'Words such as these,' lamented The Times, reflecting on Jones's sentence, 'carried rather further than the authors intended, have cost thousands of lives and millions of treasure.'[15] In the hands of the wrong people romantic rhetoric was a mighty weapon. If only Jones had remained an onlooker, a passive commentator, as his friend Archer Gurney had urged. But somewhere along the way the quietist persona of the 'Wanderer'—the poet who simply chronicles the suffering of the age—had been superseded by 'Percy Vere' and 'Carl Wonrad', engaged poetic voices for whom there could be no separation between their own personal hardship and the sufferings of the people. Jones was found guilty by a London jury on a midsummer evening in 1848, but it was almost as if the poetic vocation he had nurtured since his personal crisis of 1845 had been the principal witness in his prosecution. As Archer Gurney summed up a year later, in a poem dedicated to his godson, Llewellyn Archer Atherley Jones:

> Clouds have gather'd over thy Sire
> He, this age's professions sharing,
> Nerved with all too ardent fire
> To a course of fitful daring,
> He hath felt Misfortune's ire.[16]

---

[15] The Times (11 July 1848), 5; Walter Bagehot to Eliza Bagehot, 8 Apr. 1848 in Norman St John-Stevas (ed.), Collected Works of Walter Bagehot. 15 vols. (London: The Economist, 1965–86), xii. 274–6.
[16] 'To Llewellyn Archer Atherley' (30 June 1849), BL, Add. Ms. 61,971A. Jane copied out this poem and included it in a letter sent to Jones in prison: Jane Atherley Jones to Ernest Jones, 7 June 1850, SC.

2

Jones 'felt Misfortune's ire' for exactly two years in Tothill Fields Prison, or the Westminster House of Correction as it was officially known. Lying just off Victoria Street, at the junction with Vauxhall Bridge Road, Tothill Fields was the most central of all the London prisons, situated within the parish of St Margaret's, one of the poorest and most densely populated neighbourhoods of the borough, within earshot of the river and not too distant from the hubbub of Westminster and St James. Jones later recalled the contrast between his own dumb existence and 'the busy roar . . . booming from the streets', the 'multitudinous anthems of the steeples', 'the faint swell of festal music' from the palaces, and the sound of military parades in summer months.[17] He was in the heart of the city, yet not part of it. Jones was also, as it turned out, near the epicentre of the cholera which broke out in the late summer of 1849, sweeping through the rookeries of Westminster and leading to a mass exodus of the political classes.[18] Tothill Fields Prison was one of the newest in London, its construction, in the Panopticon style, having been completed in 1836. By the time Jones was released in the summer of 1850 the decision had been taken to make Tothill Fields a 'correctional' prison for convicted women and boys only. But between 1845 and 1850 the prison housed some 800 male, female, and boy offenders. Most of the men were convicts who had been spared transportation. The bulk of them were under sentences of hard labour, but there were also those like Jones who had been sentenced as 'misdemeanants', and there were some debtors as well.[19] The regime was harsh, the prison run like a 'garrisoned fortress' by Lieutenant Tracey, the governor. Jones was sentenced to endure the 'silent' system whereby no communication—verbal, facial, or through hand gesture—was allowed between inmates, and all prisoners were required to wear a cap with a beak-like mask.

[17] 'To the British Democracy', *NP* (17 May 1851), 62.
[18] Lying so close to the river, St Margaret's was one of the worst-hit areas of west London, with 224 deaths (73 per 10,000) from the cholera: 'Report of the General Board of Health on the Epidemic Cholera of 1848 and 1849', *Parl. Papers* (1850), xxi, Appdx. B, 201.
[19] 'Fourteenth Report of the Inspectors Appointed . . . to Visit the Different Prisons of Great Britain', *Parl. Papers* (1850), xxviii, 29–33; H. Mayhew and J. Binney, *The Criminal Prisons of London and Scenes of Prison Life* [1862] (2nd edn., London: Frank Cass, 1968), 363–5.

Middlesex County remained committed to the 'silent' system long after other London prisons, notably Pentonville, had gone over to the more expensive 'separate' confinement, and Tracey, like his fellow governor at Coldbath Fields Prison, Captain Chesterton, was one of its great advocates. Solitary confinement for minor breaches of discipline was common and visits from friends and family were limited. Furthermore, prisoners were compelled to spend most of the day picking oakum, that is, unravelling old rope-fibre from ships, under the watchful eye of the prison staff. In other words, Tothill Fields was at the forefront of metropolitan prisons in the zeal with which the new regulatory techniques of discipline were being implemented. Admittedly, Jones might have considered himself lucky. Two years after he left Tothill Fields, Tracey was trying out 'electrophrenology' on some of the convicts.[20] But between 1848 and 1850 he was the subject of the strangest of incarcerations. The real world, with its real public, lay yards away from his cell, over the prison wall. Yet the only audience he was allowed were the prison wardens who invigilated his every move. Condemned by Wilde, the judge at his trial, for using inflammatory language to 3,000 people at a 'promiscuous meeting', Jones was now under the watchful eye of a regime who came down hard on the smallest sign of 'promiscuous conversation'.[21] Total institutions leave reasonably total records, and as result Jones's two years of imprisonment are thoroughly documented from the authorities' point of view. Prison life was not at all what Jones expected.

For two years Jones was very much out of sight and out of mind. This was surprising. Traditionally, gentleman radicals like Jones had enjoyed preferential treatment whilst locked up. Horne Tooke and Burdett were sent to the Tower of London, in 1794 and 1810 respectively, but were allowed to write and communicate with relative ease, and as virtually the only inmates in the medieval fortress, were

[20] Robin Evans, *The Fabrication of Virture: English Prison Architecture, 1750–1840* (Cambridge: Cambridge University Press, 1982), 389, 397; Sean McConville, *A History of English Prison Administration*, vol. 1: *1750–1877* (London: Routledge & Kegan Paul, 1981), 244–5. Charles Dickens was a fan of the methods of Tracey and Chesterton: P. Collins, *Dickens and Crime* (London: Macmillan, 1962), 65–6. One of Jones's fellow Chartist convicts, W. J. Vernon, wrote a particularly full account of conditions in Westminster Prison in a series of articles published on his release in *Reynolds' Political Instructor* in 1850. See esp. those for 16 Feb. 1850 (p. 114) and 9 Mar. 1850 (p. 140).
[21] U. R. Q. Henriques, 'The Rise and Decline of the Separate System of Prison Discipline', *Past & Present*, 54 (1972), 73–4.

prize exhibits alongside the Crown Jewels and the animal exotica of the royal menagerie. Sentenced to Newgate in 1810, William Cobbett moved into a nice little rented cottage next to the Keeper's house, his family joined him, and he continued publishing his *Political Register* with little interference. Leigh Hunt, imprisoned for two years in 1812, took over two apartments in the prison infirmary of Surrey Gaol, papered the walls, put up trellises and planted an apple-tree in the courtyard garden, and received daily visits from his friends. In the Chartist years this liberal form of house-arrest continued, albeit not for working-class Chartist prisoners, who tended to be housed in older provincial prisons. Feargus O'Connor, imprisoned for fifteen months in York Castle in 1840–1, was housed with ordinary criminals, but was allowed to wear his own clothes and seems to have been able to communicate with the *Northern Star* without too much difficulty. Richard Oastler, the Yorkshire factory reformer, entered the Fleet debtors' prison in 1840, published his *Fleet Papers* from within, received so many visitors that a rota had to be set up, and was the recipient of such lavish gifts that he published a weekly inventory of them. Locked up in Stafford Gaol for two years, Thomas Cooper had experienced deprivation for the first two months, but thereafter was allowed to write and take his collection of books in with him, and received visitors regularly. Even in 1848 the Irish repealers, despite being sentenced to death by hanging, drawing, and quartering (later commuted to transportation), awaited their fate in the relative suburban comfort of Richmond Prison in Dublin, turning their cells into furnished study-rooms. Once in Antipodean exile, all of them, with the exception of William Smith O'Brien, were given immediate parole, free to write and publish, albeit on the other side of the world.[22] Other Chartist prisoners outside London fared better than Jones in 1848. Two of them—Peter McDouall and George White—had their poetry published in the *Northern Star* whilst inside, and the so-called 'Kirkdale' prisoners in Manchester issued a series of *Tracts for the Times*.[23] Men of letters

---

[22] Cecil Driver, *Tory Radical: The Life of Richard Oastler* (New York: Oxford University Press, 1946), ch. 31; A. J. Peacock, 'Feargus O'Connor at York', *York History*, 2 (1975), 65–75; Thomas Cooper, *Life of Thomas Cooper* (London: Hodder & Stoughton, 1872), 232–58; George Sigerson, *Political Prisoners at Home and Abroad* (London: Kegan Paul Trench & Trübner, 1890), 27–9; Christopher Godfrey, 'The Chartist Prisoners, 1839–41', *International Review of Social History*, 24 (1979), 217–21.

[23] Stephen Roberts, *Radical Politicians and Poets in Early Victorian Britain: The*

who became men in prison could still in most cases sing like birds in the cage.[24]

Jones clearly expected that he would enjoy a similar kind of existence, carrying on his literary and political vocations from within. He was naturally familiar with the details of both O'Connor's and Cooper's imprisonment, he had written a eulogistic poem about Chateaubriand's incarceration, and in the *Labourer* he had written *en passant* about the imprisonment of his hero Honoré Mirabeau in the dying years of *ancien régime* France. A month into his sentence Jones began arranging with his wife Jane for his manuscripts to be brought to the prison, and gave her a list of books and pamphlets he required to carry on with his writing. In turn she obtained copies of the *Northern Star*, intending to send them on to Jones.[25] From the outset, however, it was clear that the prison authorities were not going to allow Jones any of the privileges he had expected to enjoy. His request for pens and ink to enable him to pursue the '[l]iterary pursuits to which he had been accustomed' was turned down in the middle of July, despite him appealing to the precedent of Cooper in Stafford Gaol, and he was only given leave to write specific letters, mainly to Jane, his wife. He was given a slate and pencil after a few months. All his correspondence was vetted and all books and newspapers destined for him were inspected by the prison chaplain and usually sent back.[26] The list of books denied Jones during his imprisonment makes interesting reading: it includes innocuous titles such as *The Russian Sketch Book*, *Anecdotes of Actors*, and George Ditson's *Circassia*, alongside more subversive

Voices of Six Chartist Leaders (Lampeter: Edward Mellen, 1993), 26–7; Stephen Roberts and Paul Pickering, 'Pills, Pamphlets and Politics: The Career of Peter Murray McDouall (1814–54)', *Manchester Region History Review*, 11 (1997), 39–41; *NS* (24 March 1849), 3; (5 May 1849), 3; *Chartist Tracts for the Times*, nos. 2, 4–6 (Wortley: Joseph Barker, 1848). John Teer, one of the 'Kirkdale' prisoners, recalled having a large amount of time available for reading and writing. He later published 24 prison poems: *Silent Musings* (Manchester: Ainsworth & Cheetham, 1869), p. vi. Imprisoned in Newgate in 1848, the Chartist John Shaw was allowed writing materials: Shaw to G. J. Harney, 11 Dec. 1848, in F. G. and R. M. Black (eds.), *The Harney Papers* (Assen: Van Gorcum, 1969), 73–4.

[24] For the literary genres associated with imprisonment, see: Ioan Davies, *Writers in Prison* (Oxford: Blackwell, 1990) and Victor Brombert, *The Romantic Prison: The French Tradition* (Princeton: Princeton University Press, 1978).

[25] Jane Atherley Jones to Ernest Jones, 23 July 1848, SC; Jane to Ernest Jones, [6] Aug. 1848, CL MUN A.o.10 3/3.

[26] Visiting Justices' Minutes, London Metropolitan Archives, 15 July 1848, 5 Aug. 1848, WA/GP 1851/1.

tomes such as Louis Ménard's *Prologue d'une revolution, Février–Juin, 1848*,[27] the works of Walter Scott, Shakespeare, and Disraeli alongside newspaper-cuttings sought out by Jane.[28] The prison authorities were particularly keen to close off Jones's access to his own Chartist publications. He was refused a copy of the pamphlet report of his trial and denied the *Labourer* as well. By the end of August 1848 Jane's visits were curtailed, and thereafter she only saw him once every three months.[29]

In Tothill Fields Jones was thus treated as a common criminal and not as a martyred poet. His gentlemanly status appeared to count for nothing. As he complained in a letter to the Home Secretary in April, 1849, 'I conceive as a Political Prisoner, a Man of Character, & a Member of the English Bar, I have right to object'. In particular, Jones objected to having to keep silent, and to being kept either in separate confinement, 'or else to be associated with about 200 criminals of the lowest description, wearing the same prisongarb & particolored uniform and cap'. He complained of the limited number of visits he was allowed and the fact that all communication with visitors had to take place through a grate in his cell. And he protested vociferously over the denial of contact with his wife, especially when she fell ill in the autumn of 1848. Above all, Jones resented having to pick oakum. This punishment, which Jones said befitted 'neither a political prisoner, nor a Gentleman', could only be escaped on payment of a rather extortionate exemption fee (20s. per month), which Jones, courtesy of O'Connor, made sure he paid. Jones was clearly affronted at the total lack of respect and recognition he experienced whilst in prison. He tried to petition Wilde, who had sentenced him, seeking clarification of the terms of his sentence; he threatened to charge the prison governor, Tracey, and the local magistrates; and throughout the first year of his imprisonment he attempted to petition Parliament, although permission to do this was not given.[30]

---

[27] Visiting Justices' Minutes, London Metropolitan Archives, 25 Aug. 1849, 22 Sept. 1849, 10 Nov. 1849, 23 Feb. 1850.

[28] Jones to George Grey, 7 Apr. 1849, Jones papers, National Library of Wales, Ms 10851B. Jane also attempted to bring a volume of Cicero's *Orations*, a volume of Herodotus, two dictionaries (Greek and German), an unspecified mathematics book, Thiers's history of the French Revolution, an unnamed history of Rome, and a work of Lamartine (lent by Archer Gurney): Jane Atherley Jones to Ernest Jones, 20 Aug. 1848, 18 Dec. 1848, CL, MUN. A.o.10/5,/9.

[29] Visiting Justices' Minutes, 5 Aug. 1848; Jane Atherley Jones to Ernest Jones, 20 Aug. 1848, CL, MUN A.o.10/9.

[30] Jones to George Grey, 7 Apr. 1849, 21 May 1849, Jones to Chief Justice Wilde,

How much Jones actually suffered in prison is a topic on which fiction has usually triumphed over fact. It is questionable whether the hardship Jones endured was quite as severe as he later claimed. One of the most famous instances of this retelling of Jones's prison years came in October 1866 when, following the capture and imprisonment of several Fenians, he revealed—for the first time, or so he stated—'the sufferings inflicted' on him in 1848 and 1849. These included, Jones stated, solitary confinement in a small damp cell, denial of access to writing materials, poor diet, and unnecessary exposure to the risk of cholera. Similarly, in the sketch of his life published in 1868 his imprisonment was the centre-piece in his narrative of struggle and redemption.[31] However, the year after his release Parliament did carry out a reasonably through investigation of Jones's complaints, and the picture emerges of conditions that were better than those experienced by 'common' criminals.[32] The basic facts seem to be these. Jones was kept in a separate confinement, but at his own request, and in a gas-lit cell considerably larger than those of other prisoners. He wore prison uniform, though not the striped variety but instead a 'new suit of plain blue cloth', with as many undergarments, which were liberally supplied by his friends, as he pleased. During the winter months he was allowed his own fire in the day-room, a privilege denied other inmates. Jones received more visits than the prison regulations usually allowed: eleven in all, which worked out at a slightly more generous rate than the quarterly convention. He was excused oakum-picking except when the exemption payment ceased and when, in the spring of 1849, he made an issue of refusing to pick oakum. Excused hard labour he spent most of the daylight hours in the day-room, or exercising outside. In February 1849 the Inspector of Prisons reported that Jones had told him that although he found the prison rules severe, the staff were kind and he had no complaint. Hepworth Dixon, who undertook a survey of

19 Mar. 1849, Jones to Tracey, 19 May 1849, Jones papers, National Library of Wales; Visiting Justices' Minutes, 17 Mar. 1849, 1 May 1849, 2 May 1849, 12 May 1849. O'Connor did take up some of these grievances in the House of Commons in June, 1849: *Hansard*, 106 (12 June 1849), col. 50.

[31] Jones, 'The Prisoners of '48', *ME* (11 Oct. 1866), 4; *Ernest Jones. Who is he? What has he done?* (Manchester: The Reform League, 1868), 7–8.

[32] 'Copy of a letter, with its Enclosures, Addressed to the Secretary of State, by the Visiting Justices of the House of Correction at Westminster, with Respect to the Treatment of Ernest Charles Jones, during his Confinement in that Prison', *Parl. Papers* (1851), xlvi.

London prisons for the *Daily News*, came across Jones in 1849 and found him 'surrounded by books ... Greek and mathematics are the studies to which he seems to be devoting himself'. Jones, Dixon noted, 'walks in his yards and cell twenty miles a day, and pursues his studies. The diet, he says, is good and sufficient; the soup agrees with him well, and the chocolate is splendid'.[33] Not quite the dungeon Jones later described.

The prison authorities did confirm that on two separate occasions Jones was placed in solitary confinement on bread and water as a punishment for refusing to pick oakum. But on the first of these he proved too ill with dyspepsia and inflammation of the eyes to undertake the oakum-picking, and on the second, both hard labour and punishment were ruled out because of the cholera outbreak and also, more practically, because the supply of oakum had run out. It is true that Tothill Fields Prison was a cholera black-spot, with a mortality rate of 1.6 per hundred in 1849. Of the London prisons, only Millbank had a worse rate.[34] In September and October of 1849 there were forty cases and twelve deaths in the prison, including the passing away of Joseph Williams and Alexander Sharp, two of the other Chartist prisoners. And Jones did experience poor health during his imprisonment, spending two long periods in the prison infirmary, despite arousing suspicion that his illnesses were a sham.[35] His weight fluctuated alarmingly, although the surgeon did put him on special diets. And his sight suffered in particular. Jones claimed it was caused by the glare of the whitewashed walls, although the authorities pointed out that the inflammation of the eyelids which he experienced was already apparent when he began his sentence. Even here the prison authorities made efforts to find a remedy, although their chosen solution must have left Jones looking a rather strange bird. He wore a visor as a shade and then later on a pair of blue-stained glass spectacles. Having said that, Jane found him after four months inside decidedly thinner but 'free from the trashed &

[33] The Home Office had sent in the inspector after a intervention by Thomas Wakley: Wakley to George Grey, 13 Feb. 1849; 'Report of the Inspector of Prisons upon the alleged ill-treatment of prisoners in the Westminster Bridewell, etc' (22 Feb. 1849), PRO HO 12/2/81; Hepworth Dixon, *The London Prisons: with an Account of the More Distinguished Persons who have been Confined in them, etc.* (London: Jackson and Walford, 1850), 253–4.

[34] *Parl. Papers* (1850) xxi, App. B, 64; Report[s] of the Visiting Justices, 1 Sept. 1849, 13 Oct. 1849, London Metropolitan Archive, WA/GP 1849/9–10.

[35] Jane Atherley Jones to Ernest Jones [Mar. 1849], SC.

haggard look which latterly had unfortunately become habitual to you'.[36] And by the time of his release in the summer of 1850 he had put on weight (some four pounds) and was reportedly in good health. As to writing materials, judging from the voluminous complaints and petitions that Jones drafted from his cell these were provided, but for specific purposes only, and it was not until the September of his second year that he was allowed his own blank sketchbook. Jones was thus a sickly but obstreperous prisoner. Towards the end of his sentence the visiting justices concluded that he 'had exhibited but one feeling, that of determined opposition to all persons in authority'. But he does not seem to have been singled out for persecution. Indeed, that was the problem. Jones was not only a caged bird, he was also completely muffled. There was no point being a straitened artist if no one knew of your condition. The very ordinariness of his imprisonment tarnished his political reputation.

Denied access to the tools of his trade, Jones became marginalized as a Chartist leader whilst he was in prison. The remaining issues of the *Labourer* were published during 1848, but Jones's own contributions, clearly written before his trial and conviction, were few—limited to his piece on Mirabeau, the concluding articles of his series on 'National Literature', and a short ghost story set in Ireland: 'The murdered trooper.' Jones's editorial contributions to the *Northern Star* ended with his arrest, and Jane was left, under instruction from her husband, haggling and pleading with MacGowan, Samuel Kydd ('vulgar & presumptuous'), and George Julian Harney ('really kind & estimable') for the monies owing to Jones from the *Labourer* and the *Northern Star* as well as his salary due as a member of the Chartist executive. Jane also beseeched O'Connor to do all he could for Jones in terms of financial support, even offering him the literary services of her own father, but little seems to have been forthcoming, and in return Jane received a degree of attention from O'Connor which was as unwelcome as it was ungentlemanly. Jane also hawked Jones's remaining manuscript works (referred to cryptically in her letters as the 'bird' and the 'dog'), which MacGowan had carefully secreted away in a 'fireproof barn', around publishers such as Bohn, Newby, and Howitt. Newby indicated a willingness to take a second instalment of *My Life*, but there were no other takers. Chasing

<hr>

[36] Jane Atherley Jones to Ernest Jones, 16 Oct. 1848, CL MUN A.o.10/7.

Jones's grubby Chartist friends and Grub Street publishers was altogether too *declassé* for Jane. Soon after Jones began his sentence she wondered out loud, 'My dear Ernest, why did you not think more of us, <u>less</u> of those who care nothing for you. What wd. you say to the mother who should throw her <u>own</u> child from her breast . . . whilst she in the <u>rashness of her Philanthropy</u> ran abroad to seek & to foster the child of the stranger.'[37]

Consequently, the whole burden of parenting and running a household whilst its head was in prison fell heavily on Jane, and it no doubt contributed to her recurrent illnesses and eventual premature death in 1857. Her difficulties were primarily financial. Jones's income from his Chartist activities came too little and too late, his legal practice yielded nothing, and her own parents were unable to do more than offer kindly and pious words of encouragement. She let out rooms in their Queen's Terrace house to bring in a regular income, but by the following summer was forced to move into a smaller apartment altogether. Embittered by her distress, Jones renewed his pursuit of Uncle Hutton just before Christmas 1848, but with no success.[38] Commensurate with the worry of keeping financially afloat, Jane also faced the distress of maintaining public appearances. Jones's two elder sons enquired of her why their father was taking such an unusually 'long walk' and to which 'Government home' he had gone. Although close friends such as Michael Conan and Archer Gurney remained supportive, Jane was reluctant to seek aid from her contacts in London society, whom she knew disapproved of Jones's 'Chartist career'—'I will neither seek nor accept assistance for *your* children', she told her husband defiantly in July 1848. Following an initial flurry immediately after Jones's sentence, the round of social calls to and from Bulwer-Lytton, the Duke of Beaufort, the Stricklands, and the Manners dropped off and she was left isolated. There was little comfort for her in Jones's tactless advice not to brood on their present misfortunes: 'What has the future in store for me! Have I not been looking to the future month after month, even day by day of the last seven years. <u>You</u> know with what result . . . <u>You</u> may look to the future with more satisfaction, for your future, as much as a man's can be, is in your hands. Mine is not.'[39]

[37] Jane Atherley Jones to Ernest Jones, 23 July 1848, SC.
[38] Jane Atherley Jones to Ernest Jones, 30 Sept. 1848, 5 June 1849, SC; Ernest Jones to Hutton Annesley, 18 Dec. 1848, CL, MUN.A.0.10/10.
[39] Jane Atherley Jones to Ernest Jones, 23 July 1848, SC.

Part of Jane's dilemma was that for once Jones's gentlemanly status proved a handicap. It proved difficult for him to be included within the support campaign—the 'Victim Fund'—which the *Northern Star* newspaper organized on behalf of the families of the Chartist prisoners. The focal-point of this fundraising became the poverty endured by the wives and children, the 'starving babes', of Fussell, Williams, Cuffay, Vernon, and others, while the menfolk were under lock and key. But Jane was seldom listed in this roll-call of dependents, although she did receive some £4—'too insignificant to name'—in all from the fund. Private means, rather than public sustenance, proved the mainstay of the Jones family during his imprisonment. A poignant example of this was provided by an advert placed in the *Northern Star* by Halifax Chartists in June 1849. In aid of the family of the 'Suffering Patriot, Ernest Jones', they announced a raffle of a Chinese silk shawl, an item the well-heeled provenance of which was difficult to disguise.[40] A large rally in support of the 'political prisoners' was held at the Milton Street theatre in London in June 1849, but it was John Frost and William Jones—the transported Newport Chartists of 1839—who received top billing. And when Sharp and Williams died in prison, although there was concern at Jones's predicament, fundraising was concentrated on the widows of the two men. In April 1850 a further £4 10s. was raised by the National Charter Association at a meeting addressed by Gerald Massey (who compared Jones to Rienzi) and Bronterre O'Brien. But it was all small beer. In 1841 the Chartist 'Victim Fund' campaign had produced a petition containing 1.3 million signatures: by 1850 the *Northern Star* was lamenting the 'shameful' response of tens of thousands to Jones's plight.[41] Nor was Jones's martyrdom enhanced by his own repeated complaint that his fellow Chartist convicts were receiving more lenient treatment, including better communication with their families and, in the case of Vernon, early remission of their sentence.[42] So much for Chartist solidarity. In Parliament, a year after his release, radical MPs did argue that Jones should have been treated as a political prisoner and, in particular, should not have had the constitutional right of

---

[40] Jane Atherley Jones to Ernest Jones, 4 Dec. 1848, SC; *NS* (2 June 1849), 4.

[41] *NS* (23 June 1849), 8. The Milton Street meeting sent in a petition with 10,400 signatures to the Home Office: PRO HO 12/1/81. For later attempts to resurrect the prisoners' support campaign: *NS* (29 Sept. 1849), 8; (23 Mar. 1850) 1; (27 Apr. 1850), 1. For the 1841 campaign, see Godfrey, 'Chartist Prisoners', 213–14.

[42] Parl. Papers (1851), xlvi, 309.

petitioning Parliament withheld from him. But their case was not helped by one of them, William Williams, the radical Lambeth MP, turning out to being one of the visiting justices who had overseen Jones's imprisonment. Thomas Perronet Thompson, the veteran free-trader, spoke of the impolicy of making Jones a hero by such persecution, and forewarned that '[e]very one of those persecuted will probably make his appearance in the House of Commons'. But the outcry was muted. The carefully prepared evidence of Jones's actual treatment was hard to refute, and to a wider audience shocked later that year by William Gladstone's revelations of the brutal persecution experienced by Neapolitan deputies in the cells of King Bomba, Jones's protestations over poor food and sore eyes were hardly sensational. What did he expect, asked the MP Edward Bouverie, confidant of Gladstone and supporter of the Home Office policy on political prisoners: 'a sort of enviable retirement, where he could enjoy every luxury and indulgence?'[43]

Jones's presumption that his imprisonment would confirm his status as a martyred poet was thus confounded by his treatment inside prison and the lack of publicity he received outside. Just as the Crown prosecution had seen off his attempt during his trial to fashion himself as the voice of social conscience, so too his time spent in prison amounted to a failure. He was unable to emulate other literary captives of recent notoriety. As the debate in Parliament in the summer of 1851 suggests, Jones earned public derision rather than sympathy, a reaction nowhere better encapsulated than in Thomas Carlyle's account of his visit to Tothill Fields, during which he looked in on Vernon and Jones, two 'Chartist Notabilities'. Of Jones, Carlyle wrote:

Notability Second, a philosophic or literary Chartist; walking rapidly to and fro in his private court, a clean, high-walled place; the world and its cares quite excluded, for some months to come: master of his own time and spiritual resources to, as I supposed, a really enviable extent . . . I fancied I, for my own part, so left with paper and ink, and taxes and botherations shut out from me, could have written such a book as no reader will here ever get out of me . . . Here, alas, one has to snatch one's poor Book, bit by bit, as from a conflagration; and to think and live, comparatively, as if the house were not one's own, but mainly the world and the devil's.[44]

[43] *Hansard*, 118 (22 July 1851), cols. 1303–16.
[44] Thomas Carlyle, 'New Model Prisons', in *Latter Day Pamphlets* (London: Chapman & Hall, 1850), 7–8; Jules Siegel, 'Carlyle's Model Prison and Prisoners Identified', *Victorian Periodicals Newsletter*, 9 (1976), 81–3.

For once in his life Jones was caught out. He was too gentlemanly to enjoy the status of martyrdom accorded bona-fide working-class Chartist prisoners, and yet not gentlemanly enough to escape the rigours of mid-Victorian prison life and be left alone to write as Carlyle fancied he could. It was only with his release from prison in July 1850 that he was able to furnish the public with an account of his experiences as an imprisoned poet. And what an account it turned out to be.

3

In London Jones's release from prison on the second Tuesday in July 1850 was a quiet affair, quite unlike the cavalcade that had greeted O'Connor on his release from York Castle in 1841, or the grand reception that awaited John Frost on his return from exile in 1856. The *Northern Star* reported that after agreeing bail conditions Jones had returned home immediately, as the paper put it, 'restored to the felicity of his domestic hearth'. A few days later, at a small dinner, his compatriots in the Fraternal Democrats presented him with a pair of portraits—of himself and of Jane, his wife—and Jones in turn entertained the gathering with a reading from 'The Factory Town'.[45] The expectation seems to have been that Jones would go back, suitably chastened, to his respectable existence as a barrister and minor writer. Jones, however, had other plans. In the middle of July he was given a hero's welcome in Halifax. A week after his release a long procession of brass bands, carriages, and cheering crowds drew him, alongside Harney and his wife, from the station and into the town centre to a ticketed meeting in West Hill Park, where he thanked his Halifax supporters for sustaining him financially during his imprisonment, especially when his rich and titled relatives had ignored his plight. 'I have come upon a mission of danger', he told them, 'but of truth—once more into the social wilderness of civilised misery, proclaiming the advent of the Messiah—Freedom. Christ said to his followers "leave wife and child and follow me!" I did so and I suffered.' At this meeting, and at a later evening gathering when Jones was presented with a bag of fifty gold sovereigns, he announced that henceforth he would unfurl the 'red flag of political progression' across the countryside. We might read into these

---

[45] *NS* (13 July 1850), 1.

speeches Jones's new adherence to the principles of socialist republicanism, the turn to 'the Charter and something more' platform that is often said to have characterized late Chartism. But his appearance in Halifax in mid-July bore all the hallmarks of a religious revival, not a socialist conversion. In prison—that 'hecatomb of bleeding martyrs'—he had suffered, but out of his 'fiery ordeal of persecution' he had learned the truth. In prison, Jones had been reading his Bible:

The gospel first preached the Charter. The Messiah first preached fraternity, liberty, and equality. From the Bible itself they could refute the hierarchs of the state-church, or any other that adopt the same course . . . Christ opened the eyes of those born blind, but they try to blind those born with sight. Christ gave food to thousands in the wilderness, but they create a wilderness where God made food for thousands . . . The apostles got their call . . . by a call of grace, by the call of the Holy Ghost, but the clergy got their appointment from a city alderman, or a country-squire. What a church was this![46]

Released from prison, Jones was taking up his missionary calling once more. Over the rest of the summer he mounted an intense publicity campaign in order to give maximum vent to his new story of suffering in prison. In the *Northern Star* he published a long letter written to O'Connor, recounting the physical deprivation to which he had been subjected in prison (with no mention this time of the low criminal characters with whom he had been forced to mix).[47] And four books of new poetry and two 'sacred hymns' by Jones were advertised within days of the Halifax meeting, written, he claimed 'with the aid of blood and memory'. Turning on Carlyle, whose *Latter Day Pamphlets*, including his account of his visit to Tothill Fields, had recently appeared, Jones denied that prison was just the place to write. His writing materials, even his own bible, had been taken away from him, and yet, 'immured' and surviving on only bread and water, he had spent his hours 'writing the gospel of truth' with ink drawn from his own veins.[48] The martyr was being reinvented.

The poems that Jones claimed he had written in prison—all twenty-four of them—were eventually published in the summer of 1851, and they are discussed more fully in the next chapter. What is

[46] *HG* (20 July 1850), 6; *NS* (20 July 1850), 1; John A. Hargreaves, *Halifax* (Edinburgh: Edinburgh University Press, 1999), 139–40; Wilson, *Struggles of an Old Chartist*, 213.
[47] *NS* (3 Aug. 1850), 1.
[48] *Red Republican* (20 July 1850), 37; (10 Aug. 1850), 64; *NS* (3 Aug. 1850), 4.

worth dwelling on here is the circumstances surrounding their composition, for nothing enhanced the reputation of Jones quite so much as the dramatic revelations of how he wrote under duress. The story told was not always the same. In 1851 Jones claimed that only 'The New World' was written with his own blood, and another poem, 'Prison Fancies' was composed without writing materials whilst in solitary confinement. By the 1860s, however, the story had been exaggerated to include all the poetry Jones had written whilst imprisoned, together with a dramatic account of how Jones had fashioned a quill from a rook's feather and scrawled the verses in the pages of his bible. The story, of course, does not stand up to much scrutiny, although that has not stopped biographers repeating it verbatim ever since. First, there were obvious inconsistencies. In 1850 Jones claimed that his bible had been taken from him; in 1866 he claimed it was the only book he was allowed. In 1850 he stated that writing materials were denied for thirteen months; in 1851 it became two years of 'the pen denied', and in 1866 it reverted back to nineteen months.[49] Secondly, quite how someone who was chronically ill for much of his imprisonment was sufficiently sanguineous to yield enough blood to fill four books of poetry does test the imagination, especially when it is borne in mind that Jones was subject to frequent medical checks by the prison surgeon. Thirdly, if Jones's own chronology of when he actually wrote the poems is followed, then an interesting overlap appears between the months of their composition and the periods during which Jones was allowed writing materials in order to petition the Home Office and Parliament, or to sketch. Thus, his output peaked in the spring and early summer of 1849 (when ten poems were written) when he was busy drafting angry letters to the authorities, and again in the months following the decision of September 1849 to allow him a drawing-book (nine poems were written between this date and his release).[50] If the poems were indeed written in prison, then the evidence suggests that Jones had pen supplied, not denied.

Jones did produce something in prison: a series of landscape sketches in black ink and pencil.[51] Some were drawn from memory—

---

[49] *Red Republican* (10 Aug. 1850), 64; 'The New World', *NP* (3 May 1851), 5, 'To the British Democracy', *NP* (24 May 1851), 64; *Ernest Jones. Who is he?*, 7–8; Jones, 'The Prisoners of '48', *ME* (11 Oct. 1866), 4.

[50] The drawing-book was apparently used for poems as well: *Parl. Papers* (1851) xlvi, 337.

[51] BL Add Ms, 61,971A.

of his childhood home in Reinbek, of wicked uncle Hutton Annesley's house in Purbook. But most were allegorical. There was 'The English Town' (a vision of the factory town, with the brooding mills of Moloch, Mammon and Brothers, and of Baal and Co. dominating the foreground, and the barracks, gin-palaces, and new prison in the background, framing the parish church); 'The Prisoner's Dream' (a pastoral view through a cell window of a castle atop a hill, and a small church nestling in a village of cottages and carefully laid-out fields); 'The Grecian City' and 'Poesy and the three ages' (a triptych of 'classic', 'romantic', and 'medieval'). These were complex works of some considerable draughtsmanship, suggesting that Jones was adept at turning one pen to a variety of strokes and shades or, as seems more likely, that he in fact had a quiver-full of instruments from which to choose. They are also quite remarkable testaments of Jones's solitude and the way in which he recast personal grief, resentment, and aspiration in a visual form, opposing the pastoral bliss and feudal order of his past to the hellish condition of modern man, and also reasserting his own authority as a poet-observer. Jones's prison sketches might be read in a number of ways, but the significant point is that they were not intended for public consumption. Sketching belonged to the altogether quieter pursuits of hearth and home. On his release they were placed in an album and given to Jane as a present, and thereafter passed on to Jones's eldest son on his father's death. And there lies the conundrum of Jones's prison letters. All that can be said with certainty is that in prison he produced a series of dramatic ink-and-pencil drawings about which he remained silent, whilst he may or may not have written a hatful of poems which he never lost an opportunity to advertise. One was a very private form of atonement, even an explanation, to his wife and sons; the other was the means of recapturing the high moral ground of Chartist leadership.

Whatever the doubts about their authenticity, Jones's prison poems played an important part in the remaking of his political reputation in the ensuing months and years. In his absence new leaders such as G. W. M. Reynolds had risen to the leadership of the National Charter Association; O'Connor had begun to exert a tighter grip than ever on the *Northern Star* as well as to move back towards the more moderate reform programme of the radical MPs; and much of the momentum and personnel of Chartism had dissipated with the advent of greater opportunities for work, emigration, and, for the politically insatiable, involvement in more parochial concerns such as trade unions and town councils. Above all, as the next chapter describes, the Christian socialist movement had emerged in London, offering a mix of piety and political economy which was not altogether different from Jones's own apostolic socialism. Jones needed a gimmick to win back the sort of audience he had become used to before his imprisonment. In the longer term, and with the benefit of hindsight, Jones's suffering in prison guaranteed him inclusion in the modern pantheon of 'hunger artists'—Fenians, suffragettes, and communists—whose incarcerated bodies became noble sites of protest against the treatment meted out by the British state.[52] At the time, however, Jones's revelations, with their stories of blood, sacrifice, and salvation, belonged to a less refined and altogether more salacious tradition of prison revelations—two parts the Marquis de Sade to one part John Bunyan. It was as melodramatic a return to political life as could be imagined.

[52] For later narratives of prison suffering, see: Michael Davitt, *Leaves from a Prison Diary, or Lectures to a Solitary Audience* (Shannon: Irish University Press, 1974); Barbara Green, *Spectacular Confession: Autobiography, Performative Activism and Sites of Suffrage, 1905–38* (London: Macmillan, 1998); Maud Ellman, *The Hunger Artists: Starving, Writing and Imprisonment* (London: Virago Press, 1993).

5
The Poor Man's Editor
1850–1859

HAVING BADE farewell to his loyal supporters in Halifax, Ernest Jones returned south to spend the last week of July, 1850 *en famille* at the seaside, amongst the bourgeois bathers of Hastings. From London Bridge they travelled third class, in an 'open cattle-box without roof or sides', and found a cheap lodging 'at the back of Hastings', where Jones sat down to 'work like a galley-slave'.[1] And work he did. For the next decade Jones devoted himself to running a series of periodicals and newspapers. There were six in all: *Notes to the People* (1851–2), the *People's Paper* (1852–8), the short-lived *London News* (1858), the *Cabinet Newspaper* (1858–60), and a pair of penny papers which bombed within weeks of commencement in the spring of 1860: the *Penny Times* and the *Weekly Telegraph*. As a newspaper proprietor Jones was not a success. He fell out with virtually all of his collaborators, and ended up in court with his greatest rival, G. W. M. Reynolds of *Reynolds's Newspaper*. Absent from London for weeks on end, his marriage deteriorated as Jane bore the brunt of the family's penury, eventually dying after a painful illness in 1857. Jones came near to insolvency on more than one occasion and was finally declared bankrupt in November 1859. And although he later made political capital out of the heart-rending poverty he endured as the 'people's friend' in the 1850s, the question arises, why did he sacrifice so much for so little?

The first and most obvious answer is hubris. Much to the consternation of his family, Jones decided to rejoin the leadership of the Chartist movement. Immediately on his release from prison plans were made to establish a newspaper under the joint editorship of himself and George Julian Harney, mainly as a means of reasserting

---

[1] Jones to Harney, 22 July 1850, repr. in F. G. Black and R. M. Black (eds.), *The Harney Papers* (Assen: Van Gorcum, 1969), 26–8.

a militant tone in Chartism.[2] In the autumn of 1850 Jones resumed his itinerant life as a Chartist lecturer and in the new year of 1851 he was re-elected to the executive of the National Charter Association. By 1853, with Feargus O'Connor terminally ill, Bronterre O'Brien drinking himself into an early grave, and Harney exiled in Newcastle, Jones had no serious rivals left. As John Saville has shown, Ernest Jones and Chartism became synonymous in the mid-1850s, and his newspapers—principally the *People's Paper*—became the organ of the movement.[3] But they were non-profit-making organs. Having found his Chartist vocation just as many thousands were losing theirs, Jones was left presiding over a dwindling movement. As a newspaper proprietor he quickly became locked into a cycle of falling circulation, rising debt, and endless, exhausting forays into the provinces in pursuit of an increased readership. As his friend Karl Marx might have observed, Jones spent much of the 1850s simply working to live, his newspaper product alienating him from his very being. At the same time, Jones could not afford to give up and thereby lose face to his creditors, to his critics, and to his assailants within the movement. As ever, pride and reputation mattered most. In these circumstances the fact that the *People's Paper* lasted as long as it did is quite remarkable. Equally, it is no surprise that Jones embraced bankruptcy in 1859 with some relief.

The second reason for Jones's persistence at the press during the 1850s is that he had few alternatives. Resuming his career at the bar was not an option in 1850, at least in London, where the dust on his dispute with the Middle Temple had yet to settle. At the end of 1851 Jones did make enquiries about joining the Northern Circuit in Liverpool, but concluded that there was insufficient work.[4] Later he would claim that he had turned down the opportunity in the early 1850s to join the radical solicitor W. P. Roberts in a practice but, although the two men were firm allies, there is no evidence until the 1860s that they mixed business and friendship.[5]

---

[2] J. Sketchley, 'Personal Experiences in the Chartist Movement', *Today*, 2 (July 1884), 28–9. The paper never materialized although Jones did help edit Harney's *Friend of the People*, which began publication in December 1850.

[3] John Saville, *Ernest Jones: Chartist* (London: Lawrence & Wishart, 1952), 53.

[4] Jones to Jane, 10 Dec. 1851, SC.

[5] CN (16 July 1859), 2; Raymond Challinor, *A Radical Lawyer in Victorian England: W. P. Roberts and the Struggle for Workers' Rights* (London: I. B. Tauris, 1990), chs. 12–13.

However, Jones turned to newspapers in the 1850s above all because he believed that they were a highly lucrative form of income. As he promised his wife Jane on the eve of the first issue of the *People's Paper* in the spring of 1852, the paper would be 'the provision for the future, the £10,000 a year'.[6] There were good grounds for such optimism. The years around mid-century saw the rise of a series of entrepreneurial figures in the popular press. Men such as Herbert Ingram, Douglas Jerrold and his son Blanchard, Edward Lloyd, and Reynolds himself made a great deal of money out of newspapers and magazines which combined *actualité* with entertainment, be that illustrations, serialized novels, household advice, or the simple staple fare of yore, namely tales from the Court and from the courts. Veterans of the ribald radical journalism of the 1830s and 1840s, many of these editors had no difficulty in combining the seriousness of the political sermon with the sensation of the latest scandal.[7] This was a market into which Jones sought to tap. Although the opening numbers of his first sole editorial venture— *Poems and Notes to the People* (its original title)—were defiantly puritanical in their repertoire, by the time of the *People's Paper* Jones was dashing off his own penny-dreadfuls, reproducing Irish horror stories and French melodramas, and the goriest titbits from the assizes and police courts. Some gardening tips were thrown in for good measure too. Throughout the 1850s, as this chapter describes, Jones hoped to make ends meet by mixing the politics of the poor with the literature of the 'million'.

    [6] Jones to Jane, 4 Apr. 1852, SC.
    [7] Virginia Berridge, 'Popular Journalism and Working-Class Attitudes, 1854–86: A Study of *Reynolds's Newspaper*, *Lloyd's Weekly Newspaper* and the *Weekly Times*', Ph.D thesis, University of London (1976); Aled Jones, *Powers of the Press: Newspapers, Power and the Public in Nineteenth-Century England* (Aldershot: Scolar Press, 1996), ch. 5; Rohan McWilliam, 'The Mysteries of G. W. M. Reynolds: Radicalism and Melodrama in Victorian Britain', in Malcolm Chase and Ian Dyck (eds.), *Living and Learning: Essays in Honour of J. F. C. Harrison* (Aldershot: Scolar Press, 1996), 182–98; Ian Haywood, 'George W. M. Reynolds and the Radicalization of Serial Fiction', *Media History*, 4 (1998), 121–39. For two recent studies of Herbert Ingram's *Illustrated London News*, see: Isabel Bailey, *Herbert Ingram of Boston, Esq. MP: Founder of the Illustrated London News, 1842* (Boston: Richard Kay, 1996); Peter W. Sinnema, *Dynamics of the Pictured Page: Representing the Nation in the Illustrated London News* (Aldershot: Ashgate, 1998).

I

Jones entered a changed political landscape on his release from prison. In defeat many of the Chartist leaders had turned to a more socialist-sounding agenda: 'the Charter and something more'. It was a slogan inspired by the brief workers' republic in Paris of 1848. Jones, who resumed friendships with that hardy Jacobin Harney, with Marx and Friedrich Engels, and who in the mid-1850s took up the cause of some of the leading French exiles—most notably Armand Barbés—has often been claimed as the principal English exponent of Chartist socialism, immortalized in Marx's description of him as 'the only *educated* Englishman . . . entirely on our side'.[8] But although Jones endorsed the new programme of the 'Charter and something more' on several occasions in 1851, and indeed rubbed editorial shoulders with the great communist, his instincts on his release were to return Chartism to the political agenda of 1846, at the heart of which lay the land and the church.

The summer over, Jones returned to the lecture platform at the beginning of September 1850, undertaking an intensive tour through the Midlands, into West Yorkshire, and then on to Teesside and Tyneside. He then crossed the border into Scotland where, despite being told of Jane suffering a miscarriage,[9] he pressed on as far north as Aberdeen before returning down the west side of the country via Glasgow, Carlisle, and Lancashire, back across the Midlands, arriving in London in the second week of November. A month later, at the height of the controversy over the 'Papal aggression', Jones completed his comeback by delivering two lectures on the topic of 'Canterbury versus Rome' in the Mechanics' Institute in Chancery Lane. The tour took up where his welcome at Halifax in July had left off, especially when he reached the West Riding. There were musical bands and carriages laid on to greet him, sumptuous teas, and Sunday sermons. Outside Bingley, at a rocky outcrop known as the

[8] Friedrich Engels to Karl Marx, 29 Jan. 1869, repr. in Saville, *Ernest Jones*, 247. This line of interpretation began with Hermann Schlüter's *Die Chartisten Bewegung: Ein Beitrag zur Socialpolitischen Geschichte Englands* (New York: Socialist Literature Co., 1915), and has since been maintained by Theodore Rothstein, *From Chartism to Labourism: Historical Sketches of the English Working Class Movement* 2nd edn. (London: Lawrence & Wishart, 1983); Saville, *Ernest Jones*, 38, 40; Margot Finn, *After Chartism: Class and Nation in English Radical Politics, 1848–1874* (Cambridge: Cambridge University Press, 1993), 137–41.

[9] J. G. Atherley to Jones, 16 Sept. 1850, SC.

'Druid's Altar', Jones preached to a large gathering with such effect that it was agreed that his name and the dates of his imprisonment should be engraved onto the rock-face. At Leeds a special Chartist hymn was sung in his honour. People came from twenty miles away to hear him in Sheffield, and 12,000 gathered in Nottingham at one of his two meetings there. Much of his tour was taken up with the story of his incarceration, and from Scotland he sent back to Harney donations collected on behalf of the remaining Chartist prisoners. On other occasions he offered his reflections on 1848, concluding that without organization, people's risings were doomed to failure and betrayal. But Jones also had one lecture that he kept returning to again and again during his autumnal tour: 'Bread and Freedom.'[10] In it he described the depopulation of the countryside that was taking place, as more people were forced off the land into manufacturing, where wages were falling and starvation conditions prevailed. Delving into statistics, he argued that 'disease and crime had increased in a fearful ratio, as the people had been withdrawn from the natural labour field into the artificial labour market', and now they were heading for the 'gaol and the grave'. If only Britain, like ancient Sparta, Athens, and Rome, or modern-day Belgium, France, and Switzerland, would adopt the small-farm system, and return to an economy based on cultivation of the soil, then her current social problems would be solved. There was more than enough fertile land to go around. Jones calculated there was enough for 2 acres for every family.

Jones also turned to history in the other major theme of his come-back lectures: the state church. On two successive Sunday evenings at the beginning of December he gave long and learned (or at least heavily footnoted) accounts of the origins and first millennium of Christianity.[11] In the aftermath of the Gorham controversy and the Protestant reaction to Pope Pius IX's reassertion of the Catholic hierarchy in Britain, Jones's retort was, predictably, along the lines of a

---

[10] *NS* (7 Sept. 1850), 1; (21 Sept., 1850), 5; *Red Republican* (21 Sept. 1850), 108 (19 Oct. 1850), 140.

[11] *Lectures by Ernest Jones: Canterbury versus Rome* (London: Edwin Dipple, 1851). An abridged penny version of the lectures was published after Jones's death: *The Horrible Inquisition of Rome* (Nottingham: C. J. Shelton, 1880). Having attended the first lecture, Jenny Marx described it as 'marvellous, and by English standards, advanced, though not quite *à la hauteur* for us Germans who have run the gauntlet of Hegel, Feuerbach, etc.': Jenny Marx to Engels, 2 Dec. 1850, *MECW* xxxviii. 251.

plague on both sectarian houses. However, his lectures do make interesting reading, for the primitive apostolic Christianity that they express offers an insight into his own sense of political mission in the months after his release from prison. Jones took as his setting the city of Rome at the fall of the empire. There, in the most decadent empire, in its meanest province, and amongst its most despised people, 'rose a humanised God, a deified man, proclaiming to a bleeding and prostrate race the Gospel of peace, liberty and love'. Based on love and neighbourliness, Christ's teaching took hold, but after a century 'the beautiful fabric' began to decay as the early Christian church was overrun by the ambition and avarice of its leaders, who began to create false distinctions between laity and clergy, and who practised the sale of livings. With the death of the apostles, the priesthood took over the word of Christ and blinded people into superstition. And the doctrine of Christianity began to admit an unnecessary 'Persian dualism' of flesh and spirit, evil and good, to which the only response was a life of asceticism and monasticism. For the next thousand years the church of Rome and then, latterly, the Church of England insti-tutionalized this appropriation of Christianity, victimizing or excommunicating those valiant few, like Wycliffe, the Lollards, or the Presbyterians, who attempted a real reformation of the Christian tradition. Jones warmed up his London audience with horrific details of various tortures and burnings at the stake inflicted on religious reformers, particularly hapless Scottish women, and concluded with the declaration that only the poor remained the true apostles and martyrs of truth.

There was thus little of 'the Charter and something more' in Jones's autumnal oratory. Although he confided to Harney back in the summer that he was working his way through a two-year back-log of '105 stars' (i.e. the *Northern Star*), when the platform summoned he resorted to his old battle-cry of the meek inheriting the earth below and the heavens above. The same is true of the poetry he produced once out of prison. Nowhere is this clearer than in the long lyric poem 'The New World', which he wrote during the late summer or early autumn of 1850.[12] This poem, republished as 'The Revolt of Hindostan' in 1857, became one of the most highly regarded ever penned by Jones. It also proved to be the last long lyric that he

---

[12] 'The New World' was originally advertised for publication on 1 Sept. 1850: *Red Republican* (10 Aug. 1850), 64, but it did not appear until the first issue of the *Notes to the People* (3 May 1851), 1–15.

composed. It combined the plot of his earlier chivalric tales, such as 'Corayda' and 'Lord Lindsay', with the pastoral vision of *Chartist Poems* and a cyclical view of history which was not so much *Communist Manifesto* as a modern version of the fall of Rome. As its title suggested, the poem was both a celebration of and a warning to America, the sanctuary of fleeing Europeans, where 'kingcraft and statecraft' were absent and an empire not of arms but of 'the Saxon tongue' held sway. In the poem America is contrasted to England, and the expansion of England in the East is offered as a warning to America's bulging West, offering untold riches for 'the huxtering judge, the pandering peer, | The English pauper, grown a nabob here!' But, so the poem continues, wealth and dominion overseas bring faction at home, the country collapses, and a sad and sickly youth ascends the throne. He is conspired against by the nobles, who overthrow and execute him. The people now expected a kingless paradise, but instead are thwarted by the nobles who restore a 'tinsel crown'. However, the nobles in turn are conspired against by the middle classes, who induce the populace to turn on the landlords and '[t]he suffering masses, unreasoning in their grief, | Grasp at each straw that promises relief'. Instead, they find the middle class imposing new laws and raising prices, insisting on the emigration of labourers in sinking ships, and turning the poor into spies on their own sort. Adding insult to injury, the priesthood offer up pious support for 'reckless Mammon', admitting that:

Tis true, the Scriptures of the poor man speak—
Of lands, goods, freedom, ravished from the weak—
Of tyrants crushed—and people's fetters rent—
But all that's only *spiritually* meant

But the fable ends happily, for in '[a]n army raised and generalled of God', the people rebel and turn out the 'gold kings', paving the way for the awakening of the nations of Africa and the return of the exiled Jews. Thus a moral is proved:

Man owns no nobler name than that of MAN—
No holier law than CHRIST's great law of love,
His guide within him, and his Judge above—
Freed evermore from soldiers, nobles, kings,
Priests, lawyers, hangmen and all worthless things

Jones may or may not have been familiar with the *Communist*

Manifesto by the summer of 1850; there is a whiff of historical materialism to 'The New World'. In the poem, as in Marx and Engels' famous tract, each social order digs its own grave by allying with the forces that must inevitably destroy it. But Jones's version of the historical cycle is based on the classical trope of commerce corrupting landed virtue, and not on the emergence of modern industry. His vision of the ideal society is a Christian republic of small cultivators, not a propertyless state. And his depiction of revolution is that of a 'deluge' in which a people rediscovers its religious faith and throws off its monied and clerical oppressors, rather than a seizure of political power in which class-conscious industrial workers appropriate the means of production.

Not everyone within the remnants of the Chartist movement welcomed Jones's triumphant reincarnation as a righteous apostle. By the time he was re-elected to the executive of the National Charter Association in January 1851, there was considerable resentment amongst Manchester Chartists at the 'dictatorial' manner in which he and Harney were applying the brakes on attempts to couple Chartism to the more moderate parliamentary reform programme of the National Parliamentary and Financial Reform Association. A long stand-off ensued between Chartists in the capital and Chartists in the north-west, with Jones and Harney attempting to stymie the Manchester Chartists' conference in February, and the Manchester Chartists in turn cold-shouldering the NCA's London convention held in the Parthenium Rooms in St Martin's Lane at the beginning of April.[13] The NCA emerged victorious from the dispute, with its much better-attended convention agreeing to a twelve-point programme of principles, to be campaigned for without assistance from any other 'political movement or alloy [sic]'.[14] Reynolds, O'Connor, and other Chartist notables took part in the convention, but it was Jones who masterminded the ten days of proceedings. What he ended up committing the Chartists to makes interesting reading. It was not so much the 'Charter and something more' as the Charter and something missing.

Jones's twelve-point programme of desirable Chartist ends was prefaced with a preamble of intended means. Predictably it rejected

---

[13] For the background, see: Saville, *Ernest Jones*, 43–4; J. R. Clinton, 'The National Charter Association and its Role in the Chartist Movement, 1840–58', MPhil. thesis, Southampton University (1980).

[14] *NS* (5 Apr. 1851), 7–8; (12 Apr. 1851), 7–8.

co-operation with the middle classes,[15] and recommended that Chartists stick to the six points, contest municipal as well as parliamentary elections, and enter into discussions with trades unions. A little-known 'clause IV' called for 'missionaries' to go into the agricultural districts to address farmers and labourers, as well as the Irish people, colliers, miners, and railway workers. The programme that followed called for nationalization of the land with due compensation to current owners and the land to be let out to individuals or associations, disestablishment of the Church (with all clerical appointments reverting to congregational control), national compulsory schooling (including technical schools to replace apprenticeship), a centralized co-operative system, abolition of parochial relief and its substitution by remunerated labour on the land, taxation of accumulated landed wealth but not industry, liquidation of the national debt, unspecified currency reform, reform (but not dissolution) of the army and the navy, training in militias for all men over the age of 15, and repeal of the 'taxes on knowledge'. On industrial, urban Britain, the 1851 Chartist programme, signed, sealed, and delivered by Jones, had little to say.

No one took clause IV of the new Chartist programme more seriously than Jones. For the rest of 1851 he devoted himself to working as a Chartist 'missionary'. At the beginning of May, after plans to co-edit the *Friend of the People* with Harney came to nothing, Jones started up his own *Poems and Notes to the People* ('*Poems*' was dropped after thirteen issues), published by the Strand house of Pavey. In its political columns a largely rural agenda unfolded. And in August Jones was back on the road again, this time commencing his lectures down in the West Country and in Wales, before heading back to the Midlands and the West Riding of Yorkshire. Jones's commitment to proselytizing the cause of land reform was spelled out in the second issue of his new magazine. 'Look to the rural districts!' he declared, '[t]hey lie—those mental deserts, stretching away beneath the drought of ignorance, and thirsting for the dew of knowledge'.[16] Of all the points of the new Chartist programme, Jones gave most coverage to land nationalization. The 'earth itself is the fundamental capital', he wrote at the end of May 1851, 'the

[15] During the convention O'Connor went as far as declaring that he 'would rather see the working man represented in parliament by landlords than the middle class': *NS* (5 Apr. 1851), 7.

[16] 'The Middle-Class Franchise', *NP* (10 May 1851), 33.

capital of the human race, which in return for labour, yields them, as interest, the means of life'. The earth had been given to Adam by God as a trust.[17] Trade, by contrast, was no more than a 'flitting phantasm', which could only be kept going by war and overseas conquest—by the 'cannonballs of China' and the 'bayonets of Scinde'. Jones retold the history lesson to which he had so often turned in 1846 and 1847: namely, that the origins of the present crisis lay in the feudal lords' decision, fuelled by the arrival of Huguenot and Walloon refugees, to switch from the production of corn to the manufacture of woollen goods, thus driving men off the land and into the factories.[18] It was a mistake to believe that free trade had improved the workers' lot, as claimed by complacent MPs, whom Jones heard at first hand when he attended Parliament in the middle of July.[19] The corollary of free trade had been emigration on a massive scale. Jones began a long series on the state of the British colonies—articles he was to republish on several occasions during the 1850s—warning of the inhospitable landscapes and dire forms of misgovernment that awaited the unsuspecting emigrant. There were sketches of the Cape, where the British brutally suppressed the Boers in the name of humanity; of Australia, where convict society flourished in all its horror and Mammon controlled the ownership of land; of the rotten treatment meted out to labourers by the New Zealand Company; and of the Canadas beset with national debt.[20]

For Jones the immediate way out of the free-trade purgatory into which the British working class had been plunged was the revival of the home market. This would be achieved on the one hand by nationalization of the land, as the 1851 Chartist programme had prioritized, and by point number 4 of the same programme: a national system of co-operative production in trade and industry. Hot on the heels of his skirmish with the Chartists of Manchester, the principle of co-operation became the second battle which Jones

[17] 'Letter II on the Chartist Programme', NP (31 May 1851), 73.

[18] 'The Decline of the Middle Class', NP (21 June 1851), 154; 'A Letter to the Aristocracy', NP (5 July 1851); 'The Law of Supply and Demand', NP (13 Sept. 1851), 390–3.

[19] He went to the House of Commons to hear the debate on his imprisonment: 'The General Good: A Letter to the Secretary of the Board of Trade', NP (26 July 1851), 244.

[20] 'Our Colonies', NP (14 June 1851), 134–7; 'Our Colonies. I. The Cape', NP (28 June 1851), 170–2; 'Our Colonies. III. Australia', NP (19 July 1851), 230–4; (26 July 1851), 249–52; 'Our Colonies', NP (23 Aug. 1851), 340; 'Our Colonies', NP (27 Sept. 1851), 436–7.

fought out in the post-prison campaign to restore his political reputation. Co-operative schemes—or systems of 'associative' labour as they were also known—became widespread in some of the clothing and publishing trades at mid-century. The idea of co-operation was fairly straightforward: eliminate the middle-man, let the producers of goods do their own buying of raw materials and (especially) selling of the finished product. The origins of the co-operative movement were diverse, but the most commented-on by 1851 were those in the tailoring and printing trades of London pioneered by the Christian socialists, that is to say, the author and cleric Charles Kingsley and Edward Vansittart Neale.[21] To these men and their ideas Jones took particular exception. He objected to co-operative labour on the reasonable grounds that it upheld the profit motive, merely rewarding the few shareholders in the scheme with a dividend, and it could easily be circumvented by employers and masters, who could turn to an overstocked labour market for an alternative and cheaper supply of labour. Along the same lines, Jones spoke out in 1851—and was long remembered for so doing—against trades unions, for he believed that they encouraged sectionalism amongst the trades and made it easier for employers to undercut high wage demands by recruiting non-unionized men. Jones backed a centrally managed system of co-operation in which the profit appropriated from the middle-man was put into a central fund from which land and machinery might be purchased.[22]

Typically, Jones attacked the medium much more than the message. It was not very edifying. He warned the readers of the *Notes to the People* that the Christian socialists were 'Lawyers, Parsons, and Doctors, those still wishing to govern you even in the workshop', that their defence of the profit motive made them as bad as the usurious Jews who tyrannized the tailors of east London, and

---

[21] Edward Norman, *The Victorian Christian Socialists* (Cambridge: Cambridge University Press, 1987), ch. 5; Philip N. Backstrom, *Christian Socialism and Co-operation in Victorian England: Edward Vansittart Neale and the Co-operative Movement* (London: Croom Helm, 1974).

[22] 'A Letter to the Advocates of the Co-operative Principle, and to Members of Co-operative Societies', *NP* (10 May 1851), 27–31; 'Co-operation, What it is, and What it Ought to be', *NP* (20 Sept. 1851), 407–11; 'Trades' Grievances', *NP* (27 Sept. 1851), 421–3; 'The Co-operative Movement. Being a Letter from E. Vansittart Neale, and a Reply Thereto', *NP* (11 Oct. 1851), 470–6; 'The Co-operative Movement', *NP* (8 Nov. 1851), 543–6; 'Reply to Mr. Vansittart Neale', *NP* (22 Nov. 1851), 584–8; 'Trades' Grievances', *NP* (24 Jan. 1852), 758–64; 'Trades' Grievances', *NP* (13 Dec. 1851), 638–41.

that their evangelical piety was a cloak for hard-nosed advocacy of emigration.[23] And of course they opposed the Charter, and indeed any meaningful political reform. Kingsley, burlesqued by Jones as a parsimonious cleric, and Neale, whom Jones dismissed as an unreliable lawyer from Lincoln's Inn, were the main targets of Jones's savagery, but he also took part at Halifax in January 1852 in two nights' debate with a Manchester co-operative lecturer, the inevitably named Lloyd Jones.[24] On that occasion Ernest Jones was adamant that his was the 'policy of truth'. The co-operative system could only proceed once political power had been won. Lloyd Jones disagreed, and won a moral victory by asking the audience why his opponent spoke in such a loud voice.

At one level, the amount of vituperation directed by Jones at Kingsley and Neale is difficult to understand. To some extent there was a turf war going on, as both Jones and his Christian socialist foes vied for support amongst East End radicals such as John Bezer and Athol Wood.[25] But by the mid-1850s the differences between Jones's version of co-operation and that of the Christian socialists was minimal, with Jones's Labour Parliament of 1854 giving its backing to the very small-scale industrial associations and life-insurance schemes that Jones had attacked three years earlier. And in the West Riding of Yorkshire some of Jones's most loyal support during the remainder of his life came from the co-operative movement.[26] As ever, what lay behind Jones's animus was a sense of competition. Kingsley, the best-selling creator of *Alton Locke* (1850), acclaimed as *the* Chartist novel of its generation, and Neale, a landowning barrister, were rivals to Jones's vocation as a better sort devoting

[23] 'The Co-operative Movement', *NP* (10 Jan. 1852), 729; 'Reply to Mr. Vansittart Neale', *NP* (22 Nov. 1851), 584–8; 'A Few Words to Parson Lot', *NP* (29 Nov. 1851), 606–9.

[24] 'Discussion at Halifax', *NP* (7 Feb. 1852), 793–806; *Huddersfield and Holmfirth Examiner* (31 Jan. 1852), 8. On Lloyd Jones, see: G. J. Holyoake, *The History of Co-operation*, 2 vols. (London: T. Fisher Unwin, 1906), i. 232–3.

[25] For Bezer, see David Vincent, *Testaments of Radicalism: Memoirs of Working Class Politicians, 1790–1885* (London: Europa Publications, 1977), 149–51. Jones criticized Wood's call for a 'United Co-operative League': *NP* (20 Dec. 1851), 656–7.

[26] For the Labour Parliament, see below. For Jones's followers who were co-operators, see: Joseph Greenwood, 'Reminiscences of Sixty Years Ago', *Co-Partnership*, 16 (1910), 138; John A. Hargreaves, 'Guns and Roses: Benjamin Wilson (1824–1897) of Salterhebble, Chartist and Horticulturalist', in John Billingsley (ed.), *Aspects of Calderdale* (Barnsley: Wharncliffe Books, 2002). For Jones's changed view of co-operation in the 1860s, see: Neville Kirk, *The Growth of Working Class Reformism in mid-Victorian England* (Beckenham: Croom Helm, 1985), 151–2, 156–7, 167.

1. Ernest Jones in 1847

2. Kearsney Abbey, near Dover

3. Tothill Fields Prison, Westminster (from H. Mayhew and J. Binney,
The Criminal Prisons of London, 1862, p. 359)

4. 'The English Town' (prison drawing, 1849)

5. 'The Prisoner's Dream' (prison drawing, 1849)

6. Scene from Jones's *The Lass and the Lady* (1855)

7. Ernest Jones, Barrister-at-Law, 1866

8. Ernest Jones, Reform League lecturer, 1866

9. 'A Losing Game'
(Manchester election
cartoon, 1868)

10. 'The Manchester and
Salford Return Trip'
(Manchester election
cartoon, 1868)

their talents and wealth to the people. Amidst so many gentlemanly leaders a line of demarcation needed to be drawn, in print and on the platform.

Within a few months of commencing *Notes to the People* Jones started out on the second major lecturing tour of his post-prison years. In doing so he offered his readers some words of explanation. First, he pointed out the difficulties in the way of real bona-fide working men undertaking lectures. They could not, as they were not paid, consequently, '[t]heir cause is of a necessity entrusted to men of another class—to rich men, or to designing men, whom bribery may indemnify for expense they could not otherwise afford'. Secondly, reporting back from his tour, Jones likened himself to a missionary, comparing the people to a 'vast harp, that requires tuning into harmony'. Discord had to be overcome, and like the church there had to be 'sameness of teaching' despite there being so many sects.[27] Appropriately enough, Jones's first port of call was Exeter, where his old friend Archer Gurney was now curate. Gurney had written to Jones on his release from prison, informing him of a letter of his published in the *Leader*, and joking with him about his politics.[28] Jones lectured at Exeter on 'Class Laws versus the Law of God and Man' and, in a familiar ritual, challenged Gurney to a debate which duly took place. At Exeter Jones's bucolic obsession resumed. Around the town he found 'glorious woodlands, splendid parks, rich prairies', but not a single cottage, for the makers of this paradise were now 'dying, gasping, perishing' in the factory towns. If only, he wondered out loud, 'the dying factory child' could be brought to the 'flowery upland' of Devon.[29] From Devon he continued his journey through Bristol and into Wales where, not surprisingly, he found his name to be 'worth anything' and declared to Jane that so patriotic did he feel that he would set up a 'sovereign republic' there. To the *Northern Star* he reported back that a 'more fertile field of Democracy could not be found' than in Wales and the West Country.[30] His

[27] 'The Economy of Public Meetings', *NP* (9 Aug. 1851), 293; 'A Chartist Tour', *NP* (27 Sept., 1851), 429.

[28] Gurney to Jones [n.d, *c*.Aug. 1850], SC. Gurney quipped that Jones's children would not be 'levellers', for they had too much aristocratic blood in them, although they might erect 'an individual and Supreme Despotism for themselves over the levelled world at large'. Gurney's article defending the Sabbath appeared in the *Leader* (3 Aug. 1850), 446.

[29] *NS* (16 Aug. 1851), 1; 'A Chartist Tour', *NP* (11 Oct. 1851), 477–9.

[30] Jones to Jane, 15 Aug. 1851, SC; *NS* (23 Aug. 1851), 1. Judging from the derogatory rhyme about a thieving Welshman which was published in *Notes to the*

mood soured as he moved back into the English factory towns. Birmingham was 'infernal' and 'enough to turn a cat sick', Bury 'filthy', and he detested the Potteries. There were no more wild flowers (which he had been picking on his way and sending to Jane), and there was much apathy until he reached Peterborough, where sublime nature returned. In spite of a storm (he sheltered under an 'umbrageous oak') and the local clergy trying to scare people away, he spoke to a gathering of 500 people from the surrounding villages. Audiences improved in the West Riding and in Manchester, and Jones was particularly gratified by the temperance soirée organized for him in Bingley. But as he hurried south in the middle of September he was more convinced than ever that it was into the rural districts that Chartist missionaries needed to be sent. In 'squire-parson-farmer and lawyer-ridden' villages such as North Crowley in Buckinghamshire the real class enemy lay, and the only solution—two acres and a cottage—was to be found.[31] Jones himself could barely manage two rooms with a view. He reached London in time for the birth of his fourth son, Walter, promising Jane that they would move from their 'birds' nest' in Bayswater and that he would never venture so far and for so long again.[32]

2

As well as enrolling new Chartists, Jones's tour of 1851 was a moneyspinner, insofar as he was also enlisting new subscribers to the *Notes to the People*. Alongside its political columns and reports of trades' conditions, the magazine carried entertainment and amusement. With Parliament debating the removal of the remaining restrictions on the press, and opinion in some quarters fearing the result would be a deluge of obscene publications, Jones promised instruction and not titillation in his new title. He would not 'pander to the sensuality of the public by meretricious writing', nor would he 'degrade the literature of democracy to the level of the streetwalker'. He stood up for the poor man's reading habits, denying *The Times*'s strictures that it was all 'murder, theft, sensuality and anarchy'.[33]

People, Jones was more taken with the country than its inhabitants: 'On a Welshman', NP (11 Oct. 1851), 465.

[31] Jones to Jane, 18 Aug. 1851, 5 Sept. 1851, 14 Dec. 1851, SC; NS (6 Sept. 1851), 1; (13 Sept. 1851), 1.

[32] Jones to Jane, 27 Aug. 1851, SC.

[33] 'Words to the Reader', NP (25 Oct. 1851), p. iii; 'Copy of a letter Forwarded to

Thus *Notes to the People* carried histories—of Sparta, Rome, and Florence—a series on the 'superstitions' of different races, and, of course, poetry and novels. Much of it was a good read, some (especially the history) a hard read, but when it came to the novels it proved difficult for Jones to keep it a wholesome read.

Notes to the People began life as a vehicle for the poems Jones had written during the course of the previous year: 'The New World', the 'Beldagon church' trilogy (dedicated to his Halifax supporters), 'The Painter of Florence' (dedicated to Harney), and the cycle of so-called 'prison poems'. Rural and spiritual themes ran side by side in the poems. 'Beldagon church' appeared in the second number of the new venture and it saw Jones back to his apostolic best. In the poem he contrasted the 'deep sepulchral gloom | That turns a church into a tomb' and the lewd sculpture distracting those gathered from their prayers, with the scene outside the service, where

> Every whispering leaf's a preacher,
> Every daisy is a teacher,
> Writing on the unsullied sod
> Revelation straight from God.[34]

The 'Painter of Florence' compared a decadent modernity, personified in the ghastly Lord and Lady Devilson (he a tuft-hunting lawyer, she the daughter of a poor peer), with the virtuous nobility of medieval Florence, whom the poet-narrator had seen depicted in an Old Master on the Devilsons' wall.[35] The whole of the fourth issue of *Notes to the People* was given over to Jones's infamous prison poems, extensively advertised the previous summer.[36] Many of them were classic declarations of prison martyrdom, alternating between pathos and defiance. The 'Prisoner's Night Thought' told of '[h]is hope—to be a martyr, should he fail, | Or at best, to conquer—as he dies', whilst the 'Last Light', 'The Silent Cell', and 'Resignation' anticipated death, as did 'The Quiet Home': 'To a quiet land I'm steering; | Steering ever day and night, | . . . In a life-boat frail and slight'. Others spoke of undimmed faith in the muse, for instance,

---

the Editor of the *Times*', *NP* (27 Oct. 1851), 424. For the background, see: Ernest Jones, *Woman's Wrongs*, ed. Ian Haywood (Aldershot: Ashgate, 2001), 4–8.

[34] 'Beldagon Church, A Religious Poem', *NP* (10 May 1851), 21–7.

[35] 'The Painter of Florence', *NP* (17 May 1851), 41–7.

[36] Two poems which never appeared were also advertised the previous summer: 'Westminster Prison' and 'The Black Jury': *Red Republican*, (20 July 1850), 37; (10 Aug. 1850), 64; cf. 'To the British Democracy', *NP* (24 May 1851), 61–70.

'The Prisoner's Dream': 'Poesy! | Thro' thee I've felt my failing heart
again . . . | How care, pain, prison dwindled far behind | . . . There *is*
an empire in the mind.' The collection finished on an upbeat note,
with hopes of resurrection (described in 'St Coutts') and renewal,
summed up in 'Hymn for Lammas Day':

> Sharpen the sickle, how proud they stand,
> In the pomp of their golden grain . . .
>
> Though the ditch be wide, the fence be high,
> There's a spirit to carry us o'er,
> For God never meant his people to die,
> In sight of so rich a store.

Thereafter, *Notes to the People* featured less and less of original
poetry by Jones. There were some innocent ditties on nature: 'Sea
Shell', 'Trees', 'Too Soon', and 'To the Departed' (on flowers), 'Love
and Song' (on nightingales), and 'On Man' (on the earth as natural
bounty). And there were some weak attempts at narrative verse ('The
Slave Ship') and historical survey *à la* 'The New World' (for example,
'The Fishermen'—an analogy on the European powers). But apart
from the hard-hitting 'Marriage Feast', which was another onslaught
on clerical wickedness:

> . . . thou hypocrite priest,
> Who hast made of religion a mock!
> Who ever bade THEE to my feast,
> Over-gorged with the spoil of my flock . . .[37]

the evidence suggests that Jones's poetic fire had been extinguished.

Jones's waning faith in poetry as a political medium was gradual
but nonetheless marked. Increasingly in *Notes to the People* he fell
back on reproducing older poems of his own from the *Court Journal*
and the *Northern Star*, or published the work of foreign poets such
as Ferdinand Freiligrath and Edgar Allan Poe, other religious poets
such as Lamennais, and the great English and Irish rural poets:
George Crabbe, Tom Moore, and Jane Taylor.[38] The move was not
unheralded. Back in 1850 Jones had declared with a dramatic

---

[37] 'The Marriage Feast', *NP* (16 Aug. 1851), 314–15.
[38] For Freiligrath and *Notes to the People*, see: Christine Lattek, 'Ferdinand
Freiligrath in London', *Grabbe Jahrbuch*, 8 (1989), 101–30. On Jones and Crabbe,
see: Anne Janowitz, *Lyric and Labour in the Romantic Tradition* (Cambridge:
Cambridge University Press, 1998), 164.

flourish that his prison poems might well be his last, for '[t]he age had passed, when nations can be SUNG into liberty . . . enthusiasm is the child of an hour—conviction is the father of centuries'.[39] And now his last poems spoke of the poet as a spent force: 'We are dead and we are buried! | Revolution's soul is tamed', suggested the poem 'We are Silent', published in May 1851, whilst four months later 'The Hermit' described how 'He's buried in this gloomy den, | And he will rise—the Lord knows when'. Unusually for Jones, he allowed a contemporary to sum up his mood, republishing Robert Browning's 'Lost Leader' in the magazine at the end of November. Browning's cautionary tale of a turncoat patriot—a man whose followers '[l]earned his great language, caught his clear accents, | Made him our pattern to live and to die!', only for him to take their money and run—neatly captures the post-1848 scepticism of the younger English literary intelligentsia, and perhaps suggests that Jones was trying to distance himself from the militant politics he had espoused in 1848.[40]

The novel 'De Brassier', which began serialization in the second number of *Notes to the People*, offers the strongest proof that in 1851 Jones was endeavouring to cast off the guise he had worn three years previously. The novel, which ran over thirty issues, has been read as a moral tale on the folly of popular protest. Within months of its appearance erstwhile colleagues were rounding on Jones, accusing him of modelling his fictional characters on various living Chartists, including O'Connor and Thomas Allsop. Jones denied this, claiming that 'De Brassier' was simply a warning to Chartists not to fall in with scheming middle-class reformers.[41] Curiously, what no one then or since has really identified is the extent to which 'De Brassier' reworked themes from Jones's earlier works, conjuring up another semi-fictional, semi-autobiographical

---

[39] *Red Republican* (10 Aug. 1850), 64. Although it should be noted that a series of well-known songs by Jones do date from this period: 'The People's Anthem', *NP* (28 Mar. 1852), 933; 'The Song of the Low', *NP* (4 Apr. 1852), 953; 'The Song of the Poor', *NP* (11 Apr. 1852), 973; and 'The Song of the Future', *NP* (18 Apr. 1852), 993.

[40] Isobel Armstrong, *Victorian Poetry: Poetry, Poetics and Politics* (London, 1993), ch. 7.

[41] 'De Brassier' began life on 10 May 1851 as 'The History of a Democratic Movement, Compiled from the Journal of a Democrat, the Confessions of a Demagogue, and the Minutes of a Spy', becoming 'De Brassier, A Democratic Romance' on 7 June 1851. In 1855 Robert Gammage accused Jones of basing the eponymous villain on O'Connor in his *History of the Chartist Movement, 1837–1854*: (3rd edn., London: Merlin Press, 1976), 361. For Jones's own explanations of the purpose of the tale, see *NP* (21 Feb. 1852), 833–4.

caricature of the noble democrat. The clues are all there in the plot that unfolds.

'De Brassier' starts in a factory town, in a garret occupied by a widower, Charles Dalton, and his ailing sister Agnes, a seamstress. Dalton had been an overseer in a factory owned by Dorville, but had become involved in municipal politics, lost his job, and was now seeking parochial relief. This the guardians refused, suspicious of his claim that Agnes was his 'sister'. Caught up in the festivity of a royal visit to the town, the embittered Dalton attacks one of the poor-law officials in public, and is hauled off by the police. The royal festivities over, a people's meeting is held, and the story shifts focus to describe the man who ascends the platform to address the crowd: Simon de Brassier. De Brassier, like Percy de Vere and Carl Wonrad, is another fallen noble, though without any of the redeeming virtues of Jones's earlier characters. He is the second son of the second marriage (to a farmer's daughter) of a father who has no title but an impressive lineage. With an elder brother, Walter de Brassier, standing in the way of any inheritance, Simon de Brassier seeks a living at the bar, but becomes a gambler. With debts mounting and creditors in pursuit, he decides to try his luck in politics. Just as the people's meeting is about to get out of control, and the mayor is poised to read the Riot Act, De Brassier rises to speak, announcing that he has decided (as Jones had done in 1846) that after much deliberation he was going to set aside his wealth and devote himself to the popular cause. Denouncing the aristocracy, his former social set, and rounding on 'big-bellied' shopkeepers, De Brassier works the crowd into a frenzy, seeing off the plea made by Edward, a young mechanic, for order and calm. The scene then cuts to a pub, where a group of men end up in a drunken brawl after discussing the merits of socialism. Along with Dalton, the rioters are tried before the magistrates the next day. De Brassier unsuccessfully defends the brawlers, whilst Dalton, with his former employer Dorville, sitting on the magistrates' bench, is sentenced to transportation. Edward, the earnest young mechanic, offers to look after Agnes, although De Brassier, whose eye has been caught by Agnes's innocent beauty, offers her his assistance too.

With such a name, De Brassier is of course not all that he seems. The next of the dramatis personae to be introduced by Jones is Bludore, an unscrupulous financier, with whom De Brassier has concocted a scheme to speculate on falling stocks as civil commotion increases. The story and its sub-plots then thickened, partly because

Jones himself was then on a lecture tour and was hastily writing instalments en route. There is one sub-plot involving Cambric, the valet of De Brassier's elder brother Walter, who conspires to burn down some of the farms on the De Brassier estate. Another twist in the tale brings on William Latimer, a landed aristocrat fallen on hard times, who is the suitor of Adeline, the daughter of Dorville the factory-owner. Latimer is Carl Wonrad of 'Pride and Prejudice' redivivus, for he has been turned out of a job in the government bureaucracy for exposing corruption. He too has joined the democrats. The action now accelerates. The arson attacks on the De Brassier estate spread to Stanville Hall, the family mansion. One hundred thousand people—Edward and Agnes, now lovers, amongst them—march through the town, De Brassier at their head, demanding a sacred month of strikes. Edward again challenges De Brassier and calls for a rational plan of action, but the mob turn on him, beating him to the ground. The duplicitous De Brassier steps in to rescue him, Edward rejects his assistance, and Agnes, shocked at Edward's ingratitude is taken in by De Brassier's chivalry. The mob attacks the town's factory, but cunning Dorville has already over-insured his plant and machinery. Edward and Latimer try to restrain the violence, but are unable to prevent the death of Dorville in the fire. At this point in mid-October the serial petered out, no doubt because Jones was preoccupied with Jane's confinement and the birth of Walter, or perhaps because the somewhat incredible plot was collapsing under its own weight. 'De Brassier' resumed for five further episodes in February 1852. De Brassier summons a convention, seeking to see off his rivals amongst the democrats. There is another popular rising led by a tailor, the aptly named Hotwing, but aided and abetted behind the scenes by government-paid agents provocateurs. Many people are killed, but once order is restored De Brassier reappears, pursuing a seat in Parliament as a means of escaping the demands of his bailiffs. He makes it—just—the bailiffs appearing at the election hustings as he addresses the crowd. De Brassier identifies the poor bailiff as a spy and the crowd administer appropriate rough justice. Unnoticed, De Brassier removes the summons from the unconscious man's pocket. His place in the Commons now secure, De Brassier leaves for the Continent but hatches one last dastardly deed before he goes, precipitating an inquiry into his own election, the costs of which are eventually paid over by his opponent.

'De Brassier' can be interpreted in any number of ways.[42] To some extent it is a running commentary on the politics of the Chartist leadership in 1851–2, with Jones using fiction to make the case against hastily summoned conventions, capitulation to middle-class reform initiatives, and the radicalism of the pothouse. He was also trying to rescue democracy from the bad name that it had earned in 1848, hence the insertion into the story of Edward and Latimer, men of sense attempting to correct the 'plunder and sensuality' which characterize times of tumult. Above all, as with so many of Jones's characters, De Brassier is thinly veiled autobiography. Only Jones could construct a plot which involved scheming valets, vengeful sons denied their inheritance, claret-drinking lawyers, resilient bailiffs, and election meetings ending in injury. Life-experience was being turned into art-form. Indeed, it is hard to resist the conclusion that Jones was up to his usual tricks in offering De Brassier to his readers. After all, what was there to distinguish the story of Simon de Brassier, the well-heeled but out-of-pocket lawyer who joins the ranks of the democrats from nowhere, from the well-known story of Ernest Jones? Only one thing: their character. One epitomized duplicity, the other transparency. De Brassier's motives were those of an unscrupulous adventurer, whilst Jones's were, as he insisted throughout the disputes over the future of the Chartist organization in 1850–2, those of a patriot and beyond reproach.

Two weeks after the birth of his son Jones, the absent father and unreliable breadwinner, began a new serial in the *Notes to the People*: 'Woman's Wrongs.' In it he promised to 'paint life as it is— no poet's fancy, no romancer's dream', for 'the romance of fiction cannot equal the romance of truth'. The novel, told over the next five months, and reissued with additional chapters in 1855, was intended to 'lift the veil' on the domestic wrongs of society. Like a religious triptych or a series of Hogarthian scenes, 'Woman's Wrongs' featured separate stories from four different walks of life: the 'working man's wife', the 'young milliner', the 'tradesman's daughter', and the 'lady of title'. The plots of each, which sometimes seem to have been as carelessly constructed as that of 'De Brassier', can be briefly

---

[42] The best discussion of the novel remains Martha Vicinus, 'Chartist Fiction and the Development of a Class-Based Literature', in H. G. Klaus (ed.), *The Socialist Novel in Britain: Towards the Recovery of a Tradition* (Brighton: Harvester, 1982), 7–25.

summarized.[43] The first involves Mary, who is in a loveless marriage with Haspen, a Pimlico bricklayer. On losing his job, Haspen turns to drink and crime. He is caught, tried, and sentenced to transportation. Mary and her daughter Catherine move in with Barrowson, Haspen's former employer. Catherine is seduced by Barrowson and forced to go on the street, whilst Mary is packed off to run a pub in the country. Haspen returns and murders Barrowson in Mary's home, only to be caught by the police who are tipped off by Catherine, who saw Haspen and her mother disposing of the body. Mother and father end up on the gallows. The 'young milliner' was even more melodramatic. It begins in another garret in another part of London, this time near Gower Street, where lives a young hat-maker named Anna. She is pursued by a devious valet fallen on hard times named Treadstone, but falls in love instead with Trelawney, a young medical student from King's College. Treadstone, her land-lady, and her employer all combine to turn her out on to the street, from where the love-struck Trelawney rescues her. They enjoy a 'night of ecstasy' together, but Treadstone finds out that Anna has effectively become Trelawney's mistress. So too do Trelawney's rich parents, and he is tricked into giving her up. Back on the street, the now-pregnant Anna is taken in as a destitute by one of Trelawney's medical colleagues. The baby is lost, she dies, and in a macabre finale her body is unveiled on the dissecting table as a demonstration corpse in front of the unsuspecting Trelawney. In the 'tradesman's daughter', the third tale, pathos just about gets the better of sensation. Still in London, the reader is taken to Cheapside, to the counting-house where Laura works alongside her cousin Edward, a romantic sort from the country, 'full of enthusiasm and over-wrought poetry'. Laura, her mind dulled by repetitious work, is admonished by Edward when he catches her reading cheap illustrated romances. She confesses that her only other reading is the *Church of England Review* and the *Weekly Dispatch*, and he sets out to remedy this by lending her the 'best literature of the day' as well his own articles, penned 'in hope of literary fame'. Tragically for Edward, Laura is married off to her father's business partner, and crestfallen he gives up his office-job to try to make his name as an author. Soon he is on Grub Street, with a 'vampire' of a publisher taking his stories and repackaging them as penny-dreadfuls, and he falls into poverty and

---

[43] There is now a comprehensive modern edition: Ernest Jones, *Woman's Wrongs*, ed. Ian Haywood.

illness. But the literature he lent to Laura, 'like stray drips which ooze slowly through a rock', had awakened her feeling and now, in a loveless marriage, she falls ill pining for Edward. He seeks her out, but is turned away by a servant. She dies, he dies, but his name as an author becomes famous posthumously. The fourth tale, 'A Lady of Title' saw Jones back in 'Percy Vere' and 'De Brassier' territory in the home of the St Blaze family. At a fashionable ball Henry Darcy is pursuing the beautiful but heartless Lady Honora St Blaze. During a dramatic thunderstorm he reveals his love for her and contempt for the artifice that surrounds her. The storm abates, the quadrilles resume, and the moment is lost. For she is dissuaded from a match with Darcy, and as a mere pawn in a political intrigue, it is arranged that she marry instead Lord Parciment Cartoon, a Conservative who is attempting to relaunch his career by allying himself to Lady Honora's Whig father. Swayed by a love-letter from Darcy she resists Lord Parciment, but Parciment professes true love—expending, he confides, more rhetoric than was needed for three anti-corn law debates—and she gives in. Nine years on, the marriage is an unhappy one, she has had a string of lovers, and now proposes that her latest, Mr Vernon, move in to the house, displacing her daughter from her room. Here the serial ended in April 1852, but when Jones resumed it in 1855 Darcy reappears to marry Lady Honora's daughter.

'Woman's Wrongs' has been hailed as Jones's greatest literary achievement, insofar as it brings a strong dose of social realism and sympathy for women in dependent positions to the Chartist novel. In dramatizing the conditions of women as workers, or women as marriage chattel, Jones was contributing to a wider debate on the question of women's status in mid-Victorian Britain and, more specifically, breaking through some of the patriarchal attitudes which had long dominated the labour movement.[44] There is something in this, although it does smack of special pleading. Apart from some detail offered *en passant* about Anna's work as a milliner, there is very little about women's place in the economic system in the four books of 'Woman's Wrongs'. Moreover, there is a voyeuristic feel to all of the tales, through which women's bodies—as objects of sexual desire, marriage transaction, and corpses on the gallows—become offered up for consumption by a largely male readership.[45] Jones

---

[44] Jutta Schwarzkopf, *Women in the Chartist Movement* (London: Macmillan, 1991), 48, 51–2.
[45] *Woman's Wrongs*, ed. Haywood, 8–12.

may have been attempting to compete with other writer-editors such as Reynolds and Charles Dickens for women readers, but he ended up catering for decidedly male tastes, and capitulating to the ghoulish conventions of the melodrama.

In one way 'Woman's Wrongs' was not really about women at all. Rather than reading the novel as a pioneering example of social realism—a sort of poor man's poor Zola—we might see it instead as a further attempt by Jones to apply romantic ways of ordering the modern world. Before he launched into the fourth tale in the series, Jones explained his aims to his readership.[46] The first book, about the working man's wife, had shown the working of 'INSTINCTS' played on by misfortune. Haspen and his wife acted on impulse and were 'moulded by the rude grasp of . . . society' without a struggle. By contrast, in the tale of Anna the milliner, a class above Haspen, 'the HEART stands forth developed', but is crushed by the false sentiment or morality of society. In the 'tradesman's daughter', 'the next highest stage of prosperity', 'MIND steps into the foreground', and the heart of Laura is only reached through the brain, by exposure to Edward's poesy. Once reached, however, the feelings of the heart cannot be strangled by convention, for 'human nature is human nature after all'. Jones does not spoil the ending by revealing the moral of 'The Lady of Title', but it seems reasonable to conclude that, set in the 'loftiest platform of our social splendour', its theme would be artifice suppressing true feeling. In other words, Jones is suggesting that there is a hierarchy to the passions. The poorer the class, the ruder the impulse, and hence the more society shaped the destiny of the individual. Conversely, the higher the stage of society the more developed the heart, but also the more likely it was that feeling would be suffocated by form or convention. Thus the Edwards and Darcys of this world were required to speak to the captive heart, and free it from social constraint, but they seldom succeeded. Seen in this way, both 'De Brassier' and 'Woman's Wrongs' reveal a negative turn in Jones's continuing preoccupation with free will. In his Chartist poetry and his writings on poetics in 1846–8, Jones had seen poetry and the poet as a blunt instrument of emancipation, battering down the artificial distinctions of class and status imposed by society, and awakening the moral sentiment that lay in everyone. Now, in 1851–2, Jones's reasoning was more complex. Common

---

[46] *NP* (21 Mar. 1852), 913.

people were in too rude a state to overcome their impulses, whilst even amongst the more refined middle classes people were too bound by social convention to follow their hearts, and the nobility were too crafty and duplicitous to be trusted. In giving up the heady optimism of the lyric for the sombre inevitability of melodrama, Jones was signalling a sea-change in his hopes for humanity.

'De Brassier' and 'Woman's Wrongs' thus mark an interesting staging-post in Jones's political and literary development. Few probably noticed. *Notes to the People* sold intermittently. Jones took 250 copies with him on his lecture tour, but throughout the magazine's existence he complained of poor circulation and rivals' attempts to 'burk' advertising and sales.[47] To pay his way in the world he needed a newspaper and not a review. By the end of 1851 the prospects of this seemed as remote as ever. On the eve of the annual elections to the NCA Harney and Jones fell out over the future of Chartism: over the timing of a convention, over co-operation with other reform movements, and over Jones's plan for a small, paid Chartist executive. With O'Connor giving up the editorship of the *Northern Star* to Harney in December, Jones was sidelined. Out of the ashes a new venture arose. He reformed the defunct Chartist body in London—the Metropolitan Delegate Council—and in January 1852 announced the setting up of a fund to support a new newspaper: the *People's Paper*.[48]

3

The *People's Paper* began and ended with affidavits flying hither and thither across London. Yet for six and a half years Jones did manage to get out a weekly newspaper with a small, though constant, circulation. It never achieved the six-figure readership of *Reynolds's Newspaper* or *Lloyd's*. It did not even attain the 10,000 per week that Jones claimed at the outset he required to make a profit. And there were many weeks when sales barely nudged over the magic

[47] Jones to Jane, 11 Aug. 1851, 5 Sept. 1851, SC; 'The Burking System', NP (28 June 1851), 161; 'Words to the Reader', NP (25 Oct. 1851), pp. iii–iv.
[48] NS (29 Dec. 1851), 1; (20 Dec. 1851), 1; 'The Chartist Movement', NP (17 Jan. 1852), 743–5, 'A People's Paper', NP (24 Jan. 1852), 753–6. The battle for the Chartist leadership during the winter of 1851–2 can be followed from the different perspectives of the main protagonists in the following: Gammage, *History of the Chartist Movement*, 378–85; Saville, *Ernest Jones*, 48–9; A. R. Schoyen, *The Chartist Challenge: A Portrait of George Julian Harney* (London: Heinemann, 1958), 220–5.

3,000 mark, which Thomas MacGowan, the publisher of the *People's Paper* until his death from cholera in 1854, always said were needed in order to break even.[49] Nonetheless, the *People's Paper* found a market niche, selling somewhat more than papers such as the *Leader* and the *Nonconformist* and slightly less than the *Lady's News*. Between metropolitan free-thought and fashion, Jones thus found a place as a poor man's editor. However, there were a number of reasons why he never became rich out of the literature of the poor.

The first was capital. Throughout the previous two years Jones had been telling audiences up and down the country that the only capital that mattered was the land. But as his friend Karl Marx no doubt constantly reminded him, financial capital was crucial too. And he had none. The *People's Paper* was commenced with an appeal fund of £500 and only kept alive in the autumn of 1854 and again in the spring of 1857 by further appeals. The start-up costs of a newspaper in the 1850s were substantial. Aside from arranging advertising, printing, and publishing, under the existing law proprietors had to put up a security bond to cover any possible libel action in the courts. Although the costs to the newspaper reader came down during the mid-1850s, with the repeal of the advertisement duty in 1853 and the repeal of the newspaper stamp in the summer of 1855, for the newspaper owner the remaining taxes on knowledge—the paper duty and the security deposit—kept initial and ongoing overheads high. In 1852 Jones, whose credit was so bad that he was signing bills in his father's name, was in no fit state to take on such liability. Unlike Edward Lloyd, who only went into the business of a weekly newspaper after many years of publishing magazines and cheap novels, or Reynolds, who subsidized the early months of his newspaper with the profits from his bestselling *Mysteries of London*, Jones had no capital to plough into his new venture. Just as he had done over Kearsney Abbey in 1844, he rushed

---

[49] 'The People's Paper', *NP* (14 Feb. 1852), 813–16; Thomas MacGowan to Jones, 18 Oct. 1853, SC. For circulation figures of the leading Sundays and other popular papers up to 1855, see: 'Return of the Number of Stamps . . . Issued to Each Newspaper Published in . . . London . . . for Each Quarter in the Years, 1851–4', *Parl. Papers* (1854), xxxix; and for approximate estimates thereafter, see Virginia Berridge, 'Popular Sunday Papers and mid-Victorian Society' in G. Boyce *et al.* (eds.), *Newspaper History from the Seventeenth Century to the Present Day* (London: Constable, 1978), 247–64; Lucy Brown, *Victorian News and Newspapers* (Oxford: Oxford University Press, 1985), 52–3.

into risk when a more prudent man might have waited. In 1852 it took Jones four months to raise sufficient money to get the paper going, and much of that time was spent persuading readers of the *Northern Star* to switch their subscription to the new title.[50] Even when the stamp tax was abolished in 1855, and penny newspapers began to proliferate, Jones could not afford to lower his price. He would try enlarging the masthead, reducing the size of his typeface, chopping and changing his printers and paper suppliers, but he was never in a position to do more than just about make ends meet.

It is not surprising, therefore, that accusations of financial impropriety dogged him during the running of the paper in the 1850s. With margins so tight, borrowing here and there became the currency of friendship. Within months of the start of the paper, the committee which had managed the appeal broke out into conflict, alleging that Jones had pocketed the contributions that had poured in from different Chartist localities. The committee was led by Thomas Wheeler, the former London correspondent of the *Northern Star*, who had offered privately financial sureties of £50 to Jones, only to find himself imprisoned for debt six years later when Jones's creditors caught up with him. Jones refuted the complaints made by the committee, making the counter-claim that in fact he had put £100 of his own money into the venture, and he diligently furnished an audit of the paper's finances to support his denials. On that occasion Jones saw off his accusers, although at some price—most of them were the backbone of the Metropolitan Delegate Council.[51] In 1853 Jones was able to expand the size of the paper after receiving financial assistance from, among others, Jeremiah Briggs, a Derby solicitor. In 1854 the *People's Paper* became an illustrated weekly for several editions, following a generous input from the philanthropic stockbroker Thomas Allsop, O'Connor's friend (and said by some to be the model for Bludore in 'De Brassier'). And in 1855 Jones borrowed heavily from James Watson, the Newcastle newsagent and

[50] 'The Chartist Movement', *NP* (14 Feb. 1852), 818–22; 'The Chartist Movement', *NP* (28 Feb. 1852), 865–8; 'The Chartist Movement', *NP* (7 Mar. 1852), 880–3.

[51] Both sides of the 1852 dispute are chronicled in: 'Truth versus Falsehood' (handbill of the People's Paper Committee, 1852), SC, and *The People's Paper. Defence of Ernest Jones, as Read by Him at the Public Meeting* (London: The *People's Paper*, 1852), SC. For Wheeler's assistance to Jones: William Stevens, *A Memoir of Thomas Martin Wheeler. Founder of the Friend-in-Need Life and Sick Assurance Society, . . . with Extracts from his Letters, Speeches and Writings* (London: J. B. Leno, 1862), 76–7.

Unitarian lecturer, enabling the *People's Paper* to ride out the price wars of that year.[52] Many of these financial transactions came at some cost. Wheeler's loyalty was rewarded with the serialization of his novel 'A Light in the Gloom'. Briggs was able to conduct a long campaign for the reform of truck payments through the pages of the paper. And to Watson's benefit, Jones wrote a series of stinging denunciations of the evangelical lecturer Brewin Grant, who had taken Tyneside by storm in the early 1850s, attacking free-thought in all its different forms.[53] Some quid-pro-quo deals were manageable, others were not. Following MacGowan's untimely death in 1854 Jones returned to the publishing house of Pavey, and then in July 1857 enjoyed a temporary respite from the cheap and nasty end of the trade by giving the *People's Paper* to Holyoake and Co. to publish. Eventually in 1858 Jones 'mortgaged' the paper to the anti-sabbatarian activist and life-insurance entrepreneur J. Baxter Langley.[54] Langley exacted a higher price than previous lenders. Jones was left with two columns for Chartist news and correspondence, and had to put up with running the Political Reform League alongside Langley. Within a few years Jones had gone through a whole gamut of allies turned foes—Robert Gammage and James Finlen were two other prominent examples—and although political differences were sometimes the occasion of the trouble, money lent and not returned was usually the root.[55] By the time G. W. M. Reynolds began stirring up trouble over Jones's probity at the end of 1858, there were plenty of disgruntled witnesses ready to testify.

Part of the problem was that Jones was determined to keep up appearances. Throughout the difficult years of running the *People's Paper* Jones maintained the fiction that he was regularly dipping into

[52] Jeremiah Briggs to Jones, 28 Feb. 1853, Jones to Thomas Allsop, 2 Jan. 1854, 4 May 1854, Yale; James Watson to Jones, 3 May 1855, SC.

[53] 'The Light in the Gloom' was serialized in the *People's Paper* between 8 May and 14 Aug. 1852. For Briggs's campaign, see: *Wages of the People: A Labour Advocate and Ratepayer's Journal for the Payment of Wages without Stoppages* (Derby: W. Bemrose and Sons, London, 1858). For Jones's attack on Brewin Grant: *PP* (14 May 1853), 4.

[54] For Baxter Langley, see: J. Baxter Langley, *A Literary Sandwich* (London, 1855), and on his involvement in the anti-sabbatarian campaign, see: John Wigley, *The Rise and Fall of the Victorian Sunday* (Manchester: Manchester University Press, 1980), *passim*.

[55] In Feb. 1857 James Finlen and Robert Gammage attempted to establish a Chartist newspaper to rival the *People's Paper*. As late as 1892 George Howell found former colleagues of Jones who had retained not his only writings from the 1850s, but his IOUs as well: F. Boorman to Howell, 29 May 1892, Howell papers, BGI.

his own resources to keep the paper going. During his libel trial in 1859 he claimed that he had sunk £1,300 of his own money into the paper over the years.[56] He had not, for there were no such resources. Indeed, any profit made on the paper was earmarked for the maintenance of his family. Jones's correspondence with the long-suffering Jane is replete with details of collections made after lectures, stamps or postal orders sent home, strictures on the need for domestic frugality, and repeated promises to take the family away to the seaside. To the seaside they would go, but often without Jones. In September 1852, whilst the family went to Eastbourne, Jones remained in town fending off an unpaid butcher and informing Jane that he had not the money to pay for their return tickets. Similarly, in May 1854 Jane and the four boys enjoyed the sea air at Ramsgate, but Jones only made it as far as Chatham, where he gave a series of lectures on the state church.[57] For the most part Jones seems to have been scrupulous, only using monies raised on the lecture circuit to support the family. However, on at least one occasion he did instruct Finlen to pay Jane directly out of subscriptions for the paper.[58] Perhaps none of his Chartist followers would have minded a little embezzlement for the sake of his family, but it mattered to Jones, who not only insisted to his readers that the *People's Paper* paid its way, but that any surplus was being ploughed back into the activities of the wider Chartist movement. For Jones, poverty had to be noble and never ignominious. No wonder some readers began to get confused. Exasperated by yet another appeal for funds in 1857, a man named Wilkins from Bedminster bravely wrote into the paper asking what was happening to all the money. Jones, who had only ever mentioned Jane on one other occasion in the lifetime of the paper, played to the gallery, declaring that given his wife's precarious state of health, he needed all the pity and support his readers could muster.[59]

A second factor limiting the circulation of the *People's Paper* was its content. It was not so much that Jones should have followed his rivals like Reynolds or Lloyd in publishing a downmarket Sunday entertainment for the masses, instead of an upmarket Saturday

---

[56] *CN* (16 July 1859), 2.
[57] Ernest Jones to Jane, 20 Sept. 1852, 23 May 1854, SC; *PP* (27 May 1854), 4.
[58] Ernest Jones to Jane, 24 July 1853, SC.
[59] *PP* (11 Apr. 1857), 4. The only other occasion on which Jones mentioned Jane in the paper was to confirm that she was the last living descendant of the Plantagenets: *PP* (14 Jan. 1854), 4.

manifesto for the workers. It was simply that he should not have tried to do both. But he did. In the *People's Paper* and also in its successor, the *Cabinet Newspaper*, Jones attempted to run light amusement alongside heavyweight news, the news coverage devoted to the Chartist movement and labour conditions, parliamentary debates, and thunderous editorials from Jones. The entertainment side of the paper, which MacGowan for one much preferred, reveals Jones trying out a full range of styles and ideas, from the rational to the ridiculous. Unlike other editors, however, he never really settled on a tried and trusted formula. In the literary selections of the first two years of the *People's Paper* Jones carried on where *Notes to the People* had left off. His own poetry featured less and less. There were several republished classics from earlier collections in the *Labourer* and the first year of the *Notes of People*, but no more than a handful which seem to be new.[60] Jones continued to draw on an eclectic collection of poets. English rural utopias were out, and in their place were the plaintive Scots—David Gardiner of Dundee and Margaret Milburn. Jones kept up his penchant for Poe, and added to the ranks of the weird and wonderful with the Irish tales of Gerald Griffin.[61] He also proved to be much more mainstream in his repertoire than he had been in *Notes to the People*. Byron and Shelley featured, but they looked increasingly isolated amidst columns devoted to Elizabeth Roberts, Harriet Beecher Stowe, Charles Swain, and Martin Tupper. To his credit, Jones did make room for the poetry of working men. For example, he was an early enthusiast for the work of J. B. Leno, reproducing his 'Song of the Spade' in December 1853.[62] However, such patronage could sometimes spell trouble, as the cases of William Drew and Edwin Gill demonstrate.

William Drew was one of a growing number of working-class temperance poets emerging in the 1850s. Jones gave a great deal of coverage to the temperance and the teetotal movements in the *People's Paper*. He drew the line at prohibition—'men cannot be made sober by an act of Parliament'—but nonetheless carried on his campaign to detoxify Chartist localities. Jones reported the work of the Rochdale temperance advocate, Joseph Livesey, and he was

---

[60] The following unattributed poems were probably written by Jones: 'Our Trust' (10 July 1852), 'Song for the Next Rebellion' (14 May 1853), and 'The Reason Why' (25 Feb. 1854).

[61] On Griffin's stories see: Jacques Tissot, 'The Fantastic Vein in Gerald Griffin', *Cahiers du Centre des Études Irlandaises*, 7 (1982), 31–42.

[62] *PP* (15 Oct. 1853), 6; (31 Dec. 1853), 6.

particularly generous in the publicity he gave to St Luke's Young Man's Teetotal Society in London.[63] Drew was a member of this society, and Jones carried an appreciative review of his collection, entitled *The Poetry of Labour* (1853), which contained poems on needlewomen, American slaves, the 'Dignity of Labour', and many others with temperance themes.[64] This may not have been Jones's first acquaintance with Drew's work. In 1851 Drew had published another collection, entitled *Rhymes for the Times*. In February 1852 a set of poems with virtually the same title was published by Brettell, the Haymarket house, and credited to the author 'E. C. J'. The 1852 *Rhymes on the Times* featured seven poems, all of them doggerel satire and recognizably Jones's own work. Some, for example the verses on Derby, Palmerston, and Russell, were humorous sketches. However others, such as 'Victory of Lagos' (on the African slave squadron) and 'Reform', were racist and anti-Semitic.[65] Of course, it did not take a genius to compose a title such as *Rhymes on the Times*, though two with the almost the same name in the space of a few months suggests more than a coincidence. In the case of Edwin Gill, a power-loom weaver, Jones's relationship was more transparent. Gill's poetry was published in the *People's Paper* towards the end of 1852. Shortly afterwards, Jones took on Gill at the paper, and he was put in charge of the advertising department, much to Thomas MacGowan's despair, for Gill had a drink problem and was eventually sacked from the office two years later.[66] He too became part of the testimony against Jones in 1859.

In addition to poetry, several serial novels were also included in the first two years of the paper. As well as Wheeler's 'Light in the Gloom', there was a short story of pillage and plunder entitled 'The English in Ireland' by 'Sassenach' which ran over several issues. And Jones himself contributed three novels: 'Lovers and Husbands, or the Wrongs of Man', 'The Lass and the Lady', and 'The Maid of

<hr />

[63] *PP* (16 June 1855), 1; cf. *PP* (13 Nov. 1852), 4; (11 Dec. 1852), 6; (22 Oct. 1853), 3.

[64] William Drew, *The Poetry of Labour, With a Sketch of the Author's Life* (London: W. Horsell, 1853).

[65] 'Victory of Lagos' asked 'Why should our rulers deem it wise | To side with any dirty Black?', whilst 'Reform' asked 'What good would it do, if the oaths that are taken, | Are varied to suit every Jew upon 'Change': [Ernest Jones], *Rhymes on the Times* (London, T. Brettell, 1852). The title-page also lifted Charles McKay's 'There's a Good Time Coming'.

[66] *PP*, (18 Dec. 1852), 6; (14 July 1855), 4; Thomas MacGowan to Jones, 22 Aug. 1854, SC.

Warsaw'. The last named had been published first time around as 'The Romance of a People' in the *Labourer* in 1847. Undoubtedly stimulated by the resumption of the Russian threat and the revival of the national question in Europe, it now reappeared in 1854 as 'The Maid of Warsaw, or the Tyrant Czar: A Tale of the Last Polish Insurrection'.[67] 'The Lass and the Lady; or Love's Ladder: A Tale of Thrilling Interest' was unashamed trash: a romance of dirty dealings in high society. With a voyeuristic flourish Jones promised in its first episode that:

The truths of real life are stranger than the fictions of Romance, and, generally, far more instructive. Of such, these pages are composed. Intimate with the relations and habits of the wealthy children of fortune, the arena of the great and the domestic vices of society will be revealed by the author; and the contrast of the unsophisticated, though less educated, heart held before the reader in thrilling scenes of passion and misfortune.

'The Lass and the Lady' went on to tell the tale of Henry Grafton, son of a nouveau riche, who is engaged to Lady Flora McArthur, a descendant of King Arthur. Lady Flora's mother, the Duchess, has borrowed money on the strength of the forthcoming marriage. But Henry Grafton, inevitably, has a past. Edith, a country girl, is his former lover, and on the eve of the wedding she reappears and has his child. Grafton's valet then turns out to be Edith's father. And this was all in the first number of a serial that went on to run for twenty-two weeks. Jones could not and did not keep up the pace. Soon agents were complaining to MacGowan that the supply of 'The Lass and the Lady' was not matching the demand, despite the fact that they had paid up front for all of the instalments. The London Chartist journalist Thomas Frost was called in to complete the story, although it continued to run under Jones's name.[68] Both 'The Maid of Warsaw' and 'The Lass and the Lady' have been picked up by recent commentators on the Chartist novel. But 'Lovers and Husbands' is a new addition to the Jones canon, and is worth lingering over a little longer.

[67] It was also published separately in the same year in an illustrated edition by George Pavey.

[68] Thomas MacGowan to Jones, 21 July 1853, SC; Thomas Frost, *Reminiscences of a Country Journalist* (London, 1886), 109–10; *The Lass and the Lady* was eventually published in an illustrated cheap edition by MacGowan's firm in London in 1855, and by Ainsworth in Manchester. Each chapter was prefaced with a quote from 'Percy Vere' or another of Jones's poems.

'Lovers and Husbands'[69] took up where 'Woman's Wrongs' had left off, that is, chronicling the unhappy love-lives of the well-to-do, except that Jones now wrote from the perspective of the menfolk involved. As in 'Woman's Wrongs', a quartet of stories was featured. The first, 'The Stranger at Home; or a Husband's Autobiography', told the tale of an officer who returned from India to find that in his absence his bride Isabella has turned cold on him and, it transpired (after her death from cholera), had turned to the affections of a neighbour, Algernon Somers—a literary man. Somers, who also dies of cholera, is revealed as the true father of the boy whom the Indian officer had taken for his son. The boy is banished, the family hall auctioned off ('into the impure hands of the foul Jews'), and the officer is left to his sad memories. 'The Hen-Pecked Husband' followed, a lighter, almost Chekhovian tale of a presumptuous, nouveau-riche dry-salter—one Harvey Augustus Baysalt—who, although only five feet four, and very portly, had social ideas above his station. Baysalt pursues Helena McKinloch, a well bred but impoverished Scot, whose family of assorted military types proceed to take advantage of the suitor's hospitality and generosity whilst she flirts with her cousin, a captain in the cavalry. Baysalt's affections sour, Helena's honour is threatened, and her brother and cousin both challenge him to a duel. Baysalt tricks the rather leaden-headed cousins into fighting one another, marries his quarry, and proceeds to mix in good London society, spending freely and philanthropically (he becomes treasurer to the 'Reformed Caffarians Destitute Protection Society'). Eventually Baysalt is swamped with debt. He embezzles from the charity's funds, only to find that his wife makes off with the stolen sum to spend on diamonds for her cousin (her lover). Baysalt is caught, convicted, and imprisoned for fifteen years. The third tale in the series, 'The Man-Boy', was set in Devon and recounted the narrative of Henry, a melancholic 19-year old, very much under the thumb of his widowed mother who is conniving to marry him off to Jemima, the niece of her deceased husband's former head clerk. Into their lives comes Mrs Agatha De Lorne, a widower and the new tenant of the foreboding and dilapidated Berrydale Manor. Henry falls for her, lends her books, meets her in secret

---

[69] 'Lovers and Husbands; or the Wrongs of Man: A Romance of Truth, Passion and Incident' ran in the *People's Paper* from 23 Apr. 1853 until 14 Jan. 1854. In March 1854 it was advertised for sale in a cheap edition, although I have been unable to locate a copy: *PP* (18 Mar. 1854), 4.

liaisons in the woods, but is eventually found out by a prying local Lothario, the strapping Robert Horsefield. Horsefield not only reports Henry's amorous adventures to Henry's mother, but also finds out Agatha's secret past. Her husband is not dead, as the local villagers all believed. She has run away from him, and were he to know her whereabouts her life would be ruined. The story ended rather hurriedly with another duel, which Henry miraculously survives, Agatha fleeing the manor, observing as she bids farewell that 'the accident of time, or place, or meeting, makes all the happiness and misery of our lives', and poor, pale-faced Henry is left to marry Jemima. 'Lovers and Husbands' concluded with 'Lady Olympia's Loves', the story of a dark-eyed, raven-haired, society beauty—the daughter of Lord Clarandale—who 'trifle[s] with the sanctity of love', flirting with and capturing the hearts of a series of men in London and at the seaside, eventually falling into marriage (but not love) with Augustus Fitzplantagenet. But Olympia's conquests of the stronger sex are not indicative of any true liberty, for she quickly becomes a pawn in the stratagems of men. First, her father uses her as bait to prevent an heiress—his ward of court—from marrying, a marriage which would release her to do as she pleases with her property, Leafland Abbey, a crumbling Gothic pile which happens to sit in the middle of Lord Clarandale's estate. Olympia seduces the heiress's husband-to-be, Lionel Landrescourt, the heiress dies, but redemption comes when Lionel commits suicide in front of Olympia during a medieval masquerade held to celebrate her majority. Of this incident Jones spared no detail: 'her bosom . . . [was] . . . covered with one mass of blood.' In a second episode of false love and conspiracy, Lord Clarandale is blackmailed into allowing Sir Henry Beaugard, an MP, to marry Olympia (Jones seems to have forgotten that she was already married). Beaugard had tried to marry Olympia's virtuous (slight, fair-haired, blue-eyed) sister Madelaine, but she had taken fright and fled (and been banished forever by her affronted father). Beaugard, of course, only wants Olympia's money and once married he takes up with a marchioness in Paris and tries to have Olympia sectioned as a lunatic. Illness intervenes and Beaugard dies. Lady Olympia never remarries, nor has children. She returns to the Clarandale country seat, builds a church and school, and lives long enough to see Leafland Abbey pass to her sister, now married to the local vicar, with whose affections she had once trifled.

The plots were formulaic, the scenery predictably monochromatic (mystical wooded countryside versus the shiny and artificial metropolis), and the characters one-dimensional—no more than ciphers of good and evil, free will and circumstance. In 'De Brassier' and 'Woman's Wrongs' Jones had attempted some sophistication in his description of the psychology of insurrection or the taxonomy of the passions. But in 'Lovers and Husbands', as with 'The Lass and the Lady', he capitulated to melodramatic form. The four tales do of course say something about the predicament of the modern woman in the years before the reform of the property laws, dependent on fathers and husbands (or even cousins and brothers) for financial independence, personal security, and an honourable reputation. But Jones was hardly pushing back the frontiers of sexual emancipation by implying that in order to subvert convention, women could only be scheming sirens or pious plain Janes.

As the serialization of 'Lovers and Husbands' came to an end in the new year of 1854, Jones began to plan another attempt to expand circulation: going illustrated. MacGowan pointed out that this would not be cheap, especially if photographs rather than woodcuts were used.[70] Jones set about raising funds, and secured assistance from old friends such as the Vandenhoff family, Thomas Allsop, W. P. Roberts, and from two MPs, Charles Lushington and William Williams. By April Jones was promising his readers that the result would be 'the largest paper in the world'.[71] The first pictorial edition duly appeared at the beginning of May, and the paper was certainly larger and more expensive. Pictures—mainly of military manoeuvres in the Crimea, of Russian peasants, and of the Crystal Palace—appeared in a separate supplement alongside an expanded literary section. The pictures were not of good quality, and it is likely that they were copied from originals in the *Illustrated London News*. However, after only six weeks (including one issue which lacked illustrations), the experiment came to an end, although the higher price remained. By August MacGowan was complaining that the paper's weekly 'deficit is formidable'.[72]

Despite this setback, Jones went on combining entertainment and politics in the *People's Paper* for another three years, until Pavey gave up the publishing to Holyoake and Co. in the summer of 1857. There were fewer original serials. 'The Insurrection of the

[70] Thomas MacGowan to Jones, 19 Dec. 1853, SC.
[71] Jones to Thomas Allsop, 4 May 1854, Yale; *PP* (8 Apr. 1854), 1.
[72] Thomas MacGowan to Jones, 15 Aug. 1854, SC.

Working Classes', Jones's long history lecture from the *Labourer*, was republished in a new section of the paper headed 'The Library of Romance'. And a topical tale by John Harwood, 'The Serf Sisters', ran for six months from the summer of 1855. By and large, however, Jones gave up serials for shorter stories and excerpts, falling back on French dramas such as those of Henri Murger (best known as the author of stories used as the basis of Puccini's *La Bohème*), tearjerking stories of Irish peasant life from William Carleton, and more respectable historical tales from authors such as Harrison Ainsworth and Bulwer-Lytton. Jones also remained faithful to the literature of labour, featuring the relatively obscure, such as the temperance authors James Hillocks and Robert Gibbon,[73] as well as cashing in on the success of men such as William Cox Bennett, Sheldon Chadwick, Charles Mackay, and Gerald Massey.[74] There was an irony in all this. Jones was helping to further the reputations and literary careers of men whose poetical style was inimical to his own. J. B. Leno later recalled Jones complaining to him that Robert Burns had destroyed the chance of lyricists ever acquiring 'a big reputation'.[75] The poetry of Leno, Bennett, Massey, and their like proved Jones's point. It was patriotic—some of these men became involved in the Burns centenary of 1859 and the Shakespearean tercentenary of 1864. Such poetry was politically quietist. It celebrated the stoic dignity of labour rather than its exploitation, and it was roundly praised for evoking the rhetoric of class co-operation rather than conflict. And, of course, it lacked good stories of chivalric young men.

The alliance of literature and politics in the pages of the *People's Paper* eventually came to a close in 1857. With Holyoake and Co. and then Langley as his publishers, rather than the predominantly commercial houses he had used hitherto, Jones may have been under less pressure to reflect literary fashion. The only reviews he now inserted tended to be of titles put out or penned by his new

---

[73] *PP* (22 Nov. 1856), 5; (22 Aug. 1857), 5. James Hillocks's *Life Story* (London: W. Tweedie, 1860), became better known after it was serialized in the *Commonwealth* in 1856. Robert Gibbon's work appeared in 1868: *Reflections From Nature: Collection of Poems and Songs* (Bishop Auckland: G. E. Briggs, 1868).

[74] *PP* (4 Nov. 1854), 5; (12 Jan. 1856), 5; (19 Jan. 1856), 5; (25 Oct. 1856), 4; W. C. Bennett, *Poems* (London: Chapman & Hall, 1850); id., *Anti-Maud* (London: E. Churton, 1855); Sheldon Chadwick, *Poems* (London: David Bogue, 1856); Charles Mackay, *Collected Songs* (London: G. Routledge, 1858); Gerald Massey, *War Waits* (London, David Bogue, 1855); id., *Craigcrook Castle* (London, David Bogue, 1856).

[75] J. B. Leno, *The Aftermath* (London: Reeves & Turner, 1892), 90.

publishers.[76] A year or so later when he launched the *Cabinet News-paper*, published by Wilks from an alley off the Strand, any pretence at uplifting or original literature was given up altogether. The new paper, which ran from November 1858 through to February 1860, gave a third airing to Jones's 'History of Florence', and featured a section that often took up a third of an issue, entitled the 'Black Calendar'. This part of the paper was devoted to the choicest stories from the police courts. Jones had often resorted to filling the columns of the *People's Paper* with real-life tales of seduction, wife-beating and child-murder taken from the court reports, but never in such a sustained manner. The 'Black Calendar' offered a relentless diet of drunken clergy, cats being skinned alive, children poisoned with gin, lawyers consorting with rough trade, and, to Jones's evident delight, a violent affray involving the Duke of Beaufort at Brighton: 'a precious insight into the dirty blackguardism of the English aristocracy.'[77] How far the Beauforts, one of whom had presented Jones to Court in 1841, had fallen. And how low Jones could go.

4

Ultimately, it was not Jones's inability to settle on highbrow or lowlife entertainment that proved the undoing of the *People's Paper*. The paper was the organ of the Chartist movement, and its sales moved when the Chartist body had life. There was very little life left in Chartism in the 1850s. Jones's victory over his main rivals in the NCA executive elections at the end of 1851 was pyrrhic. He had won control of an army that had lost the battle. Jones, to be fair, did recognize this. His reluctance to convene the NCA in 1851 and 1852 stemmed from his belief that the work of awakening Chartism from its slumber would take time, and required effort across the country-side on a missionary scale. In such circumstances thinly attended meetings in the capital were of little use.[78] Until the summer of 1854 Jones was as good as his word. He undertook three more lecture

---

[76] *PP* (9 Jan. 1858), 5; (6 Mar. 1858), 5.

[77] *CN* (18 Dec. 1858), 5. The 'Black Calendar', warned Jones, offered instruction: 'we propose, as far as possible, to respect the purity of our pages': *CN* (27 Nov. 1858), 5. Jones's view of the Beauforts may have dipped irrevocably after his wife's death, when the Duke of Beaufort sent him £10 for the sake of his 'four little motherless girls [*sic*]': Beaufort to Jones, 19 Sept. [1857], SC.

[78] 'I am heart-sick', Jones wrote in November 1851, 'of sitting Wednesday after Wednesday with numbers insufficient to form a quorum': *NP* (22 Nov. 1851), 581.

tours: two in 1853, both concentrated in the villages and small towns straddling the Pennines, and a third the following summer, again to Lancashire and Yorkshire, and also to Belfast. And he used the columns of the *People's Paper* to report the doings of Chartist folk, as well as those of the co-operative and temperance societies and the trades unions.

Even in the old heartlands of Chartism, however, it was clear that the great popular acclaim Jones had enjoyed four years earlier had subsided. In the summer of 1852 Jones contested Halifax in the general election, this time on his own. Despite regaling audiences with stories of the tortures and deprivation he had suffered in prison, and despite (or perhaps because of) his relentless exposure of the hypocrisy of Sir Charles Wood and Frank Crossley, the two Whig–Liberal candidates, Jones fared poorly, coming bottom of the poll with only thirty-seven votes. Jones complained that his voters had been 'bottled', and in a famous account of the Halifax elections Karl Marx gave credence to the claim, comparing the election proceedings to the bacchanalian feasts of ancient times. Jones might have done better had he answered the question which was frequently put to him throughout the campaign, namely, for whom would he advise his voters to give their other vote.[79] The following year Jones returned to the Chartist northern circuit, using the death of Benjamin Rushton and subsequent funeral march to Blackstone Edge to 're-inaugurate' the Chartist movement (it was 'a burial and a birth'), under the itinerant leadership of himself and Robert Gammage ('a very obliging and attentive companion', Jones informed his wife).[80] His summer tour of 1853 wound up back in London, at Bishop Bonner's Fields, which was enough to alarm Jane. 'Don't get yourself into a scrap', she pleaded. But although Jones's return to the public platforms of the capital was closely watched, it aroused little concern. PC Seaward of 'G' Division reported back to the Home Office that in Finsbury Jones's audience behaved in an orderly fashion and, perhaps more significantly, 'there were no foreigners present'.[81]

[79] *PP* (17 July 1852), 1; *HG* (3 July 1852), 5; (10 July 1852), 6–7; Benjamin Wilson, *Struggles of an Old Chartist*, repr. in David Vincent (ed.), *Testaments of Radicalism*, 217–18; Karl Marx, 'The Chartists', *MECW* xi. 332–41; id., 'Corruption at Elections', ibid. 342–7.

[80] *PP* (2 July 1853), 1–2; Jones to Jane, 1 July 1853, SC.

[81] Jane to Ernest, 7 July 1853, SC; 'Report of P. C. Seaward' (3 Aug. 1853), PRO HO 45/5128K.

Some foreigners were present at the 'Labour Parliament' which Jones spent the weeks around the new year of 1853–4 organizing, and which met daily in the People's Institute in Manchester for two weeks in the first half of March. The agenda of the Parliament had been set partly by Jones's ongoing support in 1853 for an end to the 'stoppage' system in the coalfields, whereby miners were docked for incidental items, and also by his support for the lock-out dispute ('ten per cent and no surrender') in the mill-towns north of Manchester. The thirty-five delegates who attended the Parliament, in addition to the honoraries—Louis Blanc, Karl Marx (who sent a letter), and Martin Nadaud—agreed a four-point programme, committing the Chartist movement to raise through weekly contributions a national labour fund for supporting strikes, for the purchase of land and for establishing co-operative workshops. Inevitably, the absences from the conference were as noticeable as the notables present. For example, there were no delegates from Halifax, where Chartists were still pinning their hopes on a revived NCA. Marx dubbed the meeting in Manchester 'the Parliament of the poor', whilst Jones, typically extravagant, referred to it as the 'mass movement'.[82] In fact, the main legacy of the Manchester sittings was the establishment of the 'United Brothers Industrial, Sick Benefit and Life Assurance Society',[83] the advertisements of which began to nudge out chatty Chartists in the correspondence columns of the People's Paper over the next few months. Even Jones's own supporters preferred making ends meet to making revolution.

In the summer of 1854 Jones ventured out again for a short but eventful tour in Lancashire and Yorkshire, with a quick hop over the Irish Sea to Belfast. Jones fell in love with Belfast, much as he had with Wales, sending Jane long, illustrated letters praising the sublime beauty of Loch Neagh and the simple, good-natured Irish people. His favourable impressions were not dimmed by a lecture platform collapsing beneath him during his visit.[84] Someone was trying to tell

---

[82] PP (10 Mar. 1853), 1; (11 Mar. 1854), 5; (18 Mar. 1854), 4–5; (25 Mar. 1854), 1; Marx, 'Letter to the Labour Parliament' (9 Mar. 1854), in MECW xiii. 57–8; Reg Groves, 'Marx and the Labour Parliament of 1854', Labour Monthly, 12 (1930), 172–6. For Nadaud, see: Martin Nadaud, Léonard, Maçon de la Creuse (Paris: Découverte, 1998), 302. For the non-involvement of Halifax Chartists, see: Kathleen Tiller, 'Working Class Attitudes and Organisation in Three Industrial Towns, 1850–1875', DPhil. thesis, Birmingham University (1975), 432–4.

[83] PP (20 May 1854), 4.

[84] PP (19 Aug. 1854), 1; Jones to Jane, 18 Aug. 1854, SC.

him something. A week later, back in England, a man stood up at the close of Jones's lecture in the People's Institute in Manchester, shouted 'you will never talk in this town again', and fired a shot at him.[85] It missed, the assailant escaped, but for the next five years Jones's public appearances outside London were kept to a minimum. Apart from would-be assassins, Jones was at last beginning to take seriously the precarious state of Jane's health, which began to deteriorate from the summer of 1854 onwards.

As provincial Chartism contracted, the capital became Jones's political base. He became involved in a series of short-lived radical organizations occasioned by Britain's involvement in the Crimean War. From relatively early on in 1853 Jones had called for British intervention in the Russo-Turkish dispute, on the reasonably consistent grounds that the alliance of the Greek 'papacy' and the Russian 'despot' needed to be destroyed from without. Along with Karl Marx and many others, he followed the Russophobic David Urquhart's line on British 'secret' diplomacy, attributing British chicanery over the Eastern question to a desire to control the supply of grain from the lands around the Black Sea, thereby benefiting the mercantile classes at the expense of the consumer.[86] Once the war began Jones took exception to Britain's fighting partners—the Austrians and the French. He used the *People's Paper* to give full backing to the French republican exiles' campaign against Napoleon III, a campaign which peaked in the weeks leading up to the visit of the Emperor to London in the spring of 1855. Jones proved a vocal and generous political host to Armand Barbès, the French socialist recently released from prison, and he translated the protests of the exiles in Jersey, whom the Home Office sought to deport.[87] Out of the opposition to Napoleon's visit emerged the International Committee (a forerunner of the First International), for which Jones acted as chairman for a short period.[88] Surprisingly, he was less

[85] *PP*, (2 Sept. 1854), 1.

[86] *PP* (20 Aug. 1853), 4; (5 Nov. 1853), 2.

[87] *PP* (21 Oct. 1854), 4. Marx reckoned Jones had confused Barbès with Auguste Blanqui: Marx to Engels, 2 Dec., 1854, *MECW* xlix. 474; F. Pyat *et al.*, *The Letter of the Jersey Exiles to the Queen of England* trans. Ernest Jones (London: E. Truelove, 1855); K. W. Hooker, *The Fortunes of Victor Hugo in England* (New York: Columbia University Press, 1938), 112–32.

[88] Much to Marx's annoyance, Jones appeared alongside the Russian émigré Alexander Herzen at the committee's launch: *PP* (3 Mar. 1855), 4–5; Marx to Engels, 13 Feb. 1855, *MECW* xlix. 522–3; A. Muller Lehning, 'The International Association, 1855–59', *International Review of Social History*, 3 (1938), 185–286.

active in the revival of domestic radical politics which took place in the capital as Lord Aberdeen's coalition government fell at the beginning of 1855. It was not until July that Jones threw in his lot with the State Reform Association, a group centred on the *Illustrated London News*. At its public meetings Jones called for manhood suffrage, whilst in private he appealed to the newspaper's editor to run a feature on him as a 'literary man'.[89] Towards the end of the year Jones also took part with the currency reformer and *Illustrated London News* journalist Jonathan Duncan in the 'People's Provision League'. As bread shortages set in, the League, in a series of meetings in Hyde Park, called for the establishment of public granaries and a revision of the Turkish tariff.[90]

Apart from refugees from abroad and illness at home, Jones was kept in London from the summer of 1854 onwards by his efforts to restart his literary career. In June 1854 Jones wrote to Bulwer-Lytton seeking an introduction to George Routledge and Co., in whom he hoped to arouse some interest in an edition of his poems. The ground prepared, Routledge perused the selection that Jones sent in, but by the end of July had decided to decline publication. In December, however, the firm changed its mind, and in the new year of 1855 Jones began negotiations over royalties and advertising.[91] What prompted Routledge's change of heart was probably Jones's willingness to bear some of the costs of the publication, as he had done fourteen years earlier with *The Wood Spirit*. For in November 1854 Jones made the first of two applications to the Royal Literary Fund for pecuniary assistance. Armed with testimonials from, amongst others, Archer Gurney and Bulwer-Lytton, and supported behind the scenes by Richard Monckton Milnes, Jones sought the means to 'enable me to devote myself successfully to literature'. His referees supplied the now familiar background story of a literary vocation derailed by family misfortunes and political misadventure, and Jones detailed his present poverty.[92] £50 was granted, and consequently he was in a better position to prepare a new edition of his poems,

---

[89] *PP* (21 July 1855), 4; (28 July 1855), 1; Jones to Charles Mackay, 9 Aug. 1855, repr. in Charles Mackay, *Forty Years Recollections*, 2 vols. (London: Chapman & Hall, 1877), ii. 59–62.   [90] *PP* (3 Nov. 1855), 4.

[91] Jones to Bulwer-Lytton, 1 July 1854, Bulwer-Lytton Mss, Hertfordshire RO, D/EK, C4/128; George Routledge to Jones, 29 July 1854, 30 Dec. 1854, 10 Jan. 185[5], IISH.

[92] Thomas W. Porter, 'Ernest Charles Jones and the Royal Literary Fund', *Labour History Review*, 57 (1992), 84–94.

provisionally titled 'The Poetical Works of Ernest' which in June 1855 he began to advertise as forthcoming.

The faltering fortunes of the *People's Paper* were certainly one reason for Jones's resurrection of the muse. The continuing literary success of his old friend Archer Gurney was another. In the spring of 1855 Gurney brought out his own new collection of verse, *The Transcendentalists*. It included an appreciative poem about Jones, and Jones reviewed it appreciatively. Gurney was particularly productive in 1855. His tragedy *Iphigenia* came out in the summer, and later in the year another work, *The Ode of Peace*, appeared.[93] Jones urged Routledge to speed up their production of the edition of his poems, so it would not lag behind Gurney's *Iphigenia*.[94] With his laments over Greek beauties sacrificed in war and his prayers for peace, Gurney had caught the moment well, reflecting a public war mood in 1855 that was oscillating between despair (Sebastopol the previous November) and elation (Sebastopol the following September). Tennyson's *Maud* appeared in July, and although it was unhelpfully ambiguous on the correct posture to be adopted towards the war, it spawned a season of patriotic lyrics, including collections by W. C. Bennett and Gerald Massey.[95] Jones saw his opportunity, and quickly instructed his publishers to repackage 'The Poetical Works of Ernest' as *The Battle Day*. The collection duly appeared in July 1855, and so bald was the makeover that even Jones felt obliged to explain to his readers that *The Battle Day*, which included only two new verses, was in fact 'Lord Lindsay' (now called 'The Battle Day, or the Lost Army') and 'The Painter of Florence' (now called 'The Cost of Glory'). As to the rest, there was 'Percy Vere' (now 'The Peer's Story') and a smattering of his greatest hits from the Chartist years.[96] The collection was fairly well received: some reviewers regretted Jones separating his politics from his poetry, others

---

[93] Archer Gurney, *Transcendentalists*, 2nd edn. (London: Thomas Bosworth, 1855); *Iphigenia at Delphi: A Tragedy* (London: Longman, Brown, Green & Longmans, 1855); *Ode of Peace* (London: Longman, Brown, Green & Longmans, 1855). *Transcendentalists* appeared originally in 1853, when Jones reviewed it: *PP* (6 Aug. 1853), 6.

[94] Jones to George Routledge, 25 May 1855, IISH.

[95] W. C. Bennett, *War Songs* (London: Effingham Wilson, 1855), *Anti-Maud*; Gerald Massey, *War Waits*; Cynthia Dereli, 'Tennyson's *Maud*: Ambiguity and the War Context', *Tennyson Research Bulletin*, 7 (1997), 1–6.

[96] Jones, *The Battle Day; and Other Poems* (London: George Routledge & Co., 1855); Jones to George Routledge, 25 May 1855, IISH; *PP* (7 July 1855), 1. Only 'The Cry of the Russian Serf' and 'The Italian Exile to his Countrymen' were new poems.

welcomed the move.[97] Flattered and inspired, Jones followed up in the new year of 1856 with a shorter volume of completely new verse, *The Emperor's Vigil*. This was unremitting war poetry. With its depictions of heroic British tars, the 'fettered millions' of peasant Russia, and its plea for a war of nationalities, *The Emperor's Vigil* had a democratic refrain. But critics sensed that Jones was simply chasing the bandwagon of battlefield verse of the previous year. The *Leader* lamented over Jones's verse, describing it as 'nauseous commonplace', whilst the *Athenaeum* regretted that Jones was turning out books 'as quickly as Birmingham machines do steel pens'. Of all the poetry produced by Jones, *The Emperor's Vigil* remains the most ephemeral.[98]

The revival of Jones's literary reputation was not accompanied by the revival of Chartism. The State Reform Association wound up as the last summer of the Crimean War drew to a close, Jones gave up being chairman of the new International Association on the grounds of ill-health, and turned down a request to contest Cheltenham at a by-election.[99] The *People's Paper* maintained the illusion of a national movement. Jones picked editorial fights with Chartists in Aberdeen and journalists in Nottingham, and he covered John Frost's welcome-home tour through the English provinces.[100] In 1857 the paper boasted a circulation as far afield as 'Australia, New Zealand, Canada and Sierra Leone',[101] but in truth Jones was dictating to a very small audience from his desk in the Strand. In February 1856 he proposed that he and James Finlen should be vested with sole authority as the Chartist executive, and in April, at the anniversary dinner of the paper, even Karl Marx seemed overly optimistic in assuring his audience that the 'first born sons of modern industry . . . will not be the last in aiding the social revolution'.[102] Not that Jones became any more interested in co-operation with other radicals. In May 1856 he politely but firmly turned down G. J. Holyoake's invitation to attend a meeting 'of all classes of reformers'

[97] *Spectator* (11 Aug. 1855), 838–9; *Athenaeum* (15 Sept. 1855), 1048–9.

[98] Jones, *The Emperor's Vigil and the Waves and the War* (London: George Routledge & Co., 1856); *Leader* (26 Jan. 1856), 92; *Athenaeum* (24 May 1856), 647.

[99] John Coward to Jones, 4 July 1855, SC; *PP* (19 May 1855), 5.

[100] *PP* (3 May 1856), 1; (23 Aug. 1856), 4; (30 Aug. 1856), 4–5; (6 Sept. 1856), 1, 4; (20 Sept. 1856), 4.

[101] Charles Mitchell (comp.), *Newspaper Press Directory* (London: Charles Mitchell, 1857), 110.

[102] *PP* (2 Feb. 1856), 1; Marx, 'Speech on the Anniversary of the People's Paper' (12 April 1856), *MECW* xiv. 655–6.

aimed at starting up an agitation for the suffrage. Jones reminded Holyoake that there was no need to meet, 'as the Chartist organisation is now rapidly progressing towards national ascendancy'.[103] Anyone who picked up a copy of the *People's Paper* that month and found its columns devoted to the Rugeley poisoning might have begged to differ.

By the autumn of 1856 Jones was hunkered down in London, his energies and allies flagging. With Jane ailing rapidly an extra servant was taken on at home. At work Finlen gave up his post as Jones's 'henchman' (Leno's description), sold up his possessions, and headed north to cheaper company.[104] In response Jones fell back on his greatest instant resource—his oratory—and organized a series of weekday soirées at St Martin's Hall in London. These 'evenings for the people' ran at intermittent intervals from early October through to the end of the following January. They were, in Jones's words, 'an attempt to combine elevating Recreation with Political Instruction— to raise Politics from the Sphere of the Tavern, by associating them with the refinements of Music of the choicest character, the finest Professional Talent, Vocal and Instrumental, being engaged for each Soirée'.[105] The songs of choicest character were supplied gratis by Jones and sung by John Lowry. They were Jones's own verses, a mixture of old and new. In the heart of the metropolis the songs conjured up the rustic bliss of the countryside:

> God gave us hearts of ardour,
> God gave us noble farms,
> And God has poured around us his paradise of light:
> Has he bade us sow the sunshine and only reap the storms?
> Created us in glory, to pass away in night?[106]

Each of the five soirées began with a recital and then proceeded to the

---

[103] Jones to George Jacob Holyoake, 7 May 1856, repr. in Fritz de Jong, 'Ernest Jones and Chartism, c. 1856', *Bulletin of the International Institute of Social History*, 2 (1950), 99–104.

[104] *PP* (26 July 1856), 4; (27 Sept. 1856), 4; Leno, *The Aftermath*, 54–5.

[105] Although nine lectures appeared in the ensuing volume, there were in fact only five soirées: *Evenings with the People* (London: *People's Paper*, 1856–7). One of the lectures, 'The Unemployed', was the text of Jones's speech at Smithfield in Feb. 1857; two others, 'Emigration' and 'Our Colonies', reproduced earlier material from *Notes to the People*; and the two lectures on 'The State Church' provided a résumé of *Canterbury versus Rome* from 1851.

[106] Jones, 'Song of the Poor', in his *Songs of Democracy* (London: John Lowry, 1856–7).

main event: Jones's lecture. Few of the lectures broke new ground. The first, entitled 'The workman and his work', was a passionate attack on factory 'slavery', with illustrations drawn from conditions in the factories of Jones's old *bête noire*: the Crossleys of Halifax. This lecture and the one that followed—'The hereditary landed aristocracy'—detailed Jones's familiar remedy: breaking up the great estates of the country and bringing the waste land under cultivation so that there were sufficient smallholdings for every family. Jones's third lecture, on 'The state church', repeated verbatim large chunks of *Canterbury versus Rome* of six years previously, whilst the fourth, 'The franchise and taxation', was a clear and reasoned restatement of the six points of the Charter. In the last of the actual lectures, on 'Foreign Affairs', Jones gave his account of the global battle-lines that had been established by the Crimean War: the Anglo-Saxon empire now faced off against the Slav. His listeners might have thought he was reading from one of the more racy episodes of *The Lass and the Lady*:

the two widest spread races the world has ever seen—the former squandered across the earth—the latter concentrated on one block of territory—hanging like an avalanche from the starry heights of the north over the sunny regions of the south and the green vallies [*sic*] of the west;—the former having least power of projection where it needs it most—losing itself in unequal contests on the fringes of its dominions, as in China, Persia and Cabul, the latter thrusting the huge weight of its protruding head hardly and heavily into the midst of its weaker foes.

And he warned of Britain's shameful dependency on her spurious allies: the empire of 'shreds and patches' that was Austria, the 'penniless gambler' Louis Napoleon, and the 'human champagne bottle' the King of Prussia. Freedom to the oppressed nationalities of Europe and an end to British colonial wars was Jones's climax to this lecture. 'Look at home' remained his panacea, however. Revival of the home trade was preferred to the opening up of markets overseas. Even if there was little novelty, there was plenty of stirring entertainment. *The Times* reported Jones working an initially 'listless' audience into 'a band of enthusiasts', but the numbers attending were few and the series came to a premature end in the new year.[107]

If 1856 represented something of a dead-end for Jones, both as a

---

[107] *The Times* (9 Oct. 1856), 5. One old adversary could not resist a dig at Jones, ridiculing his 'Hereditary Landed Aristocracy' lecture: 'Ode to Ernest Jones', *Punch* (15 Nov. 1856), 199.

Chartist leader and as a popular author, then 1857 proved a fresh start. It began inauspiciously enough, with Jones appearing at a rowdy meeting of the unemployed in Smithfield Market in February,[108] and unsuccessfully contesting Nottingham in March. Jones had come to know Nottingham well since O'Connor's death, but the Nottingham electors had not come to know Jones, and he polled only 614 votes at the end of a campaign in which he uncompromisingly promised the nationalization of the land.[109] However, in the months that followed the tide of fortune began to turn his way. In the middle of April Jane finally died, aged 39, after 'three years of affliction', and though her death robbed four boys of a mother and homemaker, it did allow Jones to get out and about more. The crab-like posture he had increasingly adopted since 1854 was dropped and by the summer of 1857 he was beginning to lecture again, on happier and less confrontational topics such as 'The causes leading to a union of the classes'.[110]

One cause leading to a union of the classes for Jones was his switch of publishing house from Pavey to Holyoake and Co. in the middle of July 1857. Jones had usually enjoyed good relations with Holyoake. Although they had differed over Chartist strategy in 1848 and again in 1851–2, there was never any of the invective or class tension that soured Jones's friendship with men such as Harney or Gammage. Besides which they were Fleet Street neighbours for most of the decade, so that when Jones moved the home of the *People's Paper* in the summer of 1857 he was only going two doors down, from number 143 to 147. However, Holyoake's range of political friends was considerably more catholic than that of Jones. He was well connected with the editorial team at the *Morning Star*, the new Cobdenite daily which had commenced publication the previous year; he was involved with J. Baxter Langley in the anti-sabbatarian movement in the capital; and he knew the movers and shakers of London electoral politics, having been put up as a working man's candidate in the Tower Hamlets election of the previous spring. Here lay some of the materials for the new political move that Jones began planning in the summer: a conference which would bring together

[108] *PP* (21 Feb. 1857), 1.
[109] *PP* (21 Mar. 1857), 1; (4 Apr. 1857), 1.
[110] *PP* (25 Apr. 1857), 1; (2 May 1857), 4; (20 June 1857), 4. Following Jane's death Jenny Marx described Jones as 'happy as a sandboy': Jenny Marx to Engels, 14 Aug. 1857, *MECW* xl. 565.

reformers of all shades of opinion.[111] Although it did not take place until February 1858, the shift in Jones's political loyalties took shape eight months earlier.

Holyoake was one catalyst in this change, the Indian 'mutiny' was the other. For only the second time in his life, Jones's timing was impeccable. His long epic poem *The Revolt of Hindostan* was published at the beginning of August, just as the British reaction to the rebellion in May and its bloody suppression was beginning to take shape. In the same way that, eleven years earlier, Jones had appeared on Feargus O'Connor's doorstep as an aspirant poet, ready to oust Thomas Cooper from the Chartist movement, so he now capitalized on public interest in India, earning praise from a number of reviews and newspapers for the noble manner in which he dealt with the unfolding events from afar. Many applauded Jones's uncanny prescience, for in fact *The Revolt of Hindostan*, like an unmasked character in a melodrama, turned out to be something else. It was Jones's 'New World', originally written 'in blood' in prison in 1849 or, more likely, dashed off at the seaside in the summer of 1850, published first in 1851, and now remarketed with a suitably Shelleyan title as a 'remarkable prophecy'.[112] For the next few months Jones enjoyed the publicity and greater credibility that went with his latest work. He appeared in Southwark in mid-August at a meeting on India, and later in the year teamed up with Charles Gilpin, the pacifist MP for Northampton, at a demonstration critical of the manner in which the British army was putting down the rebellion. In the new year of 1858 he spoke at a meeting called by the proprietors of the East India Company to oppose the government's proposed transfer of power from the Company to the Crown.[113] Jones had his own ideas on 'how to secure India': he believed that once English lives had been secured, the states should be given independence, allowing peaceful commerce to flourish between Britain

---

[111] According to one intermediary, talks between Jones, Baxter Langley, and other London radicals dated back to the previous autumn: Frederick Chesson diaries, 8 Sept. 1856, 18 Dec. 1857, John Rylands Library, Univ. Manchester.

[112] Jones, *The Revolt of Hindostan; or the New World. A Poem* (London: Effingham Wilson, 1857); *PP* (8 Aug. 1857), 1. Jones dedicated the work to his deceased wife: 'Born and reared in wealth, she shared without a murmur the poverty created by my adherence to a great and sacred cause. Few know what she endured;— but those, her own relatives, who turned from her then, in the hour of suffering and adversity, shall live to see her own name raise higher than their worn-out pedigrees or mouldering genealogies can lift their own'.

[113] *PP* (15 Aug. 1857), 4; (12 Dec. 1857), 4; (6 Feb. 1858), 1.

and the Indian princes. He welcomed the transfer of power from the East India Company, 'the thieves of the people'.[114] But of most significance were not so much his views as the forums in which they were being expressed. Jones was now speaking alongside the very parliamentary radicals and 'middle-class' reformers whom he had dismissed as the enemy for most of the 1850s. Had he moved over to their way of thinking, or had they come round to his?

5

Jones's lurch into the centre-ground of British radical politics at the week-long conference of reformers held at St Martin's Hall in February 1858 infuriated many of his contemporaries and has long perplexed historians. Karl Marx thought he was being 'very inane', although he was not willing to believe that Jones had sold himself completely.[115] G. W. M. Reynolds had no such hesitation, and from January 1858 onwards conducted a fierce onslaught on Jones, condemning his betrayal of Chartism and questioning his motives in opening up channels of communication with the monied reformers. He compared Jones to a Judas whose hands were sullied by thirty pieces of silver.[116] Other stars of the Chartist firmament such as James Finlen, Thomas Frost, J. B. Leno, and Thomas Wheeler all voted with their feet, finally forsaking Jones in the months after the conference and forming a Chartist movement of their own, the National Political Union. On the face of it, Jones's *volte-face* did seem complete. He invited any- and everyone to his conference: from John Bright to Robert Owen, from J. A. Roebuck to Lord Harrington, from A. J. Ayrton to William Newton—industrialists, socialists, old radicals, old Whigs, bankers, and engineers—all were summoned in the attempt to find common ground on the issue of parliamentary reform.[117] Reynolds's accusations stoked rumours that Jones had accepted a loan to prop up the keeling *People's Paper* in return for preaching political harmony. And so when J. Baxter Langley, a political moderate, took over the publishing of the *People's Paper* within months of the conference, critics put two and two together and concluded that Jones had sold out to him. Poison-

[114] *PP* (1 Aug. 1857), 4; (8 Aug. 1857), 1; (6 Feb. 1858), 1.
[115] Karl Marx to Friedrich Engels, 24 Nov. 1857, *MECW* xl. 208–10.
[116] *Reynolds's Newspaper* (31 Jan. 1858), 8–9.
[117] *PP* (2 Jan. 1858), 1.

pen letters crossed Jones's desk, addressed to 'Earnest [*sic*] Jones Esquire, BBBL'—that is, 'bought by Baxter Langley', and Jones, not for the first time, was forced to defend himself against his detractors with as much energy as he expended on the conference itself.[118]

Did money change hands? Jones would certainly have liked it to have done. As the conference approached he was as strapped for cash as ever. He appealed to his readers for funds, as well as to old backers such as Holyoake and new backers such as Joseph Cowen jr. in Newcastle. A clandestine £45 was slipped his way by the secretary to Prince Radziwill, a very old and very distant friend. However, the bulk of these contributions were publicly accounted for in the pages of the *People's Paper*, and bribery on a grand scale did not take place.[119] Indeed, not very much took place. Of the long list of invitees, only a small proportion made it to the actual conference, mainly loyal Chartists such as Edward Hooson of Manchester, representatives from some of the London trades, and several of Jones's critics such as James Henriette. The octogenarian Robert Owen graced the proceedings, as did a deputation led by Samuel Morley from the Parliamentary Reform Association. For his pains Owen was hounded with begging letters from Jones for the remaining months of his life (the poor man died in November), and Morley and his colleagues were given a public dressing-down by Jones, who refuted their household suffrage proposals.[120] Otherwise, parliamentary radicals were probably scared off by Jones advertising it as a Chartist conference, and Chartists alienated by his referring to it as a 'union of the classes'. It was difficult to please everyone. Anyway, in the middle of February there was a much more interesting show going on in town a few streets away in the House of Commons, where Lord Palmerston's government fell over the Conspiracy to Murder Bill, introduced in the wake of Felice Orsini's attempted assassination of Napoleon III with British-made bombs. Jones's conference concluded not in union but in discord. Moderate reformers

---

[118] [Anon.] to Jones, n.d. (1858), Holyoake coll., COSL, fos. 1027a, 1065; *PP* (6 Mar. 1858), 4.

[119] Jones to George Jacob Holyoake, 3 Dec. 1857, IISH; Jones to Holyoake, 12 Jan. 1858, Holyoake papers, COSL, Manchester, fo. 1030; Prince's Secretary to Jones, 30 Jan. 1858, BJH. Jones had launched a fund for the National Chartist Conference back in July 1857 and this was subsumed into the appeal for the new conference.

[120] *PP*, (13 Feb. 1858), 1, 4–5; Jones to Robert Owen, 31 May 1858, 2 June 1858, 3 June 1858, Owen coll., COSL, fos. 2959a–c.

were appalled by what they called his 'carrot and stick' manner, whilst Chartist stalwarts objected to his dropping two of the six points (abolition of the property qualification and redistribution of seats).

Although the conference concluded with the formation of a new organization—the Political Reform League—Jones's handling of the proceedings did damage his reputation, and he spent much of the following eighteen months seeking its repair. One of the first activities of the Political Reform League was to give vocal support to the defence of the English radicals caught up in the Orsini bombs scandal. This brought Jones into contact with Edwin James QC, another political barrister with a colourful past, and renewed his friendship with some of the French refugees in Jersey.[121] But still the *People's Paper* was finding it hard to pay its way. In March 1858 Jones announced a new newspaper initiative: a penny paper, which would appear in four separate weekend editions alongside the *People's Paper*, its projected circulation of 16,000 per week allowing the older paper to come down in price.[122] This was a variation on the winning formula that Reynolds had hit upon in 1850 with his *Reynolds's Miscellany* running alongside *Reynolds's Newspaper*. However, Jones's new title, *London News*, which was launched in May, failed to make a sizeable impact in what had become a competitive London press in the years since the repeal of the stamp tax. In June Jones sold both titles to J. Baxter Langley for £64, disposed of his printing type, and laid off the remaining employees of the *People's Paper*, reserving for himself two columns or so to deal with Chartist news. It was not a happy business arrangement. Within weeks Baxter Langley and Jones were at loggerheads, with the former accusing Jones of doctoring the letters that were sent in from working men. By the end of the year they had fallen out politically, spelling the effective end of the Political Reform League, with Jones accusing Baxter Langley of taking a paid lectureship in support of the moderate parliamentary programme of household suffrage.[123]

In the new year of 1859 Jones was back on the boards again, this time leading the campaign for manhood suffrage. By manhood suffrage Jones of course meant the old Chartist war-cry of one man, one vote. By 1859 he had also begun to embrace newer definitions of

---

[121] *PP* (20 Feb. 1858), 4; (1 May 1858), 1.
[122] *PP* (20 Mar. 1858), 1; (17 Apr. 1858), 1.
[123] *PP*, (20 June 1858), 1; (7 Aug. 1858), 5; *CN* (18 Dec. 1858), 3.

manhood suffrage, identifying it not only as right, but also a reward for services rendered to the nation. In a speech at the Guildhall in London at the beginning of February he singled out working men for the nobility of their labour and for their contribution to the making of the national wealth. And throughout the year he spoke up for the rifle movement. Having ridiculed the invasion-scare mania in one of his 'Evenings with the People' lectures the previous winter, Jones now recommended the working-class volunteer movement, and even became involved in the establishment of a City of London rifle corps.[124] His real object, however, remained the suffrage, and in this his main opponent was John Bright, the Birmingham MP, whose plan for parliamentary reform was unveiled in a provincial speaking tour during the winter and in a 'bill' published in January. Jones followed in Bright's footsteps, speaking in Bradford and Glasgow where Bright had been, as well as in London, Derby, and Huddersfield where he had not. In Birmingham at the beginning of March Jones attempted to speak on the same stage as Bright, but was manhandled out of the meeting, his clothes torn from his back, he alleged.[125] A week later Jones was also prevented from speaking at London's Guildhall, when the Mayor, who a few weeks earlier had allowed a manhood suffrage meeting to take place, now, in the wake of the violence at Birmingham, refused to give permission for the use of the building. Jones reacted by going out-of-doors, holding meetings in Hyde Park and Bishop Bonner's Fields, where he denounced the 'ticket patriots' who surrounded Bright and the mainstream London reformers. He also laid into the Conservative reform bill, which Benjamin Disraeli had introduced into the Commons, citing with approval Bulwer-Lytton's denigration of it as 'a middle-class bill with aristocratic drag-chains'. Clutching at the coat-tails of the nobility, Jones also announced his approval of Lord Teynham's alternative reform measure.[126] In April Jones contested Nottingham again, not on the Chartist land nationalization platform of two years earlier, but instead in support of the four-point programme agreed at

---

[124] *CN* (12 Feb. 1859), 3–4; (4 June 1859), 1; Ian F. W. Beckett, *Riflemen Form: A Study of the Rifle Volunteer Movement, 1859–1908* (Aldershot: The Ogilby Trusts, 1982), 111, 298. On the legacy of Chartism for the volunteers, see: Hugh Cunningham, *The Volunteer Force: A Social and Political History, 1859–1908* (London: Croom Helm, 1975), 27–8.

[125] *CN* (11 Dec. 1858), 4; (29 Jan. 1859), 3; (5 March 1859), 3; (12 March 1859), 1; (19 March 1859), 1–3.

[126] *CN* (12 Mar. 1859), 5; (26 Mar. 1859), 1–2.

the St Martin's Hall conference, namely, registered manhood suffrage, triennial parliaments, a more equal distribution of constituencies, and the ballot. Now his tone towards Bright became more conciliatory: 'if you desire to strengthen the hands of Mr. Bright in any Reform struggle, the way to do it surely is not to elect men who will oppose him for going too far, but to elect men who will go as far or further.'[127]

The Nottingham election was a disaster for Jones. He polled only 194 votes, and perhaps should have taken up offers to stand in other constituencies, such as Cheltenham. Despite spending nine days in the Midlands town during two separate visits, and scrambling together a 'National Manhood Suffrage Association' to provide election funds (only £6 was raised), he fared worse than in 1857, when he had fought a comparatively desultory campaign. His Nottingham agent put his finger on the problem: the accusations of impropriety still hanging over Jones from the reform conference of 1858.[128] The feud had simmered away during the days of the Political Reform League, with militant Chartists such as James Henriette and James Savage claiming that Jones had abandoned Chartism, and with Reynolds resuming his attacks on Jones's personal character in September 1858, when it was mooted that Jones might stand for Greenwich at a by-election. As he recommenced his political lecturing in the new year of 1859, Jones found himself being labelled not Chartist enough by a noisy few and too Chartist by the chattering many. His response was to launch a libel action against Reynolds in January.[129] Eventually in July, almost exactly eleven years to the day after Jones was sentenced by Chief Justice Wilde, the libel action came to court.

Forty years earlier Jones and Reynolds might have settled their differences with a duel; forty years later the W. T. Steads of this world might have launched an undercover investigation to dig out the awful truth about both men. But in 1859 the obvious place to defend honour was in the theatre of a courtroom. And as courts go, the assembled cast in the Queen's Bench division on that midsummer morning were an interesting crew. The case was heard before Chief

---

[127] Jones, 'Electors and non-Electors of Nottingham' (14 Apr. 1859), East Midlands Collection, University of Nottingham; *CN* (2 Apr. 1859), 5; (9 Apr. 1859), 1; (16 Apr. 1859), 1.

[128] James Ellerthorne to Jones, 30 Apr. 1859, SC; *CN* (7 May 1859), 1.

[129] *Reynolds's Newspaper* (5 Sept. 1858), 11; *CN* (1 Jan. 1859), 1.

Justice Cockburn, who had prosecuted Palmer in the Rugeley poisoning trial two years earlier, and who would, fourteen years later, preside over the trial of the most notorious Victorian case of social imposture: the Tichborne claimant. Jones's counsel was Edwin James, late of the successful defence of Simon Bernard in the Orsini affair, also a counsel in the Rugeley poisoning, and recently elected MP for Marylebone. Two years later James was disbarred for professional misconduct and fled to America, where he divided his time between the stage and the courtroom. Reynolds's team was headed by Sergeant Shee, the most famous Roman Catholic barrister of his generation, who had defended Palmer in the Rugeley poisoning trial, and who would be mooted as a possible counsel alongside Jones in the Fenian trial in 1867. At this time the bar made no distinction between expertise in civil and criminal litigation. The same combination of forensic evidence and character assessment over which judge and jury ruminated in a murder trial was put before the court in a libel action. In reaching a verdict some familiarity with the facts was required, together with a thorough grounding in the life history of the plaintiff. Jones had found his *métier*.

Jones prepared assiduously for the libel trial. As the writ was served he established a fighting fund, and of all the various appeals he made in the 1850s it proved the most successful, with over £100 raised in a fortnight.[130] Once the Nottingham election was over, and he had given a brace of speeches in the West Riding denouncing factory-owners old (Crossley) and new (Titus Salt), he returned to London, handed over the *Cabinet Newspaper* to be run by John Watts, and began sifting his way through nine years of newspaper accounts and a decade of calumny which was embodied in the witness statements assembled by Reynolds's legal team. He gave James names and addresses of men who would vouch for him—the various auditors of the accounts of the *People's Paper*, dependable friends such as James Bligh and James Watson—and he drummed up enough evidence of atheism and drunkenness on the part of Reynolds' witnesses to make their testimony seem dubious without them ever entering the court.[131] Jones ventured from his desk only once—to Manchester in the middle of May—to give a speech in which he defended the reputation of Feargus O'Connor from a local

---

[130] *CN* (24 Jan. 1859), 4; (5 Feb. 1859), 4.
[131] *CN* (30 Apr. 1859), 5; 'Ernest Jones versus G. W. M. Reynolds. Collection of Evidence' (1859), SC.

vicar who had accused the dead Chartist leader of 'sponging on the poor for a living'. Jones's speech, in which he told the story of O'Connor the noble patriot—'descended from an ancient honourable stock, sprung from a line of kings', who entered the people's movement a man of fortune but left it a pauper, twice imprisoned (first in jail, and lastly in an asylum), and bequeathed only his teachings on the Charter and the land—can be seen as a rehearsal for his own performance in the dock two months later.[132]

After several postponements the libel trial took place on the second Saturday in July.[133] All Jones's careful preparation paid off, for the prosecution focused on Reynolds's libellous accusation that Jones had swindled the Chartist organization out of thousands of pounds throughout the 1850s, only to join up with the Manchester liberals in 1858 and pocket the proceeds of the conference. Jones took the judge and jury through a minute examination of the finances of the *People's Paper*, the O'Connor funeral fund, and through the accounts of the 1858 conference. He claimed that he had favoured a union with the middle classes ever since 1848, although, he hastened to add, not a 'sham union', and he denied that financial inducements had been offered to him by Herbert Ingram in 1855 or Baxter Langley in 1858. He described his insolvency and also the personal financial hardship he had suffered. From the factual, the trial passed to the farcical and fictional, as Reynolds's defence team took over. Was it true, they asked Jones, that the character of Simon de Brassier was based on O'Connor? Had Jones really dined at the Queen's table? Who was his uncle and how much was he worth? Was Jones actually related to the Plantagenets? Witnesses were summoned, but after hearing of Jones's prudence and probity from various accountants, the jury intimated that they had heard enough to convince them of his stainless behaviour. The judge asked if Shee wished to proceed, he consulted with Reynolds, and the libellous charges were withdrawn, with the claim that no 'personal imputation' had been intended. On the contrary, declared the judge, every 'personal imputation' about Jones had been meant, and he awarded costs against Reynolds and insisted on a full retraction in his newspaper. Vindicated, Jones left the court to the sound of cheering crowds.

With his victory in the libel trial Jones won back those most

[132] *CN* (21 May 1859), 1–2.   [133] *CN* (16 July 1859), 1–2.

precious of political commodities: his character and reputation. A few days later, in a dramatic flourish before his readers, he revealed in the *Cabinet Newspaper* that in the trial he had been forced to speak for the first time of the great sacrifices he had made on the working man's behalf.[134] This was patently untrue. Although Jones had never given a full resumé of his misfortunes of the previous decade, he had offered plenty of snippets and hints. Now the court-room had confirmed as authentic the version of his life-story that he had offered so often. But victory came at a price. For whilst Jones's reputation as an honourable if misguided gentleman was vindicated, that of the wider Chartist movement was tarnished. The *Saturday Review*, for example, reported the outcome of the trial, warming to this 'history of the English demagogue' and praising his career of 'disinterested devotion', but also pointing out that the half-a-million readers of *Reynolds's Newspaper* had hardly proved themselves deserving of the vote if they believed such muckraking.[135]

Over the rest of the summer Jones basked in his refashioned repu-tation as a political martyr. There was choreography. At a celebra-tory meeting on Copenhagen Fields a few days after the trial, James Bligh read out loud to the audience the article from the *Saturday Review*. Halfway through his recitation a murmur went through the crowd as Jones was spotted from a distance walking to the platform. Spontaneous applause broke out before he had spoken a word. And there was more hagiography. In the middle of August Jones attended the unveiling of the memorial statue to Feargus O'Connor in the Nottingham Arboretum, praising again the way in which the Irish-man had given up his wealth for the people.[136] But the bills still would not go away, and a few weeks after his libel victory a testimonial appeal was launched, its committee chaired by the former Irish MP, Patrick Murrough. Testimonials for public figures in need were not unusual: both Richard Cobden and George Thompson enjoyed the proceeds of similar appeals in 1859. But few men were quite as over-dramatic as Jones in describing their services. Jones's testimonial committee put out an appeal in a flysheet, which is worth quoting at

---

[134] *CN* (16 July 1859), 1.

[135] *Saturday Review* (16 July 1859), 72. Jones had the transcript of the trial and the *Saturday Review* article republished in a pamphlet: *Libel Exposed: Being a Full Report of the Action for Libel, Ernest Jones v. G. W. M. Reynolds, etc.* (London: Wilks & Co., 1859). For Reynolds's retraction: *Reynolds's Newspaper* (17 July 1859), 6, 8.

[136] *CN* (30 July 1859), 8; (27 Aug. 1859), 1.

length for the flashbacks it offered of Jones's life-story. The gaze was turned back on Jones:

Look back and see him when, fourteen years ago in 1845, he first entered the political movement of the working classes, full of youth and vigour, and with active perseverance and mental capacity of no common order; see him on the platform teaching the men with horny hands their political and social rights with clear and intelligent argument;—see him at his desk, studying to improve the minds of the working classes, as editor of the *Northern Star* and the *Labourer*;—behold him giving up his means of living to serve as an unpaid delegate at the Conference of 1848, and rejecting a large practice which (as Barrister of the Middle Temple) was offered him by an eminent Solicitor;—follow him to Kennington Common and Bonner's Fields, to brave the dangers of lying spies and Government persecution;—follow him to Manchester and see him at the People's Institute, and think you hear him in one of his energetic speeches calling on the people to stand forward boldly to obtain their rights;—see him at midnight dragged from his bed, brought before a Government tribunal, and sentenced for more than two years to a felon's cell for serving his country according to the best of his judgement;— see him, after undergoing his cruel punishment of solitary confinement on the silent system, with all his prospects blasted, again enter the field of political agitation, sacrificing his opportunity of taking his position once more in aristocratic society, to serve the people's cause;—see him the sole heir to his uncle, worth £2,000 a year, refusing to give up his political advocacy that he may inherit that fortune—and behold him disinherited accordingly.[137]

The midsummer appeal was to no avail. Jones petitioned for bankruptcy in October and issued a final call for funds, small—in his newspaper—and large—from various literary folk, including a cheeky appeal to Thomas Carlyle.[138] Letters of support now flooded in, principally from working men in towns and villages that he had visited earlier in the decade during his tours of the Pennines, Scotland, the Midlands, the West Country, and Belfast. Many of the writers were obviously moved by his tale: one man from Windy Nook confessed that it pained him 'that a man who has made so many sacrifices for the Benefit of the Oppressed Class of this Country is to be crushed down'. Another supporter from Rawtenstall was moved to verse which began:

[137] 'To the Friends of Progress, Truth and Honesty' (handbill, 1859), CL; *CN* (30 July 1859), 1.
[138] *CN* (15 Oct. 1859), 1; Jones to Thomas Carlyle, 19 Oct. 1859, Carlyle papers, National Library of Scotland, Ms 1767, fos. 228–9; Jones to Thomas Allsop, 19 Oct. 1859, Yale.

O cruel falsehood vile
Behold thy waning power,
The sun of Truth divinely shine
In this thy fading hours.

But although these loyal supporters were able to scrape together some financial contributions to Jones's cause, they were unable to offer him much political cheer. Many reported that their local associations were dormant or dead. Perhaps the most poignant letter came from John Snowden in Halifax, Jones's adopted political home. Even in Halifax, Snowden reported, emigration and apathy had killed off the movement. Nonetheless, Snowden wished Jones well, and signed off 'with the ardent wish that you will in future look to your own personable interest and work for yourself regardless of the multitude'.[139]

Jones's bankruptcy in November revealed gross debts of £1,900 which, although relatively small, were enough to take the *Cabinet Newspaper*, now losing £4 an issue, off the newsstands the following February. In November Jones, assisted by a further £20 secured from the Royal Literary Fund, concluded a contract with Kent and Co. for a new collection of poems entitled *Corayda*, although only one poem, the aptly titled 'Too Late', was newly penned.[140] Then in the new year Jones gave some more political speeches on the reform question and the volunteers—in Newcastle, London, and Nottingham.[141] He had one last go at newspapers, venturing into the market with the *Penny Times* and the *Weekly Telegraph*, which were published simultaneously (they both carried the same contents) for a fortnight at the end of February. The second and last issue of the *Penny Times* carried domestic advice ('The Housewives' Corner'), reports of clergy misbehaving with the destitute ladies of London,

---

[139] John Oxberry to Jones, 19 Oct. 1859, CL, MUN A.0.10.6/18; John Mills to Jones, 18 Oct. 1859, CL, MUN A.0.10.6/8; John Snowden to Jones, 16 Oct. 1859, CL, MUN A.0.10.6/1. For an account of this appeal and the response it generated, see: John Saville, 'Some Unpublished Letters from Working Men to Ernest Jones in 1859', (unpublished typescript, c.1950).

[140] W. Kent and Co. to Jones, 2 Nov. 1859, IISH; Jones, *Corayda: A Tale of Faith and Chivalry, and Other Poems* (London: W. Kent & Co., 1860); Porter, 'Jones and the Royal Literary Fund', 91–3. *Corayda* was dedicated to Bulwer-Lytton. He had approved the dedication, providing the volume was 'free from political matter', but had refused to write on Jones's behalf to various publishers: Jones to Bulwer-Lytton, 26 July 1858, Bulwer-Lytton Mss, D/EK O25/244.

[141] *CN* (21 Jan. 1860), 1; (18 Feb. 1860), 1; Jones to Walter Jones, 16 Jan. 1860, BJH; Jones to George Jacob Holyoake, Holyoake coll., COSL 1175.

excerpts from a tale entitled 'The Jew's Murder', Jones's own poem 'The Factory Child', and an advertisement for a pamphlet penned by Jones in reply to the *Manchester Examiner and Times*, called *Political Conversations: Taxation and Wages*.[142] It was all a long way from Blackstone Edge in the summer of 1846. The great orator had become a mere conversationist, hacking out a living at the lower end of Grub Street.

By the spring of 1860 Jones had reached the end of his tether. Ten years of being a poor man's editor had brought neither fame nor fortune. The yardstick by which Jones always measured his life's achievements was not his ascent in the republic of workers so much as in the republic of letters. Chartism had not revived in the 1850s, but in many ways that was the least of Jones's failures. Following his release from prison he had tried all manner of means to succeed as a Fleet Street entrepreneur. After 1851 he laid on one side his own aspirations as a political poet and devoted his time to publishing a variety of entertaining literature. Like Reynolds, he hoped that the lighter instructive and amusing content might sugar (and subsidize) the more serious political material. At times Jones strained to keep it clean, with his facility for gushing prose leading to downmarket melodrama, and his eye for intrigue in high places making him pad out his columns with the dirt from the police courts. As he experimented, Jones found the world of poetic fashion passing him by. The emergence of a new generation of male working-class poets, their verses evoking patriotic, temperate, and dignified labour, was championed by Jones, but at the expense of his own brand of chivalric lyricism. He tried too late to reclaim his place in the pantheon of democratic poets with editions of his work which were little more than old wine in new bottles. Throughout all this Jones's commitment to Chartism remained undimmed, but also undiluted. His social and economic vision in the 1850s—centred on land reform as the gateway to an Arcadian paradise—was no different from the heady pastoralism he had articulated on entering the movement in 1846. Marx's mate he may have been, a Marxist he was not. Furthermore, the fate of the Chartist organization under Jones's leadership became inseparable from the complicated business deals to which he was forced to resort in order to keep his newspapers going. Ingram at the *Illustrated London News* and J. Baxter Langley of the *People's*

---

[142] *Penny Times* (3 Mar. 1860), 1–3.

Journal were just two of the less likeable figures into whose orbit Jones and Chartism were both drawn by the dash for cash. And yet Jones ended the decade with his reputation as a political martyr intact. Reynolds was certainly the wealthier man—as Marx tartly observed, he 'is a far greater rogue than Jones, but he is rich, and a good speculator'[143]—but Jones's victory in his libel action against him proved that Jones was the more honest. For all this herculean effort, Jones still ended up bankrupt and eager to find a vocation that paid. 'The papers are dead so much for the support of the working classes', he declared in April 1860, 'I adhere to the Charter as ever, & I shall work in it anew—at the same time that I shall recommence practising at the Bar'.[144] To the bar, or more precisely the Northern Circuit in Manchester and Liverpool, Ernest Jones went a few months later.

---

[143] Karl Marx to Friedrich Engels, 8 Oct. 1858, *MECW* xl. 345–7.
[144] Jones to Thomas Hinde, 3 Apr. 1860, Howell papers, BGI.

6

The People's Advocate, 1860–1865

IN 1854 JONES published an amusing little verse in the *People's Paper* entitled 'Attorneys':

> Friends, neighbours, countrymen, I take
> The liberty to warn ye,
> Against that universal scourge,
> A rascally Attorney . . .
>
> So may I lead a pious life,
> That when to die my turn is,
> My soul may find a resting place,
> Where there are no attorneys.[1]

There were plenty of attorneys in Manchester, and in the early winter of 1860 Jones became one of them. He had in fact resumed at the bar in London in May, taking on a series of briefs passed over to him by busy barristers in the various police and county courts of the capital.[2] Ironically enough, he did two midsummer stints at the Central Criminal Court, the scene of his own trial twelve years earlier. However, the Northern Circuit beckoned. Jones's best contact in the profession was W. P. Roberts, whose practice was based in Manchester. After successfully defending a large group of weavers at Blackburn in August, Jones returned to the north-west in October, stopping off at Hawarden to present in person a copy of *Corayda* to the chancellor of the exchequer,[3] before appearing in court at Preston. Initially he lived out of a suitcase, and then in the spring of 1861 he moved with his family to Manchester. For the next five

---

[1] *PP* (18 Feb. 1854), 5.

[2] The principal source for details of Jones's legal practice between 1860 and 1866 is the case-diary he kept: Jones, Legal Diaries, MCL (hereafter EJLD).

[3] *MG* (9 Aug. 1860), 2; Gladstone, diary entry for 4 Oct. 1860: H. C. G. Matthew (ed.), *The Gladstone Diaries, 1855–60* (Oxford: Clarendon Press, 1978), 523.

years Jones became a familiar figure in the city's courts. As *The Times* recalled on his death in 1869, 'he got a good practice, became florid and stout'.[4] Indeed, the very success of Jones's practice was eventually to prove a handicap, for when he contested the constituency of Manchester in the 1868 election, many Liberals objected on the grounds that he was a lawyer, and a trade-union lawyer at that. Others rumoured that he made his living out of the unrespectable end of the police courts. This chapter chronicles how Ernest Jones, the people's martyr, became Ernest Jones, bespectacled barrister-at-law. Like any lawyer he followed the cab-rank tradition, taking whatever work came along. Unlike most lawyers, however, Jones seldom missed the opportunity to turn the ordinary into the theatrical. And in the sad and sorry tapestry of life filtering through the courtrooms of northern England there was much material for his colourful imagination.

I

The lower courts of the mid-Victorian English provinces were not quite the harsh dispensaries of class law that they sometimes appear. Although judges and juries tended to uphold with vigour the letter of the law of capital against the rival claims of labour, outside the sphere of industrial relations justice was meted out with a medicinal spoon. A mixture of paternalism and pragmatism was often applied, particularly when it was felt that those in the dock required the protection and not the censure of the law. Women and first-time offenders did rather better out of the legal system than contemporary novelists and historical orthodoxy suggest.[5] There were a number of reasons for this. Influenced by the evangelical campaign to clean up the capital code and to end the barbaric ritual of public executions, and also keen to save money, successive governments in the 1850s and 1860s revised the criminal code, reclassifying offences.[6] The

---

[4] *The Times* (26 Mar. 1869), 6.

[5] Margot Finn, 'Women, Consumption and Coverture in England, c. 1760–1860', *Historical Journal*, 39 (1996), 703–22; id., 'Working-Class Women and the Contest for Consumer Control in Victorian County Courts', *Past & Present*, 161 (1998), 116–54. For areas where 'class law' did apply, see: Paul Johnson, 'Class Law in Victorian England', *Past & Present*, 141 (1993), 147–69. And for the far more summary jurisdiction meted out to juveniles, see the London study of Heather Shore, *Artful Dodgers: Youth and Crime in Early Nineteenth Century London* (Woodbridge: Boydell & Brewer, 1999).

[6] Randall McGowen, 'Civilizing Punishment: The End of the Public Execution in

magistracy itself often proved a restraining force. Many large mid-Victorian cities did not have their own assize—Manchester only became an assize in 1864—meaning that urban offenders were often tried in the assizes of the older county towns, where the local gentry on the magisterial bench were often reluctant to rubber-stamp the class law of their urban brethren.[7] At the same time, the idea of a 'criminal class' certainly existed and was widely commented on in the mid-Victorian years, but for the most part it described a border between rough and respectable behaviour. Those who transgressed its boundaries were weak characters, and not, as they tended to be viewed later in the century, a degenerate race outside the pale of civilization. In other words, in the mid-Victorian courts souls might be saved and characters redeemed. It all depended on the sorts of stories that counsel could tell about the lives of the defendants and plaintiffs.[8]

The bulk of Jones's busy practice—a total of some 320 cases a year—involved defending those caught up in petty crime. Apart from a case involving a friendly society in January 1865, Jones never took part in a trial in which a point of law was debated.[9] And with the exception of acting as a junior to a couple of QCs at the York Assizes in March 1864, he never acted in any widely reported cases.[10] The Fenian trial of November 1867 altered that score on both counts, but by then he had given up his Manchester practice. For six years Jones bumped along the bottom of courtroom business, taking on cases involving rape, assault, garrotting, murder, manslaughter, obtaining goods under false pretences, coinage forgery, poaching, and petty theft of all descriptions. He defended robbers of earrings, lead, linen, watches, trousers, jewels, tobacco, coal, Venetian-blinds, slippers,

England', *Journal of British Studies*, 33 (1994), 257–83; V. A. C. Gatrell, *The Hanging Tree: Execution and the English People, 1770–1868* (Oxford: Oxford University Press, 1994), 589–611.

[7] C. H. E. Zangerl, 'The Social Composition of the County Magistracy in England and Wales, 1831–87', *Journal of British Studies*, 11 (1971), 113–25.

[8] Martin J. Wiener, *Reconstructing the Criminal: Culture, Law and Policy in England, 1830–1914* (Cambridge: Cambridge University Press, 1990), ch. 3; id., 'The Sad Story of George Hall: Adultery, Murder and the Politics of Mercy in Mid-Victorian England', *Social History*, 24 (1999), 174–95; Susan Steinbach, 'The Melodramatic Courtroom: Breach of Promise and the Performance of Virtue', *Nineteenth Century Studies*, 14 (2000), 1–34; Jan-Melissa Schramm, *Testimony and Advocacy in Victorian Law, Literature and Theology* (Cambridge: Cambridge University Press, 2000).

[9] EJLD 9 Jan. 1865.

[10] EJLD 19 Mar. 1864.

and even waste. He acted for prostitutes, bigamists, and brothel-keepers, for absconded prisoners, organizers of dog-fights, a klepto-maniac, and the occasional perpetrators of middle-class crime: a bailiff, a former mayor, a town councillor, some priests, and several bankrupts. There were assorted civil cases as well: bastardy claims, licensing applications,[11] and maintenance orders. Sometimes the court must have felt more like a farmyard than a place of justice. Jones defended cattle-rustlers, fish-thieves, a seller of geese, and the owner of an unfortunate horse killed by a runaway train.

Occasionally, however, the court felt like theatre. Jones was invariably counsel for the defence, but not too much should be read into this, for his legal diary reveals that many of his cases were 'dock briefs', that is, he was effectively the duty barrister, taking the case on the day as no one else had been found or instructed. This placed a premium on Jones's ability to master his brief quickly and extemporize accordingly. And in doing this he seemed to find his natural milieu. Particularly during the first months of his practice, Jones's diary records, in addition to the dry details of his case-load, what happened during the trial. Early on in his advocacy he was struck by the importance of impressing not only the judge and jury, but also the audience in attendance in the courtroom. In one of his first cases, in which a woman, found guilty of embezzlement, could not be sentenced as she had a hysterical fit in the dock, Jones described how she was dragged away brutally, her cries from the street outside audible to everyone for several minutes: '[n]o more heart-rending scene was ever witnessed in a court of justice', he noted. Several months later he described how responsive a Manchester courtroom audience had been to his own speech: 'immense attendance of all classes. Great applause. Immediate acquittal.' The following summer, in the same court, having successfully defended a man on a charge of selling goods under false pretences, Jones noted how '[o]n hearing the verdict, the audience burst into deafening cheers'.[12] These comments are significant for they are almost identical to the language used by Jones to describe the impact of his speeches when he joined the Chartist movement in 1846.

[11] In Aug. 1862 Jones, the erstwhile temperance advocate, defended a series of applications for licences from local clerical opposition. He appeared with J. P. Cobbett, another local barrister. Cobbett complained that Manchester still had the same number of public houses as in 1842, despite the increase in population. EJLD 20 Aug. 1862; MG (21 Aug. 1862), 3.

[12] EJLD 19 June 1860, 23 Nov. 1860, 24 June 1861.

Jones was also impressed by the grandeur of the principal courts in which he acted, describing the pomp and ceremony to his youngest sons. The Liverpool Assize was: 'a very grand affair. The Halls are gorgeous in the extreme, the Judge sits enthroned in bright scarlet and snow white ermine. The High Sheriff stops at the Adelphi Hotel, and accordingly we have, morning & evening, guards of Javelin Men at the doors, & great crowds to see the daily departure & return of the said functionary. The trumpets sound beautifully every morning.' And he made similar observations of the York Assize, which was opened by a service in the cathedral, the barristers joining a procession behind the judges, with a vast crowd filling the pews for the 'imposing ceremony'.[13] In 1864 Manchester finally got its own taste of Gothic splendour. The York Assize was annexed to the Midland Circuit the previous year, and the new Manchester Assize courts, designed by Alfred Waterhouse, opened for business in the midsummer of 1864. They were regarded as palatial, and they certainly afforded plenty of room for barristers keen to play to the gallery, having enough seating for up to one thousand spectators.[14] Jones was thus provided on his own doorstep with an ideal stage for turning the mundane into the extraordinary, although in fact it was at the Liverpool Assize in 1863 when he did this to greatest effect.

Amongst the hundreds of cases that Jones handled in the 1860s were several murder trials. Two of the most notorious were the so-called 'Ribchester murder' and the 'Shudehill murder', both tried on the same day in March 1863 at the Liverpool Assize. Jones was defence counsel on both occasions, and the proceedings in court and the wider publicity they generated reveal his unrivalled ability to make a drama out of a crisis. Duncan McPhail, one of the two men charged with the murder of an old widow in a lonely farmhouse at Ribchester, near Preston, was arrested and committed for trial in December. Levi Taylor was committed two months later for murdering his wife in a pub off Shudehill, one of the tough working-class districts of downtown Manchester. In both cases the evidence of guilt was overwhelming, so the chief task facing Jones was to have the charge reduced to the lesser crime of manslaughter, or to plead for clemency when the judge came to pass sentence. In each case

[13] Jones to Walter Jones, 12 Dec. 1860, 10 Mar. 1862, BJH.
[14] Colin Cunningham and Prudence Waterhouse, *Alfred Waterhouse, 1830–1905: Biography of a Practice* (Oxford: Clarendon Press, 1992), ch. 5; 'A Visit to the Assize Courts', *Freelance* (3 Aug. 1867), 101–3.

Jones painted as rosy a picture of the two men's lives as possible. To save them from the gallows he turned their life-stories into parables of well-meaning misadventure. McPhail, Jones revealed to the court, had started out in life with good prospects and a respectable pedigree. His father had once been a dissenting minister, and although as an apprentice McPhail had been convicted of stealing money from his employer, on his release he had married a respectable woman and set himself up in business as a tailor and draper. This business failed and he then went into a partnership in the drink trade in Clitheroe. His business colleague proved a shady character, recounted Jones, and McPhail was convicted of theft and sentenced to transportation. In Dartmoor, however, reprieve lay at hand, for he fell under the influence of the prison chaplain, and he was allowed to serve his sentence out on parole, as a 'ticket-of-leave' man. He returned to Blackburn, but despite his best efforts he failed at every trade to which he turned: tailor, coal-dealer, cheese-maker. In the last of his doomed business ventures he fell out with his partner, and the murder was the result. Try as he could, Jones was unable to wring sufficient mitigating virtue out of McPhail's biography. He was found guilty, sentenced to death, and executed a few weeks later. A local paper, informed but not impressed by Jones's summing up, commented that '[t]he dishonest career of Duncan McPhail . . . might be expected to have a tragical termination'.[15]

Jones fared rather better with Levi Taylor.[16] Unlike McPhail, Taylor was not a middle-aged recidivist whose crime was carefully planned with an accomplice. Taylor was a young man who had killed his wife, Mary Ann, in a fit of rage, having discovered her returning to her old ways of prostitution in a local bawdy-house. All the same, the murder—her throat was cut—was particularly brutal, and the odds on a sentence of death were short when Jones rose to address the jury for the final time. Taylor, declared Jones, was no common culprit, 'but the unhappy victim of a lofty passion, a passion arising from the highest source'. His crime had not been premeditated, and although he confessed 'I have murdered her' to a policeman shortly afterwards, what did a poor man know of the

[15] EJLD 8 Dec. 1862, 21 Mar. 1863; MG (31 Mar. 1863), 3; Manchester Courier (4 Apr. 1863), 7.

[16] EJLD 4 Feb. 1863, 21 Mar. 1863; MG, (28 Mar. 1863), 5; ME (28 Mar. 1863), 4; The Trial for Murder. Reg. v. Levi Taylor: Speech in Defence of the Prisoner, by Ernest Jones, Esq (Manchester: John Heywood, 1863).

distinction between manslaughter and murder? Jones proceeded to argue that Taylor was temporarily insane, his mind 'poisoned' by extreme provocation. His provocation was that he 'was a respectable young man, of the best and highest character, who became in love with a beautiful young girl of the most vicious habits', Jones went on. His was, 'the holiest, purest love. Had it been a mere sensual passion he might have gratified it . . . He need not have married her. But he was virtuous and good . . . he endeavoured to reclaim her from her mode of life . . . his friends . . . implored him not to link his fate to hers—but he was deaf to all their prayers—and he the honest, upright, virtuous young man married the prostitute.' Within half-an-hour of the wedding Mary Ann was back drinking in a brothel. Taylor pursued her, but she escaped. After several days of looking for her, including walking thirty miles barefoot, Taylor found her, settled in Manchester with her for two days, and then realized his only hope was to remove her from the sinful city and start over again. Out of his meagre wages he rented furnished lodgings in a village outside Manchester. 'See how', Jones emphasized, 'he strains every nerve, see how he exhausts his poor resources, to make a happy little home'. But Mary Ann left two days later and returned to the brothels of Manchester. He followed but eventually gave up the chase, announcing his intention to leave her forever. Before he left he asked for a farewell song—thereby 'showing a touch of poetry in his soul', Jones explained: 'A song! Something pure to remember him by, amid all that chaos of vice and sin by which she was surrounded. Some poor rude melody to haunt his after life—something sweet, and kind, and dear, for memory to sing to him at midnights far in some Australian settlement.' Then Taylor took her upstairs to her room, 'and the last act of the long tragedy approaches'. The deed done, Taylor made no attempt to escape, but was overcome with genuine remorse.

Baron Martin, the judge in Taylor's trial, thought Jones's defence of temporary insanity was nonsense, and told the jury so. But Jones's pathos had worked its old magic nonetheless. Although the jury took only ten minutes to find Taylor guilty of murder, they made a strong recommendation of mercy. Taylor fainted on hearing the verdict, the judge donned his black cap, many of the jury were in tears, and Jones's publishing friends back in Manchester busied themselves putting the final touches to two penny-dreadfuls describing the whole trial. Po-faced and pious, John Heywood, the Manchester publisher, explained that the narrative of the trial 'may be a useful warning' to those who rushed to support capital punishment, but in truth, in the light of the jury's recommendation for mercy, Heywood's pamphlets were an attempt to put further pressure on the judge to show leniency towards Taylor. And he did. A week later the sentence was commuted to life imprisonment.[17]

At one level Jones's defence of McPhail and Taylor simply shows a canny lawyer at work. On closer inspection, however, it is clear that he was deploying some of the same stock literary devices of romanticism that he had used in his poems and novels in the later 1840s and 1850s. For example, Levi Taylor was not merely caught up in a crime of passion and unreason, but he had embarked on a mission to save and redeem his wife from the sinful environment of the city and return her to the innocence of the countryside. Bidding her goodbye in the pot-house, he summoned from nature a melody. Thus passion is double-edged. Love, whilst natural and elemental, can also be delusionary. Similarly, poverty and adversity can condemn their victims to sin and desperation, but straitened circumstances can also produce nobility of sentiment, especially through exposure to religion or poetry. Jones turned Taylor's life into melodrama, and invited the jury to compose the final scene.

2

Jones thus proved on occasion to be a successful people's advocate, in the sense that he incorporated narrative styles drawn from popular literature and drama into the courtroom. To what extent was he a people's advocate in the more obvious sense: that is to say, what did he do for the workers in the industrial-relations litigation in which he became involved in the 1860s? It was a labour dispute in Blackburn that first brought Jones to the Northern Circuit in the summer of 1860, and although petty crime did predominate in his practice thereafter, there were three high-profile trials in which Roberts and Jones acted on behalf of strikers and trade unions against employers. The first came a year into Jones's Manchester

---

[17] *Trial for Murder*; cf. *The Manchester Murder. Antecedents of Levi Taylor: His Birthplace: His Exemplary Life; His First Acquaintance with Mary Ann Bradbury; Her Strange Career; Taylor's Fascination, and its Consequences. Their Marriage, the Wife's Irregularities; the Husband's Struggles to Reform her; His Journey to Bakewell, Barefoot; His Subsequent Eccentricities; The Last Link of Love, The Murder!,* etc. (Manchester: John Heywood, 1863); *MG* (9 Apr. 1863), 2.

practice in November 1861. When the brief reached his desk it must have appeared a mouth-watering prospect, for the plaintiffs were none other than the family firm of John Bright, the carpet manufacturers of Rochdale. Although Bright himself had no direct dealings with the business, Jones clearly approached the dispute with a score to settle, his memory of their altercation in 1859 fresh in his mind.[18] His four defendants had been 'locked out' (effectively sacked) from the factory after demanding higher wages subsequent to a new power-loom being introduced. The Bright firm replaced them with other workers, and the four sacked men picketed outside the factory and were joined by workers from another *bête-noire* employer: the Crossleys of Halifax. Courts made no distinction between picketing and unlawful assembly in the early 1860s, and thus Jones found himself defending his clients from the charge of inciting a crowd. However, he chose as his field of judicial battle the laws of political economy, arguing that the carpet-workers had a 'natural right' to claim part of the profit generated by the introduction of the new loom. Provocatively, Jones accused the opposing counsel of being at 'war with the Manchester School, and with his clients, Messrs Bright' in denying such a right. The attempt to make the Rochdale Police Court a theatre of class war failed, and Jones's defendants were convicted. Earlier that year Jones had also tried to bring radical political economy to the service of a client. He defended a Manchester book-hawker from the charge of operating without a licence by claiming that the poor had a right to ply their trade as best they could, and if his client were barred from selling literature on the street he would end up a vagrant. The magistrate found Jones's argument 'ingenious' but convicted the man nonetheless.[19]

From experiences such as these Jones seems to have concluded that radicalism was no useful ally in fighting capital in the courts. In the two other notable labour disputes of his legal practice during the 1860s he put on one side attempts to turn the principle of the law upside-down in the interests of the working man, and concentrated instead on uncovering mitigating evidence. In the summer of 1864 Jones was brought in to defend fourteen Barnsley miners from a series of charges of conspiracy to riot and assault. The case arose out of a dispute at Oaks Colliery, one of the largest in the county, where miners, backed by the recently reorganized West Yorkshire Miners

---

[18] EJLD 15 Nov. 1861, 22 Nov. 1861; *MG* (23 Nov. 1861), 5.
[19] EJLD 10 July 1861; *MG* (11 July 1861), 2.

Association, were pressing for payment by weight rather than measure of coal collected. The men came out on strike in February, the colliery owners began evicting them from their cottages, and soon the fields around the mine filled up with tents in which the evicted men camped out with their families, as 'blackleg' labour was brought in from Staffordshire and elsewhere.[20] Here was fertile territory for Jones's literary imagination, radical agenda, and legal expertise. The miners were a semi-agricultural labour force, ripe for insertion into the romantic pastoral canon. The feudal working conditions imposed by 'King Coal' had been the target of Jones's censure in the pages of the *People's Paper* in the early 1850s. And W. P. Roberts had built his reputation as a miners' lawyer. Yet Jones devoted his defence to providing counter-evidence against the charge of conspiracy, which ironically meant playing down the collective strength of the Miners' Association, for the burden of Jones's argument was that the disorder accompanying the strike was spontaneous and not premeditated. He succeeded. The summons for conspiracy was withdrawn, and although some of the miners were committed for trial at the Leeds Assizes on assault charges, by the winter of 1864–5 a compromise had been reached between the colliery owners and the Miners' Association.

Similarly, Jones opted for circumstantial evidence in his defence of the men caught up in the brick-making 'outrages' in Manchester, which reached the courts in 1864, and which three years later became part of the remit of the commission appointed by Parliament to investigate trade unions nationwide, but with special reference to the Sheffield cutlery trades and the brick-making trades of Manchester.[21] Jones's two clients, Holland Cheetham and Walter Slater, respectively president and treasurer of the Stockport Brickmakers' Union, were charged with assault against a fellow worker

[20] EJLD 28 July 1864; *Barnsley Times* (30 July 1864), 2; Frank Machin, *The Yorkshire Miners: A History* (Barnsley: National Union of Mineworkers, 1958), chs. 3–4; Helen and Baron Duckham, *Great Pit Disasters: Great Britain, 1700 to the Present Day* (Newton Abbot: David & Charles, 1973), ch. 6. Jones returned to Barnsley the following winter, defending trade unionists in a series of cases involving charges of assault and intimidation: EJLD 6 Dec. 1865, 12 Dec. 1865; *Barnsley Times* (16 Dec. 1865), 3.

[21] EJLD 3 Dec. 1864; *MG* (8 Dec. 1864), 3; 'Report Presented to the Trades' Unions Commissioners, by the Examiners Appointed to Inquire into Acts of Intimidation, etc. . . . in Manchester and its Neighbourhood (2 vols.,), vol. i, p. viii, *Parl. Papers*, xxxix, (1867–8); Richard Price, 'The Other Face of Respectability: Violence in the Manchester Brick-Making Trade, 1859–70', *Past & Present*, 66 (1975), 11–32.

who had refused to join their union during its strike. Jones pleaded to no avail that the charge rested on a simple case of mistaken identity. The two men were convicted and sentenced to long terms, of which they served only two years before being pardoned when further evidence revealed them in fact to have been elsewhere at the time of the assault. Again, resorting to the law rather than to class war had paid dividends and brought Jones the esteem of the labour movement. By 1867 he had been elected to the executive council of the Operative Bricklayers' Association, in September of that year he appeared before the Trades Unions Commission on behalf of the Manchester and Salford Operative Brick-makers' Burial Society, and by 1868 he was being sought out for his expertise on labour law by the new wave of labour politicians such as Robert Applegarth.[22] Was it all a case of mistaken identity? Jones was certainly a less radical labour lawyer by 1864. Equally he was more successful, and in the years before the legal recognition of trade unions in 1868 that probably counted for more.

Indeed, by the mid-1860s Jones seems to have learned the lesson that the most effective people's advocate need not be the most political nor partisan. The law did not allow for much choice of case-load, especially in new or small practices such as Jones's was at the outset of the decade. From his own calculations of income and expenses at the end of 1860 it is clear that he was barely breaking even. He had to take work as it came in, and sometimes found him-self on the wrong side of progress. For example, in July 1861 he and Roberts defended a group of anti-Catholic rioters in Oldham, and so eloquent was Jones's testimony that the accused had no long-term ill-feeling towards their Irish brethren that only a very light sentence was passed. The accused partied all the way back to Oldham, denouncing the Irish members of the town's police force, singing 'England for the English, and Ireland for the Irish', and raising cheers for Roberts and Jones.[23] Equally, attempts to wrong-foot the law on the grounds of principle, as Jones tried in the Bright carpet-workers' case, did not work. So although Jones was always ready to take up popular causes in the courts—and often gave pro bono advice—he

---

[22] Operative Bricklayers' Society, *Nineteenth Annual Report* (London: Operative Bricklayers' Society, 1867), SC; 'Report Presented to the Trades' Unions' Commissioners', ii. 32; Jones to Robert Applegarth, 26 Aug. 1868, Frederic Harrison papers, British Library of Political and Economic Science, London, 5/1/49.
[23] EJLD 10 July 1861; *Oldham Chronicle* (13 July 1861), 3.

achieved most when he was least radical.[24] His practice could be all things to all people. To some of his colleagues at the bar in Manchester his was an unrespectable practice,[25] to others he became renowned as a reliable advocate of the trade unions, but to the wider world he appeared to be just another attorney.

3

Public notoriety went alongside increasing domestic bliss for Jones during the 1860s. In the spring of 1861 he moved permanently to Manchester, having fallen for the suburban charms of Higher Broughton a few months earlier.[26] Lying in the curve of the River Irwell, looking westwards towards Salford, 1 Upper Compton Street was a desirable middle-class home in a relatively new part of the city. Three of his sons joined him, with Beaufort (that is, the eldest, Ernest) remaining in London, where his father had helped him find employment at the Board of Trade. Jones was also joined some time in 1861 by Elizabeth Darbyshire, a farmer's daughter from Failsworth near Oldham, whom he eventually married at the end of 1867. After a time the whole family moved to Wellington Street, on the other side of the Bury Road. His two youngest boys—Llewellyn and Walter—were sent to Manchester Grammar School, and Jones tried hard, although apparently unsuccessfully, to find gainful employment at the Foreign Office for his other son, Edmond. Beaufort became a particular source of worry for Jones. He lodged with Jane's ageing parents in London, complained of being passed over for promotion at work, and fell into bad ways of drunkenness and debt, eventually returning to Manchester for training as an accountant.[27]

Jones entertained the highest hopes for his own career-advancement as well. In May 1862 he applied for appointment as a judge, and two months later for the coveted position of revising barrister for the Northern Circuit. Nothing came of either approach. Despite

[24] Pro bono work included a poaching case in Loughborough, and advice to the Sowerby Co-operative Society: EJLD 4 June 1862, 10 June 1862.

[25] In April 1867 a local solicitor accused Jones of keeping an 'unrespectable' practice: *Solicitors' Journal* (13 Apr. 1867), 556. The accusation may have stemmed from an incident several years earlier when the two men were present at a fight in the robing room: EJLD 3 Oct. 1861.

[26] Jones to Walter Jones, 12 Jan. 1861, BJH.

[27] Henry Cockcroft to Jones, 19 May 1862, SC; Mrs Atherley to Jones, 17 July 1865, SC; Lord Clarence Paget to Jones, 18 March 1863, BJH.

soliciting the support of Gladstone and Lord John Russell, Jones found in his way Baron Wilde, the son of the judge who had sentenced him back in 1848, whose patronage was key to any promotion in the north.[28] Instead of judicial honour, Jones came to rely on the minor trappings of civic life. He joined local dinner tables with the mayors of Manchester, Salford, and Bolton, visited London for the Handel Festival at the Crystal Palace, became president of the Crichton Club, a working man's literary society which met in Chorlton Mechanics Institute, and gave occasional lectures on literature, including one on 'Fiction-writing versus fiction-writers', which he delivered in February 1866.[29] The previous year he also returned to novellas, turning out 'The Guardian Angel' for a new paper, the *Bradford Times*, in June.[30]

Inevitably, however, it was into the cosy, male, and upper-class camaraderie of the Northern Circuit that Jones was most drawn. He frequently appeared in the lampoons of the local satirical paper, the *Freelance*, which started up in 1866. In a skit of August 1867 entitled 'The Northern Circuit', Jones is described alongside the dozen or so other leading lights of the Manchester Bar: 'there's the Jones who pleads for suffrage manly, | How Jones do like eye-glasses.'[31] And an even more telling record of Jones's incorporation into the world of wig and pen is provided from his appearances at the barristers' 'mess' on the Northern Circuit, that is, the dinners that concluded the day's proceedings in court. Between the summer of 1863 and the summer of 1867 Jones was a fairly frequent diner at the 'mess' when the assizes were held in Lancashire, taking part in the forfeits, games, mock trials, and impromptu humour that was a feature of these occasions. On two nights in 1867 it all got rather out of hand, revealing Jones and the company he kept at their very worst.

In March 1867, at the height of the public outcry over Governor Eyre, the colonial official responsible for the killing of 439 Jamaican blacks in 1865, the 'mess' of the Northern Circuit held a mock debate

[28] Jones to Edward Cardwell, 13 May 1862, BJH; George Elliot to Jones, 22 May 1862, 11 July 1862, BJH; Charles Ryan to Jones, 9 July 1862, BJH; Lord Stanley to Jones, 15 May 1862, BL Add. Ms., 52,484, fo. 33.

[29] The club also reprinted three of Jones poems in the *Crichton Annual*: 1 (1865–6), 31: 'The Silent Cell', 86 ('The Legacy'); 2 (1866), 58: 'The Stars', trans. from von Arndt, and: 67: 'To the Departed'. Details of Jones's social calendar are taken from menus, invitations, and programmes in SC, 1862–6.

[30] 'The Guardian Angel', *Bradford Times* (24 June 1866), 3.

[31] *Freelance*, (3 July 1867), 37.

over the rival claims of 'our great negrophilists and philanthropists',
Mr Hopwood and Mr Stanley (two local barristers), who had both
'fallen in love with the same nigger lady'. 'Mr. E. J.' was called upon
to supply a verse in defence of Stanley. It went as follows:

> An ardent love consumes my soul
> A fiery passion thrills my frame
> My fancies warm refuse control
> For Quashie's lit the magic flame
>
> Her ebon cheek doth brightly shine
> Her ample mouth with nectar flows
> Her full thick lips, inviting mine
> Do tempt me neath her broad flat nose
>
> Against her swelling bosom pressed
> And clasped within her circling arms
> Sweet rapt'rous privilege thus to rest
> Or e'en to kiss her hindmost charms
>
> If lech'rous Hopwood (damn his eyes)
> With tongue so smooth and lips so civil
> Attempt to rob me of my prize
> I'll pitch him forthwith to the devil
>
> Has he not Fleet Street and the Strand
> Where he can pick and choose at leisure
> Yet he would back the 10th command
> And steal away my peerless treasure
>
> Unless he stops his little game
> And shows me signs of true repentance
> I'll brand him with a traitor's name
> And cut his beard, on his acquaintance[32]

A few months later the same 'mess' held another mock debate, this
time in the aftermath of a Manchester meeting on the Conservative
government's reform bill, then going through the House of
Commons—a bill to which John Stuart Mill had added an amendment to extend the vote to women (effectively to older women who
owned property in their own right). The Manchester meeting had
been addressed by Jones and John Bright, and they were both ridiculed by the 'mess'. The 'Attorney General' for the evening declared

---

[32] Northern Circuit Minute Books, 18 Mar. 1867, pp. 331–2, Greater Manchester
County Record Office, G/NCO/1/30.

his views on women's suffrage: 'he considered a woman at 40 was like a bank note which had better be changed for two twenties.'[33]

What is particularly revealing about these two occasions when Jones joined in with *in camera* chauvinism, pouring venom and spite on the very heart and soul of Liberal piety, was that he did not need to be there. By March 1867 it was several months since he had given up his practice in order to become a full-time lecturer for the Reform League. Although he returned to court famously for the Fenian trial in November 1867, in the spring and summer of that year he was, by day, doing the platform circuit of the parliamentary reform campaign alongside working men, suffragists, and some of the very 'philanthropists' he denounced by night. In returning to his old haunts at the bar he was exercising a choice about the kind of company he wished to keep. By 1867, in Manchester if not elsewhere, Jones was known chiefly as an attorney, and as this chapter has shown, he was associated with some of the virtues and a few of the vices of that profession. Like a character in one of his melodramas from the mid-1850s, Jones had put his past behind him and created a new world, its boundaries neatly defined by his family villa in the Manchester suburbs, his office downtown, and the new assize courts a few blocks away. In his mid-forties Jones had at last found some of the fame and fortune he craved as a young man. He now had more luck as a poor people's advocate than he had previously as a poor man's editor, although some of the ways in which defended his clients suggest he could not always discriminate between the romance of fiction and the romance of fact. Despite being involved in some of the major industrial disputes of the early 1860s, he was less notorious as a working man's lawyer, quickly giving up the attempt to challenge the orthodoxies of political economy in the court. With modest success at the Manchester bar came the recognition of his peers, but also seduction into the claret-laden cynicism of a professional clique in the provinces. No wonder that in 1868 voters in Manchester were beginning to ask who was Ernest Jones and what had he done? By the time he came to contest the Manchester parliamentary election, Jones was to find that his legal career had furnished one identity too many.

[33] Northern Circuit Minute Books, Summer 1867, pp. 364–5. For the background to the Reform Bill, the women's suffrage campaign, and the Governor Eyre controversy, see: Catherine Hall *et al.*, *Defining the Victorian Nation: Class, Race, Gender and the British Reform Act of 1867* (Cambridge: Cambridge University Press, 2000), chs. 3–4.

7
The People's Champion, 1866–1867

IN 1865 ERNEST Jones returned to the field of political agitation. He joined the parliamentary reform campaign, initially under the auspices of the Manchester Manhood Suffrage League, and then from the autumn of 1866 as a paid lecturer of the Reform League. Jones took part in one of the defining moments of the reform struggle—debating the merits of democracy with the Scottish scholar J. S. Blackie over two nights in Edinburgh in January 1867, and along with Edmond Beales and John Bright, he became one of the most indefatigable and in-demand speakers in the months leading up to the passage of the Second Reform Bill in July 1867. To some, Jones appeared as a relic from another age. Early on in the campaign he gave a lecture at Huddersfield, where the audience was reported to be comprised of '[o]ld veterans grown grey in the service of Reform . . . [who had] . . . walked many miles to have one more glimpse of Mr. Jones, and it was largely in recognition of his past labours that the Reform League made him an honorary vice-president in 1865.[1] Although sixteen years younger than Beales, and Bright's junior by eight years, Ernest Jones seemed to have become a grandfather in the cause of reform, his presence on the platforms of the Reform League a symbolic reminder of radical continuity. Not that Jones was content with being a totem. In April 1866 he resigned temporarily from the League, accusing the leadership of compromising over manhood suffrage, thus underlining the gulf that persisted between the six points of the Charter and the demands of the new generation of advanced Liberals.[2] In many ways, however, Jones's role in the

---

[1] *Beehive* (9 Sept. 1865), 1.

[2] Royden Harrison, *Before the Socialists: Studies in Labour and Politics, 1861–1881* (London: Routledge & Kegan Paul, 1965), 20–1; John Breuilly *et al.* (eds.), *The Era of the Reform League: English Labour and Radical Politics, 1857–1872* (Mannheim: J. & J. Verlag, 1995), 119–20; A. D. Taylor, 'Ernest Jones: His Later

parliamentary reform movement in 1866–7 went well beyond that of a Chartist legend. Far from being ossified by the reform debates of the mid-1860s, Jones, the man of letters and fallen peer, found himself restored to his element. For the 1867 Reform Act was not only a 'leap in the dark', it was also a leap into the past, as scholars, statesmen, and scribes looked to classical and medieval examples in order to vindicate democracy in the present. The most modern instances of democracy—imperial France, war-ravaged America, and Jamaica under martial law—offered little comfort to advocates of an extended franchise in Britain and Ireland, and ammunition to its opponents such as the 'Adullamites' led by Robert Lowe, who combined with the Conservative opposition to defeat the Liberal party's Reform Bill in June 1866. In their *Essays on Reform* of 1867 some of the liberal intelligentsia of Oxford and Cambridge took refuge in antiquity in order to assuage modern dilemmas over democracy. Other Liberals, such as Bright, appealed to the example of the English Commonwealth in the 1640s.[3] In Jones, who twenty years earlier had enthused late Chartism with lyrical tales of chivalric knights and Roman plebeians, the Reform League found their own in-house historian, willing and able to locate the suffrage question within a suitably heroic and romantic setting. They also found in Jones a window on the workings of the aristocracy. By the time the Conservatives returned to office in the summer of 1866, the question of parliamentary reform was no longer about when, but about whether a party headed by some of the oldest landed families in the country would heed the popular demand for constitutional change. Jones, who the *Commonwealth* newspaper pointed out 'might now be sitting with Cranbornes and other "Right Honourables"' but for his patriotism and conscience,[4] once again played the part of the class traitor, the virtuous peer, questioning the sincerity of his own kind

Career and the Structure of Manchester Politics, 1860–69', MA thesis, Birmingham University (1984), 28–31; John Belchem and James Epstein, 'The Nineteenth-Century Gentleman Leader Revisited', *Social History*, 22 (1997), 174–93.

[3] Christopher Harvie, *The Lights of Liberalism: University Liberals and the Challenge of Democracy, 1860–86* (London: Allen Lane, 1976), ch. 6; F. B. Smith, 'Democracy in the Second Reform Debates', *Historical Studies (Australia and New Zealand)*, 11 (1964), 306–23; Catherine Hall *et al*, *Defining the Victorian Nation: Class, Race, Gender and the Reform Act of 1867* (Cambridge: Cambridge University Press, 2000), 25–6; Patrick Joyce, *Democratic Subjects: The Self and the Social in Nineteenth Century England* (Cambridge: Cambridge University Press, 1994), 194, 197.

[4] *Commonwealth* (27 Oct. 1866), 1

and urging the League's supporters to keep up their pressure from without. Thus, in 1866–7 Jones had rather more than his Chartist past to recommend him. In April 1866 Benjamin Disraeli defended his Conservative party's approach to parliamentary reform, promising to follow where Simon de Montfort and Henry III had led, enfranchising 'these skilled artizans, these handicraftsmen of the Plantagenets'.[5] When it came to dignifying the modern struggle of labour versus capital, of peers versus the people, with the halo of olden-time history, Disraeli had few equals. Ernest Jones, possibly the last living descendant of the Angevin kings, was one.

I

As with many of his contemporaries in the mid-1860s, Jones found his way back into the parliamentary reform question via foreign affairs, namely the American Civil War and the Schleswig-Holstein dispute. In so doing he slipped quietly into the grooves of mainstream Manchester liberalism. In January 1863 Edward Greening and other erstwhile members of the Manchester Manhood Suffrage League helped establish a branch of the 'Union and Emancipation Society' in the city. Greening became secretary whilst Thomas Bayley Potter, son of the former mayor, served as president.[6] The main aim of the society was to counter the pro-southern states propaganda being disseminated by Confederate agents, and the implicit hostility to the north being articulated by various Liberal and Conservative politicians, ranging from the unambiguous, such as J. A. Roebuck, the Sheffield MP, to the apparently neutral, like William Gladstone, who the previous November had called for recognition of the Confederacy's claim to constitute a new nation. A week before Christmas 1862 John Bright had launched a fierce attack in Birmingham on pro-Confederate opinion. He argued that the secession of the southern states from the Union had nothing to do with sovereignty and everything to do with maintaining slavery. Bright championed the north, praising its prosperity and calling it the 'lifeboat' of Europe, where emigrants could find the land, liberty,

---

[5] *Hansard*, 3rd ser., 183, (27 Apr. 1866), 97.

[6] *ME* (24 Jan. 1863), 4; Tom Crimes, *Edward Owen Greening: A Maker of Modern Co-operation* (Manchester: The Co-operative Union, 1923), 30–2. For the connections between late Chartism and support for the Union, see: Eugenio F. Biagini, *Liberty, Retrenchment and Reform: Popular Liberalism in the Age of Gladstone, 1860–80* (Cambridge: Cambridge University Press, 1992), 72–3.

and independence denied them in the old world.[7] This was a message which proved particularly controversial in the textile districts of Lancashire, where the war against the Confederacy meant a stoppage of the cotton supply, with workers laid off, soup kitchens established, and the rules of parochial relief relaxed in order to provide sustenance for the thousands thrown out of work. Lancashire was thus considered fertile ground for the agents dispatched to Europe by the Confederacy, and by the Southern Independence Association, formed by Lord Wharncliffe in the autumn of 1863.[8] Jones was quickly drawn into the activities of the Manchester Union and Emancipation Society. He appeared at meetings in February and April 1863 (alongside Francis Newman and Goldwin Smith at the latter), and in November 1863 gave a long lecture to the Ashton-under-Lyne branch of the Society, entitled 'The Slaveholders' War'.[9]

Without mentioning Bright by name in his lecture, Jones went over substantially the same ground as his former foe. Like Bright he poured scorn on the idea that the Confederacy was upholding the principle of national sovereignty or even free trade. Like Bright he praised the economic powerhouse that was the north, and pointed to the way in which states of the Union acted as a 'magnet' to the poor emigrants of Europe. He ridiculed the feudal aristocracy that ran the southern states, and appealed to the bonds of Anglo-Saxon unity which existed between the men of England and the peoples of the Union. Jones concluded his speech by hoping for the continuation of the patriotism of their race on both sides of the Atlantic: 'there in America, its armed resistance to insurgent crime; here in England its moral endurance of unmerited privation; here the battle of patience against suffering; there the conflict of patriotism against rebellion.'[10] Indeed, so Bright-like was Jones's stance that in March 1864 he was invited to give the same lecture in Bright's home-town of Rochdale. Although he kept aloof from party politics, the road was clearly open

[7] James E. Thorold Rogers (ed.), *Speeches on Questions of Public Policy by John Bright, MP*, 2 vols. (London: Macmillan, 1869), i. 197–225; R. J. M. Blackett, *Divided Hearts: Britain and the American Civil War* (Baton Rouge, La.: Louisiana State University Press, 2001), chs. 1–2; Duncan Campbell, *English Public Opinion and the American Civil War* (Woodbridge: Boydell & Brewer, 2003).

[8] Mary Ellison, *Support for Secession: Lancashire and the American Civil War* (London: University of Chicago Press, 1972).

[9] *ME* (25 Feb. 1863), 3; (7 Apr. 1863), 5; Jones, *The Slaveholders' War: A Lecture Delivered in the Town Hall, Ashton-under-Lyne* (Ashton-under-Lyne: Ashton-under-Lyne Union and Emancipation Society, 1863).

[10] *Slaveholders' War*, 44.

for Jones's enthusiasm for liberty abroad to be hitched to the cause of parliamentary reform at home. At Rochdale he concluded by observing that although he had last addressed them in the 'stormier times' of Chartism, he had 'not forgotten the men of Rochdale, their love of freedom and truth', and he trusted that 'those who are now struggling, honourably and constitutionally for the freedom of the black will join in every effort for a fresh instalment towards the Charter of an Englishman's Liberty'.[11]

A month earlier Jones had appeared at the Manchester Town Hall alongside notable local liberals such as Thomas Bazley (one of the town's MPs), Absalom Watkin, and George Wilson at a meeting called to oppose British intervention in the Danish and Prussian dispute over the north German states of Schleswig and Holstein.[12] Jones was not one of the famous three whom Lord Palmerston quipped were the only people who understood the complexities of the Schleswig-Holstein question (one had gone mad, one—Prince Albert—was dead, and the other—himself—had forgotten the details). But having 'resided for a great number of years' in Schleswig and Holstein Jones claimed special acquaintance with the topic. He took his audience back to the fourteenth century and recited a long list of treaties since then which confirmed the inseparable nature of the territories of the two states and the inadmissibility of Denmark's claim to Schleswig. He explained how the crisis had arisen as the Danish throne recognized the female line, but under the Salic law the German duchies did not. And he likened the chicanery of the Treaty of London of 1852, in which the Danish claim was supported by the other European powers, to a father cutting off the entail of his estates without consulting his only son and heir. Again Jones concluded with a moral for domestic politics, hoping that the working men in the audience would turn their attention away from the 'balance of power' in Europe to the question of the balance of power at home, warning that if the word 'reform' was not mentioned in the Queen's Speech, it must be mentioned in louder tones by the people. There was little of old Chartism in all of this, and a great deal of modern Manchester liberalism. 'Three cheers for John Bright' shouted out a somewhat confused voice from the crowd at the end of Jones's Town

---

[11] Jones, *Oration . . . on the American Rebellion, Delivered at the Public Hall, Rochdale* (Rochdale: Rochdale Union and Emancipation Society, 1864), 16.

[12] Jones, *The Danish War* (Manchester: repr. from the *Manchester Examiner and Times*, 1864).

Hall speech. Nearly twenty years earlier Jones had denounced British ministers for standing aside whilst Poland and Italy lay prostrate under the Romanov and Habsburg yokes. Now there was little to choose between his stance on international affairs and that of Cobden and Bright. Of course, Jones's appearances on a public platform during 1863–4 were limited. He was frequently on assize and other court business, and the few lectures he gave, with their long excerpts from the newspapers and other contemporary sources, suggest hastily put-together performances, probably at the prompting of Greening. At the same time, when the parliamentary reform campaign began to revive locally in the spring of 1864, Jones found himself being painted into a Liberal corner largely of his own making.

2

Not for the first time in Victorian Britain, the provinces led and London followed in the reawakening of the parliamentary reform question in the mid-1860s. It was the Leeds MP Edward Baines who brought in a bill for franchise reform in May 1864, and a month earlier the remnants of the Anti-Corn Law League in Manchester formed the National Reform Union, choosing George Wilson as its first president. Jones attended this inaugural meeting too, but was unsuccessful in carrying an amendment making registered manhood suffrage the principal aim of the new organization.[13] Ever since 1848 there had been a substantial difference between what the provincial industrial towns wanted out of franchise reform and what London desired. The effect of lowering the household rental franchise on the electorate of the booming capital was always going to be far less dramatic than in places such as Leeds and Manchester where property prices had remained more static. Hence provincial liberals such as Wilson and Baines were not prepared to go much further than a new rental franchise of £6 per annum, whereas in London for the best part of a generation household suffrage had been a consistent radical demand. In throwing in his lot with the parliamentary reformers of Manchester Jones was very much in the wrong place at the right time. His suspicions of the moderate Manchester Liberals and their influence over the London reformers threw a shadow over

---

[13] *ME* (20 Apr. 1864), 3; *Manchester City News* (23 Apr. 1864), 3.

his early involvement with the Reform League, which was established at a great meeting in the capital attended by trade unionists, the London Working Men's International Association, and assorted radicals in London in February, 1865.[14]

From the outset, Jones felt that the Reform League was too equivocal in its support for manhood suffrage. 'London must give the signal', Jones wrote to Karl Marx in February 1865, explaining that 'if London could take the initiative in holding a great Manhood Suffrage meeting . . . it would be like a spark to a mine, and the whole people would awake from one end of the country to the other'.[15] Impatient at the slow progress in the capital, Jones helped resuscitate the Manchester Manhood Suffrage League in April 1865, and at its first meeting in Failsworth he spelled out just how far the MMSL meant to go with franchise reform: '[b]y manhood suffrage they did not mean that every man should immediately become possessed of the vote, but get it under certain restrictions; that he should be registered as a resident, not a householder, for a certain number of months in the borough where he claimed to vote, before he could exercise the vote; that he should be twenty-one years of age, and that he should be untainted with crime.'[16] Unfortunately, the candour of the MMSL was not contagious. When some of the London-based members of the Reform League came north to attend the National Reform Union's Manchester conference in May, Jones found them reluctant to come out for manhood suffrage pure and simple. Edmond Beales and Peter Taylor jr. would only sign up to a resolution which echoed William Gladstone's call for all those morally fitted to be brought within the 'pale of the constitution', and promised at best household suffrage based on payment of poor rates.[17] Jones did emerge from this meeting with recognition of a sort. In June he was elected vice-president of the Reform League.

[14] F. M. Leventhal, *Respectable Radical: George Howell and Victorian Working Class Politics* (Cambridge, Mass.: Harvard University Press, 1971), 56; Breuilly *et al.*, *Era of the Reform League*, 114, 131–2; Henry Collins and Chimien Abramsky, *Karl Marx and the British Labour Movement: Years of the First International* (London: Macmillan and Co., 1965), 63–4.

[15] Jones to Karl Marx, 10 Feb. 1865, repr. in Dorothy Thompson, 'Letters from Ernest Jones to Karl Marx, 1865–1868', *Bulletin of the Society for the Study of Labour History*, 4 (1962), 13–14.

[16] *Beehive* (1 Apr. 1865), 1. Earlier Jones had mentioned six months' residence in a letter to Marx: Jones to Karl Marx, 10 Feb. 1865, repr. in Thompson, 'Letters from Ernest Jones to Karl Marx', 13–14.

[17] *Beehive* (20 May 1865), 1; Jones to Karl Marx, 17 May 1865, repr. in Thompson, 'Letters from Ernest Jones to Karl Marx', 19–20.

Nonetheless, the MMSL went into the general election held in July 1865 in a mood of sectarian defiance. Jones informed George Howell, the Reform League's secretary, that the NRU—'the middle-class Election men'—were showing no sign of life, and that the MMSL's own candidate, Abel Heywood, stood a very good chance of victory.[18] In the event Heywood came bottom of the poll, to the evident surprise of Jones's colleague Edward Greening, who saw the success of the moderate Liberal, Edward James, as bitter confirmation of the ascendancy of the NRU. It was, he confided to his wife, 'a great triumph for the *Manchester Guardian*'.[19]

Throughout the autumn of 1865 Jones and George Howell continued a game of cat and mouse. Anxious to secure as broad a base of provincial reformers as possible, Howell sounded out Jones and Greening on the possibility of joint action with the NRU, urged them not to show public hostility towards the rival organization, and promised a disbelieving Jones that Beales would not commit the Reform League to anything less than its publicly declared support for household suffrage—of some sort. For his part, Jones maintained his view that the NRU was 'impracticable' and 'dying out', whereas his lectures for the MMSL were going down a storm in the textile towns of the Pennines.[20] It was an uneasy relationship, with neither side able to make much more than symbolic concessions. The Reform League refused to join the NRU's deputation to meet Lord John Russell in the new year of 1866, making a separate visit later in the month, whilst Jones agreed to attend the League's February conference at St Martin's Hall in London, scene of his own 'Evenings with the People' nearly a decade earlier. But when the executive of the League decided to give its backing to the Russell ministry's reform bill in March 1866—a bill which proposed lowering the borough franchise only to a £7 rental—Jones resigned not only the vice-presidency but his membership of the League as well. In signing up to the Liberal bill, Jones argued, the Reform League was sanctioning legislation which would see the working class lose what

[18] Jones to George Howell, 12 June 1865, Howell papers, BGI, Letters (1864–8), fo. 19.
[19] Greening to his wife, 14 July 1865, Edward Greening papers, COSL, Manchester, EOG/1/1.
[20] George Howell to Jones, 9 Oct. 1865, Howell papers, BGI, Letter-book 1 (1865–6), fo. 5; Howell to Edward Greening, 16 Oct. 1865, ibid., fo. 16; Howell to Jones, 16 Oct. 1865, ibid., fo. 18; Howell to Greening, 6 Nov. 1865, ibid., fo. 41; Jones to Howell, 12 Oct. 1865, ibid., Letters (1864–8), fo. 1.

little political power it had gained since 1832 and which would greatly increase the grip of the 'monied class'. Jones gave the Reform League and the readers of the *Commonwealth* a lesson in class relations:

up to a certain point, the interests of the middle class and working class are identical, and beyond that point they diverge. For instance, anything that opens new fields for the capital of the rich, anything that spreads commerce and even what encourages speculation, while immensely benefiting the capitalist, also benefits the working man by promoting employment. But as soon as a certain point is reached, as soon as competition begins to tell in the markets of the world, as soon as capital amassed in a few hands, commences to monopolise the machinery it develops, so soon the community of interests ceases, and capital begins to fight its battles with the weapon of cheap labour, and every victory of *money* is purchased by the defeat of *man*.

In this way, working-class support for the Liberal franchise bill was a 'hallucination' and a 'scandalous delusion'. Just as in 1832, popular pressure would yield temporary social and economic benefits, but in the longer term the only class to gain would be the capitalists: the Gilpins, Goschens, and Stansfelds of this world.[21]

The Reform League and its organs were thunderstruck by Jones's resignation. Howell, who had a soft spot for Jones, regretted that he had joined the 'obstructive party'. The council of the League were officially polite: '[t]heir esteem for your long, faithful, and talented services, as one of the most devoted friends of the People, renders your retirement of much painful interest to them', but Beales took it more personally, pointing out to Jones that the League had consulted widely and democratically in arriving at their decision to support the government reform proposal in an 'open and straightforward manner'.[22] The editor of the *Commonwealth* (probably Marx and Engels' compatriot and friend, J. G. Eccarius) took issue with Jones's depiction of the bill as only serving the interests of the monied class. The monied class was not interchangeable with the middle class, pointed out the paper; indeed, they only comprised a small part of the middle class, and more often than not 'having become great

---

[21] *Commonwealth* (21 Apr. 1866), 5; (12 May 1866), 6; Jones to George Howell, 4 May 1866, 12 May 1866, 17 May 1866, Howell papers, BGI, Letters (1864–8), fos. 2–4. Jones effectively gave up the MMSL as well, for Greening and Hooson remained supportive of the Reform League's position: Jones to Karl Marx, 22 May 1866, repr. in Thompson, 'Letters from Ernest Jones to Karl Marx', 20–1.

[22] George Howell to Jones, 7 May 1866, Howell papers, BGI, Letter-book 1 (1865–6), fo. 310; Edmond Beales to Jones, 14 May 1866, ibid., fo. 318.

magnates, have ceased to belong to the middle class altogether'. The majority of the middle class, declared the *Commonwealth*, were 'on the contrary, hard up for money'. The real class enemy remained the landed aristocracy.[23] Jones had got his political sociology all wrong

Within a few months, however, Jones was back on track. By the autumn of 1866 he had not only rejoined the League, he had even given up his Manchester practice and returned to the full-time lecturing circuit as the employee of the League, and moreover, he began to appear on platforms alongside the untrustworthy Beales, and also John Bright—by name, if no longer by association, the personification of Manchester liberalism. How are we to account for this turnaround, which even by Jones's elastic standards of consistency seems unusually complete? One answer, as always, was money. At the end of October 1866 the Reform League streamlined its system of payments to its lecturers, providing a salary of £2 a week (quickly raised to £2 10s.) with all travel, business, and incidental expenses thrown in, as well as a returnable £10 advance and 20 per cent commission on all monies received following lectures.[24] Toeing the League's line made financial sense, if nothing else. Lecturing for the League also got Jones out of Manchester, and to a large extent got Manchester out of Jones. That is to say, he no longer saw the reform struggle as a straight fight between the metropolitan rich and the labouring poor, a view hardened perhaps by too many dock briefs in the assizes of Manchester and Liverpool. As he toured the country, resuming his acquaintance for the first time in over a decade with the agricultural Midlands and Scottish Lowlands, with the industrial villages of the north-east and Yorkshire, and with reformers as far afield as Dublin, Jones's old Chartist agenda began to re-emerge in his speeches—the tried and trusted vision of a virtuous people in thraldom to a landed elite. Above all, Jones's rapprochement with the Reform League resulted from the sea-change in the reform debate brought about by the defeat of Russell's government in the summer of 1866, and its replacement by the Conservative administration of the 14th Earl of Derby. For much of 1865 and 1866 the breach between the MMSL, the NRU, and the Reform League was symptomatic of the wider tensions within the Liberal party over where the limit of the suffrage should be drawn.

[23] *Commonwealth* (21 Apr. 1866), 4.
[24] Reform League Executive Committee Minutes, 27 Oct. 1866, Howell papers, BGI; Leventhal, *Respectable Radical*, 80.

Should the vote be extended to the £7 or to the £6 tenant, or should simple occupation of a household suffice, or should there not even be a 'bricks and mortar' household franchise at all, but a residential one which might embrace lodgers and compound householders (i.e. those who did not pay their poor rates in person)? As statisticians stacked up scenarios of an electorate swamped by the urban poor, Liberals divided and their reform bill was lost. With the Conservatives in office, however, the stakes were rather different. The prospect was raised of Lord Derby's cabinet forestalling on constitutional change altogether, and stifling the reform movement as well. Within weeks of the Conservatives taking office, a Reform League demonstration in Hyde Park ended with mounted policeman charging at the assembled crowds. The moral was obvious, and Jones was quick to draw it: the landlord class would not give up their power without a fight.[25] When the railings of Hyde Park came tumbling down, so too did the divisions between moderate and radical parliamentary reformers.

Thus, there was no real surprise when, six months after taking his leave of the Reform League, Jones joined Beales and John Bright at a series of monster meetings and banquets in the late autumn of 1866. At Birmingham, Manchester, Leeds, and Glasgow the League turned on the spectacle and carnival of a bona-fide people's movement. In Manchester caps of liberty festooned in Reform League colours were worn by the estimated 80,000 demonstrators, and photo-montages of the Hyde Park victims were borne aloft. In Leeds an orderly procession, some 20,000 strong, of trades societies, masons, miners, town and village committees, sixty musical bands, singing troupes, and gaily caparisoned carriages and gigs made their way from the town centre to Woodhouse Moor. The plain white banners with red lettering put out by the National Reform Union predominated along the route, and unanimity of sentiment characterized the speeches, with Jones and Beales taking up the denunciation of aristocratic power where John Bright had left off. There was a similar procession of 50,000 tradesmen at Glasgow, carrying examples of their handicraft, where Jones seconded the resolution of thanks to Bright.[26] At these meetings Jones remained third on the bill behind Bright and Beales—and sometimes further down still if there were prominent

[25] *MG* (11 Aug. 1866), 4; *ME* (11 Aug. 1866), 5.
[26] *Beehive* (13 Oct. 1866), 6, (20 Oct. 1866), 6; *MG* (25 Sept. 1866), 5; *ME* (25 Sept. 1866), 5–6; *Scotsman* (17 Oct. 1866), 7.

local speakers. But there were signs that his status within the parliamentary reform movement was growing week by week. In October he posed for a studio portrait and had the photograph sent on to Howell so that the engraver of the *Illustrated London News* might turn it into a copy capable of reproduction and dissemination nationwide.[27] A fortnight later the *Commonwealth* carried a short biographical account of Ernest Jones. Noting that its gallery of eminent characters was usually made up of men from humbler walks of life, the paper praised Jones as an exception to the rule that 'upper class morality' only bred worship of money and power: 'Born in the ranks of the aristocracy, nurtured in wealth, with the glittering prospect of fortune and luxury before him, he hesitated not to sacrifice his personal interests at the shrine of principle, and to devote his energies, comfort and liberty, and almost his life itself, for the benefit of his suffering fellow country-men.' The biographical narrative followed the usual journey through Jones's 'life', although certain aspects were given topical emphasis, such as his marriage to Jane, who, it was pointed out, was related to the senior branch of the Stanley family, thus sharing in the pedigree of the new prime minister. Also highlighted was the fact that Jones was imprisoned merely for advocating the points of the Charter, principles which only 'Adullamites' like Robert Lowe now opposed. A degree from Göttingen University was thrown in for good measure, the verdict—though not the anti-democratic caveat—of the *Saturday Review* in 1859 added, and the piece concluded by equating the death of Chartism with the cycle of Christianity which ended with the death of Christ. The six points were no longer talked of, but the principles of democracy they enshrined lived on.[28] In November Jones received perhaps the ultimate accolade of radical Liberal acceptance, dining at the Potters' Manchester table with none other than John Bright.[29]

It was in Edinburgh in the new year of 1867 that Jones showed his true value to the Reform League. Following the League's demonstration and banquet in Glasgow back in November, John Stuart Blackie, Edinburgh University's Professor of Greek and an opponent of manhood suffrage and the ballot, threw down a gauntlet to the reform movement, challenging them to put forward a 'Bright, or

[27] Jones to George Howell, 11 Oct. 1866, Howell papers, BGI, Letters (1864–8), fo. 16.

[28] *Commonwealth* (27 Oct. 1866), 1.

[29] Thomas B. Potter to Jones, 8 Nov. 1866, SC.

Beales, or Jones or McLaren' in order to debate the merits of reform. '[W]ith Aristotle in one pocket and Plato in the other, and a great deal of Scottish rummlegumption in the front battery', Blackie boasted, 'I think they will find me a sharp customer.' Through the auspices of the Scottish branch of the Reform League, Jones took up the challenge, insisting that the debate covered not only Athens and New York, as Blackie had suggested, but democracy in general, otherwise Athens and New York 'might supply a kind of *kuma hata thalassan* argument in which the *kuma* might not be a fair specimen of the great sea'. His linguistic credentials intact, Jones stated that he had 'some slight knowledge of Aristotle and Plato', but was unacquainted with 'Scottish rummlegumption'. Jones's acceptance took Blackie by surprise. He attempted to wriggle out of the debate, insisting that the arrangements be made by the Edinburgh Working Men's Institute, where he had originally issued his challenge, and not by the Scottish branch of the Reform League, whose existence he claimed ignorance of. Baiting Jones, he said he wanted to hear a 'calm and philosophical statement of both sides of the case, not a vulgar show of political pugilism' or 'a vulgar fight between two political combatants to gratify the mob'. But Jones gave as good as he got, denying that an audience of respectable working men would turn into a mob, and raising the stakes further by inviting Blackie to speak first, with Jones following the next evening, having had only twenty-four hours to read, absorb, and reply to the learned man's lecture.[30] It would be the ultimate exercise in extempore.

The two nights' debate duly took place at a ticketed meeting in the Edinburgh Music Hall at the beginning of January.[31] Ladies were present, and on the platform Blackie and Jones were joined by the city's Liberal worthies, including Duncan McLaren (Bright's brother-in-law), David Masson, the Shakespearean scholar, and Peter Lorimer, the Presbyterian minister whose own oratory had so inspired Jones two decades earlier. On the first night Blackie's three-hour speech ranged over many examples of democracy ancient and modern, concluding that all the most notorious examples of the republican system—Greece, Rome, Venice—had ended in failure, or

[30] *Commonwealth* (8 Dec. 1866), 5; (22 Dec. 1866), 1; Anna M. Stoddart, *John Stuart Blackie: A Biography*, 2 vols. (Edinburgh: William Blackwood & Sons, 1895), 29–33.

[31] *Scotsman* (4 Jan. 1867), 4, 5; (Jan. 1867), 7; *Commonwealth* (12 Jan. 1867), 4; Jones, *Democracy Vindicated: A Lecture Delivered to the Edinburgh Working Men's Institute* (Edinburgh: Andrew Elliot, 1867).

worse, imperialism, whilst the two most prominent modern examples—despotic France and corrupt New York—amounted to subversions of the principle of democracy. Jones took to the stage the following evening and prefaced his lecture by denying the rumour, fuelled by the *Scotsman*, that he had been given a proof copy of Blackie's lecture several days earlier. In fact he had only received it the previous midnight, and had not read it until that morning. And yet he had managed to write out his lecture in full in time to pass copy onto the newspapers and deliver it that same evening. Having fulfilled one part of the challenge, Jones went on to meet Blackie on his own ground: 'I will go with him to ancient Greece . . . to classic Rome; I will accompany him to revolutionary France; I will walk by his side in our Australian colonies, and attend his footsteps to republican America'. Throughout he accused Blackie of making a schoolboy error of confusing the 'ochlos' (the mob) with the 'demos' (the people), and he brought on Herodotus, Thucydides, and Macaulay to demonstrate how democracy had brought glory to the ancient world, whilst aristocracy had pitched it in into war and conquest. The democracy of modern France he contrasted with the absolutism and feudalism of the Bourbon regime, the corruption of New South Wales he attributed to its origins as a convict colony. He refuted tales of Tammany Hall in New York with De Tocqueville's rosier picture of Philadelphia and Dr McCosh's (a Belfast Professor of Logic) testimony about respectable factory workers in Massachusetts. In what proved the most controversial part of his lecture, Jones concluded his survey of modern America by asserting the benefits of democracy: '[I]t takes those whom your system has corrupted, and degraded, and debased, and turns them into the worthy citizens of the happiest country in the world.' The same results might be achieved in Britain: 'Are we not the same race? Are they not of our flesh and blood—our brothers and sisters—immortal souls—those coins of Heaven's treasury, from whom by your base handling, you have effaced the King of kings, but whom the mint of freedom has re-stamped with the image of their God?' Jones went on to defend trade unions, the right of public meeting and demonstration, and the ability of working men to choose their own representatives. And in a rousing climax he rejected the wisdom of one ancient in favour of another. St Paul, he pointed out, had also spoken in Athens, and Jones rounded off his lecture with a series of apt quotes from the apostles applied to the unequal division of land-ownership, national wealth, and political power in the modern age. 'Democracy', Jones reminded his audience, 'is but Christianity applied to the politics of our worldly life.'

Jones brought off a clever piece of theatre in his Edinburgh lecture. With the assembled journalists watching carefully for any sign of rabble-rousing on what was meant to be a polite occasion, Jones turned the tables on his opponent not by cheap invective, but by easily worn learning. The only insult Jones hurled at Blackie was that he was a Whig at a time when the parliamentary reform question had come down to a straight fight between Tories and radicals. In effect Blackie might as well be a Tory. Otherwise Jones won the challenge on the grounds chosen by his antagonist. Whereas the professor had weeks to prepare carefully his text, Jones had dashed off an equally academic riposte in a matter of hours. The professor's eloquence suggested artifice—even the *Scotsman* observed that he was less 'shrewd and witty' than usual—whereas Jones's delivery seemed spontaneous and natural. The lecture revealed Jones in his favourite role—the class renegade, turning his classical education back at his own kind on behalf of the working man. But his lecture had a wider significance. Timing was all. Until Jones's lecture the Reform League had never given a proper refutation to Robert Lowe's claims of the previous year that the artisan vote meant mob-rule. Together with Walter Bagehot, the 3rd Earl Grey, Viscount Cranborne, and all the Cassandras of the reform debate in the mid-1860s, Lowe, by dint of superior scholarship and personal experience, had got away with equating democracy with ochlocracy. And to some extent the violence in Hyde Park in the summer, and the ongoing revelations of intimidation and brutality in the trade societies of Manchester and Sheffield, gave credence to his claims. Jones's was the first attempt by anyone in the Reform League to reply to this demonization of the reform struggle using the same classical and historical range of reference as the opponents of the extension of the franchise. Others quickly followed. *Essays on Reform* was published in March, and one contributor in particular—James Bryce—covered similar ground to that of the Blackie–Jones debate. Bryce agreed with Blackie that the ancient republics were not perfect cradles of liberty, but he also followed Jones in locating democracy at the dawn of Christianity.[32] Jones also pulled off a clever party-political manoeuvre. By querying

[32] James Bryce, 'The Historical Aspect of Democracy', in G. C. Brodrick (ed.), *Essays on Reform* (London: Macmillan & Co., 1867), 239–78.

Blackie's Whig credentials, Jones signalled where 'Adullamite' opposition to reform now really belonged—not on the fence, but in the Conservative camp.[33] In the weeks that followed Jones enjoyed the sort of popular acclaim that had eluded him ever since the summer of 1848. London journalists were somewhat sceptical, but across the country the reaction was overwhelmingly positive. The executive of the Reform League passed on a resolution thanking Jones for the 'able and dignified address', and similar formal addresses were sent from Bermondsey, Durham, and Rochdale.[34] A fortnight after his lecture the *Commonwealth* gave away his portrait gratis in its weekly edition, and Howell and others urged him to write a weekly column for the paper: 'to do battle against a Feudal Caste of English Thugs, the recent upholders of a Slaveholders' Bloody Rebellion.'[35] Jones was besieged with requests to speak—over one hundred invitations being sent to him by the end of March—causing much confusion between Jones and Howell over which towns were included on his itinerary.[36] A cheap edition of his Edinburgh lecture was published immediately, with the Reform League snapping up 1,500 copies for dissemination at its meetings. Jones's Edinburgh publishers floated the idea of a new cheap edition of his poems, although nothing came of this.[37] Jones appeared at all the principal set-piece events of the Reform League over the next few months—at Sheffield, Manchester, Newcastle (which he described to Howell as the largest demonstration ever known there), and before a crowd of 22,000 at the Agricultural Hall in London on the eve of the opening of Parliament. He was also a member of the Reform League's deputation to Gladstone in February.[38] And as the Conservatives' Reform Bill made its way

[33] Blackie long resented Jones's success at stigmatizing him as a Tory: A. S. Walker (ed.), *The Letters of John Stuart Blackie to his Wife with a Few Earlier Ones to his Parents* (Edinburgh: William Blackwood & Sons, 1909), 349.

[34] Reform League, Executive Committee Minutes, 11 Jan. 1867, Howell papers, BGI; Stephen Lumley to Jones, 10 Jan. 1867, John Butterworth to Jones, 11 Jan. 1867, Robert Hanford to Jones, 17 Jan. 1867, SC. For a hostile review: *Saturday Review* (12 Jan. 1867), 34–5, and for a longer and somewhat patronizing treatment from an old acquaintance: [Charles Mackay], 'Blackie and Jones—Democracy in America', *Blackwood's Magazine*, 101 (Feb. 1867), 230–40.

[35] *Commonwealth* (19 Jan. 1867); George Howell to Jones, 21 Feb. 1867, BL Add. Ms. 52, 484, fos. 34–5.

[36] Jones to George Howell, 8 May 1867, Howell papers, Letters (1864–8), fo. 10.

[37] George Howell to Jones, 27 Feb. 1867, 4 Mar. 1867, ibid., Letter-book 2 (1866–7), fos. 267, 290; Andrew Elliot to Jones, 14 Feb. 1867, SC.

[38] *Beehive* (2 Feb. 1867), 1; (16 Feb. 1867), 5–6; *Commonwealth* (26 Jan. 1867),

through its final stages in Parliament in the early summer, Jones returned to Manchester and, together with Beales and Jacob Bright, addressed a triumphant meeting of 15,000 people in Stretford, following a procession from the city centre. Jones told the crowd that 'although the shade of years was beginning to descend upon his head, he should not die until he had seen manhood suffrage'. Even the *Manchester Guardian* conceded that Jones was the true hero of the reform demonstration. He alone, the paper pointed out, had never wavered in his insistence on as wide an extension of the franchise as possible throughout the previous three years, and now found his position vindicated by the decision of Disraeli and Derby to enfranchise all heads of households and a significant number of lodgers too.[39] Admittedly, it was not universal manhood suffrage. In England and Wales the complicated residential and rating qualifications remained, voters in large, multi-member constituencies effectively lost one vote (as Jones found to his cost the following year), and rural England and Wales got off lightly, avoiding household suffrage and with the majority of its constituencies unaffected by redistribution of seats. But once the numbers were totted up it looked—and sounded—like urban, male democracy.

The Reform Bill passed, the Reform League switched its attention to other matters. The League turned to Ireland, which did not get its own separate franchise legislation until the following year. It also began attempts to get as many of its own members selected to contest constituencies at the general election which was believed to be imminent. And it tried to reinvigorate the campaign for land reform. In all of these Jones was to play a central role. At the end of August he travelled to Dublin with Beales and gave a series of lectures on 'Political Justice'.[40] From the summer of 1867 his name began to be mentioned in connection with a number of constituencies, notably Manchester, but also 'several smaller places, one or two of which hold out very alluring prospects of success'. In July he was formally adopted ahead of Abel Heywood by the Trades' Unionist Political Association and the Northern Department of the Reform League as

5; (2 Feb. 1867), 5; (9 Feb. 1867), 4; (10 Feb. 1867), 2; *The Times* (12 Feb. 1867), 12; *ME* (2 Feb. 1867), 5.

[39] *Beehive* (8 June 1867), 1; *MG* (3 June 1867), 3; (4 June 1867), 4; *ME* (3 June 1867), 3–4.

[40] *Freeman's Journal* (4 Sept. 1867), 4–5; *Beehive* (7 Sept. 1867), 1; *The Times* (3 Sept. 1867), 9; (6 Sept. 1867), 6.

the candidate for the new third Manchester seat.[41] And in October he agreed with Howell that he would speak in the League's programme of winter lectures in London on the subject of 'Labour and Capital', by which, as it turned out, Jones understood his remit to be reform of the land laws. Hoping to emulate his success in Edinburgh at the beginning of the year, Jones and Howell planned the occasion with a view to maximum publicity. St James' Hall in London's West End was booked, the ranks of the London press were invited, a publisher was lined up well in advance, and Samuel Morley, the Liberal MP for Nottingham, was invited to chair the occasion. Mindful of Jones's tactics at the 1858 conference, when he had been ambushed, Morley insisted on chairing only if he were allowed to preface Jones's lecture with a few words in favour of industrial courts of conciliation.[42] Jones gave dry-runs of his lecture in Glasgow and Manchester,[43] and the stage seemed set for a repeat of his stunning success of the new year. Jones had almost single-handedly transformed the terms of the debate over democracy. Could he do the same to the vexed question of labour and capital? Before his opportunity arose, the Fenians of Manchester intervened.

3

On 18 September 1867 Sergeant Brett, a Manchester policeman, was shot dead during a successful attempt to free two Fenian suspects, Captain Deasy and Colonel Kelly, being transported across Manchester. In the days that followed the fatal shooting many local Irish men and women were arrested, and five men—William Allen, William Gould, Michael Larkin, Thomas MacGuire, and Edwin Shore—emerged as the principal suspects in the attack on the police van. W. P. Roberts and Charles Nuttall were instructed as their solicitors, and Jones appeared on their behalf at their initial committal in September, and as junior counsel at the Special Commission held in Manchester in November. Jones also defended several of the

---

[41] Jones to George Howell, 12 July 1867. Howell papers, BGI, Letters (1864–8), fo. 36; *Beehive* (20 June 1868), 1; *ME* (8 July 1867), 4; (14 July 1867), 5. The candidature of Heywood was only revealed later: *ME* (26 Sept. 1868), 5.

[42] Jones to George Howell, 8 Oct. 1867, Howell papers, BGI, Letters (1864–8), fos. 37, 40; Howell to Jones, 7 Oct. 1867, 31 Oct. 1867, 4 Nov. 1867, ibid., Letter-book 4 (1867–9), fos. 9, 66, 76.

[43] *Glasgow Daily Herald* (11 Nov. 1867), 6; (12 Nov. 1867), 4; *ME* (29 Oct. 1867), 5.

other men accused of indirect involvement in the assault.[44] The Fenian prisoners needed Jones rather more than he needed them. The controversial trial came just as Jones was rounding off his reinvention as a respectable radical Liberal—a popular lecturer who was being widely tipped to be returned to Parliament in the near future, a veteran reformer who had left behind the hot-headed militancy of his younger days. The Manchester trial in November, followed in December by the Fenian bombing of the court-house at Clerkenwell in London, in which twelve people were killed, brought the Irish political struggle to the British mainland for the first time. These were the first organized conspiracies against the British state since the foiled Cato Street attack of 1820, and the Special Commission sent to Manchester to try the suspects was the first of its kind since the trial of those arrested after the rising in Newport in south Wales in 1839. The death of Sergeant Brett and the subsequent trial sparked alarm nationwide. London sewers were searched for bombs. The Home Office drew up emergency plans to provide the capital with electric light—deemed safer than gas in the event of a bombing campaign. All sentries in London were ordered to cease discharging their rifles whilst on ceremonial duty in case the sound of gunshots caused public panic. Extra guard was placed around the Queen, and her passage back from Balmoral in late October was carefully arranged to ensure that she would pass through Lancashire and the west Midlands during the early hours of morning, so as to lessen the chances of hostile demonstrations or even attempted kidnap. Rumours abounded of threatened Fenian risings in Lancashire if the accused were sentenced to death. There were said to be 100,000 people ready to break out in Liverpool and Manchester, and another 20,000 in Wigan.[45] Against this backdrop of sectarianism, fear, and rumour, anyone associated with the Fenian defence courted controversy. At the beginning of November the Reform League publicly distanced itself from Fenianism. A few weeks later one of Manchester's MPs—Edward James—died, and Jones, in the

[44] For the background: Paul Rose, *The Manchester Martyrs: The Story of a Fenian Tragedy* (London: Lawrence & Wishart, 1970); Hall *et al.*, *Defining the Victorian Nation*, 188.

[45] George Earle Buckle (ed.), *The Letters of Queen Victoria: A Selection of her Majesty's Correspondence and Journal between the Years 1862 and 1878*, 3 vols. (London: John Murray, 1926–8), i. 466–8; Gathorne Hardy, diary entry (20 Oct. 1867), Cranbrook papers, Suffolk Record Office, Ipswich, T501/294; Lord Derby to Gathorne Hardy, 3 Nov. 1867, ibid., T501/63.

thick of the trial, was passed over as a possible replacement. No wonder his behaviour throughout the whole proceedings was odd, to say the least.

Ironically, there might never have been a Fenian murder trial in Manchester had Jones not been so caught up in Reform League business. For it was Jones who had been originally instructed to represent Kelly and Deasy, the two suspects inside the police van. But *en route* to the Reform League conference at Glasgow Jones had forgotten his brief and not turned up at the committal proceedings. Nuttall had appeared in his place and had secured an adjournment, after which the men, still not formerly charged, were returned to prison.[46] Jones was back in Manchester, however, in time to appear for the principal accused when they were brought before the local magistrates for committal. Even then his contribution was fairly small. The hearing lasted five days, but Jones got no further than day one. On 26 September the twenty-eight men accused were brought from the jail to the Manchester police court in a series of sealed vans, under armed escort and at an early hour so as to avoid the crowds. The hearing was hardly under way before Jones protested on behalf of his four clients (Allen, Gould, Shore, and Henry Wilson) that they had been forced to remain handcuffed inside the courtroom. Once the prosecution had set out their evidence, Jones resumed his objections, pointing to the considerable pain around the wrists which the accused were suffering as a result of being handcuffed. Jones also complained about the presence of armed policeman at the side of the magistrates on the bench, and about one of the witnesses being allowed to arm himself with a pistol in the courtroom. His clients were innocent until proven guilty, and the armed police had no constitutional right to interfere with the due process of the law. Robinson Fowler, the magistrate, turned down Jones's objections, explaining that he was acting under police advice in what were highly unusual circumstances. 'Then', declared Jones, 'as a member of the English Bar, I decline to sit in any court where the police override the magistrates. I will not lend myself to any such violation of the ordinary course of justice. There is your brief, Mr. Roberts. I am sorry to return it, but I cannot disgrace the Bar by proceeding with the defence. (Loud hisses from the gallery).' Grabbing his umbrella, Jones stormed out of the court. A rather surprised Roberts conferred

---

[46] *ME* (19 Sept. 1867), 3; F. L. Crilly, *The Fenian Movement* (London: John Ouseley, 1908), 73.

with Jones's clients, and reported that they neither wanted fresh counsel nor their handcuffs removed. For the remainder of the hearing, to Fowler's evident annoyance, Allen, Gould, Shore, and Wilson, were unrepresented in court. They insisted on retaining the absent Jones, and neither allowed Roberts to cross-examine witnesses nor took up cross-examination themselves. After four more days they were all committed to trial at a Special Commission due to commence on 28 October.[47]

Jones was widely criticized for his dramatic exit from the police court. Although he did pursue his objections with Gathorne Hardy, the home secretary, his 'ostentatious and undignified petulance' was deemed to have done his clients a disservice. Legal journals conceded that whilst it might have been customary for prisoners in the dock never to be manacled or handcuffed, they had no rights in the matter and it was all subject to the discretion of the court, a view confirmed by telegram by the Home Office. Jones should have at least accepted the magistrate's decision and represented his clients as best he could.[48] The *Law Times* hinted darkly that Jones may have thrown up the brief because he did not want to offend anti-Fenian working-class opinion in Manchester, where he was expected to stand for Parliament. Jones, suggested the paper, 'may have been glad of an excuse to escape from an unpopular cause in a popular way'.[49] This was a little unfair, for Jones, along with Cottingham and Roberts, continued to press for a fairer trial. Three weeks later they asked the Home Office to postpone the proceedings until the New Year, when the mood of panic and anti-Irish sentiment might have died down. In the present circumstances, they warned, 'the innocent would, despite any effort of the learned judges, be confounded with the guilty'.[50] But there was little chance of delay. The Queen was particularly keen for a 'prompt decision',[51] and towards the end of the month the two Justices, Sir John Mellor and Sir Colin Blackburn arrived in the city and opened the Commission.

[47] *The Times* (27 Sept. 1867), 10; (5 Oct. 1867), 10; Printed Depositions, 26 Sept. 1867, Palatine of Lancaster, PRO 27/18.

[48] *MG* (5 Oct. 1867), 4; *ME* (28 Sept. 1867), 4; *Solicitors' Journal* (5 Oct. 1867), 1063; Jones to Gathorne Hardy, 26 Sept. 1867, PRO, HO 45/7799 (Pt. II), fo. 224.

[49] *Law Times* (5 Oct. 1867), 390–1. A few days earlier Jones was sent an anonymous note containing the following warning: 'Don't be a fool sympathising with a lot of murderers on purpose to please a mob of low fellows and Fenians—it won't pay nor get you better thought of in Manchester': Anon. to Jones, 30 Sept. 1867, SC.

[50] *The Times* (24 Oct. 1867), 12; (25 Oct. 1867), 6.

[51] Charles Grey to Gathorne Hardy, 14 Nov. 1867, Cranbrook papers, T501/261.

Jones played an altogether secondary part in the main trial of Allen, Gould, Larkin, McGuire, and Shore. At first it was assumed that a prominent Irish barrister, such as William Shee, would be the main defence counsel, but in the end William Digby Seymour and Sergeant O'Brien led the defence, supported by Jones and Cottingham. The attorney-general led the prosecution and twenty-three local politicians, businessmen and landowners made up the grand jury. The main business of the Special Commission lasted five days, and in the early evening of 1 November the jury pronounced a verdict of guilty. The only contribution of Jones throughout the five days was to restrain Gould during his post-verdict speech, when he began to protest to the court over the state of Ireland under the English.[52] The verdict returned, the sentence of death was passed on all five men (McGuire was subsequently pardoned), and the Commission then continued for a further two weeks, hearing the evidence against two more sets of defendants. Only in the third trial, in the middle week of November, did Jones undertake the bulk of the defence, appearing for men accused of participating in the riot that followed the attack on the police van and which provided cover for the escaping Kelly and Deasy. Jones had mixed success. Some of his clients were acquitted, others sentenced to penal servitude, but he was at least praised by the judge for his fairness and impartiality.[53]

The trial over, with the date of execution set for Saturday 23 November, Jones left for London to give his 'Labour and Capital' lecture. Not that there was any respite from the Fenian controversy there. As the Commission had begun its work in Manchester, George Odger, a member of the Reform League executive, had succeeded in committing the League to support an appeal for clemency for the Fenians, a move which, Howell confided to Jones, had lost the League some friends. Consequently, at the beginning of November the League publicly disavowed the secretive organization of the Fenians and their methods of assassination.[54] Three days after Jones's lecture a large meeting was held on Clerkenwell Green, at which speakers, including Charles Bradlaugh of the Reform League, called for a commutation of the death sentence, likening the four

[52] C. G. Smith, *The Manchester Fenian Outrage* (Manchester: Alex Ireland & Co., 1867); *The Times* (2 Nov. 1867), 7; (4 Nov. 1867), 4.

[53] *The Times* (8 Nov. 1867), 10; (9 Nov. 1867), 12; (13 Nov. 1867), 10.

[54] Reform League General Council minutes, 1 Nov. 1867, Howell papers, BGI; Howell to Jones, 29 Oct. 1867, ibid., Letter Book 4 (1867–9), fo. 59; *Beehive* (2 Nov. 1867), 1; Leventhal, *Respectable Radical*, 98–9.

condemned to Italian supporters of Garibaldi. The meeting concluded by resolving to send a deputation to the Home Office, and by giving a vote of thanks to Ernest Jones 'for the able way in which he had defended the prisoners'.[55] The following day the deputation called on Hardy, the home secretary, who refused to see them, but led by Jones's former sidekick James Finlen, they barged into Hardy's room anyway, only to be eventually ejected. 'Lawlessness', concluded the anxious Hardy, 'is indeed rife.'[56]

Thus, by the time Jones went ahead with his 'Labour and Capital' lecture in mid-November he was inextricably associated with the Fenian cause, despite the fact that his role in the defence had been rather marginal. His reputation had gone before him. In his lecture at St James' Hall he attempted to turn attention back to the reform question. Ireland was only mentioned twice, and only then in the context of land-ownership. However, some London newspapers used his purported Fenian sympathies to discredit his views on political economy. The success of his Edinburgh lecture was not repeated in the capital. In his London lecture Jones in fact offered little that was new. He began by defining labour as the man, and the principal capital as land. Animals, food, and manufactures were secondary capital, whilst money was only 'representative capital'. Poor relations between labour and capital were caused by the supply of labour exceeding demand. And this in turn was a result of the monopoly of land-ownership. Because there was not enough capital in land available, men were forced to turn to manufactures. The working class had sought various remedies for the labour surplus: co-operation, emigration, and trade unions. Of the first two, as in the early 1850s, Jones was critical, whilst he described the trade unions as offering an important palliative but not providing a solution by themselves. Indeed, Jones likened trade unions to the land monopolists. In keeping up wage-levels, and restricting entry to skilled men, they were responding in kind to the monopoly enjoyed by landowners, whose own restrictive practices were protected by the law of primogeniture and other conventions. But for the labour surplus there would be no trade unions, and with proper exploitation of uncultivated land there would be enough resources to go around—two acres for every family. Proper development of the land

[55] *The Times* (18 Nov. 1867), 9; *Beehive* (23 Nov. 1867), 3.
[56] Gathorne Hardy, diary entry (18 Nov. 1867), Cranbrook papers, T501/294; *The Times* (19 Nov. 1867), 10.

in Ireland alone, suggested Jones, might absorb the whole of the British labour surplus. There would be no need for confiscation or appropriation of existing land-holdings, for only waste-land would be turned over to smallholders. Emigration would cease: '[o]ur true goldfields are our golden fields of wheat.' The land would offer physical regeneration: 'it sends the pure current of the country air through the emaciated frame of city toil', it would create property rights for millions, and restore national pride. 'When was England truly powerful?', asked Jones at the conclusion of his lecture: '[W]hen she had her yeomanry to win an Agincourt, her peasants to fight at Crecy and Poitiers. Give us a million peasant farmers, and you have a million patriot soldiers for old England, whose every cottage is a trusty fortress, with waving cornfields for its golden glacis, and stalwart yeoman for a gallant guard.'[57]

Reporters expecting a lecture on modern trade unions heard an old declamation on the land. True, there was some evidence that Jones had modified his views. He proved less critical of trade unions in 1867 than he had been in 1851, and his information about the depopulation of the great estates was now derived from the recent 'clearances' on the Sutherland estates in Scotland (a subject which also exercised the anger of Karl Marx), rather than reliant on a hazy recall of the shift from a corn economy to a woollen one in the medieval past. But for all his contact with younger trade-union leaders such as Howell and Robert Applegarth, Jones seemed ignorant of the sea-change in the political economy of labour relations in the 1850s and 1860s. He was neither familiar with the greater credibility being attached by labour leaders to the 'wages-fund' theory which went a long way to legitimating the bargaining status of trade unions, nor was he even sympathetic, as he might have been, with emerging historicist accounts of trade unions which located their origins and functions in the medieval guilds.[58] Jones remained as hostile as ever to the whole culture of industrialism. By itself this ensured him a rough ride in the press. *The Times* found Jones's political economy full of contradictions—'[h]e is a

---

[57] Jones, *Labour and Capital: A Lecture* (London: Simpkin, Marshall & Co., 1867), 19.
[58] Eugenio F. Biagini, 'British Trade Unions and Popular Political Economy, 1860–1880', *Historical Journal*, 30 (1987), 811–40; Hall *et al.*, *Defining the Victorian Nation*, ch. 2. For the emerging historicist perspective on trade unions as guilds, see: James Thompson, 'The Idea of Public Opinion in Britain, 1870–1914', Ph.D thesis, Cambridge University (1999), 291–2.

Protectionist, a Physiocrat, Bullionist, and a disciple of M. Proudhon by turns, and all without knowing it'—and the paper also objected to the great prominence that Morley's presence and the Reform League's patronage gave to his views. The *Saturday Review* was more scathing, declaring Jones to be 'communistic', and conflated his views with the Fenian sympathizers on Clerkenwell Green and those who stormed Hardy's rooms in the Home Office. Morley himself left the meeting thinking Jones to be a 'wild Irishman'.[59] Anxious to have the last word, Jones rounded up all the reviews of his lecture, added a rejoinder to each one, and published the whole as a pamphlet the following December.

After his London lecture Jones returned to Manchester to join with Digby Seymour, Cottingham, and Roberts in one final attempt to win a reprieve for the four Fenians. They came up with an ingenious argument to the effect that the two men in the police van were not being held in legal custody, so it followed that the assailants were justified in trying to release them. A proper warrant had not been issued and they had not as yet been charged with an offence. Therefore, the death of Brett amounted to manslaughter rather than murder, and the sentence should be set aside. On Wednesday 20 November Blackburn and Mellor reiterated that the attack was premeditated, and even if the warrant was not watertight, the charge and the verdict were proper.[60] The following day the Cabinet met, reprieved Shore, whom it had been proved was unarmed, but otherwise agreed to leave 'the law to take its course'.[61] In Salford two thousand special constables were sworn in, the streets around New Bailey were barricaded off, and the Albert Bridge over the Irwell was closed so that no one could easily cross over from Manchester.[62] Last-minute meetings were held in London, Birmingham, and Manchester on the Friday. And Jones, who had properly kept his powder dry since the sentence, finally appeared in public at the

---

[59] George Howell, diary entry for 11 Dec. 1867, Howell papers, BGI. For Morley's own defence of his appearance at the meeting, see: Edwin Hodder, *The Life of Samuel Morley* (London: Hodder & Stoughton, 1887), 249–51.

[60] *The Times* (21 Nov. 1867), 10. For a harsh attack on this argument, see: T. C. Anstey, 'Legal Ethics of the Fenian State Trials', *Law Magazine*, 24 (1867–8), 278–93.

[61] Gathorne Hardy, diary entry, 21 Nov. 1867, Hardy papers, T501/294. The trial judges believed Shore to be blameable, but not guilty on the evidence. McGuire's post-sentence speech had also impressed them greatly: John Greenwood to Hardy, 6 Nov. 1867, BL, Add. Ms., 62,537, fos. 16–17; Colin Blackburn to Gathorne Hardy, 6 Nov. 1867, Hardy papers, T501/63.

[62] *The Times* (21 Nov. 1867), 10; *ME* (23 Nov. 1867), 5.

Manchester meeting at the Corn Exchange, alongside Cottingham. Jones called for mercy for the three remaining men, on the grounds that their offences were political, and that England should show generosity as a Christian nation. Poignantly, he observed that in the two adjoining boroughs of Manchester and Salford builders were at work. In the former they were assembling a hustings for the by-election occasioned by the death of Edward James; in the latter they were erecting a scaffold for the execution of Allen, Gould, and Larkin.[63] But for the Fenians, Jones might have been electioneering away in Manchester, rather than lamenting the fate of the condemned Fenians across the river. The next day, in what proved one of the last public executions in the north-west, the three men were hanged amidst the usual atmosphere of solemnity and awe. Back in London Finlen organized a mock funeral procession, starting at a foggy Clerkenwell Green. The ghost of Ernest Jones's past was again summoned to symbolize the present struggle. 'If Irishmen could be executed on the evidence of the perjured witnesses who had been suborned at Manchester', warned one of the speakers, 'Englishmen might expect that the political scaffold would soon be erected for the friends of freedom here, and that Mr. Ernest Jones or some other champion of the people's rights, would be chosen as the first victim.'[64]

A year later Jones added the Fenian trials to his curriculum vitae, and in subsequent decades his role became part of the muddled hagiography associated with his name. In 1867 the story was rather more complex. Fenianism in any shape or form compromised the respectable, middle-of-the-road radical liberalism to which Jones had hitched his fortunes a year earlier. And whilst it seems unlikely that his melodramatic exit from the committal proceedings was a ploy to escape from the taint of terrorism, it did point to the difficulty Jones faced in trying to accommodate the Fenians within his political repertoire. His flamboyant advocacy won him new friends in Ireland, and revived memories in London of his own martyrdom twenty years earlier. In sectarian Manchester, however, his defence of the Fenians did little to raise his reputation.

The Fenian trial also dampened the Reform League's enthusiasm for Jones. In early December, just as the dust was settling on events in Manchester, the bombing of the Clerkenwell court-house in

---

[63] *MG* (22 Nov. 1867), 3; *ME* (22 Nov. 1867), 8.
[64] *The Times* (25 Nov. 1867), 5.

London took place, and the capital became caught up in the wave of panic and anti-Irish bellicosity which hitherto had been most intense in the Midlands and north-west. Jones chose this moment to urge the Reform League to allow him to deliver a follow-up lecture in the capital, this time on 'The Hereditary Land Caste, How they got the Land, and the effects of the monopoly'. George Howell delayed and eventually deflected Jones's request, saying the League's lecture season was already booked up and there was not enough money to fund more lectures.[65] Nine months earlier the League could not get enough of Jones; then Howell had entreated him to come to the capital at every opportunity. Now he was rebuffed and deemed less than useful. Jones was not quite *persona non grata*, but further appearances in London were viewed as unhelpful.

Unperturbed as ever, Jones took his follow-up lecture north, not south, and delivered it instead in Glasgow the following February. In between times he made an honest woman of his partner Elizabeth Darbyshire, sealing the knot at St John's, Broughton, at the end of December and snatching a holiday in Spain.[66] As it turned out the lecture was a reheated version of the second of his 'Evenings with the People' series of 1856–7.[67] Once more the British political system was unveiled as a Gothic ruin. He invited his audience to listen in as he would be:

touching an ancient fabric, founded in the darkness of the middle ages. Time and storm have shaken its haughty towers, but ivy clings upon its shattered walls, veiling their deformities. Around it, art and literature, arms and trade, have twined their varied growth—but the upas and the hemlock flourish in its shadow. Within it, are the glittering bowers of pomp and pride—but there are also the dungeons of suffering and want, the garrets of penury and despair. Alas! the vaults that confine the sighs of misery, supply the arches that support the halls of splendour. That fabric is the BRITISH CONSTITUTION.

At the outset of the lecture Jones eschewed different theories of government, ideal constitutions, and the notion of abstract rights.

---

[65] Jones to Howell, 9 Dec. 1867, Howell papers, Letters (1864–8), fo. 47; Howell to Jones, 10 Jan. 1868, ibid., Letter-book 4, fo. 228.

[66] They were married on 28 December. 'In Spain. Vacation notes, 1867', MCL, Ms. F821.89/J5/47.

[67] Two nights earlier the Scottish National Reform League presented Jones with a congratulatory address: *Glasgow Daily Herald* (13 Feb. 1868), 3; (15 Feb. 1868), 2; 'The Hereditary Landed Aristocracy' was also later reprinted in a penny edition: *Speeches and Lectures of the Late Ernest Jones* [n.d., n.p.].

No-nonsense utilitarianism was called for: '[t]he right of man—is to be happy, so long as that happiness is founded on obedience to the laws of God.' In its current state the constitution did not provide this, hence his exposition, which would: 'throw back the shutters that keep out the light of day—that you, who stand beyond the pale, may look on its interior. The owls of the Church, the bats of the land, the spiders of usury and the ear-wigs of the law, will make a stir among its ivy, but public opinion, like a clear breeze, shall come pouring through its halls with the breath of heaven, the people's voice, which is the voice of God.' The lecture then gave a familiar résumé of Jones's guide to English history since the Norman Conquest, its main theme being the emasculation of freeholders by greedy knights and enterprising Huguenots, its climax coming with a call for a reform of the land laws and the opening-up of uncultivated land to the poor of the industrial towns. There lay the 'promised land', Jones concluded, and to enter it required not so much the invasion of Palestine, but the reconquest of Canaan. Of course the real question remained, could Jones retake Manchester after his exodus with the Fenians?

8

Manchester, 1868

ERNEST JONES was first approached to contest Manchester in the summer of 1867. The invitation came from local trade unions and from the northern department of the Reform League. Jones, it was believed, would be tempting bait for the new working-class electors of the great city, who after 1867 had three MPs to choose instead of two. The people's champion would become the people's choice. But there was a catch. Manchester was one of the testing-grounds of the new minority clause of the 1867 Reform Act, whereby in multi-member constituencies each elector had one less vote than the number of seats. This clause had been introduced late on in the parliamentary debates over the Reform Bill. It was supposed to ensure that smaller parties, such as the Conservatives, were not completely swamped in the big cities. So in Manchester after 1867 electors had two votes to distribute between three choices. The local Liberal party was presented with a problem. The more candidates the Liberals started, the more their vote would divide, and the greater the prospect of a single Conservative sneaking victory. Liberals in Lancashire already faced a resurgent Conservatism in the wake of Gladstone's Irish policy. In Manchester the Conservative challenge was given a slide-rule stimulus as well.[1] John Bright once famously observed that the new minority clause amounted to 'making the last in the race the winner'.[2] For Ernest Jones, it was as though he had reached the end of a marathon only to find the finishing-tape even further away. In order to ensure that the Liberals won all three seats in Manchester, Jones had to become part of the local election machine and fall in with the political credo of Thomas Bazley and

[1] John Vincent, The Effect of the Second Reform Act in Lancashire', *Historical Journal*, 11 (1968), 84–94; Derek Fraser, *Urban Politics in Victorian England: The Structure of Politics in Victorian Cities* (Leicester: Leicester University Press, 1976), 192.

[2] *Hansard*, 3rd ser., 130 (16 Feb. 1854), 735. Bright warned Jones that it would be difficult to return three Liberals in Manchester because of the new 'crippled vote': John Bright to Jones, 4 Oct. 1867, BGI.

Jacob Bright, the two other 'United Liberal Party' candidates. For someone who had made a career out of noble independence, and who was a veteran of one-man election campaigns, it was a bitter pill to swallow, and it turned out to have a nasty aftertaste. No one was convinced by his performance. Erstwhile radicals accused him of compromising and betraying his Chartist principles, whilst moderates suspected him of still being a Jacobin on the loose, or too pro-Fenian. Jones himself was uncomfortable. Unconvinced that he would win easily in Manchester, he explored election possibilities elsewhere—in Dewsbury, Edinburgh, and Carlisle—and in so doing managed to raise even more doubts about his political integrity. Throughout the attacks and slurs of his 1868 election campaigns Jones kept turning to his principal asset: the story of his life and the parable of virtuous consistency that it embodied. In 1868, however, Jones found his past catching up with him.

I

As Disraeli's government struggled to remain in power during the summer of 1868, it was not Manchester but the newly created constituency of Dewsbury in the West Riding of Yorkshire which occupied Jones's attention. The new seat straddled the adjacent towns of Dewsbury and Batley, and at the end of June the Liberal voters of the Batley portion of the constituency held a public meeting and selected Handel Cossham, a Bristol alderman and colliery-owner, as their candidate.[3] Affronted at their neighbours' haste, the Dewsbury Trades Council contacted Jones, asking him if he would come forward as their candidate as there was no unanimity over Cossham. Jones agreed, on condition that a majority of the electors pledged their votes to him. He criticized the 'hole-and-corner representation dictating to the working classes' which had selected Cossham.[4] A comedy of men and manners then ensued, with the two candidates competing for the favours of the two towns, whilst agreeing to stand aside if the other proved more popular. A meeting was arranged in Dewsbury for the middle of July, with Jones's appearance advertised by placards comparing his martyr-like devotion to the people's cause with those few 'who had sacrificed the

---

[3] For the background, see: Christopher J. James, *MP for Dewsbury: One Hundred Years of Parliamentary Representation* (Brighouse: privately printed, 1970), ch. 4.

[4] *Leeds Mercury* (1 July 1868), 4; (4 July 1868), 8; *MG* (8 July 1868), 5.

manhood of the country for their own behests'. Some 15,000 people gathered in the town centre, and heard Cossham contend that Jones was a lawyer and there were too many lawyers in the House of Commons already. It was a challenge that Jones was to face repeatedly during 1868, and his retort became just as commonplace. He had been called to the bar in 1844, he confirmed to the crowd, but had not practised again until 1861, and he need not remind them how he had spent the intervening years, for they were all familiar with his past history. Jones then sketched out his advanced liberalism: support for reform of the church and land in Ireland, support for the trade unions and for abolition of the game laws. The question of who should be candidate for Dewsbury was then put to the vote. Six-to-one the show of hands was in favour of Jones, and the scene seemed set for his adoption by the new constituency. Even the Baines-owned *Leeds Mercury* cooed with enthusiasm. Jones, the paper declared, could hardly be bettered as the 'impersonation . . . of the wants and feelings of the working man'.[5] Within a week, however, Jones had withdrawn from the selection battle and retreated back to Manchester. Having undertaken a thorough canvass, his election committee could only muster 2,700 pledges (out of an electorate of just over 7,000), confirming what some had observed at the Dewsbury meeting the previous week—that many of those who raised their hands for Jones had been brought in from outlying villages beyond the new constituency boundaries. It was even rumoured that Jones had done his own canvassing, and when shown the humble cottages from which his own committee was drawn wisely decided to stay with the wealthier United Liberal Party of Manchester.[6]

Jones emerged from his dalliance with the electors of Dewsbury with his honourable credentials intact—just. But he was less successful in his negotiations with local politicians in Edinburgh and Carlisle, from where soundings about his possible candidature also emerged in the early autumn. Having relinquished Dewsbury, Jones published his address to the Manchester electors on 11 August 1868, simultaneously with the addresses of Bazley and Jacob Bright. It called for abolition of the ratepaying and minority clauses of the recent Reform Act, and an end to the distinction between county and

---

[5] *Leeds Mercury* (8 July 1868), 4.
[6] Ibid. (16 July 1868), 4; (17 July 1868), 4; (18 July 1868), 5; (24 July 1868), 4; (4 Sept. 1868), 4; MG (24 July 1868), 4.

borough franchises, introduction of the secret ballot, redistribution of seats, church reform and tenant right for Ireland, compulsory education and legal protection of trade-union funds. Jones also promised to give up his legal practice when Parliament was in session.[7] Still he toyed with electoral chances elsewhere. At the beginning of September he travelled to Scotland to give a lecture in the capital to the Edinburgh Temperance Electoral Association, in the Circus on Lothian Road, on 'The Politics of the Day'.[8] The lecture fleshed out the main points of his address. Jones called for a further reform of Parliament, one which obliterated the distinction between the borough and county franchises and introduced the secret ballot, so that the Commons was not monopolized by wealthy men. The election, Jones pointed out, offered a stark choice for the electors of Britain: between Disraeli and no reform, and Gladstone's Liberal party, which was 'synonymous with the people of the United Kingdom'. For the first time Jones came out in support of women's suffrage, and then settled into his favourite theme: the land. To the usual panacea of cultivating the waste land of the country in order to cure urban malnutrition, prevent the need for trade unions, and improve the condition of Ireland, Jones added a topical plea. The monopoly of land-ownership, he claimed, created a proliferation of alcoholic drinks, for too much corn production was turned over to malt and barley. The lecture proved something of a success, for it was rumoured that an attempt might be made to get Jones to run for Edinburgh, although nothing came of this.

Backing out of Edinburgh, Jones should really have returned to Manchester, where even if the 'United Liberal Party' election band-wagon was not under way, that of its rivals certainly was, and Jones's position was vulnerable. However, he was waylaid by Carlisle. Earlier in the summer Jones had been approached by the radical wing of the Carlisle Liberal party, who were unhappy at the way in which Sir Wilfrid Lawson, the town's former MP, had been selected once again, despite having lost the seat in 1865. Sensing a repeat of the situation in Dewsbury, Jones rebuffed the idea of contesting Carlisle, but in September accepted an invitation from Lawson's committee to give his 'Politics of the Day' lecture in the town. It was an insensitive move, for the Carlisle radicals turned out in force to disrupt the

---

[7] *ME* (11 Aug. 1868), 1.
[8] Jones, *The Politics of the Day: A Lecture* (Edinburgh: Edinburgh Temperance Electoral Association, 1868); *Scotsman* (3 Sept. 1868), 2.

mainstream Liberals' meeting on 29 September. Jones, who on this occasion was accompanied by Elizabeth, his second wife, duly gave his lecture, only to find a local man, John Hargreaves, heckling him for being a Whig stooge. Hargreaves quoted excerpts from Jones's debate with J. S. Blackie back at him, and although Jones handled the objections from the floor with his usual aplomb, worse was to follow.[9] So incensed was Hargreaves that he started up a newspaper to denounce Jones. The *Democrat* only ran for two issues, but it dug up enough dirt on Jones to last a season, providing anti-Liberal papers in the town with material with which to denigrate their opponents. Hargreaves used the *Democrat* to pursue his charge of hypocrisy against Jones. He retold the story of how Jones had rejected his own invitation to contest Carlisle as a radical, only to reappear in the north, 'coquetting at Edinburgh' and turning up for money when requested by the Whigs of Carlisle. In the *Democrat*'s view Jones was a political renegade, and now the mask was dropping. The paper attacked the recently published *Ernest Jones: Who is He? What has he Done?*, claiming that it only proved one thing, that its subject 'is of a highly imaginative temperament, with a disposition to romance and exaggerate'. And then the mud really began to be slung. A friend of Hargreaves revealed himself to be one John Scott, who had lent Jones money back in 1859 and who still held the IOU to confirm the debt. Further revelations followed. Placards appeared, reproducing Jones's and James Finlen's announcement in the *People's Paper* of 1856 of a Chartist dictatorship, and Jones was declared guilty by his association with Finlen, still notorious from his pro-Fenian histrionics in London the previous year. Scott followed up with the cautionary tale of Jones's treatment of the late Thomas Wheeler.[10] The *Democrat* disappeared from view, but the damage was done. The *Carlisle Patriot* reproduced the sordid essentials, and the other local Tory paper, the *Carlisle Standard*, poked fun at the Liberal committee, revelling in the impropriety which Jones's depiction as a 'discomfited barrister' now brought on their campaign.[11] As for Jones, he replied as best he could to Hargreaves's charges, denying that he had been paid for his visit to Carlisle or that he had chosen to contest Manchester because

---

[9] This account is drawn from the following: *Carlisle Journal* (19 Sept. 1868), 3; (2 Oct. 1868), 7; *City of Carlisle Liberal Club Circular* (3 Oct. 1868), 1.

[10] *The Democrat* (10 Oct. 1868), 1–5; (24 Oct. 1868), 1–4.

[11] *Carlisle Patriot* (2 Oct. 1868), 4–6; *Carlisle Standard* (15 Oct. 1868), 4.

of the promised financial support, and repudiating any friendship with Finlen, whom he had known only when he was still a 'respectable character'.[12] After Carlisle, Jones ventured out of Manchester no more. Trading on his life-story was proving a liability, and in his haste to find a constituency question-marks about his commitment and sincerity were being raised all round.

2

And so Jones turned instead to play his part in the 'United Liberal Party' election campaign in Manchester. By the second week of October, when the Bazley, Bright, and Jones bus began running at full speed, Manchester was, for Jones, not so much the 'best way to get what he wanted' but perhaps the only way, for elsewhere he had alienated erstwhile radicals and confused moderate Liberals.[13] Since issuing his election address back in August, Jones had been absent from the city's political stage, appearing only once to address a meeting in Hulme towards the end of August.[14] Jones's neglect of Manchester during the late summer opened the door to Mitchell Henry, former surgeon and partner in a local textile business, whose candidature as an 'independent Liberal' proved the undoing of the united Liberals.[15] In a predatory fashion Henry seized upon Jones, the weakest of the three 'official' Liberal candidates, and pursued his quarry relentlessly. Henry's campaign had one aim: to destroy Jones's credibility as the third Liberal. Henry's purported politics were actually quite similar to those of Jones. He was for retrenchment, reform of the Reform Act, and extensive changes to the government of Ireland. He too was an advanced Liberal, and indeed

[12] *Carlisle Examiner* (10 Oct. 1868), 5.

[13] There are several good accounts of the Manchester election, and Jones's role within it: A. D. Taylor, ' "The Best Way to Get What he Wanted": Ernest Jones and the Boundaries of Liberalism in the Manchester Election of 1868', *Parliamentary History*, 16 (1997), 185–204; John Walton, *Lancashire: A Social History, 1558–1939* (Manchester: Manchester University Press, 1987), 258–9; H. J. Hanham, *Elections and Party Management in the Time of Disraeli and Gladstone* (London: Longmans, Green & Co., 1959), 302–22.

[14] *MG*, (24 Aug. 1868), 3.

[15] For the announcement of Henry's candidature: *ME* (18 Aug. 1868), 6. Surprisingly, Jones's eldest son (Ernest jr.) appeared on the platform amongst Henry's backers, but whether by mistake or malice is not clear. On Henry, see: W. W. Bean, *The Parliamentary Representation of the Six Northern Counties of England, etc.* (Hull: privately pub., 1890), 366; T. Swindells, *Manchester Streets and Manchester Men*, 2 vols. (Manchester: J. E. Cornish, 1907), ii. 16–18.

he made efforts to drive a wedge between the local trade unions and Jones, describing at an early election meeting how Jones had defended a local trade-union official accused of fraud. So rather than fight on the ground of Jones's political principles, Henry turned to his opponent's character. He accused Jones of having remained an old Chartist, whom the Liberals would have rejected had they known his real views, and he declared him to be the choice of the Reform League clique, and not that of the local Liberal party as a whole.[16]

Weary of election bickering and backbiting in Carlisle and Dewsbury, Jones initially rose above Henry's insults. For the first month of the campaign he appeared on almost a daily basis alongside Bazley and Bright, and did little to dissent from the advanced Liberal agenda. He spoke out for class harmony and fell in behind his colleagues on matters such as Irish reform, trade unions, and colonial defence.[17] There was some variation—Jones advocated manhood suffrage, the removal of the bishops from the House of Lords, pointed to the continuing problem of surplus labour, and mounted his old hobby-horse of 'back to the land'. For instance, he told a meeting of the Manchester building trades that the monopoly of land-ownership affected them too, for in the agricultural counties they would find:

the nobleman's mansion, the parson's house, the lawyer's villa— (laughter)—the bastille or poorhouse, and the prison; but only at great intervals did they see the cottage of the labourer. (Hear, hear). Let them go three or four miles and they would see a country village full of hovels, or some little county town, with crooked lanes and tumble-down dwellings in its back slums and alleys. That was where the labourers lived. The agricultural labourer had to walk from three to six miles, sometimes eight miles, every morning to the scene of his daily work, because the landed aristocracy had pulled down the labourers' cottages.

But for the landowners, Jones declared, the builders of Manchester could be busy erecting cottages throughout the countryside.[18] However, both by design and by default Jones stuck closely to the

[16] *MG* (18 Aug. 1868), 6; (20 Aug. 1868), 5; (25 Aug. 1868), 6; (27 Aug. 1868), 5; (29 Aug. 1868), 5; *ME* (25 Aug. 1868), 6; (27 Aug. 1868), 8; (29 Aug. 1868), 5.

[17] *MG* (8 Oct. 1868), 5; (13 Oct. 1868), 7; (15 Oct. 1868), 4; (20 Oct. 1868), 5; (22 Oct. 1868), 5; *ME* (8 Oct. 1868), 5; (15 Oct. 1868), 4; (20 Oct. 1868), 5; (22 Oct. 1868), 5.

[18] *MG* (10 Oct. 1868), 5; (12 Oct. 1868), 3; (23 Oct. 1868), 3; *ME* (10 Oct. 1868), 5; (12 Oct. 1868), 3; (23 Oct. 1868), 4.

common ground of the 'United Liberal Party'. And that was the part of the problem. For once in his life, Jones was in danger of appearing too ordinary. To potential new allies he was too orthodox: the women's suffragist Lydia Becker attended his opening campaign speech, and found it 'full of claptrap . . . things just said to catch the audience', whilst the local Conservative sketch, the *Freelance*, found him too stagy, criticising his descent into 'beggarly jokes' and 'gratuitous buffoonery'.[19] Jones needed a makeover, a new persona, in order to differentiate him from his worthy Liberal colleagues.

At the end of September the northern department of the Reform League rushed into print a copy of *Ernest Jones. Who is he? What has he Done?* Dictated to James Crossley by Jones, it pulled together all the material from earlier renditions of Jones's life: most notably, the 1859 libel case, the article in the *Commonwealth* in 1866, and the entry in *Men of the Time*, published at the height of the Fenian trial in 1867. In the longer term the pamphlet became the main biographical source for Jones's life.[20] But in the immediate context of the Manchester election in 1868, *Ernest Jones. Who is he?* had a different purpose, namely, to reveal its subject as a model of democratic consistency and as a bona-fide working-man's candidate. Thus the account sketched lightly over the familiar years of Jones the Manchester barrister, and even Jones the Reform League orator. The bulk of the work was devoted to his youth in Germany, his literary aspirations, his conversion to Chartism, and, as a centrepiece, his suffering in prison. The pamphlet closed with a statement of Jones's financial independence. Although a barrister of note, it claimed that Jones was also heir to an estate in Cumberland, and had investments in the funds. To some extent the pamphlet achieved its aim. The *Manchester Examiner and Times* welcomed the revelations of Jones's early life up to 1850, and the *Manchester City News* found his life 'a very remarkable story'. The paper went on: '[i]t reads like the adventures of Baron Trenck, or the story of Silvio Pellico.' The paper likened Jones's imprisonment to that of the famous Neapolitans, and declared that it would be 'poetical justice' if Jones ended up in the House of Commons.[21]

---

[19] Lydia Becker to Mrs Jacob Bright, 8 Oct. [1868], Manchester Society for Women's Suffrage Papers, MCL, M50/1/3, fo. 65; *Freelance* (24 Oct. 1868), 337.

[20] See above, Introduction.

[21] *ME*, (1 Oct. 1868), 2; *Manchester City News*, (7 Nov. 1868), 2. Baron Friedrich von der Trenck (1726–94) suffered several spells in prison, during which he wrote poetry, before becoming a diplomatic agent in revolutionary Paris, where he was

However, there were just as many who contested the Reform League's endorsement of this saintly veteran of democracy. A week after Jones joined in the Liberal campaign proper, another voice from his past spoke out. On 13 October William Stokes, local Peace Society activist and sometime member of the Manchester Manhood Suffrage League back in its first manifestation in 1859, nailed his colours to Henry's mast in a pamphlet.[22] Stokes's main charge against Jones was that he was a lawyer and there were too many lawyer MPs as it was. Worse still, he was the trade unions' candidate, and would be too partisan to be of service to Manchester in the Commons. Henry, in contrast, was a local merchant, familiar with the business of the city, and had come forward independently of any local party organization. Quoting John Hampden, Stokes reminded the electors of Manchester that 'clever lawyers' were not the 'most fitting law-makers'. The 'best law-makers are plain honest men'. Jones, the slur continued, was a jobbing lawyer and it was questionable whether he had the financial means to support himself. It was even suggested that he was already planning to do Commons committee work at £5 per day to earn his parliamentary keep. Jones rallied with the same riposte he had used at Dewsbury—that he had only practised at the bar since 1861, and that his toil and sufferings of the previous decade-and-a-half were so well-known as to preclude comment. However, the attacks on his profession continued. Stokes's challenge was followed a few days later with another attack, this time from the editor of the *Hulme Advertiser*, who repeated the aspersions about Jones being a lawyer and ridiculed the story of his life. Eventually Jones was forced to resort to defending the usefulness of his vocation, arguing rather desperately that he could be of help to his constituents precisely because he was a lawyer.[23]

As election-day approached, Jones was challenged on all sides.

eventually executed. His *The Life and Adventures of Baron Trenck* was published in 1787. Silvio Pellico (1789–1854), Italian patriot and member of the *Carbonari*, was imprisoned by the Austrian authorities in the 1820s. His 1832 autobiography *Le mie Prigioni* (My Prisons) was widely read.

[22] William Stokes, *The Representation of Manchester: Who Shall be its Third Member? A Letter Addressed to Sir Elkanah Armitage . . . Chairman of the United Liberal Party* (Manchester: privately pub., 1868).

[23] 'To state as clearly as may be the grounds upon which Mr Jones rest his claims to our suffrages, they are these:—That he was born in Berlin, and had a king for his godfather': [Anon.], *Mr. E. J. and his Candidature: A Reply to Ernest Jones: Who is he? What has he Done?* (Hulme: Hulme Advertiser, 1868), 7; *MG* (26 Oct. 1868), 3; *ME* (26 Oct. 1868), 3.

Henry's single-minded assault had continued, and meanwhile two Conservative candidates—Hugh Birley, a local magistrate, and Joseph Hoare, a London banker—had emerged. In the last week of the campaign the gloves came off, and Jones faced up squarely to Henry, appearing alone for the first time at an election meeting on 9 November, when he took his audience, point-by-point, through the rival claims of himself and Henry to their suffrages. Jones pointed out that he was not, like Henry, a 'state churchman', but rather a 'Christian dissenter'. He supported shorter parliaments and life peerages. Above all, he had been supporting the trade-union cause for twenty-five years: working for them 'when Mr. Henry was writing prescriptions for lackadaisical ladies in London'.[24] The following day Jones, again alone and conscious of the canvass returns, took on the Tories, denouncing their policy towards Ireland.[25] On 11 November, five days before polling, disaster struck. Henry had been sent copies of the Carlisle *Democrat*, no doubt by a bitter Hargreaves, and Henry's supporters and the Manchester Tories quickly placarded Manchester with copies of the offending *People's Paper* article from 1856.[26] The careful choreography of the 'United Liberal Party' had lost all its rhythm.

Jones thus cut rather a forlorn figure at the election nomination in Albert Square on 16 November. In his introductory speech Edward Hooson defended Jones from the charge that he was a mere lawyer, arguing that it was no more a disqualification for Parliament to be a lawyer than to be a doctor. Besides, Hooson went on, Jones was an 'experienced politician' who was 'at one with the great commercial community' he sought to represent. Moreover, for a quarter-century he had worked for the working classes. 'One day's work from them was a poor return for 25 years' labour', stated Hooson. Jones went along with the sentiment, summoning his vote with an 'appeal to their memory'.[27] But a few weeks' work by his opponents had already undermined Jones's campaign. Polling confirmed what the last weeks of meetings and canvassing had indicated. Jones lost votes to Henry, who withdrew from the poll at 1.00 p.m., and the struggle to squeeze four Liberals into the two selections of each voter let in Birley, the Conservative candidate, who eventually topped the poll

[24] *MG* (11 Nov. 1868), 6.
[25] Ibid. 8.
[26] *MG* (12 Nov. 1868), 5; (14 Nov. 1868), 7; *ME* (16 Nov. 1868), 4.
[27] *MG* (17 Nov. 1868), 6.

with Jones lying in fifth place, some 1,800 votes behind the other Conservative candidate. Had Henry not stood Jones would have pipped Hoare to the third seat, but if Henry had not appeared the experiences of many other large Liberal boroughs in the pre-caucus elections of 1868 and 1874 suggested that another independent Liberal candidate might have emerged anyway.[28] After all, had not Jones mooted that very idea at Dewsbury four months earlier?

3

Plenty of post-mortems were offered following Jones's failure to win the third Manchester seat. Having initially backed Jones against Mitchell Henry, the *Manchester Guardian* criticized the folly of the local Liberal committee in forcing Jones upon the electorate in defiance of the opinions of a large section of the Liberal party. The *Manchester Examiner and Times* denounced the 'three-cornered' system which had been imposed upon Manchester. Most London papers attributed the result to Lancashire's general drift towards Toryism.[29] Jones himself was more conspiratorial, attributing his defeat to a rumour that he had retired from the election, and to the fact that many electors kept voting for Henry long after he had withdrawn from the poll.[30] The truth probably lay somewhere in the middle. Intrigued by prospects elsewhere, Jones came too late to the campaign in Manchester. By the time he appeared on the city's hustings in October, Henry had enjoyed an open season of chipping away at his reputation. And even when Jones did finally get his Manchester campaign going, he probably spent too much time agreeing a united front with Bazley and Bright, and not enough defending an exposed flank against Henry's accusations, now spiced by the damaging revelations from Carlisle. Jones, an old master at puffing up and putting down, had been beaten at his own game. Several abiding images of Jones in the Manchester election have been left by the cartoonists and songsters of the contest, and in their different ways they point up the difficulty he faced as well as any political narrative. In one broadside Jones was a failed pugilist,

---

[28]   Michael Hurst, 'Liberal versus Liberal: The General Election of 1874 in Bradford and Sheffield', *Historical Journal*, 15 (1972), 669–713.

[29]   *MG* (18 Nov. 1868), 5; (2 Dec. 1868), 4; *ME* (18 Nov. 1868), 4–6; *Spectator* (21 Nov. 1868), 1361.

[30]   Jones to Howell, 18 Nov. 1868, Howell papers, BGI, Letters (1864–8), fo. 17.

brought in to fight dirty for Bazley and Bright, but out-punched by
Henry. A few verses will suffice:

> Now, this Jones is a source of much physical force,
> And can give a straight tip on the nose,
> But when at Carlisle, he was so full of bile,
> That he hit both his friends and his foes.
>
> Now these three 'United', appear much delighted,
> And declare they will throw all their might in
> The battle to gain, and to save so much pain.
> They will pay Jones to do all the fighting.
>
> But a novice came out, though little but stout,
> With notions so fearless and free;
> And he said 'twas a shame, and if no-one else came,
> He would venture to fight the whole three.
>
> He is quite a trump card, and he hits very hard,
> And so manly and frank his behaviour;
> That crowds are beginning, to bet on his winning,
> And are giving long odds in his favour.[31]

One cartoon depicted the election as a cock-fight, with Jones in the
pen with the Liberal and Tories, but reluctant to join in their dispute,
and with Henry sitting on the fence beckoning to Jones, '[l]et's get
out of it'. Equally telling was a cartoon which showed the disunited
Liberal stage-coach being pulled off-course by Jones, one of the four
horses. And summing up Jones's misery was a cartoon by John
Rothwell, depicting the 'Manchester and Salford return trip' balloon
ride. Jones, in his spectacles and barristers' bands, remains on the
ground as the balloon ascends. At his side is a packed trunk, labelled
'Ernest Jones, QC, London', but he is shouting out in vain at the
other Liberals in the balloon's basket: 'Now then pals o'mine where
are you. I've got my luggage here. You said you'd take me with
you.'[32]

In defeat Jones was despondent. He told George Howell that '[a]
political career, that might have done something, has been stopped'.[33]
Nonetheless he remained positive, looking for opportunities to

---

[31] 'Bazley, Bright and Jones, versus Henry: A New Song', Broadside coll., MCL,
1868/5/I.

[32] 'The Contest', ibid., F1868/12; 'A Losing Game', ibid., F/1868/5/G; 'Up in a
Balloon: the Manchester and Salford Return Trip', ibid., F/1868/15.

[33] Jones to Howell, 18 Nov. 1868, Howell papers, BGI, Letters (1864–8), fo. 17.

contest other seats as soon as the chance arose. He nagged Howell about the possibility of standing in Greenwich, should Gladstone choose to represent South Lancashire, where he had also been elected. Jones told Howell he would stand aside and let Edmond Beales or Baxter Langley fight the Greenwich seat instead in the Reform League interest. But should John Stuart Mill stand he would oppose him, on the grounds of Mill's opposition to the ballot and his support for the minority clause. Mixed in with the usual bravado was a new note of desperation. Jones told Howell to telegraph him and he would appear in Greenwich the very next day: 'I am now within a few weeks of 50, and if ever I am to make a Parliamentary career for these Principles which we want, it must be now.'[34] As it happened, Gladstone opted for Greenwich, Mill came in for Westminster, and Jones remained in Manchester, where a few weeks later his fortunes turned in one final twist.

In the middle of December it emerged that Hugh Birley, the successful Conservative candidate at Manchester, was in fact a government contractor and therefore ineligible to sit in Parliament, where his presence would breach the conventions, such as they were, on conflicts of interest. The Manchester Liberal committee began the process of petitioning against his election, and also began to consider who might contest the seat in the event of the petition being upheld and a by-election taking place. Fair play suggested there should be only one candidate, so naturally two emerged. Jones was put forward, but so too was Thomas Milner Gibson, former MP for Manchester. The pall of disunion still hanging over them from the November election, the Liberal committee opted for a pre-selection election. As an educative experience, voting would take place by secret ballot, and to prepare the men of Manchester for the novelty an illustrated circular was sent out to 18,000 voters in the new year of 1869.[35] Jones welcomed his second chance, delighted to be the subject of the first ever semi-official ballot for a parliamentary election. It was a 'glorious experiment', he told a meeting at Bradford at the end of December. And two days before the vote he declared to a meeting at Chorlton that after Ireland, the redistribution of seats

---

[34] Jones to Howell, 21 Nov. 1868, Howell papers, BGI, Letters (1864–8), fo. 16. Jones told Karl Marx that he *would* challenge Langley: Jones to Marx, 21 Nov. 1868, repr. in Dorothy Thompson, 'Letters from Ernest Jones to Karl Marx, 1865–1868', *Bulletin of the Society for the Study of Labour History*, 4 (1962), 22.

[35] *MG* (19 Dec. 1868), 5; (23 Jan. 1869), 5.

and the secret ballot were the next most important issues on which Parliament had to legislate. He himself, he added, had waited twenty-five years to join the Commons. He had contested Halifax and Nottingham as a younger man, but now he was anxious to go to Westminster before what life left in him was taken away.[36] Polling took place over two days (22 and 23 January) at twenty-two different stations dotted around the city. Although the turnout was low, Jones won comfortably, receiving 7,282 votes to Milner Gibson's 4,133. In Manchester the *Guardian* and the *Courier* sniped at the result, pointing out that Jones had polled fewer votes than in the real November election and that overall only one-quarter of the entire Manchester constituency had turned out and voted for him. However, *The Times* welcomed the result, concluding that it would be useful to hear Jones's voice in the Commons.[37]

It was not to be. Jones caught a chill shortly after the Chorlton meeting and retired to his bed with a recurrence of the pleurisy which had dogged him for much of the previous decade. This time he could not shake it off and full-blown pneumonia set in. Over the next few days, as Jones lay dying, ghosts of past, present, and future seemed to gather around his bedside in Higher Broughton.[38] On Thursday, despite doctor's orders for calm, Jones's son Walter read to him press reports of his prophetic speech at Chorlton. On Friday, a deputation waited upon him from a new Dublin-based organization, the 'Society for the Release of Political Prisoners', seeking his patronage. The same day Liberals from Drogheda in Ireland sent word that they wanted him to stand for election there, in the event of a successful petition against the new MP. News of his own success in the Manchester ballot and news of his son Llewellyn's success in entering Brasenose College, Oxford, were reported to him on Saturday, and that same evening Llewellyn arrived home. In death, it seemed, everyone wanted a piece of the life of Ernest Jones. But there was no life left. On Tuesday afternoon, the day after his fiftieth birthday, he rose from his bed, felt faint, and died immediately. Newspapers busy hailing or lamenting his success in the Manchester ballot turned to reporting his death. Howell wrote one day to congratulate Jones on

[36] *ME* (1 Jan. 1869), 2; (21 Jan. 1869), 5.
[37] *MG* (25 Jan. 1869), 3; *Manchester Courier* (26 Jan. 1869), 5; *The Times* (25 Jan. 1869), 8.
[38] *ME* (27 Jan. 1869), 5; *Manchester City News* (30 Jan. 1869), 2; Walter Jones to Llewellyn Jones [22 Jan. 1869], BJH.

the test ballot, and to wish him well in the event of a real election, and wrote to Greening two days later to enquire about funeral arrangements.[39] Everyone seemed stunned by the rapid, almost fateful turn of events. Old adversaries struck a note of sorrow. The *Manchester Guardian* stated that a void would be left by a man whose life had been lived in the 'public eye'. Robinson Fowler, the stipendiary magistrate, ended court proceedings early so the bench could express its regret at the loss of a familiar advocate.[40] Faithful friends such as Steinthal and Hooson rallied around the bereaved family. The Reform League dispatched Beales, Odger, and Howell to attend the funeral, but left the northern department to make the arrangements.[41] A week after Jones appeared to be on his way at last to the world of Westminster, he was laid to rest in Ardwick cemetery.

[39] Howell to Jones, 25 Jan. 1869, Howell to Greening, 27 Jan. 1869, Howell papers, BGI, Letter-book 5, fos. 20–1.
[40] *MG* (27 Jan. 1869), 4; (29 Jan. 1869), 3.
[41] Reform League General Council Minutes, 27 Jan. 1869, Reform League papers, BGI; Howell to Mrs Ernest Jones, 1 Feb. 1869, Howell papers, BGI, Letter-book 5, fo. 28.

9
Epilogue

SO ENDED THE life, or rather the lives, of Ernest Jones. In the event, no petition was brought forward from Manchester to contest Birley's election, and in March 1869 the Reform League, which had done so much to resurrect Jones's political career, shut up shop. Nonetheless, had he lived, somewhere, somehow, in 1869 or in the early 1870s, Jones would no doubt have been returned to Parliament. His life outside the Commons would have been a hard act to follow inside. It is not difficult to see him occupying the same political ground as Sir Charles Dilke.[1] Jones would have been expected to spearhead the ongoing campaign to complete the unfinished business of the Second Reform Act. His seasoned views on land reform would have made him a desirable acquisition for the Land Tenure Reform Association, alongside John Stuart Mill. Jones might have made the same outspoken intervention on the monarchy as Dilke in 1871, and he would have proved a friend of Ireland and a defender of the Paris Commune. Conversely, as the 1868 election had proved, Jones was never good at sharing political space with anyone else and he might equally have ended up on the margins of radical liberalism in the age of Gladstone. It is also difficult, in the light of his experiences in 1868, to see how Jones would have coped with the caucus organizations which came to dominate the Liberal party machines in the big cities in the 1870s, cramping the independent radicalism of men such as Joseph Cowen jr.[2] Equally, Jones's political style—that of the gentleman radical—would have been difficult to maintain in later Victorian Britain, as aristocratic decline and bourgeois aspiration combined to reconfigure the whole ethos of the gentleman. To pass

---

[1] For Dilke's radicalism, see: David Nicholls, *The Lost Prime Minister: A Life of Sir Charles Dilke* (London: Hambledon Press, 1995), chs. 3–4. Perhaps in homage Dilke acquired a manuscript copy of Jones's 'Italy and her Masters' (1856): Dilke papers, BL, Add. Ms. 43,909, fo. 237.

[2] Joan Hugman, 'Joseph Cowen and Radical Liberalism', Ph.D thesis, Northumbria University, 1993).

oneself off as a 'fallen peer' in the 1840s and 1850s, when aristocratic society appeared to be an impenetrable caste, was indeed a novelty. By the 1870s, with old landed family fortunes falling, and new industrialists putting their profits into country estates, it had less purchase. Gentlemanly status came to be measured by acreage and assets, and not by books and breeding. Not until the mid-twentieth century, in a national mood of post-war imperial nostalgia, would the character of the 'gentleman' be reinvested with the hallmark features of daring, chivalry, and altruism that Jones had claimed for so much of his life.[3] Ultimately, such speculation is unrewarding. The gods favoured Jones's reputation by an early death, allowing posterity to elaborate a legend unspoilt by an inconsequential ending.

Jones might well have ended up out of place in the world of later Victorian radical liberalism, but as this book has tried to show he caught the mood of the moment during the twilight years of Chartism and again, more fitfully, in the reform revival of the mid-1860s. His fame did not come from his familiarity with Marxist socialism at home and abroad, as twentieth-century assessments of his life have often claimed. The chemistry between the two men owed something to Marx's own youthful acquaintance with Lutheran evangelism and romanticism, and a great deal to Jones's proficiency in German. The more confident Marx became in English, the less confident he became in Jones. Jones's real impact stemmed from his deep immersion in the lives and letters of European romanticism. At one level, the influence of the romantics on Jones was very simple. He aspired to be a Byronic man of the people—a levelling lord, a reincarnation of Shelley's poet as the 'legislator of the world'. But Jones also absorbed other influences within the diverse range of romanticism. He grew up amidst the intellectual and religious reaction against the French Revolution, and this left its mark on him in two main ways. First, he was touched by the evangelical revival, both in its Lutheran form in Holstein, where he spent his childhood and adolescence, and again in London as a young man, through his

---

[3] On the changing ethos of the gentleman, see: Penelope J. Corfield, 'The Rivals: Landed and other Gentlemen', in Negley Harte and Roland Quinault (eds.), *Land and Society in Britain, 1700–1914: Essays in Honour of F. M. L. Thompson* (Manchester: Manchester University Press, 1996), 1–33; Martin Wiener, *English Culture and the Decline of the Industrial Spirit, 1850–1980* (Cambridge: Cambridge University Press, 1981); Marcus Collins, 'The Fall of the English Gentleman: The National Character in Decline, c. 1918–70', *Historical Research*, 75 (2002), 90–111.

friendship with Archer Gurney and exposure to the urban missions of Baptist Noel. Secondly, Jones was schooled in an anti-French version of nationalism, in which local custom and ancient kingship was preferred to universal rights of man and elective assemblies. Jones was no Jacobin. His French heroes always remained misunderstood *artistes*, such as Chateaubriand and Mirabeau, and misunderstood monarchs, such as Charles X and Louis Philippe. It was out of materials such as these, rather than acquaintance with Marxism, that Jones fashioned his version of Chartist democracy.

Jones idealized the 'people'—the heart and soul of the Chartist movement—because, like the evangelicals, he saw the working classes as the embodiment of simple Christian faith, uncorrupted by the artifice of modern society. The people were governed by their hearts and not their heads. God had created in mankind a natural love of humanity, which a secular lust for power and material gain had taken away from all but the redemptive poor. Jones also idealized the people as the working classes, for like other proponents of the English Gothic he saw them as the bearers of England's medieval heritage, the sole survivors of a pre-lapsarian land of plenty, in which paternalistic nobles and sturdy peasants provided the sinews of the nation. Hence his appearance amongst the Chartists in 1846 as 'Percy Vere'. Only a poet—for poetry spoke to the heart and not to the head—could truly speak to the humane poor. And only a descendant of the feudal order could remind the modern workers of the bonds of loyalty and duty that had attached their ancestors to the nation. Jones's vision of Chartist democracy thus combined evangelical idealism with patriotic history. In a movement dominated, especially in its early years, by a succession of evangelical preachers—Joseph Rayner Stephens, Humphrey Price, Thomas Cooper, and Arthur O'Neill—it is perhaps no surprise that Jones was an instant success. And to Chartist followers accustomed to locating their struggles within a long line of English dissent—the 'Norman yoke', Wat Tyler, and the Commonwealth—Jones told a familiar historical tale.

Even with these humane and chivalrous credentials, Jones still had to bridge the gulf between his patrician social status and the working-class character of his Chartist following. In its wake the French Revolution had left the enduring image of the demagogue: the man of letters as mob-agitator, the *philosophe*, *littéraire*, or lawyer as revolutionary speculator. As late as 1844 Thomas

Macaulay was still demonizing the Jacobins as immoral mountebanks, and Thomas Carlyle's *Latter Day Pamphlets* (1850) can be read as a diatribe against the alliance of the pen and the barricade.[4] In order to deflect such criticism from his own chosen course, Jones turned to another resource within the repertoire of romanticism: autobiography. He told tales about his own life as a parable of noble sentiment and righteous suffering, and in stories such as 'De Brassier' he caricatured the fine line between demagogic and honest leadership. Through his monologue poems ('Percy Vere', 'The Better Hope', 'Corayda'), his novels, his libel action against Reynolds in 1859, and finally in his debate with Blackie in 1867, Jones the writer invented Jones the patriot, his virtue confirmed by the contrasts furnished by literary idlers such as Reynolds or Blackie. In turning to tell tales about his life, Jones was tapping a rich seam. Mid-Victorian bookstalls heaved with gallows confessions, religious tracts telling of souls saved, self-improvement literature dominated by plebeian accounts of lives redeemed from poverty by knowledge, and respectable lives and letters of great men and women. Even if the Victorians did not invent autobiography, they perfected the art of writing about the self in a manner which by no means revealed all, but proved their subjects to be models of consistency.[5]

When Chartism failed Jones kept faith with romantic literature as the agent of radicalism, but the emphasis gradually shifted from humane, uplifting verse and novellas to demotic tales of a more sensationalist kind. 'Woman's Wrongs', with the natural passions of its characters reined in by their environment, marks the transition from Jones using the serial novel as a form of social critique to his

---

[4] Thomas Babington Macaulay, 'Barère' [1844], in *The Works of Lord Macaulay*, 12 vols. (London: Longmans, Green & Co., 1898), iv. 168–279; Thomas Carlyle, *Latter-Day Pamphlets* (London: Chapman & Hall, 1850), esp. chs. 1, 5.

[5] For the shift from the autobiography as introspection to the autobiography as public, objective history, see: James Olney, 'Autobiography and the Cultural Moment: A Thematic, Historical and Bibliographical Introduction', in Olney (ed.), *Autobiography: Essays Theoretical and Critical* (Princeton: Princeton University Press, 1980), 5–6; Howard Helsinger, 'Credence or Credibility: The Concern for Honesty in Victorian Autobiography', in George P. Landow (ed.), *Approaches to Victorian Autobiography* (Athens, Ohio: Ohio University Press, 1980), 39–63; J. H. Buckley, *The Turning Key: Autobiography and the Subjective Impulse Since 1800* (Cambridge, Mass.: Harvard University Press, 1984), 19; Linda H. Petersen, *Victorian Autobiography: The Tradition of Self-Interpretation* (London: Yale University Press, 1986); David Vincent, *Bread, Knowledge and Freedom: A Study of Nineteenth-Century Working-Class Autobiography* (Cambridge: Cambridge University Press, 1981).

cranking out light melodramas such as 'The Lass and the Lady' and 'Lovers and Husbands'. As in his earlier stories, Jones peopled these later melodramas with characters with hidden pasts and improbable pedigrees, but neglected to add men of heroic destiny, whose virtue amidst so much vice pointed to a happier future. In the 1850s Jones's novels, much like his own wider fortunes of the decade, ended not with a moral bang but with a whimper. In the early 1860s he turned his literary talents to the defence of the poor in the courts. Taking advantage of the enhanced role being given to defence counsel in mid-Victorian trials, he told tales about the life-stories of murderers in order to win them some clemency. Ironically, this proved to be one twist of romanticism too far, for in 1868 the Manchester electorate rejected Jones largely on the grounds that he was a barrister, and barristers were unreliable on matters of truth and consistency.

The romance of politics, or rather the ways in which romanticism contributed to Victorian political style, did not die with Jones. After all, the years after his death were dominated by two political heavy-weights—Gladstone and Disraeli—who, in very different ways, fashioned their public personalities out of similar materials to those selected by Jones. Gladstone, with his evangelical moralism and a stagy, gesticulatory speaking style honed over the years and in imitation of the great tragedian actors of the day, articulated a political rhetoric in which the forces of humanity and the heart vied with the evils of artifice and greed.[6] Facing him in the gaze of the new urban electorate of the post-1867 era was Disraeli, like Jones a connoisseur of continental belles-lettres, and like Jones an outsider who used the Gothic past to denizen himself in the English political present.[7] Further afield, the evocation of workers' rights through medieval motifs can be seen in the writings of John Ruskin and in the work of

[6] Patrick Joyce, *Democratic Subjects: The Self and the Social in Nineteenth-Century England* (Cambridge: Cambridge University Press, 1994), 104–16; Eugenio F. Biagini, *Liberty, Retrenchment and Reform: Popular Liberalism in the Age of Gladstone, 1860–1880* (Cambridge: Cambridge University Press, 1992), 396–7; D. A. Hamer, 'Gladstone: the Making of a Political Myth', *Victorian Studies*, 22 (1978), 29–50; Glynne Wickham, 'Gladstone, Oratory and the Theatre', in Peter J. Jagger (ed.), *Gladstone* (London: Hambledon Press, 1998), 1–31. The classic account of personality politics in the age of demos remains Richard Sennett's scintillating *The Fall of Public Man* (London: Faber & Faber, 1986), esp. chs. 8–10.

[7] Paul Smith, *Disraeli: A Brief Life* (Cambridge: Cambridge University Press, 1996); Charles Richmond and Paul Smith (eds.), *The Self-Fashioning of Disraeli, 1818–1851* (Cambridge: Cambridge University Press, 1998); Todd Endelman and Tony Kushner (eds.), *Disraeli's Jewishness* (London: Vallentine Mitchell, 2002).

Pre-Raphaelites such as William Morris, both of whom exerted considerable influence on the outlook of the early Labour party. Medievalism was also writ large in the Conservatives' Primrose League, established in 1883, with its organizational hierarchy of 'knights' and 'dames', and its love of pageants.[8] This is not to assert any connection between Ernest Jones and these later manifestations of romanticism, which after all were politically quietist in a way Jones had never been. It is merely to offer a reminder that the grip of the pre-industrial past held firm amidst so much Victorian modernity, and in that sense Jones's career mirrored the mores of his age.

A final thought. As this book comes to a close it is tempting to drop the biographer's mask of detachment and ask an obvious question: was Ernest Jones all that he seemed? Even if the conventions of romanticism required Jones to blur fact and fiction, he still emerges at times as duplicitous and unpleasant: in short, a liar, a cheat, an anti-Semite, a racist bigot, an absent father, and a neglectful husband. In his defence, Daniel Defoe once observed that 'necessity makes an honest man a knave', and it is certainly the case that it was financial hardship and family tragedy that started Jones out on the long road to political notoriety. Or perhaps Jones simply learned the necessary lie at the heart of the modern democratic condition, that is, the need to avoid the truth, but to do so with the greatest possible conviction. Whatever the explanation, it is fitting that Jones should have the final word: 'As soon as we stand on the stage of public life, the most honest man becomes an actor, not from any want of sincerity, but from a love of approbation.'[9]

[8] Florence S. Boos (ed.), *History and Community: Essays in Victorian Medievalism* (London: Garland, 1992); R. J. Smith, *The Gothic Bequest: Medieval Institutions in British Thought, 1688–1863* (Cambridge: Cambridge University Press, 1987); Tim Hilton, *John Ruskin*, 2 vols. (London: Yale University Press, 2000); Peter Stansky, *Redesigning the World: William Morris, the 1880s and the Arts and Crafts* (Princeton: Princeton University Press, 1985); Martin Pugh, *The Tories and the People, 1880–1935* (Oxford: Blackwell, 1985), 20–4.

[9] 'Lovers and Husbands', *PP* (13 Aug. 1853), 6.

Bibliography

This bibliography refers only to primary manuscript and printed materials relating directly to Ernest Jones. For fuller references please consult the footnotes.

I. MANUSCRIPT COLLECTIONS RELATING TO ERNEST JONES

i. London

Bishopsgate Library, Bishopsgate Institute
    George Howell papers
    Ernest Jones papers
    Reform League correspondence and minute books
British Library of Political and Economic Science
    Frederic Harrison papers
Department of Manuscripts, British Library
    Add. Ms. 43, 239: Ernest Jones, 'Italy and her Masters' (1856)
    Add. Ms. 43, 909: Aberdeen papers
    Add. Ms. 52, 477: Thomas Serle papers
    Add. Ms. 52, 484: Ernest Jones correspondence
    Add. Mss. 61, 971A–C: Ernest Jones album (1849)
    Add. Ms. 70, 772: Ernest Jones, 'Song of the Factory Slave' (1858)
London Metropolitan Archive
    Visiting Justices' minutes
Middle Temple Library
    Minutes of Parliament, Middle Temple
Public Record Office
    Treasury Solicitor papers
    Home Office papers
    Palatine of Lancaster papers (Fenian Trials)

ii. Outside London

Department of Manuscripts, National Library of Wales, Aberystwyth
    Ernest Jones prison correspondence
Department of Manuscripts, National Library of Scotland, Edinburgh
    Thomas Carlyle papers

Hertfordshire Record Office, Hertford
    Bulwer-Lytton papers
Department of Manuscripts and Archives, Brynmor Jones Library,
University of Hull
    Ernest Jones family correspondence (microfilm)
Department of Manuscripts and Archives, Manchester Central Library
    Ernest Jones manuscript poems
    Ernest Jones diaries, 1839–47
    Ernest Jones legal diaries, 1860–6
    Ernest Jones miscellaneous correspondence
    A. B. Wakefield correspondence
Chetham's Library, Manchester
    Ernest Jones correspondence and papers
Co-operative Society, Manchester
    George Jacob Holyoake papers
    Robert Owen collection
Greater Manchester Record Office, Manchester
    Northern Circuit minute books, 1860–8
Tyne and Wear Archives, Newcastle
    Joseph Cowen papers
East Midlands Collection, University of Nottingham
    Election broadsides (1859)
Nuffield College, Oxford
    Ernest Jones Manuscripts
    G. D. H. Cole collection
Staffordshire University Library, Stoke
    Dorothy Thompson collection

iii. Overseas

International Institute for Social History, Amsterdam
    Ernest Jones correspondence
Stadtarchiv, Lüneburg
    St. Michael's College Manuscripts
Department of Manuscripts, Yale University Library, New Haven
    William Harrison Riley papers
Department of Rare Books and Manuscripts, Columbia University Library,
New York
    E. R. A. Seligman collection

2. LIST OF ERNEST JONES'S PUBLISHED WORKS

i. Poetry

Infantine Effusions (Hamburg: F. H. Nestler, 1830)
 Rodriguo. A canto imitated from a celebrated author
 Lines on seeing a vessel in a storm
 Lines written 23rd July 1828
 Emblems of Morning
 Extracts from a poem called Rodolski
 Lines on England
 The Minstrel: A Ballad
 Lines written when eight years of age
 Henriade 1st Canto: Translated from the French of M. de Voltaire
 Pyrenean Adventure
 Lines on the death of Lord Charles Murray in Greece
In the *Court Journal*
 The Dying Girl (12 Sept. 1840)
 Lines on Lady Stepney's New Work (28 Nov. 1840)
 Lines on the Brocken (22 May 1841)
 The Goodwin Sands (2 Oct. 1841)
 To Her (8 Jan. 1842)
 The Sun (15 Jan. 1842)
 The Rainbow of Hope (29 Jan. 1842)
 Lines to Charles Kean, esq., on his Marriage with Miss Ellen Tree (19 Feb. 1842)
 Geister-Ahnung (5 Mar. 1842)
 Der Glocken-ruf (26 Mar. 1842)
 Lines on Miss Adelaide Kemble (7 May 1842)
 Das Lebens-Ziel (2 July 1842)
In the *Morning Post*
 To Chateaubriand. A Voice from England to the Stranger Bard (13 Dec. 1843)
 New Year's Eve (1 Jan. 1844)
In the *Deutsche London Zeitung* (25 Apr. 1845)
 Der Deutsche Sprachschatz
 Politisches
 Licht und Sprache
Percy Vere (pseud.), *My Life* (London: T. C. Newby, 1845)
Chartist Poems (London: MacGowan and Co., 1846)
 The Better Hope
 Our Summons
 Our Rally

Our Warning
Our Destiny
The Two Races
Labour's History
Chartist Chorus
Blackstone Edge
O'Connorville
The Coming Day
Onward and Upward
In the *Northern Star*
  A Chartist March (13 June 1846)
  England's Greatness (4 July 1846)
  Britannia (18 July 1846)
  Liberty (25 July 1846)
  A Song for the Road (15 Aug. 1846)
  St. Stephens (26 Sept. 1846)
  Maid of the West (10 Oct. 1846)
  The Poet's Mission (17 Oct. 1846)
  Our Cheer (21 Nov. 1846)
  Age of Peace (4 Dec. 1847)
  New Year's Cup (1 Jan. 1848)
  Blind Boy's Song (15 Jan. 1848)
  Patriot's Test (29 Jan. 1848)
In the *Labourer*
  A Christmas Carol (Jan. 1847)
  The Factory Town (Mar. 1847)
  Life of a Flower (Mar. 1847)
  Song for May (May 1847)
  Royal Bounty: A Legend of Windsor (May 1847)
  War, Love and Liberty (June 1847)
  Onward (July 1847)
  The Change (July 1847)
  The Sketch (Aug. 1847)
  Lord Lindsay (Sept. 1847)
  The Bard's Lament (Nov. 1847)
  Age of Peace (Dec. 1847)
  The Funeral of the Year and its Epitaph (Jan. 1848)
  The March of Freedom (Mar. 1848)
  The Song of the Gaggers (May 1848)
In *Notes to the People*
  The New World (3 May 1851)
  Beldagon Church (10 May 1851)
  The Painter of Florence (17 May 1851)

Bonnivard (24 May 1851)
The Prisoner's Night Thought (24 May 1851)
Hope (24 May 1851)
Prison Bars (24 May 1851)
Poet's Parallel (24 May 1851)
Prison Fancies (24 May 1851)
Mariner's Compass (24 May 1851)
Steed and the Rider (24 May 1851)
Last Light (24 May 1851)
Languages (24 May 1851)
Where (24 May 1851)
What (24 May 1851)
Garden Seat (24 May 1851)
Earth's Burdens (24 May 1851)
Silent Cell (24 May 1851)
Prisoner's Dream (24 May 1851)
Resignation (24 May 1851)
Quiet Home (24 May 1851)
The Legacy (24 May 1851)
To Wordsworth (24 May 1851)
St. Coutts (24 May 1851)
Easter Hymn (24 May 1851)
Hymn for Ascension Day (24 May 1851)
Hymn for Lammas Day (24 May 1851)
The Harper Wind (31 May 1851)
We Are Silent (31 May 1851)
Sea Shell (14 June 1851)
Trees (14 June 1851)
Fine Young Foreign Gentleman (21 June 1851)
Too Soon (28 June 1851)
Love and Song (18 June 1851)
Rebecca of the Well (12 July 1851)
To Her (26 July 1851)
To the Departed (9 Aug. 1851)
The Marriage Feast (16 Aug. 1851)
Christian Love (23 Aug. 1851)
The Prisoner to the Slaves (23 Aug. 1851)
The Fishermen (30 Aug. 1851)
Life, Hope, Truth and Love (13 Sept. 1851)
On Man (13 Sept. 1851)
A Song for the Great Exhibition (13 Sept. 1851)
The Hermit (27 Sept. 1851)
On a Welshman (11 Oct. 1851)

The Slave Ship (18 Oct. 1851)
To My Sister (15 Nov. 1851)
The Old Man's Song of the Old Year's Dying (3 Jan. 1852)
The People's Anthem (28 March. 1852)
The Song of the Low (4 Apr. 1852)
The Song of the Poor (11 Apr. 1852)
The Song of the Future (18 Apr. 1852)
Rhymes on the Times (London: T. Brettel, 1852)
   The Invasion
   The Quack
   Victory of Lagos
   Reform
   The Farmers' Last New Song
   Lord Palmerston's Song
   Lord Derby
In the *People's Paper* [unattributed, but in Jones's style]
   Our Trust (10 July 1852)
   Song for the Next Rebellion (14 May 1853)
   The Reason Why (25 Feb. 1854)
The Battle Day; and Other Poems (London: G. Routledge & Co., 1855)
   The Cost of Glory
      The Country House
      The Visit
      The Pictures
      The Painter of Florence
   The Battle Day; or the Lost Army
   Plough and Loom
      Leawood Hall: A Christmas Tale
      The Factory Town
      The Cottage and the Factory
      The Peasant
   Cries of the Nations
      Liberty
      The Cry of the Russian Serf to the Czar
      The Italian Exile to his Countrymen
      Onward and Upward
      The Coming Day
   Echoes from Within
      The Better Hope
      The Poet
      New Year's Eve
      Last Light
      Languages

The Harper Wind
Moonrise
The Steed and the Rider
The Life of a Flower
Percy Vere: The Peer's Story
Emperor's Vigil and the Waves and the War (London: George Routledge &
Co., 1856)
  The Waves and the War
    The Baltic Fleet
    The Baltic
    The Arrival
    The Words of the West
    The Emperor's Vigil
    The Sailor's Night Watch
    The Return
    Prayer for Peace
  Waifs
    Songs of Glory
    Calls to Battle
    Helping Hands
    Peace and War
    Brother-lands
    The Fountains of History
Songs of Democracy (London: John Lowry, 1856–7)
  Song of the Poor
  The Fishermen
  Song of the Day Labourers
  A Song of Resurrection
  Song of the Lower Classes
  A Song of Cromwell's Time
  The Marriage Feast
  Song of the Factory Slave
The Revolt of Hindostan; or the New World. A Poem (London: Effingham
Wilson, 1857)
Corayda: A Tale of Faith and Chivalry, and Other Poems (London: W. Kent
and Co., 1860)
  Corayda. Parts I and II
  Scatterings
    Bard's Lament
    On Hearing of a Poet's Death
    Hope
    Earth's Burdens
    The Sea Shell, or the Desert

The Trees
The Last Light
The Wayside Porch
The Factory Child
Too Soon
Too Late
Where
What
To Her
Agatha
Mine
Village Courtship
The Lords of Italy
The Last Battle
New Year's Morn
Percy Vere. A Day of Youth
Transmarine

ii. Dramas

The Student of Padua (1836), a tragedy in five acts, is attributed to Jones by
the British Library, but I have discovered no manuscript or other contemporary evidence to corroborate his authorship. The date and the style
make it doubtful that it was composed by Jones.
St John's Eve, *Labourer* (Oct.–Nov. 1848)

iii. Novels and Short Stories

The Invalid's Pipe in *Ackermann's Juvenile Forget Me Not* (London: R.
Ackermann, 1830)
The Wood-Spirit: A Novel (London: Boone & Co., 1841)
Confessions of a King, *Court Journal* (28 Jan. 1843–25 Feb. 1843)
The Romance of a People, *Labourer* (Jan. 1847–Jan. 1848), republished as
The Maid of Warsaw, or the Tyrant Czar: A Tale of the Last Rebellion
(London: George Pavey, 1854)
The Charter and the Land, *Labourer* (Jan. 1847)
The Jolly Young Poacher, *Labourer* (Feb.–June 1847)
An English Life, *Labourer* (June 1847)
The Glorious Privilege: A Tale of Our Days, *Labourer* (Aug. 1847)
The Price of Blood: A Tale of the South, *Labourer* (Sept. 1847)
Pirates' Prize, *Labourer* (Mar.–Apr. 1848)
The Meal Mongers; or Food Riots in Ireland, *Labourer* (Apr. 1848)
The London Doorstep, *Labourer* (May 1848)

De Brassier, A Democratic Romance, *Notes to the People* (10 May 1851–4 Apr. 1852)

Woman's Wrongs, *Notes to the People* (1 Nov. 1851–25 Apr. 1852), republished as *Woman's Wrongs: A Series of Tales* (London: n.p., 1855)

Lovers and Husbands, or the Wrongs of Man, *People's Paper*, (23 Apr. 1853–14 Jan. 1854)

The Lass and the Lady; or Love's Ladder. A Tale of Thrilling Interest (London: Thomas MacGowan, 1855)

The Wood Spirit: A Romance of the Feudal Era, and the Priestly Age (n.p., 1855)

The Guardian Angel, *Bradford Times* (24 June 1866)

iv. Newspapers

Northern Star (1846–8)
Labourer (1847–8)
Poems and Notes to the People (1851–2)
People's Paper (1852–8)
London News (1858)
Cabinet Newspaper (1858–60)
Penny Times (1860)
Weekly Telegraph (1860)

v. Lectures

Canterbury versus Rome (London: Edwin Dipple, 1851)
Evenings with the People (London: *People's Paper*, 1856–7)
  1. The Workman and his Work
  2. The Hereditary Land Aristocracy
  3. The State Church. Part I
  4. The State Church. Part II
  5. The Franchise and Taxation
  6. Foreign Affairs
  7. The Unemployed
  8. Emigration
  9. Our Colonies, Their Climate, Soil, Produce, and Emigrants
The Slaveholders' War: A Lecture Delivered in the Town Hall, Ashton-under-Lyne (Ashton-under-Lyne: Ashton-under-Lyne Union and Emancipation Society, 1863)
Oration . . . on the American Rebellion, Delivered at the Public Hall, Rochdale (Rochdale: Rochdale Union and Emancipation Society, 1864)
The Danish War (Manchester: repr. from the *Manchester Examiner and Times*, 1864)

Democracy Vindicated: A Lecture Delivered to the Edinburgh Working Men's Institute on the 4th January 1867 (Edinburgh: Andrew Elliot, 1867)

Labour and Capital: A Lecture (London: Simpkin, Marshall & Co., 1867)

The Politics of the Day: A Lecture (Edinburgh: Edinburgh Temperance Electoral Association, 1868)

The Horrible Inquisition of Rome, etc (Nottingham: C. J. Welton, 1880). An abridged version of *Canterbury versus Rome.*

'The Hereditary Landed Aristocracy', in *Speeches and Lectures of the Late Ernest Jones* (n.p., n.d.).

vi. Ephemera

'King's Ernest's Accession', 'King's Ernest's Arrival', 'King Ernest in his Dominions', *Morning Post*, (10 Apr. 1841–7 May 1841)

The Queen against Ernest Jones: Trial of Ernest Charles Jones for Sedition and Unlawful Assembly at the Central Criminal Court before Wilde (C. J.), July 10, 1848 (London: MacGowan & Co., 1848)

Defence of Ernest Jones, as Read by him at the Public Meeting in the South London Hall (London: *People's Paper*, 1852)

F. Pyat et al., *The Letter of the Jersey Exiles to the Queen of England*, trans. Ernest Jones (London: E. Truelove, 1855)

Libel Exposed: Being a Full Report of the Action for Libel, Ernest Jones v. G. W. M. Reynolds, etc. (London: Wilks & Co., 1859)

The Trial for Murder. Reg. v. Levi Taylor: Speech in Defence of the Prisoner, by Ernest Jones, Esq (Manchester: John Heywood, 1863)

Ernest Jones. Who is he? What has he Done? (Manchester: Reform League, 1868)

Index